DESERT PEOPLE

Desert People

A study of the Walbiri Aborigines of Central Australia

by

M. J. MEGGITT

THE UNIVERSITY OF CHICAGO PRESS

CHICAGO AND LONDON

Library of Congress Catalog Card Number: 66-11884

THE UNIVERSITY OF CHICAGO PRESS, CHICAGO 60637
The University of Chicago Press, Ltd., London W.C. 1

Reissued 1965
Originally published 1962 by Angus & Robertson, Ltd., Sydney, Australia
© 1962 by M. F. Meggitt. All rights reserved
Second Impression 1968
Printed in the United States of America

FOREWORD

By A. P. Elkin

Although much has been written about the Australian Aborigines, their social organization, totemism, mythology and ritual, intensive accounts of individual tribes are rare. The classic is Spencer and Gillen's description of the Arunta in their *Native Tribes of Central Australia*, published in 1899. This was based partly on Mr Gillen's experience for many years in the Alice Springs district and on two periods of field research by Professor Baldwin Spencer. The book did not give that detailed analysis of social organization which is now considered essential, but it did show how the kinship and subsection systems were mechanisms in living situations, both social and ritual. Above all, it made a great impact on comparative studies of religion through its vivid description of initiation and totemic ceremonies. It was a remarkable pioneering work.

Pastor C. Strehlow, in *Die Aranda und Loritja Stamme in Zentral-Australien* (published by the Frankfurt Museum in five parts, 1907-20), added much authoritative information about the mythology and social system of the western division of the Arunta but did not succeed in presenting a picture of a living culture.

In the major part of their second book, *The Northern Tribes of Central Australia*, 1904, Spencer and Gillen gave an account of the Warramunga tribe around Tennant Creek, comparable to their description of the Arunta though not as good with regard to social organization. For the rest of this book and also for Spencer's *The Native Tribes of the Northern Territory of Australia*, 1914, we are given comparative descriptions of the ceremonies, myths, social systems and material culture of several tribes. A. W. Howitt's *The Native Tribes of South East Australia*, 1904, is similar.

The next book to give an intensive study of a tribe or group of related clans was W. L. Warner's *A Black Civilization*, 1937, based on field-work (1926-9) amongst a people he named the

Murngin in the Millingimbi district of north-eastern Arnhem
Land. This very scholarly description, analysis and interpretation showed the advance in methodology since the days of Spencer
and Gillen. It was particularly welcome, too, because it dealt with
a tribe living in a well-watered tropical coastal region—a very
different environment from the semi-arid and frequently drought-
stricken country of the Arunta.

Dr Phyllis Kaberry's *Aboriginal Woman*, 1939, and Dr Cath-
erine Berndt's *Women's Changing Ceremonies in Northern
Australia*, 1950, dealt with one aspect of Aboriginal society and
culture in north-western Australia, while Dr R. M. Berndt's
Kunapipi, 1951, and *Djanggawul*, 1952, were concerned with a
special cult and an epic myth respectively in the north of the
Northern Territory. On the other hand, R. M. and C. H.
Berndt's *A Preliminary Report of Field Work in the Ooldea
Region, Western South Australia* (reprinted from *Oceania*, 1942-5)
does give a reasonably rounded account of groups from culturally and regionally related tribes settling together in a new district to which they had recently migrated. The same authors'
Sexual Behaviour in Western Arnhem Land (Viking Fund Pub-
lications in Anthropology, No. 16, 1951) describes the social
organization of two tribes but mainly from the point of view
of the relations of the sexes.

This survey shows that Spencer and Gillen's books of 1899
and 1904, Warner's of 1937 and, to a lesser degree, the Berndts'
on Ooldea, 1945, and Western Arnhem Land, 1951, make up
the total of worth-while accounts of individual Australian tribes
so far published. Unfortunately, the opportunities for the study
of individual tribes living in their own country, and altogether
or mainly within their own cultural tradition, have been few
and have ever been on the decrease since 1926, the year in which
the Australian National Research Council commenced its planned programme of research in Aboriginal Australia. The separate tribal organization has usually broken down very quickly on
contact with White settlement, and the field-worker has found
himself mostly amongst remnants of a tribe or of several tribes
around a Mission, Government settlement, pastoral station,
or township.

However, a few tribal groups have remained, until quite

recently at least, sufficiently independent of the effects of contact to provide the opportunity for a full tribal study. Such a group was the Walbiri, or Wailbri as it has often been called, in the arid-to-desert region north and north-west of Alice Springs. The Walbiri had kept themselves fairly well intact, as the author of this book shows.

I was, therefore, very pleased when Dr M. J. Meggitt, after completing a brilliant undergraduate course, decided in 1953 to work amongst this tribe, first intensively at Hooker Creek and then amongst the other Walbiri groups at Yuendumu, Phillip Creek and elsewhere. He was ably assisted by his wife. Mrs Meggitt got on well with the Aborigines and gathered, with and through the women, information which male anthropologists are not able to observe or to obtain.

Every chapter reveals Dr Meggitt's thoroughness and the care with which he has observed, inquired into, discussed and checked the field data so that his interpretation of Walbiri social structure would be soundly based. Where possible he has used the statistical method. Even more helpful are the many actual examples of behaviour, which enable the reader to draw his own conclusions and also to get the "feel" of the living, pulsating society.

Dr Meggitt, too, aimed at throwing light on unsolved problems and debated points while he was in the field. He refers to some of these in the Preface. An important one is concerned with local organization, that is, the subdivision of the tribe into localized groups. The somewhat academic view, and yet one which has seemed quite realistic, was that each tribe was (and is) divided into localized food-gathering hordes, patrilineal and exogamous in structure. Further, each of these was considered to be confined to its own part of the tribal territory, except when on a visit to a relative's "country" or when gathered with other hordes for ceremonies.

Evidence coming to hand, however, has indicated that this is not the real picture, that unless drought causes the temporary separation of the tribe, or of a community of the tribe, into small food-gathering bands, each consisting of a family or of two or three closely related families, the whole tribe, if a small one, or else a geographical division of the tribe, habitually camp, hunt, move to fresh grounds, and corroboree together.

On the other hand, each small, patrilineal group is particularly associated through the doctrine of pre-existence and through totemic cult affiliations with a definite site of mythological and doctrinal significance. This site, quite small in area, is called by the members of the group concerned their "country".

In addition, several such groups, forming a community of the tribe, refer to their total territory as their "country". So the question arises: is the everyday, functioning group a small food-gathering band of a man and his brothers and sons with their families, or is it a much larger and more complex, endogamous community?

Dr Meggitt shows conclusively that for the Walbiri the latter is the fact. His marshalling and analysis of the data on this matter are an important part of the book. We see from it that the Aboriginal social order is a rational one. The Aborigines of a tribe are all relatives; moreover they are a sociable people. They have no villages, but they like to be together for hunting and food-gathering, for protection against the dangers of the dark, and for the corroboree—in fact, just for the sake and interest of being together. After all, field-workers have always seen them in complex, community formation, apart from small groups in the camps on the smaller pastoral stations.

In spite of this, we have been inclined to infer that such a state of affairs was caused by the influence and attraction of the Mission, Government settlement, or large pastoral station, and that previously the Aborigines moved about in small bands over comparatively small parts of the tribal territory. Dr Meggitt's study of the problem, in a region where investigation was still possible, suggests very strongly that this "cell-like" formation was an anthropological abstraction.

The author's chapter on Walbiri ethnocentrism is significant, for it ties up with the conviction which the tribesmen possess that they will not die out but rather will increase. There is no reason to doubt them. They are virile; they are loyal to their social order, with 91 per cent of marriages conforming to the ideal rules; and they believe in stable marriages, particularly in the interests of the children.

Without going into further detail, I simply draw attention to the outstanding thoroughness with which the kinship and subsection systems are described and analysed, and to the ample illustrative material. There is also the important discussion of the constitution of the patrilines and matrilines and of their function in social and religious life. Initiation ritual and the ritual that follows death are fully described, for in them we see as it were the social structure in action—respectively taking in a new member and adjusting itself to the loss of a member.

Finally, Dr Meggitt realizes that he is describing a phase in a process, not a static situation. He gives, therefore, in chapter II a concise history of Walbiri contact up to date; and in the final chapter he deals with the present phase of contact, particularly with the implementation of declared Government policy.

As one who has been associated with anthropological research amongst the Aborigines for 30 years, and with movements for the development of Aboriginal policies for more than 25 years, I take heart from Dr Meggitt's concluding words regarding the goal of assimilation. He writes: "I believe that the prospects of successful, long-term assimilation are nowhere brighter than among the Walbiri."

I congratulate Dr Meggitt on this book and commend it to all who desire to have more than superficial knowledge about the Aborigines. In particular, I commend it to all social anthropologists for its soundness and for its value to anthropological theory. I hope that the author will continue and finish the task so ably begun in this volume by giving us a sequel on Walbiri totemism and ritual. I am indeed pleased to have been associated in some small way with Dr Meggitt's anthropological initiation.

Sydney

PREFACE

Anthropological field-work carried out over the last fifty years has given us a comparatively deep understanding of the culture and social organization of a number of Aboriginal tribes west of the Great Dividing Range.

Howitt, Elkin, Tindale and the Berndts have published detailed reports on several South Australian tribes. In the Kimberleys, tribes distributed from the Fitzroy River to the Ord River have been investigated from various points of view by Elkin, Piddington, Capell, Phyllis Kaberry, Worms, Lommel and Petri. Stanner has worked with groups north-east of the Kimberleys. The published accounts of the Arnhem Land Aborigines provide what is probably the most comprehensive documentation available for any Australian tribes; Warner, Elkin and the Berndts have analysed in detail the native culture and social organization and the people's reactions to European contact. Extending east from the Overland Telegraph Line through the Barkly Tableland and into the Gulf and Channel countries of Queensland are the Aborigines described by Spencer and Gillen, Roth, Elkin, Stanner and Sharp.

The great, semicircular sweep of these northern tribes from the Kimberleys to Queensland encloses a region still remembered as the domain of Spencer and Gillen—the Centre, stretching more than 500 miles from the Finke River north to Newcastle Waters. As early as 1896, these indefatigable pioneers were recording the striking features of Aranda tribal life; and their descriptions of Aranda, Kaitish and Warramunga culture have remained mines of valuable data for later Australian field-workers. Their researches were followed by those of the Strehlows, father and son, of Roheim and of Olive Pink, all of whom reported on various aspects of Aranda culture; but little more was written about the northern congeners of this tribe.

The earlier field-workers, however, were chiefly concerned to describe Aboriginal cultures, in particular, totemic ritual and religious belief, rather than to analyse social organization and structure in any systematic fashion. Their approach reflected the prevailing theoretical interests of the time. As a result, the structure of Central Australian society is still imperfectly understood, for the only evidence available comprises passing comments made in various contexts by Spencer and Gillen and by T. G. H. Strehlow.

It is now too late to repair the omission with respect to some of the tribes already mentioned, for these bore the brunt of early European settlement in the central region. The Walbiri, however, who lived farther to the west, had fewer contacts with Europeans during that period, and their traditional tribal organization survived relatively unaltered. Despite the occurrence of certain superficial cultural changes, the significant social groupings within this tribe function today much as they did in the past. Moreover, incidental remarks in the earlier accounts of the Aranda and Warramunga suggest that, although the two peoples in some respects differed culturally from the Walbiri, all three societies were structurally similar. My main object, therefore, is to undertake a detailed analysis of Walbiri society, for I believe that this may provide reference points that will facilitate the placing of the central tribes in an over-all comparative framework.

Within this broad approach, I intend to deal with several more specific problems. The first concerns the significance of actual and putative genealogical connection in orienting Aboriginal social behaviour. One point of view is succinctly expressed in Radcliffe Brown's proposition that "in Australian tribes the arrangement of marriages is carried out by reference to genealogical relations of kinship" (1951, p. 38). Most Australian anthropologists who have investigated Aboriginal societies would, I think, accept this statement. On the other hand, Americans, such as Lawrence and Murdock, reject it explicitly; they argue instead that membership in social "classes" (that is, sections and subsections) is the significant determinant of marriage choice. As the Walbiri possess an elaborately organized system of kinship behaviour as well as an established system of subsections, it should be possible to test both propositions in the light of evidence from this society.

I shall analyse in detail a number of institutionalized situations that the people regard as significant (birth, betrothal,

initiation and death) in order to determine the relative importance of locality, genealogy and subsection affiliation in organizing
social behaviour. I intend to examine not only the sort of proposition advanced by Radcliffe Brown concerning kinship and
marriage but also the problem of the significance of kinship in
Walbiri totemic organization.

Concomitantly with this I shall examine the widely-held
assumption that, in societies typified by the Australian Aborigines, unilineal descent groups have little or no structural
significance.

Finally, I shall discuss the changes in Walbiri society and
culture that have occurred in response to contact with Europeans
and with other Aboriginal societies. To do this, it will be necessary to draw together as much as possible of the history of Walbiri-European intercourse, a task whose performance has intrinsic
merits in providing comparative data for other anthropologists.
I shall relate this sort of evidence, together with my own observations on Walbiri acculturation, to a diachronic analysis made
by Elkin of the course of such contacts elsewhere in Australia,
so that the generality of his approach may be tested.

I welcome the opportunity to acknowledge here my great
debt to Professor Elkin, under whose guidance I first read
anthropology. His lectures and seminars were largely responsible for my acquiring an interest in problems of social structure
and organization. As well as providing such broad stimulation
for his students' researches, he has always been generous in
sharing the knowledge he has derived from many years of first-
hand acquaintance with Aborigines. Thus, my decision to undertake field-work among the Walbiri was made after many discussions with Professor Elkin, during which the research poten-
tialities of a number of Australian societies were carefully
weighed.

I received financial support from the Research Committee of
the University of Sydney, which granted me a Research Student-
ship and expense funds. This enabled me to spend 15 months in
the Northern Territory in 1953-4 and 1954-5. I thank the Committee for its assistance.

On the first of my visits I was accompanied by my wife, who
worked intensively with the Walbiri women to obtain the sorts

of information that Aboriginal women are generally reluctant to divulge to men, whether Aboriginal or European. Many of the data incorporated in my descriptions of child-birth, child-rearing, women's food-gathering activities and the like are the results of her patient observations.

The Department of Native Affairs (now the Welfare Branch) of the Northern Territory Administration gave me the most valuable co-operation, both formal and informal. The directors (Mr F. Moy, Mr R. McCaffery, and later Mr H. Giese) facilitated my entry to the Walbiri settlements; Ted Evans, district super-intendent at Darwin and later at Alice Springs, organized trans-port and accommodation for me. The settlement superintendents —Joe Mahood and Jack Hawley at Hooker Creek, Tom Wake at Phillip Creek and Jack Newham at Yuendumu—patiently bore with the inquisitive stranger. Without their help, as well as that of the patrol officers Les Penhall and Creed Lovegrove, I could not have covered so much country nor contacted so many of the Walbiri.

The interest that all these officers, and others such as Gordon Sweeney, Bill McCoy and Harry Kitching, showed in my work was most stimulating, and we had many illuminating discussions on the practical problems involved in the administration of Aboriginal communities. I hope that my account of Walbiri society will be of interest to the Welfare Branch, so that I may repay in some measure the assistance I received from its officers, as well as lighten my debt to those Walbiri who so cheerfully "looked out" for my wife and myself.

Other departments of the Administration also facilitated my research. The Lands Office in Darwin gave me access to its archives, thus enabling me to trace the course of early European settlement in and around the Walbiri territory. School-teachers of the Commonwealth Office of Education helped me to admin-ister psychological tests to Aboriginal children and also discussed with me the problems connected with educating these children. George Chippendale, botanist, and Warren Hitchcock, biologist, of the Animal Industry Department, went to great trouble to advise me on the identification of Walbiri flora and fauna.

To these, and the many other Territory people who gave me such friendly help, I offer my sincere thanks.

In conclusion, I should point out that the "ethnographic present tense" used in this book refers primarily to the period from 1953 to 1955. Since that time there have been important developments in Walbiri-European inter-relationships, generally in the direction of a greater integration of the Walbiri into the total society of the Northern Territory. The Welfare Branch has achieved a significant extension of educational facilities and employment opportunities for the people as a whole, and the general standard of Walbiri living is rising. More particularly, the Branch has made material improvements to the Aboriginal settlements, the most spectacular involving the establishment of a new settlement at Warrabri to which the Phillip Creek Walbiri moved in 1956.

In the summer of 1959-60 I revisited the Walbiri, both to observe the effects of such changes and to verify certain aspects of my earlier field-work. As it was by then too late to incorporate the additional data on socio-cultural change in the present volume, I can only state briefly that the developments I observed, especially in the patterns of employment, leadership and local identification, accorded well with the kinds of predictions I had ventured earlier. Moreover, this recent field-work has satisfied me of the validity of my analysis of Walbiri social structure and institutionalized behaviour.

M.J.M.

Sydney

CONTENTS

I The Physical Environment of the Walbiri   1
    Climatic Conditions
    Topography
    Flora
    Fauna

II Historical Background   16

III The Present Distribution of the Tribe   30

IV The Tribe and its Congeners   34
    Ethnocentrism
    Intertribal Relations
    Summary

V Local Organization   47
    The Major Tribal Divisions
    Totemic Countries
    Summary
    Recent Changes in Local Organization

VI The Residential Family Unit and the Kinship System   75
    Dwellings
    The Occupants
    The Kinship System

VII Intrafamilial Relationships   85
    Husband–Wife
    Co-wives

VIII Intrafamilial Relationships (*continued*)   115
    Father–Children
    Mother–Children
    Siblings

IX Extrafamilial Relationships   137
    Father's Sister—Brother's Children
    Mother's Brother—Sister's Children
    Father's Father—Son's Children; etc.
    Father's Mother—Son's Children; etc.
    Mother's Father—Daughter's Children; etc.
    Mother's Mother—Daughter's Children; etc.
    Wife's Mother—Daughter's Husband; etc.
    Husband's Mother—Son's Wife; etc.
    Wife's Father—Daughter's Husband; etc.
    Husband's Father—Son's Wife; etc.
    Wife's Brother—Sister's Husband
    Husband's Sister—Brother's Wife
    Cross-cousins

 X The Subsection System   165

XI Moieties and Descent Lines   188
    Grouped Alternate Generation-Levels
    Matrimoieties and Matrilines

XII Moieties and Descent Lines (*continued*)   203
    Patrimoieties and Patrilines

XIII Gradations of Age and Maturity   233

XIV Government and Law   242
    Government
    Law

XV Betrothal, Marriage and Child-birth   264
    Betrothal
    Marriage
    Conception and Child-birth

XVI Initiation   281
    Circumcision
    Subincision and After

XVII Death   317

XVIII "Reaction and Interaction"   331

    Bibliography   341

    Index   343

ILLUSTRATIONS

Ngama, a valley rich in game   28

Paintings at Ngama cave   28

Yarry djabangari—a man of uncertain temper   29

A decorated Walbiri man   29

Wally djabaldjari—a redoubtable fighter   44

Bulbul djabaldjari—a man of many talents   44

Making the sacred incised boards   45

Walbiri men preparing to meet visitors   45

Men acting the wild melon totemic ritual   76

Gadjari ritual cycle   76

A totemic ceremony   77

Chest cicatrised with a flake of glass   77

Medicine-man and ritual leader   92

Mess-hall at Warrabri settlement   92

Preparation for the mustering season   93

Roping a beast in the stock-yard   93

The shaded section denotes the area discussed in this book

CHAPTER I

THE PHYSICAL ENVIRONMENT OF THE WALBIRI

The exact boundaries and area of the Walbiri tribal territory are not easily delimited. The country that the people regard as traditionally their own lies in the central-western part of the Northern Territory. It occupies a pentagon, about 200 miles from north to south and about the same at its widest from east to west, with an area of between 35,000 and 40,000 square miles. Recent movements of the people, however, have added two more tracts to this territory—one extending to the headwaters of the Victoria River in the north and the other extending to Teatree on the Stuart Highway in the south-east. These additions together comprise some 15,000 to 16,000 square miles, which the Walbiri now consider to be their own country.

Climatic conditions. Despite the extent of the tribal territory, local differences in environmental conditions are not as marked as might be expected. Most of the country lies within the five- to ten-inch rain-belt, although the northern (Hooker Creek) region enters the fifteen-inch belt. Annual rainfalls vary considerably throughout the area. Thus, about seventeen inches of rain fell at Phillip Creek in the east in the summer wet season of 1952-3, but only about two inches in the season of 1953-4. About twenty inches fell at Hooker Creek in the 1952-3 wet season, but only about five inches in the 1953-4 season. Sweeney (1947) gives rainfall figures for other localities.

TABLE 1

Rainfall

Locality	Period	Annual rainfall		
		average	maximum	minimum
Conistan	7 years	9·17″	15·92″	4·34″
Mount Doreen	11 years	9·50″	16·72″	3·82″
The Granites	8 years	6·90″	15·73″	3·53″

Chewings (1930), who travelled through the north-eastern parts in 1909, estimated the average rainfall there to be between ten and twelve inches and the annual evaporation rate to be about twelve feet.

Seasonal variations in temperatures are also extreme. The sultry summer heat experienced before the breaking of the rains can be well-nigh insupportable for Aborigines and Europeans alike. At Hooker Creek, in the summer of 1953-4, for instance, the shade-temperature hovered between 100 and 115 degrees F. for about two months; one thermometer outdoors burst at 140 degrees. Shade-temperatures of 115 to 118 degrees were also common at Phillip Creek and Yuendumu in the summer of 1954-5. During the rains, and for a short time afterwards, the temperature drops to between 85 and 90 degrees. In the couple of months that may be counted as winter, Europeans find the climate pleasant, but the Aborigines detest the cold nights. Winter temperatures range from about 50 to 85 degrees. Unfortunately, these agreeable conditions are offset by persistent, strong winds laden with fine dust, which blow from the south-east, east and north-east. The south-east winds occasionally bring light but useful rains. The summer winds, although more variable than the easterlies, usually blow from the north-west quarter and are the main rain-bearing winds. Should they fail to bring rain, Europeans and Aborigines may expect a disastrous year.

Topography. The rainfall and temperature figures indicate that much of the country can be regarded as desert; but not all of it is like conventional pictures of African and Asian deserts. Sandhills devoid of vegetation occur only in a few localities, chiefly between the Hanson and Winnecke creeks and south of the Granites. Other extensive red-sand and loam areas, lying between the Treuer Range, the Reynolds Range and the headwaters of the Victoria River, are clothed with spinifex grasses and stunted acacias, grevilleas and hakeas, interspersed with occasional eucalypts. Much of this undulating, sandy country is between 1000 and 1500 feet above sea-level. But, despite the elevation, there are few drainage lines other than the great "flood-outs" of the Lander and Hanson creeks, desiccated swamps now supporting brakes of teatrees.

There are outcrops of sandstone in the east and of granite and quartz reefs in the west. The depth of subterranean waters varies from a few feet near the Hanson to between 100 and 150 feet towards the Granites. Although the Hooker, Winnecke, Lander and Hanson creeks are significant topographical features, they are dry for six to nine months of the year, except for occasional tree-sheltered, deep billabongs. The ubiquitous xerophilous scrubs and herbage give an illusion of plenty; but the lack of dependable surface waters for most of the year presents a real obstacle to travel. The Aborigines overcome this in part by digging for soaks in suitable places in creek-beds and by remembering the locations of tiny rock-holes and rock-seepages. The desert is latticed with native tracks following the lines of such waters, which in quantity and quality are generally inadequate for the needs of European stock-raisers.

The auriferous Tanami-Granites area differs considerably from the central sandy country. It is part of a long belt of slate, quartz reefs and granite outcrops and supports fewer and smaller trees than do the other sections. From Winnecke Creek northwest to the Victoria River the red sand and sandstone give way to shale, ferruginous sandstone and ironstone, which meet the Victoria River basalt ridges.

The hills in the east and south are at most 1000 and 1500 feet above the surrounding country, but they form rugged, tangled complexes that are hardly to be penetrated by motor vehicles. Only since the introduction of four-wheel-drive trucks have the pack-horse and camel been superseded as a reliable means of transport for Europeans in much of the Walbiri territory. The Reynolds Range, mainly granite gneiss, covers an area of about 50 by 20 miles. Tin has been mined here. The range tails away for some 90 miles in an irregular line of granite hills, including Mount Eclipse, Mount Hardy and Mount Doreen, which are all important totemic sites. Wolfram, mica and copper occur in some of the southern hills that join the Treuer Range, but only the wolfram has been mined commercially.

Flora. To the superficial gaze, the local bush is a dreary monotony of drably-coloured spinifex-grass and stunted trees, studded with innumerable termite mounds. But closer examination reveals a great variety of floral forms, most of which the Walbiri exploit. Moreover, the stretches of spinifex are punctuated by small, treeless plains of light brown loam, on which grow sweet grasses that provide edible seeds for Aborigines as well as fodder for game and cattle.

The following list, pp. 5-9, which is by no means complete, indicates the uses to which the people put the vegetation. (In the native terms used in this account, *j* is prounced as y, as in "yet"; ŋ as in "singer"; ŋg as in "finger"; *a* as in "father"; *ai* as in "time"; *au* as in "now"; final *i* as in "feel"; non-final *i* as in "fit"; *o* as in "saw"; final *u* as in "rude"; and non-final *u* as in "put".)

There are significant differences in the distribution of many of these plants. For instance, cypress-pines and wild figs are found on granite hills, and the wild orange is also a hill-dweller. The bean-tree, which hugs the creek-banks, is rare in the north. Coolibahs and river red-gums are watercourse trees, whereas the ghost-gum favours drier sites, especially on hill-sides. Bloodwood and blue mallee also thrive in the drier localities. Desert-plum and plum-bush grow in sandy loam, often in company with mulga and witchetty-bush; all tend to be confined to the southern regions. Cassias and eremophilas, hakeas and grevilleas are widely distributed, as are conkerberries and most of the acacias. The natives are aware of such local differences and in the past organized their food-gathering itineraries accordingly.

Fauna.   As I spent most of my time in permanent native camps of some size, I can give only a sketchy account of the wild life. Inevitably, there is little game within a radius of ten to fifteen miles around these camps, which is the range of daily food-gathering excursions. My longer journeys away from the camps were usually in motor-trucks or on horseback and, consequently, were unsatisfactory from the point of view of game-watching. It is, moreover, almost impossible to identify animals and birds with certainty from native descriptions. The following lists, pp. 10-15, therefore include some genera identified only tentatively from observation and description.

In general, it may be said that the Walbiri at one time or another eat most of the birds, animals and reptiles frequenting their territory, except a few species that they avoid for magico-religious reasons. In good seasons, when food is plentiful, the smaller and less palatable creatures may be ignored; but in times of scarcity even the humblest insects are eaten.

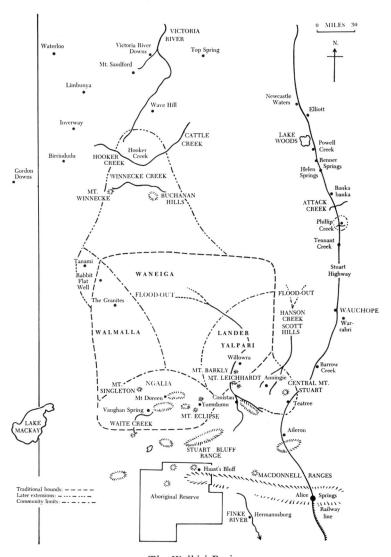

The Walbiri Region

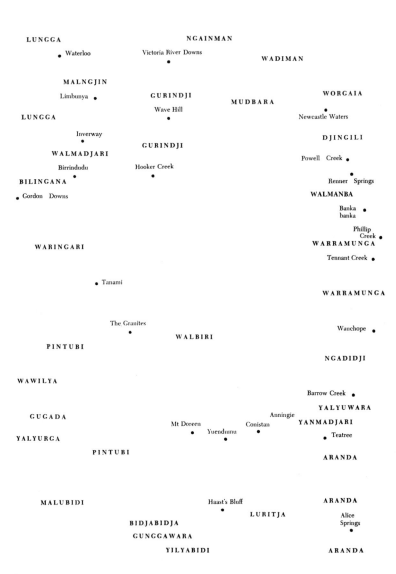

LUNGGA

• Waterloo

NGAINMAN

Victoria River Downs
•

WADIMAN

MALNGJIN

Limbunya •

GURINDJI

Wave Hill
•

MUDBARA

WORGAIA

•
Newcastle Waters

LUNGGA

Inverway
•

WALMADJARI

Birrindudu
•

BILINGANA

• Gordon Downs

GURINDJI

Hooker Creek
•

DJINGILI

Powell Creek •

•
Renner Springs

WALMANBA

Banka •
banka

Phillip
Creek •

WARRAMUNGA

Tennant Creek •

WARINGARI

• Tanami

WARRAMUNGA

The Granites
•

WALBIRI

Wauchope •

PINTUBI

NGADIDJI

WAWILYA

Barrow Creek •

GUGADA

Mt Doreen
•

Anningie

Conistan
•

YALYUWARA

YANMADJARI

YALYURGA

Yuendumu
•

Teatree •

PINTUBI

ARANDA

MALUBIDI

Haast's Bluff
•

ARANDA

LURITJA

Alice
Springs
•

BIDJABIDJA

GUNGGAWARA

YILYABIDI

ARANDA

YARABAN

The approximate distribution of neighbouring tribes
according to the Walbiri

TABLE 2

Walbiri flora

TYPE	WALBIRI NAME	USES
Acacia ancistrocarpa (wattle)	birauru	Edible seeds; wood for implements.
Acacia aneura (mulga)	mandja	Ditto.
Acacia coriacea (wattle)	baŋguna	Leaves used medicinally.
Acacia dictyophleba (wattle)	bilbirinba	Wood for implements and sacred objects.
Acacia estrophiolata (ironwood)	jadanbi	
Acacia farnesiana (wattle)	budumari	Edible seeds; trunk harbours witchetty grubs.
Acacia kempeana (witchetty-bush)	ŋalgiri	
Acacia notabilis (wattle)	mandala	Edible seeds, gum; wood for implements.
Acacia sp. (wattle)	badudu	Wood for spear shafts.
Acacia sp.? (wattle)	biliŋarba	
Acacia sp.? (wattle)	budjubanda	Edible seeds.
Acacia sp.? (wattle)	ganalarambi	Wood for spear shafts.
Acacia sp.? (wattle)	jalbiljaru	Trunk harbours witchetty grubs.
Acacia sp.? (wattle)	minjana	Edible seeds; wood for implements.
Acacia sp.? (wattle)	waralga	Trunk harbours witchetty grubs.
Acacia spondylophylla? (wattle)	bundaldji	
Acacia tetragonophylla? (wattle)	gurara	Edible seeds.
Acacia victoriae (wattle)	ganabargu	

TYPE	WALBIRI NAME	USES
Aristida sp.? (mulga-grass)	**jibiri**	Edible seeds.
Atalaya hemiglauca (whitewood)	**wanaguru**	Trunk harbours witchetty grubs.
Bassia bicornis? (goathead prickle)	**njili**	Nectar from flowers eaten.
Bauhinia hookerii	**gundji**	Edible roots.
Boerhavia diffusa (creeper)	**waijibi**	Wood for implements.
Callitris glauca (cypress-pine)	**wajari**	Ditto.
Callitris hugelii (pine)	**wajari**	
Calocephalus platycephalus (small flowering plant)	**julbaiyi julbaiyi**	Dried flowers produce down for decorations.
Canthium latifolium (plum-bush)	**jauwagi**	Edible fruit.
Capparis mitchelli (wild-orange)	**wadagi**	Edible fruit.
Capparis nummularia	**mingiljanaŋa**	
Capparis sp.? (wild-orange)	**djuguru**	Edible fruit.
Carissa lanceolata (conkerberry)	**managidji**	Edible fruit; wood for spear-heads.
Cassia artemisoides	**warii**	Leaves for ritual decorations.
Cassia desolata	**bumada**	Ditto.
Cassia eremophila	**warii**	Ditto.
Cassia pleurocarpa	**galbigalbilba**	Ditto.
Cassia sp.?	**buijulbuijulba**	
Cassia sp.?	**djaganba**	
Casuarina decaisneana (desert-oak)	**gulgabi**	Wood for implements.
Casuarina sp.?	**gunjangunjanba**	
Cienfugosa gossypoides (desert rose)	**binambali**	
Clerodendrum floribundum	**dadubidji**	Edible roots.
Crinium sp.? (lily)	**jalilgaliligi**	

6

TYPE	WALBIRI NAME	USES
Cymbopogon sp. (grass)	jindjiri	Shafts for children's toy spears.
Cyperus rotundus (onion grass)	djanmara	Edible roots.
Dactyloctenium sp.? (button grass)	wulia bundaru	
Duboisia sp.? (pituri)	djumbunbu	Chewed as narcotic.
Ehretia sp.?	ŋauwuljawulja	
Eremophila duttonii?	jagundji	Edible flowers, leaves.
Eremophila freelingii	mianba	Ditto.
Eremophila latrobei	janjiliŋi	Leaves for ritual decorations
Eremophila longifolia (emu-bush)	ŋalulbu	and uses.
Eremophila sp.?	wadiamu	Edible flowers,
Eremophila sp.?	wagabadari	Ditto.
Eremophila sturtii?	jagundji	
Erythrina vespertilio (bean tree)	jenindi	Wood for implements.
Eucalyptus camaldulensis (river red-gum)	ŋabiri	Edible flowers; wood for implements.
Eucalyptus gamophylla (blue mallee)	jilaŋgurunju	Wood for implements.
Eucalyptus microtheca (coolibah)	wabaliŋgi	Ditto.
Eucalyptus pachyphylla? (mallee)	walalju	Ditto.
Eucalyptus papuanas (ghost-gum)	wabamuŋgu	Ditto.
Eucalyptus sp.?	wadaruru	Medicinal use of leaves.
Eucalyptus sp.? (box)	wambalba	Wood for implements.
Eucalyptus sp.?	walandja	Ditto.
Eucalyptus sp.?	wuralu	Wood for implements; trunk harbours wild bees.
Eucalyptus sp.?	gidji baridji	Wood for implements.
Eucalyptus terminalis (bloodwood)	wilgali	Wood for implements; trunk harbours wild bees.

TYPE	WALBIRI NAME	USES
Ficus platypoda (wild-fig)	**widjirgi**	Edible fruit.
Grevillea junctifolia	**walunari**	Leaf-ash chewed with tobacco; wood for implements.
Grevillea sp.?	**djirindi**	Wood for implements.
Grevillea striata (beefwood)	**jildilba**	Edible flowers.
Grevillea wickhamii (holly grevillea)	**lagabara**	Ditto.
Hakea intermedia	**jargambi**	Stems used as rope.
Hakea lorea	**biriwa**	Edible tubers.
Hoya australis (vine)	**galjabi**	Edible seeds.
Ipomea costata ("yam")	**jala**	Edible flowers.
Ipomea muelleri	**judadjidi**	Edible leaves, fruit.
Loranthus sp. (mistletoe)	**njanjagiri**	Bark used for blankets, packages, coverings.
Marsdenia australis (bush-banana)	**jubali**	Juice used medicinally.
Melaleuca lasiandra (paper-bark)	**bagali**	Leaves and stems chewed as narcotic.
Melothria micrantha	**julgari**	Ditto.
Nicotiana ingulba? (tobacco)	**djuɲarai djuɲarai**	Wood for spear-shafts.
Nicotiana sp.? (tobacco)	**djanjuɲu**	Dried powder used for decoration.
Pandorea doratoxylon? (spear-bush)	**winbiri**	Dried flowers produce down for decoration.
Parkinsonia aculeata	**murulumbu**	Edible seeds, stems.
Podaxon sp.? (fungus)	**jagiraru**	
Portulacca sp.?	**maraguru**	
Portulacca sp.? (pig-weed)	**wagadi**	
Salsola kali (buckbush)	**bundunari**	

8

TYPE	WALBIRI NAME	USES
Santalum lanceolatum (plum-bush)	**mugagi**	Edible fruit.
Santalum sp.? (plum-bush)	**moiju**	Ditto.
Scleroderma sp.? (truffle)	**wiljari**	Edible.
Solanum ellipticum (desert raisin)	**garaba**	Edible fruit.
Solanum petrophilum	**waragalugalu**	Inedible.
Solanum sp.?	**waŋgi**	Edible fruit.
Solanum sp.?	**mandaru**	Inedible.
Tecoma sp.?	**juwunbiri**	Wood for spear-shafts.
Tinospora smilacina (vine)	**waraldji**	Stems used as rope.
Tribulus sp.? (bullhead prickle)	**djilgali**	
Trichinium sp. (hairy-tail)	**wanabanaba**	
Triodia pungens (grass)	**jibiri**	Resin used as adhesive.
Triodia spp. (spinifex-grass)	**mana**	
Ventilago viminalis (supplejack)	**walagari**	Wood for implements.
Vigna lanceolata ("yam")	**wabidi**	Edible roots.

TABLE 3
Walbiri fauna

TYPE	WALBIRI NAME	USES
Anas superciliosa (black duck)	**gidingidinba**	An uncommon but highly-prized food.
Artamus spp. (wood-swallow)	**binbaladjalba**	Rarely eaten.
Barnardius zonarius (Port Lincoln parrot)	**labadji**	Often eaten.
Calyptorhynchus banksi (black cockatoo)	**jirandi**	Eaten; plumes prized.
Corvus spp. (crow)	**waŋala**	Never eaten.
Cracticus sp.? (butcher-bird)	**njurba**	Occasionally eaten.
Dendrocygna arcuata (whistling tree-duck)	**djibilagu**	Highly-prized food.
Dromaius novae-hollandiae (emu)	**galaija**	Highly-prized food; plumes highly-valued.
Egretta alba (white egret)	**galwa**	Occasionally eaten; plumes prized.
Epthianura tricolor (crimson chat)	**djindjiwanu**	Rarely eaten; ritually important.
Eupodotis australia (bustard)	**barulga**	Highly-prized food.
Eurostopodus guttatus? (nightjar)	**jingadagudagu**	Rarely eaten; ritually important.
Falco berigora (brown hawk)	**gilgilari**	Occasionally eaten; plumes pri ed.
Falco hypoleucus? (grey falcon)	**winjinba**	Rarely eaten.
Fulica atra (black coot)	**galadjaraburuburu**	An uncommon but prized food.
Geopelia cuneata (diamond-dove)	**gulugugu**	Occasionally eaten.
Grallina cyanoleuca (magpie-lark)	**djarawanu**	Rarely eaten.
Gymnorhina sp.? (magpie)	**gulbaru**	Rarely eaten.

TYPE	WALBIRI NAME	USES
Halcyon pyrropygius? (kingfisher)	lunba	Rarely eaten.
Haliastur sphenurus (whistling eagle)	gilgilandji	Occasionally eaten; plumes prized.
Histriophaps histrionica? (flock-pigeon)	wadugulbari	Prized food.
Hylochelidon ariel (fairy-martin)	jagirigi	Rarely eaten.
Kakatoë leadbeateri (Major Mitchell cockatoo)	gagalala	Occasionally eaten; plumes prized.
Kakatoë roseicapilla (galah)	galilgalilba	Occasionally eaten; plumes prized.
Kakatoë sanguinea (corella)	baŋara	Occasionally eaten; plumes prized.
Leptolophus hollandicus (cockatiel)	djarula djarula	Occasionally eaten.
Lophophaps plumifera (spinifex pigeon)	juburu	Prized food.
Malurus cyanotus (blue-and-white wren)	djiwiljiriljiri	Never eaten.
Megalornis rubicundus (brolga)	worgali	Highly-prized food.
Melopsittacus undulatus (budgerigar)	gumiljuru	Frequently eaten.
Merops ornatus (bee-eater)	djubudu	Occasionally eaten.
Milvus migrans (kite)	bula bula	Never eaten.
Ninox sp. (owl)	gurulgurulba	Occasionally eaten; plumes prized.
Notophyx novae-hollandiae (blue crane)	galwa	Occasionally eaten.
Notophys pacifica? (heron)	galwa	Occasionally eaten.
Ocyphaps lophotes (crested pigeon)	ŋabalgiri	Prized food.
Oreoica gutturalis (crested bellbird)	gubalabala	Rarely eaten.
Pelecanus conspicillatus (pelican)	jundjari	Eaten, but rarely encountered.
Podargus sp.? (frogmouth)	gabululu	Rarely eaten; ritually important.

TYPE	WALBIRI NAME	USES
Podiceps ruficollis (grebe)	wilaŋana	Prized food.
Pomatostomus rubeculus (babbler)	djuwaiagiri	Rarely eaten.
Querquedula gibberifrons (grey teal)	djibilagu	Prized food.
Rhipidura leucophrys (wagtail)	djindidjinilbra	Never eaten.
Smicrornis sp.? (weebill)	bimiri bimiri	Occasionally eaten.
Taeniopygia castanotis (zebra finch)	jindjinmari	Occasionally eaten.
Threskiornis molucca? (ibis)	walabara	Rarely eaten.
Threskiornis sp.? (ibis)	windigi	Rarely or never eaten.
Turnix velox? (quail)	bundaru	Frequently eaten.
Tyto sp.? (owl)	wiriŋari	Rarely eaten.
Uroaetus audax (wedge-tailed eagle)	walauwaru	Rarely eaten; plumes prized
Bettongia sp.? (wallaby)	mala	Prized food.
Canis dingo (dingo)	maligi	Rarely or never eaten.
Canis familiaris (dog)	maligi	Rarely or never eaten.
Dasyurinus geoffroii (wild-cat)	guninga	Rarely eaten.
Dasycercus cristicauda (crest-tailed mouse)	dadjina	Often eaten.
Felis catus (feral cat)	ŋaija	Occasionally eaten.
Largochestes sp. (wallaby)	wombana	Prized food.
Macropus robustus (euro)	ganala	Highly-prized food.
Macropus rufus (kangaroo)	malu	Highly-prized food.
Macrotis sp. (bandicoot)	walbadjiri	Prized food; tails used for decorations.
Mus musculus? (mouse)	djuŋanba	Occasionally eaten.
Notomys sp.? (hopping-mouse)	djuŋanba	Occasionally eaten.
Notoryctes typhlops (mole)	bidjabidjaba	Prized food.
Nyctophilus sp.? (bat)	ŋalamanmanba	Rarely eaten.
Oryctolagus sp. (rabbit)	jurabidi	Prized food.

TYPE	WALBIRI NAME	USES
Perameles sp. (bandicoot)	baguru	Prized food.
Petrogale sp.? (wallaby)	waguljari	Prized food.
Phascogale macdonnellensis (fat-tailed mouse)	ganagalimbai	Frequently eaten.
Pseudomys sp.? (bush-mouse)	minini	Frequently eaten.
Tachyglossus aculeata (spiny anteater)	jinaliŋi	Highly-prized food.
Trichosurus vulpecula (possum)	djaŋanba	Highly-prized food.
Acanthophis pyrrhus? (death-adder)	waljawalja	Not eaten.
Amphibolurus barbatus (bearded dragon)	jungadi	Frequently eaten.
Amphibolurus maculatus (lizard)	galabara	Frequently eaten.
Amphibolurus reticulatus (reticulated dragon)	ganari	Frequently eaten.
Amphibolurus sp.? (lizard)	galandjiri	Frequently eaten.
Amphibolurus sp.? (lizard)	ganu	Frequently eaten.
Amphibolurus sp.? (lizard)	djiniŋandji	Frequently eaten.
Aspidites melanocephalus (black-headed snake)	muljugunja	Frequently eaten.
Ceramodactylus sp.? (gecko)	ragalara	Frequently eaten.
Chiroleptes sp.? (burrowing frog)	janagiri	Squeezed to produce potable liquid.
Demansia sp. (green snake)	bilgari	Not eaten.
Demansia sp. (snake)	lowanu	Not eaten.
Diplodactylus sp.? (gecko)	ŋuwa	Rarely eaten; ritually important.
Diplodactylus strophrurus (gecko)	walura	Frequently eaten.
Dtella sp. (gecko)	walwara	Frequently eaten.
Egernia kintorei? (skink)	warama	Frequently eaten.

13

TYPE	WALBIRI NAME	USES
Gymnodactylus sp.? (gecko)	**juduwaruwaru**	Frequently eaten.
Liasis childreni (snake)	**radalba**	Frequently eaten.
Limnodynastei spencerii (burrowing frog)	**djaldji**	Squeezed to produce potable liquid.
Lygosoma sp.? (lizard)	**liwiringi**	Frequently eaten.
Moloch horridus (mountain-devil)	**minjiri**	Not eaten.
Nephrurus aspa (gecko)	**jumarimari**	Frequently eaten.
Nephrurus levis (gecko)	**jumarimari**	Frequently eaten.
Notaden nichollsi (sand-toad)	**burugulja**	Not eaten.
Physignathus sp.? (lizard)	**gandjinari**	Frequently eaten.
Pseudechis sp.? (venomous snake)	**liɲa**	Not eaten.
Python sp.?	**jarabiri**	Prized food.
Sphenomorphus sp. (skink)	**borli**	Frequently eaten.
Tiliqua occipitalis? (skink)	**luŋgara**	Frequently eaten; fat a purgative.
Typhlops endoterus (snake)	**binbara binbara**	
Varanus acanthurus (goanna)	**njindjiri**	Prized food.
Varanus giganteus (pirinti)	**bulalba**	Prized food.
Varanus sp. (goanna)	**bildja**	Prized food.
Varanus sp. (goanna)	**djarambai**	Prized food.
Varanus sp. (goanna)	**luwadjiri**	Prized food.
Varanus sp.? (goanna)	**warungaruɲa**	Prized food.
Varanus sp.? (goanna)	**wilina**	Prized food.
Arbanitis sp.? (spider)	**mamuburunba**	Not eaten.
Campanotus sp.? (ant)	**biɲi**	Not eaten.
Cerambycidae larvae? (witchetty-grub)	**mijamija**	Prized food.
Cossidae larvae? (witchetty-grub)	**ŋalgari**	Prized food.

TYPE	WALBIRI NAME	USES
Eutermes sp.? (white ant)	jarinju	Occasionally eaten.
Eutermes sp.? (flying ant)	bandjidi	Occasionally eaten.
Gryllotalpa sp.? (mole-cricket)	lirinba	Not eaten.
Melophorus inflatus? (honey-ant)	jirambi	Prized food.
Melophorus sp.? (honey-ant)	jagula	Prized food.
Musca domestica (house-fly)	jimaɲi	Not eaten.
Musca vetustissima? (bush-fly)	jimaɲi	Not eaten.
Myrmecia sp.? (ant)	gadili gadili	Not eaten.
Psyllid lerp (manna)	jiljalbu	Frequently eaten.
Trigona sp. (wild bee)	munagi	Honey prized food; wax for adhesive.
Moths, butterflies	bindabinda	Not eaten.
Blackbeetles	birailji birailji	Not eaten.
Grasshoppers	djindilga	Occasionally eaten.
Scorpions	garaɲara	Not eaten.
Mosquitoes	giwinjiwinji	Not eaten.
Spiders	jinarɲi	Not eaten.
Centipedes	jirindji	Not eaten.
March-flies	judulu	Not eaten.
Mantis	julduldju	Not eaten.
Caterpillars, grubs	ladjul	Some eaten.
Cicadas, crickets	lirinba	Occasionally eaten.
Weevils, lice	lodu	Occasionally eaten.
Hornets	murururururu	Not eaten.
Phasmids	njinɲa	Not eaten.

15

CHAPTER II

HISTORICAL BACKGROUND

In general we know little of even the recent history of most Australian tribes, and this is true also of the Walbiri. They have few myths or legends that can be sifted for hints of early movements or contacts with other tribes.

The absence of such material can be construed, perhaps, as evidence of the people's long residence in the one area. As far as they themselves are concerned, the tribe has always existed as a distinct group connected by religious (that is, totemic) ties with most of the desert country it now occupies. We can infer that certain features of the social structure and culture, such as the subsection system and the moiety division, the Gadjari or Big Sunday ceremonial cycle and the use of particular implements, have been imported from other tribes. But the Walbiri tend to regard these things (insofar as they think about their origins at all) as local and internal developments that occurred in the long-past dreamtime.

The people's association with Europeans has been comparatively limited as a result of the location of the tribal country in relation to the prevailing pattern of European settlement in the Northern Territory. High costs of transport, difficulties of communication, unreliable rainfall, absence of lasting surface-waters, relative infertility of the soil, and, not least, the later reputation of the Walbiri as truculent "myalls" all combined to delay pastoral settlement in this area until the more suitable land closer to Alice Springs had been selected. The few Europeans who visited the tribal territory in early years were explorers and prospectors and were not interested in Aborigines except as potential obstacles to the fulfilment of their tasks. Consequently we have few records of the first encounters of the Walbiri with Europeans.

Exploration from the south did not penetrate the Northern Territory until 1860, but there had been earlier attempts to open up the country from the north. Thus, in 1855, a party led by A. C. Gregory landed at the mouth of the Victoria River in search of land suitable for pastoral use (vide Calvert, 1901). They explored the river to its headwaters and reached a point 18° 12′ S., 130° 39′ E., which is roughly the position of the present Hooker Creek Walbiri settlement. In those days, however, the locality was part of the Gurindji tribal territory, and Walbiri country lay about 150 miles to the south. In his subsequent journeys Gregory came no closer to the Walbiri.

J. M. Stuart, on the fourth of his remarkable attempts to cross Australia from south to north, took his companions in 1861 through the Hugh River gap in the Macdonnell Ranges into Yanmadjari country. They then travelled along Hanson Creek to Central Mount Stuart. The many tracks and fires Stuart observed there led him to assume that the area supported a large Aboriginal population. He saw only a few of the people themselves, who were probably Ngadidji (Kaitish), the eastern neighbours of the Walbiri.

Stuart turned west to Mount Denison, whence he pushed on to Mount Leichhardt and camped by permanent water. He saw signs of many Aborigines, who were probably Lander Walbiri or, as they are sometimes called, Ilpirra. He went on to Mount Barkly and Mount Arthur, but the arid spinifex-grass country forced him to return to the Hanson. Stuart eventually reached Attack Creek, north of Tennant Creek, where he encountered a large gathering of armed Warramunga. Turning back to avoid clashing with them, he retraced his steps to Mount Stuart and the Hanson. On the way he was followed by parties of armed natives (probably Ngadidji), but they did not molest his small band. Aborigines were also numerous between Hanson Creek and the Reynolds Range, and he conjectured that the seasonal drying-up of waterholes had forced them to congregate at permanent soaks and rockholes.

After replenishing his supplies in the south, Stuart returned to Attack Creek in 1861 by much the same route, then travelled north through Walmanba and Djingili country to Newcastle Waters. The impenetrable hedgewood scrub there forced him to turn south again. He saw few Aborigines in the Hanson area on this trip. His final journey in 1862 took him once more across Reynolds Range and along the Hanson. He encountered many

Aborigines around the waterholes. They were unfriendly at first but became less suspicious when Stuart made it clear that his party would not take all the limited amount of water that was available (vide Stuart, 1864).

It seems clear that Stuart was the first white man seen by the Walbiri. They were fortunate that it was Stuart, rather than some other of the early explorers, for throughout his journeys he took great care to avoid conflict with Aborigines.

The next Europeans to enter the region formed the supply and working parties engaged in the construction of the Overland Telegraph Line between 1870 and 1872. The line ran through the Macdonnells to Mount Stuart, thence to Barrow Creek, Tennant Creek, Powell Creek and Darwin. The presence of so many white men, with their array of horses and equipment, must have greatly puzzled the Walbiri who lived nearby. Unfortunately, there are no records of the course of contacts between Aborigines and Europeans in this area during these years.

After Stuart's successful crossing of Australia from south to north, people in the southern colonies became interested in the possibility of crossing the continent from east to west. Several attempts were made, but few succeeded. Between 1872 and 1874, for instance, Giles and Gosse tried to find routes from the Overland Telegraph Line to the Western Australian coast. Both failed. The explorations of Giles were made in Pidjandjara tribal territory, about 60 or 70 miles south of Walbiri country, and so they do not directly concern us. Gosse set out from a point about 40 miles south of Mount Stuart and skirted the Reynolds Range west-north-west through Yanmadjari and Walbiri country. He then travelled south-west through Yanmadjari and Pidjandjara territory until he entered the same area that Giles was traversing. Gosse apparently had friendly dealings with the few Aborigines he encountered, but Giles was attacked at least nine times by the Pidjandjara (vide Calvert, 1901; Giles, 1875; Rawson, 1948).

In 1873 a party led by Warburton left Alice Springs and headed west along the northern rim of the Macdonnells to Mount Wedge in the Stuart Bluff Range on the south-eastern border of Walbiri territory. The explorers then passed through the heart of the Ngalia Walbiri country as they travelled via Mount

Eclipse and Mount Hardy to Mount Stanley. To judge from Warburton's journal (1875), they met no Aborigines at all in this region. From Mount Stanley the party went to Eva Springs, near Mount Davenport, then turned north to Waterloo Wells in Walmalla Walbiri country. Here they saw several camps of a score or more Aborigines, whom Warburton describes as naked, bearded, well-built and healthy, and armed with clubs and spears. There were also women and children present. The people lived mainly on wallabies. The travellers camped at the wells for several weeks, without conflict with the natives, and while there found two incised stone bullroarers that had been hidden in the spinifex nearby. From this base camp the explorers tried unsuccessfully to find a practicable route through Walmalla territory near the Granites. Lack of water eventually forced them to push on west, and finally, after many hardships, which included having to eat their camels, the party reached the coast at the Oakover River.

All the reports of the western desert country were so adverse that few Europeans visited it during the next 15 years. But from 1880 to 1900 there was much activity north of Winnecke Creek on the northern border of Walbiri territory. Pastoralists such as the Buchanans, the Gordons, the Farquharsons and the Duracks were moving great herds of cattle from the Barkly Tableland and seeking new land along the Victoria, Stirling and Ord rivers. These men laid the foundations of the big cattle-stations that now adjoin Walbiri country on the north and north-west.

Nat Buchanan selected Wave Hill in 1880 and, with the Gordon brothers, grazed the first cattle along the Victoria in 1883. At that time Delamere station, 200 miles to the north-north-east, was the nearest white settlement to Wave Hill. The Gurindji and Mudbara tribesmen living near Wave Hill were from the start more or less friendly, although the settlers shot a number of them for spearing cattle. In 1884 Buchanan drove more Queensland cattle to the Ord, via Gill Creek and the Negri, and in 1886 opened up the Murranji track as part of a stock route between Powell Creek and Wave Hill. The Duracks took up Lissadell in 1885, and other stations soon grew up around Sturt Creek and the lower Ord.

By 1890, despite the effects of the Hall's Creek gold-rush of

1885-6, the pattern of European settlement in the northern desert had been established. Then, in 1913-14, the Australian Investment Agency (Vesteys) bought Wave Hill and Gordon Downs, eventually becoming the greatest landholders in the Northern Territory. By 1937 they exploited nearly 25,000 square miles of grazing land, much of which lay along the northern and western edge of Walbiri territory. These stations today are among the main employers of Walbiri labour.

While he was establishing Wave Hill station, Nat Buchanan carried out a series of explorations of the desert to the south. In 1896, accompanied by a Warramunga man, he rode from Tennant Creek telegraph-station to Hooker Creek, via the Buchanan Hills, and then on to Sturt Creek, seeking a new stock-route. His journey took him along the north-eastern and northern edges of Waneiga Walbiri country. In 1897 he and Farquharson searched the desert east of Tanami and near Waneiga territory for mica deposits, but they found none of commercial importance. Buchanan followed this with another trip from Sturt Creek to the Winnecke (vide Buchanan, 1933).

Meanwhile settlement along the telegraph-line had proceeded more slowly. Banka Banka was selected in about 1866 and Powell Creek in 1897; but the arid country south of Tennant Creek attracted few pastoralists. Some took up land along the Hanson and Lander creeks in the 1890s, but few selectors actually stocked their properties with cattle. One intrepid nomad named Brown grazed cattle in the desert between Sturt Creek and the Lander, in Waneiga and Walmalla Walbiri territory, but this venture did not last long. It was he who opened up the J.B. track from Tanami to Conistan station. The severe drought of 1902-5 seems to have forced the few smallholders out of the Lander-Hanson area. Between 1908 and 1910 small selections were taken up around Teatree and Ryan's Well, adjoining the Lander Walbiri territory. South of the Walbiri country, on the northern side of the Macdonnell Ranges, there was apparently no settlement during this period.

The Hall's Creek gold-rush of 1885 had led to renewed interest in the Northern Territory as a gold-producing area, and in 1900-1 a geologist named Davidson prospected the desert from Barrow Creek to Tanami, including Winnecke Creek. He reported that, although he had found gold at Tanami and the Granites, the deposits were too small for profitable exploration. But by about 1907 the Hall's Creek field was worked out and many miners sought employment. A number moved to the Tanami area. Impressed by their success, the South Australian official geologist announced in 1909 that gold existed there in worthwhile quantities. In the subsequent rush, according to the late W. Braitling who was present, there were at least 500 men on the field.

The local Aborigines, mainly Walbiri, at first avoided this large group of strangers at Tanami and for a time there seems to have been little conflict between the two peoples. But in 1910 Walmalla Walbiri surprised two miners prospecting at the Granites and, in an attempt to seize their stores, speared one to death. The policeman who was stationed at Tanami led a party of miners in pursuit of the killers. A number of Aborigines were captured, none of whom, as far as I can discover, was involved in the murder. Those caught by the policeman were escorted to Darwin and tried on charges of murder. They were discharged for lack of evidence and turned loose on the outskirts of the town. They were never heard of again. The natives seized by the miners simply vanished. Walbiri who remembered the affair told me that, although the Granites was an important ritual centre, most of the tribe avoided the place for years afterwards.

Concerned at the number of inexperienced bushmen who were attempting to cross the desert to try their luck at the Tanami field, the Government in 1909 arranged for wells to be sunk along the most dangerous approaches. A party led by Pierce constructed a chain of wells from Wave Hill to Tanami, via Hooker Creek, along a route skirting the western Waneiga country. At the same time another team under the guidance of Chewings sank wells from Barrow Creek to Wave Hill. This party followed the native tracks from the Hanson through the north-eastern corner of Waneiga Walbiri territory to the Winnecke and Wave Hill. At End Well, in the sandhills, they met a group of Aborigines (almost certainly Waneiga) who accompanied them for some days as guides. Chewings (1936) reports that the natives used boomerangs and spears with great accuracy to secure an enormous number of lizards, rats and feral cats. Although the Aborigines were more or less friendly, they remained wary of the strangers and would not come close to the camp.

The new tracks to Tanami were little used, however, for the rush had ended in 1910. A few optimistic miners remained, laboriously digging enough gold to pay for food; but when Wilkinson, an itinerant priest, visited Tanami in 1914, he found only six miners on that field. There was none at the Granites. He saw no Aborigines in the area (vide Smith, 1947). Only occasional prospectors and geologists continued to visit the locality until 1932, when the Granites gold-rush occurred.

The political status of the Northern Territory had changed several times during the 60 years to 1914. From 1827 to 1863 the Territory was nominally part of the State of New South Wales. The government took little interest in this distant and unexplored possession and was more than willing to cede it to the young State of South Australia when the latter, on no evidence at all, decided that occupation of the northern regions was necessary to that State's development. The main concern of the new government was to make the Territory pay its way quickly. Consequently, in order to encourage rapid settlement, the Administration in Darwin at first gave local pastoralists and prospectors a free hand to exploit the country, and conflicts between Europeans and Aborigines were usually settled in favour of the former. In any case, the great distances, poor communications and shortage of administrative personnel made it almost inevitable that the settlers would take the law into their own hands.

But by 1890, partly in response to local economic factors and to humanitarian outcries from the south, the Administration was expressing its concern for the fate of the Aborigines. It nominated police officers as Protectors of Aboriginals and in 1892 proclaimed several areas as Aboriginal reserves on which the natives could, if they wished, live without molestation. The Government Medical Officer became the Chief Protector of Aborigines in 1894. Later, the Administration urged the South Australian Parliament to legislate for the regulation of Aboriginal-White intercourse. Parliament rejected the recommendation on the grounds that recognition of Aboriginal rights would discourage Europeans from settling in the Territory.

One result of the Government's failure to intervene was that conflicts between pastoralists and northern Aborigines were exacerbated. A number of settlers had so many cattle speared that they had to abandon their stations. In a few instances, the natives' persistent ambushing and murdering of station-hands drove the Europeans away.

South Australia was prepared by 1910 to write off the Territory as a bad investment. Local conditions combined with economic crises in other states had caused the plans for extensive settlement to fail, and there was no prospect that the Territory would ever become self-supporting, let alone a profitable asset. South Australia, having but a small population, could not afford to pay out subsidies indefinitely, so in 1911 induced the Commonwealth Government to take over the area.

Federal Parliament quickly passed laws specifying the conditions under which Aborigines were to be employed, and in 1912 appointed an eminent biologist and anthropologist, Baldwin Spencer, as Chief Protector of Aboriginals in the Northern Territory. During the year he held that position, he set up an Aborigines Department and made many recommendations for the amelioration of native conditions. These formed the basis of new legislation passed in 1918 covering various aspects of Aboriginal employment, residence, health and morality. Most of these ordinances remained in force until amended in 1933.

Such changes in administrative policy, however, meant little to the Walbiri. Their associations with Europeans were still mainly limited to casual contacts with the cattle-stations adjoining the tribal territory. A few young men were beginning to visit the stations occasionally to work in stock-camps or simply to satisfy their curiosity; but pastoralists could not force them into regular employment. At the first signs of pressure the visitors retired to their homeland, much of which was still inaccessible to Whites. In this respect the Walbiri differed significantly from the Aranda and tribes to the east who were already congregating around the townships and cattle-stations that had been established in their territories.

Walbiri men have told me that they were content to maintain

this pattern of sporadic contacts with Europeans indefinitely. It enabled them to obtain supplies of the new goods they desired, such as axes, knives and blankets, without having to relinquish the independence they still value so highly. But from 1924 to 1929 Central Australia suffered the most severe drought in its history. After the first two years, food and water were so scarce that only a few Walbiri dared to remain in the desert. A number of these perished. The rest of the tribe was forced to disperse and seek food from the white men they had hitherto avoided.

Some walked to Birrindudu and Gordon Downs stations, others crossed Hooker Creek into Wave Hill, where Bleakley (1928) remarked on the arrival of one party of 50 Walmalla who were almost starving. Other groups moved to the Granites and Tanami to beg from the few prospectors. One big party reached the police ration depot that had been set up for the distressed Warramunga at the Tennant Creek telegraph-station. Many Walbiri made for the cattle-stations in the better-watered Hanson and Lander district. The influx of so many hungry and unemployable Aborigines seriously embarrassed the cattlemen, who were themselves in difficulties, and relations between the two peoples soon became tense.

At this time an old prospector named Brooks was camped at a soak near Conistan station, and a number of Walbiri, mainly Walmalla, set up camp nearby. He shared food with the visitors at first but, when he could no longer afford to do so, they clubbed him to death, rifled his stores and fled north along Lander Creek. In the same year (1928) another group of Walbiri wounded and robbed a solitary settler farther north on the Lander. These attacks, together with other thefts of food from cattle-stations, incensed many of the local Europeans. A policeman led a small punitive expedition to the Lander, where he surprised several Walbiri camps and shot the occupants. Mission organizations protested strongly at the harshness of these measures and asked the Administration to investigate the matter. An official enquiry followed, in which a board comprising a Queensland police magistrate, a South Australian police inspector, and the Central Australian chief of police publicly heard evidence at Alice Springs. The policeman, who admitted to killing 17 natives, was exonerated. The board's findings are of interest:

> The evidence of all witnesses was inconclusive, and, after exhaustive enquiry lasting three weeks, the Board found the shooting was justified and that the natives killed in the various encounters were all members of the Walmulla tribe from Western Australia who were on a marauding expedition with the avowed object of wiping out the white settlers and native boys employed on these stations. (Report on . . . Central Australia, 1929).

Meanwhile, the Walbiri in the Lander district had scattered to avoid further reprisals. Some travelled along the Hanson to Wauchope and from there gradually drifted into Tennant Creek. The rest returned to the desert and to the Vaughan Springs-Mount Singleton-Mount Doreen area, where a few Ngalia Walbiri were then living. Some continued on to the Granites and Tanami. The shootings left the people with a long-standing distrust of Europeans and to an important degree reinforced the authority of the older men of the tribe who had previously tried to dissuade their juniors from becoming entangled with white men. The effects of this attitude are seen today in the continued adherence of many Walbiri to the traditional rules and values.

In 1928 Terry led a geological survey party from the Kimberleys through Tanami and the Granites to Conistan (vide Terry, 1930). Although his reports on the Tanami-Granites area were discouraging, prospectors still sought gold there, and in 1932 news reached the south of a rich strike at the Granites. By November 1932 there were about 200 men on the field. The Administration, doubtless recalling the Brooks' Soak incident, stationed a policeman to keep all Aborigines beyond a 10-mile radius of the miners' camps.

The official reason given for this segregation was that many Walmalla Walbiri were believed to be infected with venereal granuloma (vide Baume, 1933; Madigan, 1944), a statement which implied that miners were cohabiting with the native women. The Walbiri say that this was so. They also assert that at this time miners shot one Walbiri man dead and wounded several others for stealing provisions. I have not discovered any

official confirmation of this allegation. A party of Walbiri supposed to have been involved in the affair migrated to Birrindudu
and Gordon Downs, where they still live. Whether or not this
shooting actually occurred, the people now firmly believe that
it did.

The white population of the Granites had dwindled to 10
by late 1933 and rarely exceeded that figure during the next
seven or eight years. As the policeman had been withdrawn,
a few Walbiri remained at the fields and became casual labourers. In the meantime, smallscale mining of wolfram had
begun at Mount Hardy in about 1931 and later extended to
Wolfram Hill, near Mount Doreen, and Mount Singleton. A
number of Walbiri worked at these diggings. In 1933 W. Braitling settled permanently at Mount Doreen. His cattle-station
became the home of a large group of Ngalia Walbiri, many of
whom now work in the stock-camps.

In the same year rich deposits of gold were found at Tennant
Creek and a rush followed that soon increased the population
of the township to over 500. Walbiri in the area congregated
around the town, either to work or simply to beg. The price of
wolfram had also risen at this time, and there were as many
as 30 to 40 miners digging on the eastern Wauchope and Hatches
Creek fields. Some of the Walbiri obtained work there as labourers.

Partly as a result of these mining developments and partly in
response to changes in public opinion in other states, the
Administration in 1933 introduced new legislation to redefine
the status of Aborigines in the Territory. Employers were to
pay natives a prescribed minimum wage and to feed and clothe
their dependants. The illness of any native had to be reported
and, if necessary, the patient carried free to hospital. The newly-
established Aerial Medical Service could be asked to provide
transport. Police and medical officers, who were Protectors of
Aborigines, could prosecute negligent or defaulting employers.
Moreover, to ensure that native morals would not be impaired,
Aborigines were forbidden to receive liquor or to consort with
non-Aborigines. Many desert Aborigines had settled around
Alice Springs during the drought of 1924-9 and become beggars,
scavengers and prostitutes. The Administration sent all these

people back to their tribal territories, where good seasons had replenished food supplies.

The Aborigines Branch, which was then part of the Medical Department, appointed its first patrol officer, T. G. H. Strehlow, in 1936. His duties included not only the supervision of the welfare of Aborigines, especially in Central Australia, but also the recording of native customs. In 1938 the Branch became the Native Affairs Branch and functioned independently of the Medical Department. One of its first undertakings was to plan the establishment of a number of new settlements for Aborigines who were not completely detribalized.

For the Walbiri, the period from 1936 to 1940 was marked by an increase in mining activity in and near their territory. Men now worked on the wolfram-fields at Mount Hardy, Mount Doreen, Mount Treachery, Wauchope and Hatches Creek, the gold-fields at Tanami, the Granites and Tennant Creek, and at the newly-opened tin-mines near Anningie and Conistan. At the same time more young men were joining the stock-camps at Mount Doreen, Conistan, Anningie, Willowra and Wave Hill cattle-stations. It is impossible to say accurately how many were then employed, but the figure must have been relatively small. Even in 1954 only about 25 per cent of the tribe worked casually for Europeans. The significant point is that, once the drought of 1924 had forced the people to live on cattle-stations and near mines, they became too much accustomed to the new foods, warm clothes, steel axes and the like to wish to return permanently to the rigorous life in the bush. Everyone now desired these commodities, which could be regularly obtained only as long as some at least of the tribe accepted European employment.

The war had little direct effect on the Walbiri. Although the Australian Army was by 1944 employing more than 1000 Aborigines, mainly as unskilled labourers, few of these were Walbiri. The younger men continued in their pastoral and mining occupations, and a few of the wives worked as station domestic servants. Most of the older men remained unemployed, largely because they had no need to work. Younger men, under the existing kinship system, were bound to supply them with the white man's commodities.

Wartime financial retrenchments restricted the activities of the Native Affairs Branch, but it was able nevertheless in 1941 to proclaim the Haast's Bluff Aboriginal Reserve of some 7000 square miles and in 1942 to build a ration depot and trade store there. The depot was intended to halt the eastward drift of Pidjandjara to the towns, but it also attracted many Ngalia Walbiri from the Mount Doreen area.

The N.A.B. then decided to establish a settlement for the Walbiri and Warramunga living in the vicinity of Tennant Creek township. Only a few of these natives could find work in the town, and the police ration depot at the telegraph-station was not equipped to support large numbers of unemployed. The new settlement was formed at Phillip Creek, about 30 miles north of Tennant Creek. At first it was staffed by members of a Protestant mission, who issued food and clothing (supplied by N.A.B.) to the 275 Aborigines and provided them with limited medical attention and elementary schooling. N.A.B. took over the running of the settlement in 1951, following an unsavoury scandal involving the missionary and the native schoolgirls. By 1955, however, it was clear that the lagoon on which the settlement depended for water could not long meet the requirements of the growing population. A new settlement called Warrabri was established east of the Stuart Highway, between Wauchope and Barrow Creek, and the natives moved to it in 1956.

Meanwhile, a sharp drop in wolfram prices at the end of the war had closed most of the small mines. The Walbiri who were thrown out of employment had no wish to return to a nomadic life in the desert. In 1945 N.A.B. set up a ration depot at Bullocky Soak, near Teatree, for these men and their dependants, but, when the numbers being supported reached 120, this ceased to be a practicable arrangement. So an area of 200 square miles around the Rock Hill bore on the newly-opened stock-route from Alice Springs to Mount Doreen was proclaimed in 1946 as the Yuendumu Aboriginal Reserve. All the Walbiri at Bullocky Soak were sent there, as well as unemployed Walbiri living on neighbouring cattle-stations. N.A.B. had earlier established a ration depot at Tanami for western Walbiri but in

Ngama—the site of the cave-paintings—a valley rich in game.

Paintings at Ngama cave, near Yuendumu. They represent snake,
dingo and wallaby totems.

Yarry djabangari—a man of uncertain temper.

A Walbiri man decorated for a public meeting.

1945, a drought year, the only well had failed. The depot was moved to the Granites and later to Yuendumu.

By the end of 1946 there were about 400 Walbiri at Yuendumu, including representatives of all the traditional local divisions of the tribe. Old feuds soon came to life and a long series of quarrels split the settlement into armed factions. Obviously another settlement was needed if bloodshed was to be avoided. Vestey's grazing lease on the Catfish block of 845 square miles at Hooker Creek had expired in 1945, so, in the face of strong opposition from the pastoral company, N.A.B. had that area proclaimed an Aboriginal Reserve in 1948. The Hooker Creek settlement was established there with a nucleus of about 25 Walbiri in 1949. A small herd of cattle and a plant of stock-horses were driven on to the property in 1951, and in the next year about 150 Walbiri arrived from Yuendumu settlement. Finally, the few Walbiri remaining at the Granites were sent to Hooker Creek and Yuendumu.

Thus, by 1955 about two-thirds of the tribe lived on settlements under the direct supervision of N.A.B. officers; almost all the other Walbiri lived on cattle-stations, where patrol officers visited them regularly to investigate their welfare.

Recent legislation has given Northern Territory Aborigines the status of wards of the Commonwealth Government. They are under the protection of the Department of Welfare (a new department that includes the former Native Affairs Branch) whose ultimate aim is the assimilation of Aborigines into Australian society. The Department may recommend that Aborigines who attain certain standards of living be exempted from the provisions of the Welfare Ordinance and granted full citizenship. I do not know of any Walbiri who have been exempted.

CHAPTER III

PRESENT DISTRIBUTION OF THE TRIBE

The exact size of the tribe is not yet known. The people are highly mobile and considerable difficulties attend the making of an accurate census. Although most Walbiri now regard particular government settlements and cattle-stations as their usual "countries" of residence, they spend much time visiting relatives in other localities. Men usually take their families with them on such journeys and may be absent from the home camp for months at a time.

At Mount Doreen cattle-station in the summer of 1955, for instance, I saw a party of men, women and children arrive from Hooker Creek settlement, en route to Yuendumu settlement. In appalling heat they had walked more than 200 miles across the desert in a fortnight in order to bring a youth to be circumcised in the presence of his father. People constantly travel between Hooker Creek and Wave Hill station (a distance of about 80 miles), and there is much visiting among the groups at Tea-tree, Anningie, Willowra and Conistan stations, as well as among those at Mount Doreen station, Yuendumu and Haast's Bluff. Movement is usually greatest in summer, when initiates are taken on the grand tour before circumcision.

Some men work on cattle-stations many miles from their camps for six to nine months of each year. They do so not only for the wages they receive, but also for the pleasure of travelling and seeing new places at the white man's expense. Men who are competent stockmen are in demand, especially on the stations in the north-west where local tribes are declining in numbers. Thus, Hooker Creek men are regularly employed at Wave Hill, Limbunya and Waterloo. For the past few years small parties of Yuendumu men have travelled over 300 miles to the Gallipoli and Soudan stations on the Barkly Tableland, although Yuendumu stockmen normally work nearer home—at Mount Denison, Mount Allan and neighbouring stations. Many droving-plants that cross the Territory to Queensland railheads employ Walbiri stockmen, usually recruited from Phillip Creek settlement.

An added obstacle to my estimating the population of the tribe was the fact that, at that time, no census had been made simultaneously on all the cattle-stations where Walbiri were thought to be employed. Consequently, a number of families might have escaped the counting. Bearing in mind these sources of error, I shall present the figures at my disposal (for many of which I am indebted to N.A.B.) and make the best estimate I can of the size of the tribe.

TABLE 4

Estimated Walbiri population, 1954

Locality	*Number of Walbiri residents*		
Government settlements	*Male*	*Female*	*Total*
Hooker Creek	78	87	165
Yuendumu	146	207	353
Phillip Creek	184	159	343
Bungalow, Alice Springs	18	7	25
Total	426	460	886
Percentage	48	52	100
Cattle-stations, mines			
Total	187	201	388
Percentage	48	52	100
Both			
Total	613	661	1,274
Percentage	48	52	100

There are also a few Walbiri living permanently at Conistan, Wave Hill and Gordon Downs stations and at Haast's Bluff and Bagot (Darwin) settlements who are not included in the above table. I have no accurate figures for these people but, from the evidence of genealogies and the like, doubt that they exceed 150 in all. Combining all these figures, then, I take the total population in 1954 to be about 1400. This means that the tribe today is one of the largest in the Northern Territory.

After examining various factors, such as the high birthrate, improved diet and extended medical services, that have affected the population during the past decade, I conclude that, before the arrival of the Europeans, the tribe numbered about 1000—at most 1200. The average density of population was thus about one person per 35 square miles, a figure that reflects the difficulties of maintaining a food-gathering economy in the Australian desert. Similarly, the Aranda, who in the past occupied more than 25,000 square miles of rather more productive country nearby, probably numbered fewer than 2000.

These figures may be compared with estimates made of Aboriginal populations in less rigorous environments. Elkin (1932, p. 297) reported that in the Kimberleys about 10,000 natives, comprising at least 30 tribes, lived on about 65,000 square miles. Some of this area was sea-coast, which provided regular and copious supplies of food. Stanner (1936, p. 187) stated that the Murinbata group of 100 or more occupied only 500 to 700 square miles of the fertile Daly River country. Warner (1937, p. 16) estimated that in north-eastern Arnhem Land the Aboriginal population averaged about one person to eight or nine square miles. It is clear that desert tribes needed much greater areas to support them than did tribes nearer the coast.

It is reasonable to assume that the ratio of males to females shown in Table 4 approximates the true Walbiri ratio. The masculinity rate of 93 in the sample does not differ significantly from the rate of $100 \cdot 4$ in the Commonwealth population of 1947 (which excludes all Aborigines; vide the Year Book for 1951). Among the Australian population the masculinity rate tends to be positively correlated with the birthrate, but this does not appear to be so among the Walbiri.

TABLE 5

Walbiri births and deaths

	Locality			
	Hooker Creek 1952-4	Yuendumu 1952-5	Phillip Creek 1952-4	Common-wealth 1947
Period				
Births				
male	8	27	?	
female	9	29	?	
total	17	56	25	

Deaths

male	4	16	?	
female	2	15	?	
total	6	31	12	
Estimated population	165	350	340	
Crude birthrate per 1000	72	62	32	24·1
(averaged over 12 months for Walbiri)	(all settlements—52)			
Crude deathrate per 1000	24	34	14	9·7
(averaged over 12 months for Walbiri)	(all settlements—24)			
Rate of natural increase per 1000	48	28	17	14·4
	(all settlements—28)			
Masculinity rate (approx.)	89	70	115	100·4
	(all settlements—90)			

Whereas the figures for births and deaths in Table 5 are accurate, the rates for birth, death and natural increase are approximations and probably under-estimate the true state of affairs. It would be unwise, however, to assume that a high rate of natural increase exists also among Walbiri on cattle-stations; my impression is that the rate there is lower, although I have no reliable evidence to confirm this view.

Walbiri men, especially those living on settlements, firmly believe that whatever adjustments the tribe might have to make in the face of European pressures, it will continue to increase in size and will remain an identifiable society distinct from all others. The figures I have presented here offer some support for their optimism.

CHAPTER IV

THE TRIBE AND ITS CONGENERS

Ethnocentrism. The Walbiri are aware that, in terms of material possessions, power and prestige, they rank low in the hierarchy of social statuses in contemporary Northern Territory society.

At the top they see the "Whitefellow", who, they believe, commands almost unlimited wealth and power. This power has many expressions. The Whitefellow has policemen ready to enforce his commands, he has complete freedom of movement, he can manipulate symbols on paper so that other people (especially Aborigines) are made to act in ways often uncongenial to them. A long way below stand the "Yellowfellows"—half-caste Aborigines, so-called Afghans and other Asians. They are thought to have fewer material possessions and less money; they have much less power, and Aborigines often have claims over them arising out of consanguineal and affinal ties. Whitefellows who through marriage or consorting with Aboriginal women are liable to the same sorts of claims tend to be placed in the Yellowfellow category. At the bottom of the scale is the "Blackfellow", with few possessions and little money, prestige, or power.

A dispassionate analysis of Territory society indicates that this classification is fairly accurate. It also raises the point, too often overlooked in discussions of social attitudes and prejudices, that a stereotype need not be distorted simply because it is maintained with conviction.

The Walbiri mainly invoke this class stereotype and its concomitant rules of action when dealing with non-Aborigines. When associating with Aborigines they work within a simpler frame of reference. "There are two kinds of blackfellows," they say, "we who are the Walbiri and those unfortunate people who are not. Our laws are the true laws; other blackfellows have inferior laws which they continually break. Consequently, anything may be expected of these outsiders." This ethnocentrism leads them to patronize other Aborigines in a lordly fashion whenever they meet; but, such is the Walbiri reputation for aggressiveness and fighting ability, the victims generally swallow the sneers in silence.

The Walbiri maintain their identity wherever they settle. When one takes a wife from another tribe, the children are Walbiri, no matter if the couple live in the wife's tribal territory or even in the same camp as her near kinsmen. Sooner or later the father takes his children back to Walbiri country for a lengthy sojourn. He goes to great trouble to have his sons initiated into his own totemic lodge and into the Big Sunday rituals, to ensure that the boys will follow "the true line of the Walbiri law". The people cannot believe that a person fortunate enough to be born a Walbiri would ever allow his "citizenship" to lapse, and I have never encountered a Walbiri who has done so.

Intertribal relations. The Walbiri recognize many distinct tribal groups outside their own borders. Their attitudes to these people vary considerably. Some they regard as friends and relatives, some as traditional enemies, and towards others they remain neutral. Of the outlying tribes they rarely know more than the names and approximate locations; but this does not prevent them from imputing to the strangers cannibalism, incest and other practices that the Walbiri deem disgusting.

Relations with northern tribes. In the past the Walbiri boundary lay south of Winnecke Creek, and the Gurindji and Mudbara tribes formed the main ceremonial and trading links with other northern groups. The presence in Walbiri culture of the Big Sunday religious complex, Waranggan dancing and certain kinship terms, as well as the use of bamboo spear-shafts and iron "shovel-nose" spear-heads, suggests that these contacts were extensive and of long standing. Today the Gurindji still act as agents for the Walbiri in dealings with tribes farther north on the major ceremonial and trade routes.

Until recently, however, intermarriage between Gurindji and Walbiri was infrequent; and the Gurindji, Mudbara and Malngjin tribesmen still tend to regard the Walbiri as uncouth trouble-makers, although they respect the desert people's strict observance of tribal laws. Thus, at Limbunya, Malngjin men and women vehemently assured me that nothing would induce them to visit Hooker Creek; "those long-haired myalls there would murder us!" The Walbiri, on the other hand, consider the Victoria River natives to be soft and over-sophisticated, and they are shocked at the ease with which unsubincised youths there gain access to women. At the same time, Hooker Creek men are quick to attribute misfortunes, ranging from attacks of rheumatism to death, to sorcery performed by Wave Hill Gurindji.

As a result of the decline in the numbers of the Gurindji, Malngjin and Mudbara (Meggitt, 1955b), more Walbiri from Hooker Creek are working on cattle-stations in the territories of these tribes. Intermarriage is now occurring more often as the local women find that Walbiri virility has attractions outweighing the visitors' uncouthness. Moreover, Hooker Creek Walbiri and Wave Hill Gurindji meet during the summer in large numbers to share certain Big Sunday ceremonies, usually at sites midway between the two localities. The development of such ties of ritual friendship also facilitates intertribal marriage. Already a fairly large Walbiri camp has grown up at Wave Hill and some of the occupants now regard that area as Walbiri country. I think it likely that in a couple of generations or so the Walbiri will absorb their northern neighbours.

A few Walbiri men have lived for short periods in Katherine and Darwin, either to work or to receive medical treatment, and have in consequence encountered a fairly representative selection of Aborigines from tribes to the far north and northeast of the desert. Despite these contacts, most Walbiri are convinced that these people, in their own countries, make a practice of killing strangers and eating their kidney-fat. For instance, a woman had her arm broken in a camp brawl at Hooker Creek and was flown to Darwin for treatment. After a few weeks there she absconded with a northern tribesman and the authorities were unable to recover her. When the news reached Hooker Creek, her relatives at once assumed that she had been killed for her kidney-fat, and the whole camp mourned her death.

This sort of belief makes it difficult for N.A.B. officers to persuade seriously-ill Walbiri to go to Darwin; but none of the tribe objects to going to the Alice Springs hospital where other desert natives are treated.

Relations with the Djingili, Walmanba and Warramunga tribes. The people had few contacts with the Djingili in the past but, following the drought-induced migrations to Tennant Creek and the establishment of the Phillip Creek settlement, they now see much more of these tribesmen. Walbiri men from Phillip Creek who work in droving-plants occasionally visit Newcastle Waters, and Djingili men coming to Tennant Creek often spend a few days at Phillip Creek. The daily contact of the Phillip Creek Walbiri with the co-resident Warramunga, who have always known the Djingili well, has also facilitated this friendly intercourse. I have several times seen Walbiri, Warramunga, Walmanba and Djingili men participate simultaneously in Djingili *kadjiga* ceremonies connected with circumcision.

The Walbiri have apparently always been on good terms with the Walmanba and often refer to them as "half-Walbiri", whose women can be married with propriety. The languages of the two groups are similar, and the people share a number of cultural features. The Walmanba seem to have declined greatly in numbers since about 1900, and the survivors are today concentrated around Banka Banka, Helen Springs, Renner Springs and Powell Creek stations. They often visit Phillip Creek but see little of Walbiri on other settlements who are separated from them by hundreds of miles of desert.

When Spencer and Gillen were visiting the Warramunga near Tennant Creek, in 1901, they observed the arrival of a party of 16 Walbiri, including two ritual novices (vide Spencer and Gillen, 1904, p. 576). Their comments on this event implied that the two tribes were the best of friends and often visited each other, and the authors lumped the Walbiri in with the Worgaia and Djingili as members of a Warramunga "nation" of tribes (1904, p. 76). When I discussed these opinions with older Walbiri men, however, they rejected them out of hand. The Waneiga at Hooker Creek in particular often asserted that the two tribes with whom the Walbiri were usually in conflict were the Warramunga and the Waringari to the west. Indeed, they referred to these peoples as though they were traditional enemies and gave me circumstantial accounts of the raids and counter-raids that frequently took place between them and the Walbiri. The same men explicitly denied that similar disputes were common with other tribes.

The men's descriptions made it clear that the Warramunga (and Waringari) trespasses were not merely hunting forays impelled by food-shortages in the invaders' own territory but rather were raids undertaken to combine hunting for sport and the abduction of women. Often, too, the raiders were simply spoiling for a fight. They were met with force, and deaths occurred on both sides. Walbiri war-parties would then invade the Warramunga country in retaliation. If they were able to surprise the enemy camps and kill or drive off the men, they carried away any women they found.

As the kinship systems and marriage rules of the two tribes were similar, it was possible for a Walbiri raider to stand in the relationship of potential husband to the Warramunga woman he had abducted, in which case his tribesmen regarded her as his legal wife. But, if the pair were otherwise related, she could only be his concubine and other men who were appropriately related to her were likely to argue that she belonged to one of them. As a result, there was often more blood spilt over the allocation of captives than was shed during the original raid. Most of the stolen women sooner or later escaped to their own tribe when the chance offered, but a few who had borne children to their captors preferred to remain with their offspring.

Accounts such as this clearly indicate that, in the past, the relations of the Walbiri and Warramunga were by no means friendly. It is also significant that, although most Walbiri men are bi- or multi-lingual, few of them could speak Warramunga when the drought of 1924 forced them to move into the Tennant Creek area. Since that time, however, a comparatively large group of Waneiga and Lander Walbiri have lived in close contact with the Warramunga, notably at the Phillip Creek settlement, and there appears to have been little friction between the two tribes.

The friendlier associations today seem to depend on several factors. Phillip Creek is in Warramunga territory and Aboriginal courtesy demands that the Walbiri, who came there uninvited, take care not to antagonize the men who are, in their eyes, their hosts. Moreover, the immigrants now pay a kind of tribute to validate their residence in this area. The two groups have agreed that, whereas Phillip Creek Walbiri men may marry only Walbiri women, the Warramunga men are free to marry both their own and the Walbiri women. Children of these intermarriages are Warramunga.

I did not hear any Walbiri men complain about the arrangement; some indeed told me that the Warramunga are now so few (there were only about 45 at Phillip Creek) that they withdraw only a limited number of Walbiri women from circulation. Finally, both groups are under the daily supervision of N.A.B. officers, and they know that any overt displays of intertribal hostility would be quickly checked.

Relations with the Ngadidji and Yalyuwara. Although the Walbiri and the Ngadidji shared a common boundary somewhere near the Hanson floodout, the tribes apparently had little to do with each other. The Walbiri, like other Aborigines (vide Spencer and Gillen, 1904), regarded the Ngadidji (Kaitish) as a sullen, suspicious and hostile people who were best left alone, and their opinion has changed little today. They point to the behaviour of the Ngadidji in the Barrow Creek killings of 1874, of which they have a garbled knowledge from European sources, as confirmation of their attitude, and they say that the one saving grace of these Aborigines is that they were not cannibals.

Nowadays, members of the two tribes meet occasionally, especially in the vicinity of Barrow Creek, Murray Downs and Wauchope where the surviving Ngadidji are gathered. These contacts occur under the eyes of European authority and are perforce superficially friendly or neutral. However, when N.A.B. planned to replace the Phillip Creek settlement with one at Warrabri in Ngadidji territory, the Ngadidji privately approved of the proposal and said that their own numbers were now too few for them to want all the land that was once theirs. The Phillip Creek Walbiri also appeared to welcome the plan, for the new locality was much more attractive than was Phillip Creek. A few men wondered if they would have to make an arrangement with the Ngadidji to give them women, as they had done with the Warramunga, in order to live there, but none seemed perturbed by the thought.

Walbiri acquaintance with the Yalyuwara must have been limited, for the territories of the Ngadidji and the Yanmadjari separated the two tribes. During the past ten years or so, a few men have encountered occasional Yalyuwara at Murray Downs, Hatches Creek and the Bungalow (Alice Springs). Relations between them were more or less friendly until 1954, when several Yalyuwara men murdered a Walbiri man near Murray Downs. Walbiri attitudes changed sharply as a result.

Relations with the Yanmadjari and Aranda. The Yanmadjari, like the Walmanba, occupy a special place in the affections of the Walbiri, who regard them as "half-Walbiri and one people with us". (Strehlow, 1947, p. 52, noted that the Aranda also called the Anmatjira "half-Ilpara".) The two tribes have a long, common boundary; they have always traded together; they share totemic ceremonies, myths and tracks; and inter-marriage frequently occurs. Mount Barkly and Mount Leichhardt, between which the border passes, are said to represent the two tribes, each looking towards the other. Indeed, both the hills and the tribes themselves are often referred to as *djuraldja-gida*, which means two descent lines that exchange women in marriage.

Some western and north-western Walbiri would question the description of the Yanmadjari as a separate tribe, asserting instead that they are really a Walbiri community whose language has been contaminated by contact with the Aranda. But the Lander Walbiri, who probably know the Yanmadjari best, consider them to be a distinct tribe. Since the arrival of Europeans, Yanmadjari population appears to have declined and much of their territory around Anningie, Mount Esther and Teatree stations is now occupied by eastern Walbiri who regard the area as Walbiri tribal country. These movements have not caused any friction between the two groups.

Yanmadjari territory divides the Walbiri from the northern and western Aranda, and the two tribes appear to have had little direct contact. Nevertheless the Walbiri have always disliked the Aranda, who, they assert, are as unpleasant as the Ngadidji—both are too quarrelsome and unreliable. Nowadays, they see a good deal of the Aranda at Alice Springs, particularly at the Bungalow settlement, and they have found another reason for disliking them. The long association of the Aranda with white men, they say, has made them too sophisticated for their own good. Neither group attends the other's rituals at the Bungalow, although Walbiri participate in Pidjandja ceremonies held there.

Relations with the Pidjandja-speaking tribes. The Walbiri recognize several tribal groups within this general category, and their attitude towards most of them is friendly. They are all regarded as "people of the spinifex country", which establishes a bond between them and the spinifex-dwelling Walbiri. The languages are similar, and most southern Walbiri speak Pidjandja fluently. A number of important totemic tracks link the territories of both groups, so that both peoples share the custody of the related complexes of myth and ritual. The Walbiri are aware that many elements of the ceremonies are the same in both areas. Thus they say, "We Walbiri follow the same kangaroo dreaming track as do the Bidjabidja and Pintubi; we sing the same songs, recite the same myths and make the same sacred string-crosses."

But, despite the existence of these ties, the Walbiri do not consider the Pidjandjara, as a whole, to be as closely related to them as are the Yanmadjari or Walmanba, and intermarriage is less common than might be expected. Many Walbiri men say that this is because they find Pidjandjara women unattractive; some of them, they say, are bearded like men—they are covered with spinifex-grass!

I have, however, recorded a considerable number of marriages between Ngalia Walbiri and Pintubi women—more than occur with other Pidjandja-speakers. This is surprising, in that Walbiri relations with Pintubi are in many respects less happy than with the other Pidjandjara. Their attitude towards these people is tinged, if not with fear, at least with respect for their magical powers. Pintubi medicine-men are thought to be powerful and of uncertain temper; the women are believed to assume the guise of demons and eat their own children, for "they have no game in their country" (vide Meggitt, 1955a, p. 398). At the same time, perhaps as compensation, the Walbiri regard the Pintubi as naive bumpkins. Thus, if a Walbiri man commits a social blunder, others present shake their heads and murmur pityingly, *"o pintubi:i:i."*

The Walbiri continue to hold these sorts of beliefs about Pintubi today largely because, in the absence of European settlement in the south-west, they have not had free intercourse with them under the neutral authority of the white man. Farther east, the founding of the Hermannsburg Mission in 1877 and the later establishment of cattle-stations and the Haast's Bluff and Areyonga settlements have facilitated the friendly intercourse of the Walbiri with other Pidjandjara. Nowadays, Aborigines travel frequently between the Yuendumu and Haast's Bluff settlements.

Relations with the Waringari and Lungga. For as long as the Walbiri can remember they have been in intermittent conflict with the Waringari. The tribes frequently raided each other to avenge old killings and to abduct women, and neither placed any reliance on the word of the other. Matters apparently came to a head some time before the Tanami gold-rush of 1909. Until then, the Waringari had claimed the ownership of the few native wells at Tanami and the country surrounding them, but in a pitched battle for the possession of the water the Walbiri drove the Waringari from the area, which they incorporated into their own territory. By desert standards the engagement was spectacular, the dead on either side numbering a score or more. Such forcible conquest of land (or, rather, water) was, to judge from the published accounts of Aboriginal societies, most uncommon among Australian tribes; but it is possible that it occurred more often than we realize in the desert regions where water is a precious commodity.

An uneasy peace broken by raids followed this battle. Between the raids there were occasional inter-tribal meetings for totemic rituals and for trade, held mainly at Barinjanggu, an important yam totemic site between Tanami and Sturt Creek and well inside Waringari country. According to my informants, not only

Waringari and Walbiri gathered there, but also Pintubi from the south and Lungga and Walmadjari from farther north, and the groups associated amicably. The latter is difficult to believe, but Strehlow (1947, p. 65) has reported similarly harmonious meetings between the traditionally hostile Kukatja and western Aranda.

Contact with the Waringari today is confined mainly to Walbiri who work at Gordon Downs and Birrindudu cattle-stations. The rest of the tribe still dislike their former enemies and take comfort from the belief that contemporary Waringari are the worse for European contact.

The Walbiri loosely apply the name Lungga to most Aborigines living between the Western Australian border and Wyndham. They are generally thought to be cannibals and drinkers of human blood. Although the few Walbiri who meet them on droving trips to Wyndham admit that this reputation may be somewhat exaggerated, others who do not know them have given me remarkably circumstantial accounts of Lungga cannibalism, which they have obtained at secondhand from Waringari and Walmadjari. One such story ended with a bloody description of a European massacre of a party of Lungga men, women and children who were supposed to have eaten a native stockman. When I commented on the magnitude of the slaughter, I was silenced by the remark that the victims were, after all, only Lungga cannibals who deserved to be shot.

The Lungga also have a shocking reputation for lechery, and they are believed to ignore their own marriage rules and incest taboos in their attempts to copulate with women normally forbidden to them. Walbiri men speak with manifest disgust of the huge and ugly genital organs that Lungga men are reputed to possess and contrast these with their own penes, which, they assert, are of the proper size, like those of all decent desert men. It is of interest that this constellation of beliefs and attitudes, so significant in terms of psychoanalytic theory, is found among other Aboriginal tribes. Thus, the Berndts (1945, p. 20) reported that desert natives at Ooldea, in South Australia, attributed cannibalism, lechery and long penes to the alien Kukata.

Summary. This survey has demonstrated that the Walbiri

exhibited a variety of attitudes towards the members of other tribes—as indeed they still do. The evidence obviously disproves the statement of Spencer and Gillen (1904) that, among Aborigines, contiguous tribes live on friendly terms simply because they have more to do with each other than with more distant tribes. On the contrary, long-term acquaintance may just as well lead to the sort of hostility that existed between the Walbiri and the Waringari or between the Kukatja and the western Aranda. It is also clear that a wide range of factors, extending from observed cultural similarity to temperamental characteristics, may determine the attitudes that one tribe has towards each of its neighbours.

But, whether the Walbiri regard other tribes in a favourable light or not, their opinions always reveal an aggressive belief in their own superiority. As might be expected, they evaluate the behaviour and usages of other peoples in terms of the coincidence of these with Walbiri norms, and they consider any noticeable divergence of the two to be evidence of the shortcomings of the outsiders. The fact that Warramunga mortuary ritual differs from that of the Walbiri, or that the Pintubi lack a thorough-going subsection system, is thought to reflect the essential inferiority of the group in question. On the other hand, the highest praise the Walbiri can bestow on well-liked neighbours, such as the Walmanba or Yanmadjari, is to refer to them as "half-Walbiri".

Tribes who are friendly disposed, however, do not for this reason have the right to enter each other's territory at will. The Walbiri believe that other Aborigines should respect their tribal borders, no matter how recently these have been extended. Outsiders may enter the territory uninvited only in an emergency, such as when they face the threat of starvation in their own country, and they should afterwards formally compensate the hosts for this hospitality. Aboriginal movements resulting from European activities have forced an extension of the definition of emergency, but the expectation of recompense remains. By the same token, the Walbiri are prepared to meet their obligations when they have to visit the territory of another tribe.

I have seen Walbiri men travelling as assistants to an N.A.B. officer, for instance, accompany him on a patrol of Ngadidji

Wally djabaldjari—in his day, a redoubtable fighter, as his many scars indicate.

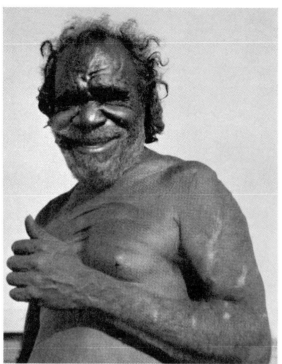

Bulbul djabaldjari—a man of many talents.

Men making the sacred, incised boards in readiness for a circumcision ceremony. The man in the foreground uses the conventional adze.

Walbiri men preparing to meet a party of Yalyuwara visitors.

and Yanmadjari country. At each camping place they offered small gifts of kangaroo-meat, flour, or tobacco to members of the local group, although the latter obviously had more of these commodities at the time than did the visitors. Even when the gifts were made ostensibly to meet kinship obligations, they were also intended to atone for the travellers' incivility in having arrived without invitation.

Outsiders may on occasions enter Walbiri territory under the protection of a "mate" or sponsor. Sponsorship is an important concept among these people, as it is, I suspect, among most Central Australian tribes. It also receives expression in the creation of ritual friendships during circumcision ceremonies and in the practice of penis-holding during the settlement of quarrels. The basic notion is that, in certain circumstances, one man may be bound to assist another, or even to substitute for him, when the latter faces trouble.

The following instance of social sponsorship reveals the technique by which strangers can be incorporated into the tribe:

A Walbiri man of the djangala subsection, who possessed considerable ritual and social prestige, worked in Darwin for several months. At Bagot settlement he made the acquaintance of an elderly man from Bathurst Island who, through the sharp practice of a Bagot resident, had been bilked of £20 paid as a deposit on a bride. When the Walbiri man was ready to return to Hooker Creek, he invited Bathurst Jack to accompany him, saying that the old man could work there for some months and save up another bride-price.

The unexpected arrival of the stranger at first disconcerted the Hooker Creek men, for his very appearance, as well as his speech, was alien to them. The djangala explained the situation, stating that he took full responsibility for the visitor. Whoever quarrelled with the outsider also quarrelled with him; if the stranger at any time behaved badly, the sponsor would take the blame. Thenceforth, everyone regarded the visitor not only as a member of the djangala subsection but also as a countryman and elder brother of his sponsor. Happily, Jack's own Bathurst Island totem was fire, which among the Walbiri was also an important totem of the djangala and djambidjimba couple of subsections.

At the time a woman of the nungarai subsection, whose husband had died about a year before, still resided in the widows' camp. The dead man had been a countryman and close classificatory brother of the djangala sponsor, who was, therefore, entitled in terms of the levirate to claim the widow as his wife. He did so and then handed her on to Bathurst Jack, who was also a potential husband for her. This action was also in accord with tribal custom. All the other men approved it, for the visitor now had no reason to interfere with their own wives. When he returned to Darwin six months later, the woman was sent back to the widows' camp. During his stay at Hooker Creek, everyone had treated him with great civility and friendship, and his departure was genuinely regretted.

The only people who may travel more or less freely between tribal territories without the need for sponsors are ceremonial messengers and ritual novices on tour with their guardians. In theory, a messenger who is decorated with totemic patterns and carries a sacred bullroarer is himself sacred, and his safety is therefore assured. As messengers are usually sent to summon only those groups who share totemic ceremonies—that is, tribes with whom the Walbiri are on more or less friendly terms—it is unlikely that the theory has often been put to the test. Novices and their guardians are also regarded as a kind of ritual messenger. It is probably significant that the party of Walbiri that Spencer and Gillen (1904, p. 576) saw welcomed by the Warramunga included two novices and their guardians.

CHAPTER V

LOCAL ORGANIZATION

The traditional local groupings of most Aboriginal tribes changed quickly and radically under the impact of European settlement. I shall, therefore, not only describe Walbiri local organization as it was until the 1930s but also indicate the sorts of changes it has since undergone. Moreover, the analysis of the kinship, subsection and moiety systems that I wish to present later must take account of the inter-relations of these sorts of categories and groups with the local groups and with the system of totemic beliefs.

In any case, there is so little reliable information about Aboriginal local organization in the literature that any new data should be recorded in detail, particularly as there is still considerable disagreement about the composition and significance of localized hordes among Australian tribes.

The major tribal divisions. Despite the displacement of people following the recent migrations, most Walbiri still believe that their territory comprises four major divisions or "countries", which were formerly occupied by the Yalpari (Lander), Waneiga, Walmalla and Ngalia subgroups of the tribe. The areas of the countries vary from about 7000 to about 15,000 square miles. On the average, they are larger than those of the Aranda, which, to judge from Strehlow's map (1947), ranged from about 3000 to 8000 square miles.

Population density varied among the territorial divisions. The country of the Lander Walbiri, one of the smallest in area (about 8000 square miles), supported a relatively large population, and the 200 or more Walbiri who still live there are almost all Yalpari. It will be remembered that Stuart, during his visits to the area in 1861-2, saw many Aborigines between Hanson Creek and Reynolds Range (Stuart, 1864). Terry also remarked on the density of the native population there in 1928 as compared with regions farther west, and Baume in 1932 observed at least 200 people camped near one cattle-station alone

(Terry, 1930; Baume, 1933). In terms of Aboriginal requirements, the country is rich in vegetable foods; game abounds, and the soaks and wells along Lander Creek hold water all the year round.

The larger Waneiga country, which lies to the north-west, lacks the variety and quantity of vegetable and flesh foods obtainable in the Lander area, and the human population was certainly sparser. Chewings, who travelled through this country in 1909, saw only a few Aborigines at the scattered wells and soaks (Chewings, 1930).

To the west, the Walmalla occupied some of the poorest and most desolate country in the Northern Territory. There are few reliable wells and soaks, and only in the wet season could the small population safely range far from the camp sites at Rabbit Flat Well, the Granites, Thompson's Rockhole, or the Newland Cave soak. In 1932, for instance, Baume encountered about 60 Walmalla at a soak that was drying up, and the party was then setting off in search of water in the western ridges. Throughout the district useful timber is scarce, vegetable foods are limited, and reptiles provide most of the scanty supply of meat. During World War II, N.A.B. had to set up a ration post in the Tanami-Granites area for the people, who then numbered about 150.

By desert standards, the Ngalia country in the south is much more attractive. The mountainous terrain supports a great variety of game and edible plants, and water supplies are generally adequate for native needs. The fact that most of the 400 or 500 Walbiri now living at Yuendumu and Mount Doreen are Ngalia indicates that the population was probably relatively dense in the past.

I have marked on my map only the approximate locations of the boundaries of the countries, for I was unable to visit all of them while I was in the desert. The older Walbiri men, however, have no difficulty in defining the limits of their own countries fairly precisely, although they may be less sure of the more distant boundaries of other countries. The positions of the boundaries are fixed, validated and remembered through the agency of religious myths. These stories not only plot the totemic tracks and centres but also specify the points at which the custody of the songs, rituals and decorations associated with them should change hands as the tracks pass from one country to another. An investigator able to spend long enough in the field could produce from such data a detailed map of the borders of the four countries.

The residents of a country, who include representatives of all the subsections and kinship categories, called each other *walaldja*, "my own countryman", a term still in common use among older men. The distinction between one's own countrymen and other Walbiri was to some extent sharpened by the recognition of minor cultural differences among the four local groups. Some of the most obvious of these diacritical marks concern linguistic variation. Thus, the Yalpari or Lander Walbiri are said to "talk light", that is, to use unvoiced consonants, and the others to "talk heavy". The Ngalia vocabulary includes a great many words common to Pidjandja languages, whereas the Waneiga frequently employ words derived from eastern Kimberley languages.

Differences of this kind helped to produce a mild local ethnocentrism in each group, and relations among the four groups in some respects resembled inter-tribal relations. But the residents of all the countries also thought of themselves as members of the superordinate Walbiri tribe, which was distinct from all other tribes. Certainly, men today can still recall occasions on which inter-country disputes flared up but, to judge from their accounts, the groups never displayed to each other the intense and continuing hostility that Strehlow (1947) has said characterized the interaction of some of the divisions of the Aranda.

The residents of a Walbiri country were normally economically self-sufficient. They were free to wander anywhere in the district, provided that the women and children kept away from certain sacred totemic sites. Hunting and food-gathering itineraries were governed mainly by local and seasonal variations in the distribution of game and plants. In the good season, which usually lasted from autumn until early winter, when billabongs were full and vegetable foods abundant, the people congregated in one or two large groups. They travelled from one waterhole to another as particular plants came into bearing and the game moved ahead of the hunters. As water and food became more scarce, the main party broke up into progressively smaller groups.

By the time of the bad season, towards the end of the dry weather in late spring and early summer, the typical food-gathering unit comprised a man, his wives and children, with perhaps an old widowed mother or father-in-law in their care. Only a group as small as this could operate effectively at a time when the day's catch might be no more than a lizard or two, a few withered yams and a handful of grass-seeds. Then, after the rains had broken and food become more plentiful, the small groups slowly converged until all were assembled again at the big waterholes.

Between autumn and summer, as the foraging groups split up, their composition did not conform to a single pattern. A number of factors determined the membership of the units at various times, as indeed they still do at Hooker Creek and Yuendumu settlements where hunting and food-gathering continue. In particular, kinship ties of one kind and another were involved.

Thus, actual and classificatory brothers, especially those who had been circumcised at the one ceremony, commonly hunted together. They did so not only because of the bonds of ritual friendship, but also because they were more willing to share wives than were more distantly related "brothers". The men could, therefore, enjoy male companionship and sexual variety simultaneously. Brothers-in-law were also likely to be good mates and suitable hunting companions, for they had shared in important ritual activities and exchanged actual or classificatory sisters in marriage.

Men related as classificatory "mother's mother's brother" and "sister's daughter's son", however, rarely joined the one small group. The wife of each was the classificatory cross-cousin of the other, and in this society such cross-cousins were (and still are) expected to engage in extra-marital sexual liaisons. Their inclusion in the one party would cause too many arguments and perhaps bloodshed. Male cross-cousins, on the other hand, generally welcomed each other's company and often hunted together. This friendship seems to have been based partly on the men's tacit recognition that they enjoy the sexual favours of each other's classificatory "sisters".

Young married men sometimes accompanied their fathers and their fathers' fathers, especially if they were still receiving instruction in their lodge mysteries, but the attraction of relaxing with coevals often induced them to travel instead with cross-cousins and brothers-in-law. Unmarried men frequently joined their parents, but once again the call of age-mates and married brothers was strong. The few unmarried women, including widows, usually remained with their parents or married sisters.

It is obviously misleading to regard these Walbiri food-gathering groups as simple patrilineal and patrilocal hordes. Their composition was too labile, too dependent on the changing seasons, the alternation of quarrels and reconciliations, the demands of non-agnatic relatives, and so on. From the point of view of the individual, the group at its greatest was the community that comprised all his countrymen and included most of his closer relatives. At its least, the group was his family of procreation or orientation. Between these extremes, the unit might perhaps be termed a horde, but it was one whose personnel were recruited on a number of different bases that varied from one occasion to the next. These might reflect consanguineal links, affinal ties, bonds of ritual friendship or obligation, the pull of temperamental compatibility—or combinations of all of them.

I shall henceforth refer to the largest group of countrymen as the community—"the maximal group of persons who normally reside together in face-to-face association" (Murdock, 1949, p. 79). This social unit possessed the following characteristics:

i. its membership was relatively stable within more or less permanent territorial boundaries;
ii. male members were generally born into the community, whereas many female members were recruited by marriage from other countries;
iii. it had a legitimate title to its domain or country, the resources of which it exploited (often co-operatively);
iv. it had custody of totemic sites within its territory;
v. it cared for aged and weak members, as a form of social insurance;
vi. it displayed in-group ethnocentrism and discovered its scapegoats in out-groups;
vii. it protected its members from external attack;
viii. it was in many respects the maximal political entity.

The labile subgroups within the community, which were larger than the residential family units, may be referred to as bands or hordes.

It is a basic Walbiri rule that people with food should share it with those who have none. If seasonal conditions were so bad that food and water became scarce in one country, its members dispersed and entered neighbouring countries, including those of the Yanmadjari. They explained their plight to their hosts and asked permission to reside with them until food was again available in their own country. Such requests often took the form of appeals to actual kinship ties and, couched in these terms, could hardly be refused. The suppliants, then or later, made gifts of weapons, hair-string, red ochre and the like to express their gratitude and, equally important, to rid themselves of feelings of shame or embarrassment. Even if the hosts' resources were also limited, they were shared until all the food was consumed. Then hosts and guests alike literally tightened their string-belts and scoured the countryside for overlooked trifles, hoping they could survive until the rains came and game returned.

The good season at the end of the wet weather was the time for visiting between countries. Small parties sometimes walked long distances simply to see kinsfolk and keep up friendships. Although the visitors arrived unannounced, they were usually expected and were sponsored by the appropriate relatives. I think that such spontaneous visiting was less common then than it is today. One deterrent was, and to a large extent is still, the people's fear that they might lack "space" or unrestricted mobility while travelling. This notion of individual mobility deserves comment.

The women in a Walbiri camp may be observed each day to set off in the same few directions in their search for food and firewood. The men do not go hunting in these directions, and, when they gather to discuss, rehearse, or enact ceremonies, they select sites on the opposite side of the camp from the areas visited by the women. The environs of the camp are thus divided into two main zones. The camp at the Hooker Creek settlement provides a typical example of such arrangements.

Within a radius of three or four miles, the neighbourhood

of the settlement includes a number of clearly defined tracts that are closed to men or to women. The men cannot wander at will in the southern and south-eastern of these—"they have no space there, for that is women's country". Any man who goes there alone is thought to be contemplating adultery. As a man usually seeks a mistress among his classificatory cross-cousins and brothers' wives, the husbands of these women are at once alarmed if they see him entering the women's country. When the women return home later in the day, their protestations of innocence are likely to be disbelieved by the husbands, who berate and often thrash the women. Indeed, the married men at Hooker Creek have good reason to distrust their wives, for the young stockmen tailing the settlement cattle often slip away from the herd to copulate with women who are gathering food in the bush. Men accompanied by their wives, however, can pass through the women's country on their way to the more distant south-eastern hunting grounds.

The northern, north-eastern and eastern environs are men's country, where most of the ceremonial activity takes place. Women have no space there, for the sacred songs and rituals are intrinsically dangerous to them. Moreover, in the old days, a woman who trespassed would have been killed; nowadays, the men are likely to thrash her with boomerangs and perhaps rape her (Meggitt, 1955a, p. 397). If women or children have to travel by motor-truck along either of the two northern roads, they must crouch face downward and cover their eyes until they have passed the men's country. They may walk along the more easterly of the roads only when accompanying their husbands or fathers on hunting trips or when groups of them are invited to attend parts of the circumcision ceremonies. They cannot walk on the other road at all.

A person's space or mobility around the camp thus varies with the locality in question, and there are some that he rarely approaches. Deviations from these norms appear to be discouraged more by the people's fear of physical punishment than by their feelings of guilt or shame or their fear of supernatural sanctions, although shame doubtless plays some part. A couple detected in amatory adventures in the women's country, for instance, may be publicly ridiculed, as well as physically attacked;

and Walbiri humour and sarcasm are extremely heavy-handed.

This notion of space also refers to inter-community relations. A party travelling unannounced through a neighbouring country in the past could not be certain of the whereabouts of all the residents. At any time the visitors might encounter people whom they should have avoided. Thus, women must keep away from all classificatory, as well as actual, sons-in-law and all secluded novices; recently circumcised youths have to avoid their circumcisers. If members of these tabooed categories were camped at the only waterhole in the area, the visitors were likely to stumble across them, to the embarrassment of all. Etiquette then demanded that the visitors at once withdraw and by-pass the waterhole, no matter how thirsty they might be. Outsiders also had the worry that during their journey they might come across men of the host group engaged in religious or magical rituals. Even if the visitors had no women with them, they would feel shame or discomfort at the encounter. They would realize that, had their neighbours wanted them to attend such ceremonies, they would have received a specific invitation to do so.

In short, the Walbiri tend to structure their socio-geographical environment into regions of greater or less space or personal mobility, which can also be distinguished in terms of the degree of embarrassment, shame, or actual fear attendant on entering them. The whole concept bears a certain resemblance to the Lewinian notion of the life-space.

Such considerations explain why the people preferred not to visit each other's countries uninvited. (Strehlow, too, has commented on the rarity of informal visiting among Aranda communities—1947, p. 52.) Nevertheless, invitations were freely extended in the ceremonial season, when food and water were sufficient to support large numbers of visitors. The main events occurring in this season were the ceremonies connected with the circumcision of pubescent boys, but the opportunity was taken to carry out other rituals, including those related to the subincision of older youths. The Walmalla and Waneiga in addition enacted the Gadjari or Big Sunday cycle of ceremonies. This pattern of activity may still be observed today.

The usual practice was to select candidates for circumcision some months beforehand so that they and their guardians could visit kinsmen in neighbouring countries and formally invite them to attend the forthcoming rituals. Among the northern communities, ceremonial messengers were (and are) also sent out to announce the holding of the Big Sunday. At the appropriate time (usually determined by counting notches cut in a message stick), the guests travelled in a body to the hosts' country.

Comparatively large groups of perhaps 400 to 500 Walbiri assembled on these occasions. I may point out here that gatherings of this size were more common in the desert than is generally realized. Thus, Strehlow (1947, p. 65) has remarked that in some localities parties of several hundred Aranda and Matuntara congregated for four or five months at a time. Similarly, the Northern Territory Administration Report of 1937 records that groups of up to 300 Pintubi were observed in the arid South-west Aboriginal Reserve as recently as 1925.

After the ceremonies concluded in one Walbiri country, the guests in turn asked the hosts to visit their own country to participate in similar activities connected with the circumcision and subincision of their own lads. Much the same sort of reciprocal visiting for ritual reasons goes on today between Hooker Creek and Wave Hill, between Mount Doreen and Yuendumu, and around Teatree, Anningie, Willowra and Conistan.

When the people gathered in this way their community affiliations were reflected in the arrangement of their bough-shades. The visitors camped apart from the hosts and oriented their camps towards their own countries, a practice that has been observed among other Australian tribes (vide Berndt, 1945, p. 49; Kaberry, 1939, p. 29). It is still kept up in the large, permanent camps on Walbiri settlements. Thus, at Hooker Creek, where three communities are represented, the Waneiga as a rule camp to the north, the Ngalia to the south, and the Walmalla between the two, although temporary rearrangements of individual families sometimes follow quarrels. Visiting Walbiri stay in the camp appropriate to their country.

In the same way, the camps at Yuendumu tend to fall into four divisions oriented to the four main countries. When men from one community section call on residents of another, etiquette demands that they wait at the outskirts of the camp until someone from the second group comes to escort them to the

shelter of the men they seek. Visiting women wait at the widows'
shelter until one of the hosts summons the women they have
come to see.

TABLE 6

*Distribution of residential family units among the four main
divisions of the Hooker Creek camp, late in 1953*

	Divisions of the camp				
	Waneiga	Walmalla	Ngalia	Employed men	Total
Number of family groups	14	7	10	6	37
Number of residents	40	37	50	16	143

Although intercommunity gatherings were held ostensibly
for ceremonial purposes, they also facilitated the making of
economic exchanges and marriages. Trade among Walbiri communities was not on a large scale, however, and had none of the
elaboration of the Daly River Kue and Merbok, for instance, or
the Kimberley Wunan transactions (Stanner, 1933; Kaberry,
1939). The nearest approach to trading based on local speciali-
zation occurred when commodities entering the tribe from one
direction were exchanged for those received from other directions. Thus, Waneiga men procured a highly-prized kind of red
ochre from the Walmanba at Banka Banka and gave some of
this to the Walmalla in return for the Kimberley-type pressure-
flaked spear-heads that the latter imported from the Waringari.

In general, there were few raw materials or finished articles
that were not available through the whole tribal territory, and
most transactions were (and are) ceremonial or gift-exchanges
intended to meet kinship and ritual obligations. Although, in
some situations, rules specify the objects or services to be exchanged, the public act of giving is usually the significant feature
of the transaction.

The matter of intercommunity marriages deserves comment.
Men have told me that community endogamy was the norm and
cited instances as confirmation of this. They asserted that the
practice was desirable because it left "outside" women free for
the men of their own communities to marry and therefore
reduced the chances of intercommunity conflict. In other contexts, the same men spoke strongly of the benefits of community

exogamy and again pointed to particular cases to demonstrate that this was the rule. Such marriages, they said, linked the communities and, by creating wide networks of affines, made intercommunity quarrels less likely. The stress in both cases on the desirability of peaceful relations among the communities is significant.

My own analysis of people's genealogies revealed that marriages made within the community slightly outnumbered those made between communities, but the difference is not statistically significant. It was also clear, from consideration of the circumstances of particular marriages, that previous obligations, current friendships and possible future disputes all had a bearing on whether a man married inside or outside his own country.

No summary formula describes the pattern of residence following marriage. When a man took a wife from his own community, the couple lived in the same country as the parents of both, so that in this respect their residence was simultaneously viripatrilocal and uxoripatrilocal. Within the country, the couple might on different occasions live alone or with the husband's father, his father's father, his brothers, his brothers-in-law, his male cross-cousins, and so on. The existence of certain rules of avoidance, however, prevented the pair from residing near the actual or classificatory mother's brothers, mothers-in-law and sons-in-law of the husband.

A girl who married a man from another community usually went to live in his country; but if she was very young at the time of marriage (say, seven or eight years old), the couple were expected to reside for the first year or so in her country. This action was intended to assuage the grief felt by the mother at losing her daughter. While the couple were in the girl's country they were free to live with, or near, any relatives they did not have to avoid. It was common also, when their first child was born, for them to return for a season or so to the wife's parents' country.

Community affiliations were, and are still, relevant to the discharge of certain kinship rights and duties. In some disputes, for instance, a man has authority over particular kin only if they are also his countrymen. Similarly, men have definite prerogatives and obligations following the death of one of their fellow countrymen. I shall discuss these matters later in their appropriate contexts.

Nowadays, camp brawls on settlements occasionally align the members of one community against those of another, but they are more likely to involve only countrymen. This limitation on the spread of quarrels is to some extent connected with the notion of personal "space" and of minding one's own business. In the past, the people's reluctance to engage in intercommunity fighting supported the institution of extracommunity refuge for social offenders. A man who was unlucky enough to kill a countryman in a mêlée (premeditated homicide is rare within the tribe) might flee to another country and beg the hospitality of close kinsmen. The men of his community who were responsible for avenging the death would hesitate to pursue the killer, for his hosts could legitimately object to the uninvited entry of an armed party into their country. At the same time the hosts did not have the right to send the man back to his death and indeed would be reluctant to suggest that he leave. If he was prepared to remain in exile from his own community for a long time, say, five or ten years, he could expect to face nothing more dangerous than a formal duel with knives on his return. In less serious matters, such as wife-stealing, a voluntary exile of a couple of years might enable the culprit to escape serious punishment.

To summarize the discussion so far—the tribe comprised four large communities, each with its own domain or "country". (The term "country" is often used as a synonym for the community.) This was not merely a formal or nominal division; community affiliations were (and often are still) an important determinant of the interactions of individuals and groups in a number of situations. The people's behaviour varied significantly according to whether they were dealing with countrymen or with other members of the tribe. Relations between communities were analogous with those of the tribe with its neighbours. Analysis of the present status of the communities must wait on a discussion of the other connotations of the Walbiri concept of country.

Totemic countries. Although the term ŋuru connotes the larger domain of the community, it also refers to various more or less discrete subdivisions of that district. To compound confusion, the latter usage has several distinct, although related, implications. A man may define a country in terms of the sub-section affiliations of the totems believed to reside there, or he may be referring to the ties that unite all the people whose individual conception-totems were found in one locality, or he may be speaking of the quasi-localization of totemic cult-lodges. Only by knowing the context of the statement can his audience be sure which connotation of ŋuru he intends.

The totems include most things occurring in the pre-European environment of the tribe—birds, mammals, reptiles, insects, plants, the sun, the moon, the stars (singly or in constellations), wind, rain, lightning, fire, and so on, as well as artefacts such as spears and digging-sticks. I do not know of any objects of European introduction that have achieved totemic status; the Walbiri simply keep them outside the system. Some totems are believed to be capable of adopting human form and habits (rain-men, lizard-women and the like), and these are thought to be simultaneously human and non-human. (The people consider human beings to differ in important respects from other living creatures.) Other totems always retain their specific characteristics; thus, a dreamtime bandicoot resembles in appearance and habit an everyday bandicoot.

There is also a category of "culture heroes" who, either singly or in groups, wandered about in the dreamtime, always in human guise. These beings, who may be male or female, adults or children, function as totems in the same ways as do other creatures and objects, but they usually occupy a much more significant place in the religious dogma.

Finally, there are malicious spirits or demons which, strictly speaking, are not totemic in the same sense as are the preceding forms (Meggitt, 1955a). All the totems have originated in the dreamtime, and each has a local reference of some kind. For the rest of this account, I shall also use the common Aboriginal term "dreaming" to refer to the totems, in order to remind readers that Australian totemism is rather more complicated than that of most other societies.

The local reference of a Walbiri dreaming may be a track, *yiriyi*, or a country, ŋuru or ŋurara, which, like *walaldja*, means "own country". Where a track is involved, dreaming-heroes or members of a dreaming-species either entered Walbiri territory from another tribal area or emerged from the earth at definite places within Walbiri bounds. They travelled about, creating topographical features, performing ceremonies, introducing customs and laws, and depositing spirit-essences. Their journeys may have covered 500 miles or more, but every place at which they halted is named and can be found today. Eventually, the dreamings passed into neighbouring tribal areas, where their tracks may be unknown to Walbiri, or entered the earth (or, rarely, ascended into the sky) within Walbiri territory.

In the case of a dreaming-country, certain totemic beings are said to have emerged from the earth at a specific locality, where they resided for some time before re-entering the earth. Although these dreamings were often mobile and creative, the area in which they moved was usually restricted to a few square miles. Such countries are also named and are known today. It is my impression that the dreamings that are supposed to have remained in a limited country are generally non-human and the countries are the places where those natural species, such as spiders, bandicoots, and possums, are common today.

All these events occurred in the long-past dreamtime, an epoch (which is also a category of existence) that not only preceded the historical past and present but also continues in parallel with them. Although the totemic beings either departed from the Walbiri territory or vanished into the earth within it during the dreamtime, they still exist and their powers and actions directly affect the contemporary society. The people believe that, by performing the appropriate rituals and songs, living men can actually "become" these beings for a short time and so participate briefly in the dreamtime.

The sites of a given dreaming are not necessarily confined to the country of one community. Thus, the track of the *maman-dabari* heroes runs south-east from Waneiga country to the Lander, swings south-west into Ngalia country, thence continues south into Pidjandjara territory where it turns north and returns to the Waneiga. The track of the two kangaroos is even longer. It starts in Waneiga country, leads west at first, then turns south through Walmalla and Ngalia country, whence it runs south-west to the Pintubi, crosses into Western Australia, turns south-east into South Australia and finishes near the Great Australian Bight. Separate budgerigar dreaming-countries are found in both the Lander and the Waneiga districts. There is a possum dreaming-country near Yuendumu, one near Mount Doreen, one on the Lander and another near the Granites.

Each community, however, tends to be concerned with some of the more important dreamings rather than with others. The Waneiga say they are most interested in the *mamandabari* heroes, the *djamala* fire and the ibis-men; the Lander Walbiri regard the two *walaŋari* heroes as peculiarly theirs; the Ngalia stress the *gumbaldja* complex of dreamings, which includes the two kangaroos, and the Walmalla the possum, yam and fire dreamings. Interestingly enough, the various rain-tracks are held to be important by all communities.

The people believe that intimate and complex relations exist between the dreamings and themselves, both as individuals, and as groups. It is not surprising, therefore, that the dreamings are incorporated into the kinship and subsection systems, as well as being reference-points in the local organization. This in turn involves what might be called a second-degree relationship between local organization and the subsection system.

Walbiri subsections are not groups but categories of people. Every member of the tribe is allocated to a subsection from birth. As a rule, the subsection he (or she) receives depends indirectly on that associated with his mother. The eight subsections, whose names have male and female forms, are arranged in the following manner:

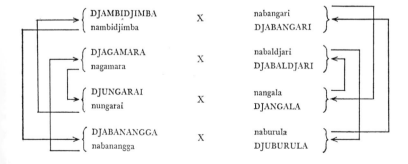

The terms in upper case denote males, and lower case females; X indicates the preferred marriage between subsections and the arrows trace the course of matrilineal descent. Thus, a djambidjimba man should marry a nabangari woman, and their children are djangala boys and nangala girls. The djangala marry nungarai women and have djambidjimba and nambidjimba children, whereas the nangala daughters marry djungarai men and have djabaldjari and nabaldjari children.

When the preferred marriage rule is followed, male members of one subsection have their actual and classificatory fathers and sons in only one other subsection, and the men of the latter division find their fathers and sons in the former. The djambidjimba and djangala subsections in this way form one father-son couple, the djagamara and djuburula subsections another, djabaldjari and djungarai a third, and djabangari and djabanangga the fourth. There are also pairs of subsections wherein the men of one are either actual or classificatory mother's mother's brothers or sister's daughter's sons of men of the other. If we take any father-son couple of subsections, their correlative mother's mother's brother-sister's daughter's son subsections themselves form a father-son couple. Similarly, the correlative father-son subsections of any mother's mother's brother-sister's daughter's son pair of subsections are in turn a mother's mother's brother-sister's daughter's son pair. Thus, as djambidjimba-djangala and djagamara-djuburula are both father-son couples, djambidjimba-djagamara and djangala-djuburula are both mother's mother's brother-sister's daughter's son pairs. These four subsections form a patrimoiety, as do the djabaldjari, djungarai, djabangari and djabanangga subsections, which are related in the same manner.

Every dreaming "belongs to" one or more of the four father-son couples of subsections in the tribe, and "belonging to" in this context can most easily be defined by denotation. Djangangulangu, a hill some three miles south of Yuendumu settlement, is a possum dreaming-place. In the dreamtime, possums emerged from this hill, lived on it and returned into the earth there. These possums were, and are still, members of the djabaldjari and djungarai subsections simultaneously. Men of both the subsections refer to them as "father", djabangari and djabanangga men refer to them as "mother's mother's brother", and the possums are said to belong to the patrimoiety composed by those four subsections. In the same way, djagamara and djangala men speak of the animals as "wife's brother", and djuburula and djambidjimba men call them "mother's brother". The various men also refer to the dreaming-site itself as "father" and so on. In everyday parlance, the Djangangulangu hill is "djabaldjari-djungarai country".

Three other possum sites with which I am acquainted (and there may be more) are also djabaldjari-djungarai. But, although the several countries associated with one dreaming-species generally belong to the one father-son couple of subsections, and hence to the one patrimoiety, there are deviations from this pattern. Thus, a honey-ant dreaming-track emerges at Yulumu, a hill about 15 miles from Yuendumu, and runs through Yuendumu towards Mount Doreen. Yulumu and all other sites on this track are "djabangari-djabanangga country". Another honey-ant track that leads south from Yuendumu to Papanya, near Haast's Bluff in Pidjandjara country, however, is "djagamara-djuburula country" and belongs to the opposite moiety to the first track.

A further complication can arise with regard to long tracks. The *mamandabari* heroes dreaming, for instance, is so important that both the djabaldjari-djungarai and the djabangari-djabanangga couples refer to it as "father". The track skirts, among other places, three native-bee dreaming-countries. Nyugulu, north of Tanami, and Yinabaga, in the Lander floodout, are both djabaldjari-djungarai, but Ngandaru, near Brooks' Well at Conistan, is djagamara-djuburula. As a result the latter site is connected with both patrimoieties. Similarly, Mount Hardy (Yarungganyi) is on the rain track, which belongs to djambidjimba-djangala, and on the initiated-men track, which belongs to djabaldjari-djungarai of the other patrimoiety. Some very long tracks, such as those of the rain and the two kangaroos, may change subsection and even patrimoiety affiliations at certain points on their courses.

Now, the use of the term "country" to denote dreaming-sites merely expresses the classificatory aspect of Walbiri totemism—the view that people, natural species and localities form an interconnected whole (Elkin, 1954, chap. VI). It does not have any necessary implications for the tribe's residential patterns. Thus although Djangangulangu at Yuendumu is regarded as djabaldjari-djungarai country, members of these subsections do not reside there exclusively. Indeed, this would not be possible, for there is no water and little vegetation on or near the hill. Nor are these people the only ones who may visit the place. Any Ngalia man has the right to camp in this country and to hunt over it, and he may extend the privilege to members of any subsection who are visiting from another Walbiri community.

The absence of an economic or residential reference in this concept of "country" is emphasized by the fact that several dreaming-sites belonging to each patrimoiety may lie in the one limited area. Within a radius of 15 to 20 miles of Yuendumu settlement, for instance, at least 14 dreamings are represented:

Dreaming	*Associated couple of subsections*
possum	djabaldjari-djungarai
moon	djabaldjari-djungarai
old woman	djabaldjari-djungarai
incestuous man	djabaldjari-djungarai
initiated men	djabaldjari-djungarai
uncircumcised youths	djabangari-djabanangga
eaglehawk	djabangari-djabanangga
honey-ant	djabangari-djabanangga
rain	djambidjimba-djangala
skink	djambidjimba-djangala
dingo	djagamara-djuburula
large snake	djagamara-djuburula
small snake	djagamara-djuburula
wallaby	djagamara-djuburula
honey-ant	djagamara-djuburula

The area might perhaps have supported 14 small hordes or bands in the past (although I very much doubt it), but it could have done so only if they had been able to forage freely over all parts.

In short, such small, named countries were not the domains of patrilineal and patrilocal hordes. They were, and are still, foci of religious reference—they are spirit-centres, at which dream-time beings have deposited part of their spiritual or dreaming-essence.

The dreamtime beings did this in several ways. The most common occurred when they decorated themselves with bird- or vegetable-down and performed ceremonies descriptive of their travels. As the actors agitated their bodies, the down was dislodged and transformed into *guruwari*, immaterial particles that entered the surrounding trees, rocks and waterholes, where they still remain and affect the behaviour of living things. The particles, although as amorphous as the down itself, are essentially of the same nature as the beings who have produced them. Con-sequently, the *guruwari* are thought to *be*, and not merely to represent, uncircumcised boys, kangaroos, hakea flowers, spears, the winds, and so on.

At Maiaragulangu near Mount Doreen, however, the *guruwari* of the wild orange tree (*Capparis mitchelli*) originated in a different manner. A dreamtime youth found many oranges growing near a rockhole. He picked some and lay on the ground to eat them. As he threw the inedible skins over his shoulders, they became the *guruwari* that now reside in the rocks and trees nearby. Other myths tell how feathers falling from birds, fragments of eggshell, and blood flowing from the wounds of fighting men became *guruwari*.

Some published accounts of the Aboriginal belief in pre-existing spirits refer to "spirit-children", a term first used, I believe, by Spencer and Gillen (1899). It would be misleading to apply this description to the Walbiri *guruwari*. They should be regarded rather as impersonal and causally-effective entities— as catalysts that, in appropriate circumstances, can set off trains of reactions. These events may culminate in successful parturi-tion, in floral reproduction, in accretions to human personalities, in the restoration of the health of individuals, in the heighten-ing of social euphoria, and so on. The *guruwari* and the dream-ings that produce them are noumena, of which the observable, contemporary natural species and objects are the phenomenal manifestations.

This statement is not intended to strain a Kantian analogy. Walbiri men versed in religious dogma also express this point of view. "The bandicoots we hunt and kill—they all sleep by day, copulate at dusk and feed at night, *because* the dreamtime bandicoots behave thus. The bandicoots we see today come from the dreamtime *guruwari*; they have that dreaming inside them."

Throughout the discussion, I shall refer to these spirit-catalysts as *guruwari* in order to distinguish them from the dreamings that produced them, as well as to avoid any suggestion that they are necessarily anthropomorphic.

The localization of dreaming-sites and the depositing of *guruwari* have two aspects relevant to the analysis of the connotations of the term "country". Every Walbiri has a conception-dreaming. This means that the foetus from which the person developed was animated by the entry of a *guruwari* into the mother's womb. The identity of the *guruwari* depends on where the mother was when that happened. If she discovered her pregnancy while camped near a kangaroo dreaming-place, the child was "found" there and henceforth has the kangaroo dreaming. In theory, this association is fortuitous; any person may have any conception-dreaming. At Hooker Creek, for instance, the man Bulbul djabaldjari had dingo conception-dreaming, whereas his two half-brothers, also of the djabaldjari subsection, had wildcat and rain dreaming respectively. All three dreamings belonged to the djambidjimba-djangala couple of subsections and hence to the opposite moiety of these men. On the other hand, Bulbul's two full-brothers had edible fungus and rat-kangaroo conception-dreaming respectively, which belonged to their own patrimoiety. This distribution of dreamings simply indicated that the parents of the five brothers were camped at a different place each time the mother found she was pregnant.

There is, nevertheless, a limited but significant correlation between the patrimoiety affiliations of individuals and of their conception-dreamings. A sample of 480 cases abstracted from genealogies presents the following pattern:

TABLE 7

The relationship between conception-dreaming and personal patrimoiety affiliation

Patrimoiety affiliation of the conception-dreaming	Patrimoiety affiliation of the person		
	Moiety A	*Moiety B*	*Total*
Moiety A	138	86	224
Moiety B	87	169	256
Total	225	255	480

chi squared $= 36 \cdot 6$, df $= 1$, p $\angle \cdot 001$; phi coefficient $= \cdot 27$

The more perceptive men realize that some such relationship exists, and they explain it as follows: camp-sites usually adjoin waterholes, most of which are dreaming-places and have *guruwari* nearby. Often, there are several dreamings of both patrimoieties near the waterhole. A woman who finds herself pregnant at such a camp could have been entered by a *guruwari* from any of the dreamings. If the dreamings are roughly equal in ritual importance, the husband usually plumps for one that belongs to his (and his children's) patrimoiety, in particular, one that also belongs to his cult-lodge. But, if none of the dreamings there belongs to his lodge, he may occasionally prefer his child to have the most important of the others, no matter to which patrimoiety it belongs.

One consequence of the Walbiri theory of conception-dreamings is that tribesmen often refer to certain people as being "really my countrymen", or "my close countrymen". They are not only all members of the one community, but they also have conception-dreamings that, irrespective of patrimoiety affiliations, relate to a comparatively limited geographical area. Thus, all the people whose *guruwari* have come from the dreamings in the vicinity of Yuendumu "have been found in the one country". The intimate bond that exists among them, however, is not reflected in special rules of behaviour or in formal groupings, whether social, economic, or religious. Rather, it is manifested in an intensification of the affection that a man feels for his wider community and its country; it expresses the ties of *die Heimat*. In this sense, the people belong to the smaller dreaming-locality just as much as it belongs to them, for it is spiritually part of them.

There is no constant demarcation of the limits of such smaller divisions of the community territory. In one context a man whose conception-dreaming is from Vaughan Springs may use the term "close countryman" to include only people with conception-dreamings from the environs of the spring. On other occasions, he may extend the term to cover people whose dreamings come from the area bounded by Gunadjari in the west, Mount Singleton in the north and Annie Spring in the east. That is to say, men are likely to define these countries in terms that best suit their purposes in particular situations—for instance, when claiming the right to dispose of a woman in marriage, when calling up support in a quarrel, or when sharing out the possessions of a dead man.

The dreamings are thought to have deposited the *guruwari* ultimately to benefit all members of the tribe, but the entities cannot be expected to function unless men provide the appropriate conditions to initiate the action. Consequently, groups of men are responsible for the regular performance of sacred songs and rituals connected with dreamings in various localities. There is a cult-lodge associated with each dreaming and, less commonly, with a group of linked dreamings. Thus, the long track of the two kangaroos passes through Walmalla country. The ceremonies, songs and myth relevant to this section of it are in the custody of a group of djabaldjari and djungarai men who have not only been initiated into that lodge at the time of circumcision, but are also closely related in the male line. From the point where the track continues into Ngalia country, a group of agnates from the djuburula-djagamara subsections assumes responsibility. Each lodge as a rule recruits its members from the men of one patriline.

Linked dreamings are those which are closely related in a variety of ways in the dreamtime. Lightning, for instance, which "splits the clouds and trees", is the penis of the rain dreaming; termites in the flying stage, which appear in swarms a few days after summer rain falls, were originally "made" by the rain dreaming. Lightning and the termites therefore belong to the rain lodges, which are either djambidjimba-djangala or djagamara-djuburula according to the sections of the track involved. At Ngama, about 18 miles south-west of Yuendumu, rock-paintings depict the snake, dingo and wallaby dreamings whose tracks meet at the cave; all three dreamings belong to one djagamara-djuburula lodge.

Although all the men of a patrimoiety have the right to participate in ceremonies performed for any dreaming in the patrimoiety, only the men of the lodge associated with the dreaming are its true custodians or "bosses". The members of a lodge regard each other as "close countrymen", even if they have different birthplaces and conception-dreamings. Similarly, when several lodges are connected with one dreaming-track, or with different countries of the one dreaming, all the members are united by a strong bond based on the possession of a shared spirit or soul. This tie tends to transcend community or country limits. A man from the Waneiga rain lodge thus expects to receive special courtesies from men of the Ngalia, Walmalla and Lander rain lodges when he visits those countries. In a spiritual sense, they are all countrymen and brothers.

There is a further complication in that the men of lodges associated with more or less contiguous dreaming-places (as, for instance, at Yuendumu) regard each other as "close countrymen", irrespective of their birthplaces, conception-dreamings, or subsection and patriline affiliations. This definition of countrymen is neither formal nor fixed but varies with the special interests of the persons involved. Moreover, there is no sure way of knowing whether a man involved in a dispute will appeal to conception or lodge classification when making a claim on another person. Indeed, he can shift from one to the other with almost bewildering rapidity.

Summary. There are four main connotations of the Walbiri term for "country". Their actual referents must be carefully distinguished if the local organization of the tribe is to be fully understood.

(*a*) The term "country" may refer to the domain of one of the four major divisions of the tribe, and it is sometimes a synonym of the latter. These divisions were stable residential groups or communities that comprised as many as 300 or 400 people of all subsections and kinship categories. They also included a number of patrilines, which were not segments of a larger patriclan but were genealogically separate, although ritually related, units within each patrimoiety. Community members could express a considerable range of residential preferences within the country limits. Community endogamy appears to have been slightly more common than exogamy. On some occasions the communities functioned as the largest economic (food-gathering and exchange) units, but more often they broke up to form a number of smaller food-gathering units.

(*b*) The term "country" may refer to a specific dreaming-site or -track, especially when the speaker wishes to stress its patrimoiety affiliation. This usage does not indicate the local or residential grouping of people but is an aspect of classificatory totemism. It has nothing to do with food-gathering as an economic pursuit, or with the composition of food-gathering units.

(c) The term "country" may refer to a specific dreaming-site, or group of sites, associated with a cult-lodge. This usage does not have an economic or residential implication but has primarily a religious and ritual significance. Indirectly, however, it recognizes that agnation is the principle on which lodge personnel are recruited.

(d) The term "country" may refer to specific dreaming-sites whose geographical contiguity provides a basis for classing together people related to the dreamings either through conception or through lodge affiliation. Such categories are informal and have no economic or residential implications. Their limits may be defined differently as people's motives vary.

Radcliffe Brown (1930, p. 35) has asserted that "the important local group throughout Australia is . . . the horde . . . a small group of persons owning a certain area of territory, the boundaries of which are known, and possessing in common proprietary rights over the land and its products . . . membership in the horde is determined in the first place by descent, children belonging to the horde of their father . . . as a normal thing, male members enter the horde by birth and remain in it till death. . . ." Aboriginal hordes are exogamous, independent and autonomous. "The horde, therefore, as an existing group at any moment, consists of (1) male members of all ages whose fathers and fathers' fathers belonged to the horde, (2) unmarried girls who are the sisters, or daughters, or sons' daughters of the male members, (3) married women, all . . . (or) most of whom belonged originally to other hordes, and have become attached to the horde by marriage."

Radcliffe Brown's definition of the horde was largely based on an interpretation of the indirect references to Aboriginal local organization contained in the descriptions of tribal life then available. With a few exceptions, these accounts of Aboriginal society, as distinct from culture, were deficient in almost every respect. Although it is likely that units analogous to such hordes existed in some tribes, Radcliffe Brown went far beyond his evidence when he assumed that these groups were to be found everywhere in Australia. In short, his notion of the horde was an ideal type, and he offered no compelling arguments to support his assumption that this group was a necessary element of Aboriginal local organization.

The only Walbiri group that possessed some of the attributes ascribed by Radcliffe Brown to the horde was the community, but this was clearly a much more extensive, populous and complexly-structured group than that which he had in mind. It was not a simple patrilineal and patrilocal band. Intracommunity marriages were as common (and as desirable) as those between communities, so that any man numbered among his countrymen many relatives who were his non-agnatic cognates. Within the community patrilineal descent was important mainly as a principle of recruitment to the cult-lodges, and the community included several of these patrilines, which were not genealogically related to each other. At the same time, residential and food-gathering units whose size and composition varied with the seasons and with other factors, formed and reformed within the matrix of the wider community. In the light of these sorts of considerations, it would be misleading to apply the term "horde", in Radcliffe Brown's sense, either to the Walbiri community or to any of its component groups.

In a later publication (1951, p. 38), Radcliffe Brown stated that "everywhere in Australia the fundamental basis of social organization is a system of patrilineal local groups or clans of small size". This is merely his earlier generalization shorn of qualifications, and, to the extent that it is unqualified, it is even less applicable to the Walbiri data. Moreover, Elkin (1953, p. 417) has demonstrated that evidence from other tribes also invalidates it.

Recent changes in local organization. The traditional Walbiri communities no longer exist as separate residential and economic units. The big, permanent camps on government settlements and on cattle-stations are taking their place, and of these groups the former are having the greatest effects on local organization.

Before the establishment of the settlements, although the people often gathered at cattle-stations and mining-camps instead of at the usual waterholes, they still tended to keep to their community domains. Thus Yalpari who moved to stations founded along Lander Creek early in this century were still more or less in their own country. Most Ngalia remained in the vicinity of Mount Doreen station and the Wolfram-diggings at Mount Hardy and Mount Singleton, and the Walmalla congregated around Tanami and the Granites. There was, however, no European settlement in the country of the Waneiga, who for years had been slowly dispersing—to the western gold-fields, the Victoria River stations and Tennant Creek.

Government intervention at the end of World War II radically altered this pattern. At least two-thirds of the tribe were placed on settlements, two of which (Hooker Creek and Phillip Creek) were far outside the old tribal boundaries. Few, if any, Walbiri now live in the Waneiga and Walmalla domains, although many remain in the Ngalia and Lander countries. There has also been an extensive reshuffling of groups in the process of moving them. All four local communities are represented at Yuendumu settlement; Waneiga, Walmalla and Ngalia live at Hooker Creek, and Waneiga and Yalpari at Phillip Creek.

The settlements, which have now been in existence long enough to be the birthplaces of many Walbiri children, will probably become the foci of new community divisions, although such a re-arrangement may not become effective until after the death of the men who still remember clearly the boundaries, dreaming-sites, and other features of the old countries. At Hooker Creek, for instance, older men rarely referred to the settlement as "their country" in any sense of the term; but the younger men occasionally did so, largely, I think, because they were used to being identified as "Hooker Creek Walbiri" when they went off to work with Europeans and other Aborigines.

A similar tendency was also apparent at Phillip Creek, although there two factors acted against it. One was the presence of the Warramunga, which reminded the Walbiri that the locality was the latter's country, and the other was the people's knowledge that they would probably move to a new settlement in the near future.

The physical separation of these two settlements from the traditionally demarcated countries doubtless facilitated the adoption of a new definition of the community. Most of the residents were unable to renew regularly social and ritual ties with their old homes. A few men had made visits, some several times, but they were drawn back to their relatives and friends on the settlement. Aborigines travelling about on jobs also kept the others informed of Walbiri news, and Tennant Creek and the Bungalow settlement at Alice Springs were clearing-houses for such gossip. But these were tenuous links. The Hooker Creek Walbiri, in particular, felt keenly their isolation from the rest of the tribe, for most of their news filtered through Newcastle Waters and Wave Hill and was remarkably distorted in the process.

Yuendumu presented a different picture. Predominantly Ngalia in composition, the settlement was in Ngalia country. To the west, Mount Doreen station, with its large Walbiri population, was within easy walking distance, and the ritually-important Vaughan Springs area was accessible from there. Lander Walbiri to the east could be reached in a series of short journeys via the camps at Mount Denison and Conistan stations. There was also a comparatively large volume of motor traffic to and from Alice Springs, where "outside" Walbiri could often be contacted. In the opinion of its residents, Yuendumu had much to recommend it as the nucleus of a new community.

Residence on settlements will probably also involve a change in the identification of "close countrymen" in terms of the common possession of contiguous conception-dreaming places. Thus all the children born at Hooker Creek had yam, mosquito, wind, or rat-kangaroo conception-dreaming, for these were the only dreamings in the area with which Walbiri were acquainted. At Phillip Creek, as far as I could discover, only two dreamings were believed to have left *guruwari* there, and these were really Warramunga totems.

In short, residence in permanent settlement camps ensures that most children are conceived within a limited radius of the camp and so share a small number of conception-dreamings. The emergence of such diacritical features is likely to sharpen the definition of a settlement as a country or community, even though the geographical grouping of conception-dreamings is not, in traditional Walbiri theory, reflected in formal social groupings.

Changes in terms of lodge-dreaming affiliation will probably occur much more slowly. In all the instances about which I could gather definite information, the youths at all settlements had been initiated at circumcision into their fathers' lodges as a matter of course. This took place despite the fact that some of the lodge-countries concerned were many miles from Hooker Creek and Phillip Creek, and the youths had never visited them. One factor likely to sustain the practice of initiating youths away from their lodge-countries is the belief that in most cases, no matter where lodge rituals and songs are performed, the performance in itself will cause the increase of the natural species in the appropriate dreaming countries. Nevertheless, unless the men adopt some novel device, such as lengthening dreaming-tracks or "finding" new dreaming-countries, it is difficult to see how the continuity of initiation into lodges can be maintained for many more generations. If this is achieved, however, it may well facilitate the development of settlements into new communities.

The fact that a comparatively large group of people resides in a settlement camp does not, *per se*, significantly affect kinship norms in general or marriage rules in particular, for large-scale assemblies were common enough in the past. But although a man should still marry a particular category of relative his actual choice of a wife may be altered. Of ten betrothals, marriages and remarriages at Hooker Creek, for instance, six involved partners who were members of the one community and the one settlement, three involved people who belonged to different communities but the one settlement, and the last concerned people who were of different communities and settlements. The sample is too small for the differences to be statistically reliable, but a tendency towards settlement endogamy seems to be emerging. If it continues, it should accelerate the identification of settlements as communities.

CHAPTER VI

THE RESIDENTIAL FAMILY UNIT AND THE KINSHIP SYSTEM

Dwellings. An outsider's first impression of a Walbiri camp is usually one of ugly disorder.

Small shelters are scattered about in apparent confusion. Dozens of gaunt and nondescript dogs scavenge and brawl through the camp area, which is almost devoid of vegetation for a radius of several hundred yards. The spinifex-grass has been burned off and the ash trampled into the hard-packed red soil. Few trees have survived the constant demand for firewood and building materials. Shallow depressions and small mounds of bones, charcoal and other rubbish mark the sites of abandoned shelters. Closer observation reveals the presence of one or two similar camps, separated from the first by narrow belts of sparse acacia and eucalypt scrub. These divisions roughly correspond to the traditional community affiliations.

The shelters nowadays conform to three main types. The most common is a roughly rectangular, flat-roofed structure, 5 or 6 feet square. Four forked corner-posts support a roof made of rusty sheets of galvanized iron or of layers of leafy branches. The rigid iron roofs are generally wired down or have heavy pieces of ant-bed placed on them as protection from the whirlwinds that daily blow through the camp. Branches are sometimes laid on iron roofs to insulate them from the fierce summer heat, or an old piece of tarpaulin is lashed over the iron to keep out both heat and rain. The roof is rarely more than 4 feet above the ground, which is scraped clean of vegetation and stones. Usually, there are three walls of galvanized iron or branches, the south side being left open. This orientation is designed to prevent the sun's rays from entering the shelter. Earth is banked against the walls to a height of about 6 inches to anchor them against the winds and to keep out storm-water.

In each community section a shelter, built on the same lines but extending 10 to 15 feet, forms the "women's camp", which

houses widows not yet eligible for remarriage and the few unmarried women not living with their parents. As far from it as
possible, although within the community area, stands a smaller,
open-sided, rectangular structure under which bachelors gather
to gossip and gamble. Married men who wish to escape from
boredom or domestic disputes often join the young men here.

Interspersed among the rectangular shelters, wherever shrubs
and tree-trunks remain, are shades simply made of leafy branches
propped butt-uppermost against a central support. In plan, the
shades are roughly semi-circular and about 6 feet in diameter;
in elevation, they are triangular and about 5 feet high. The
open side usually faces south, and earth is heaped against the
wall. This kind of shelter is most often seen today in camps in
the bush and was the typical house-form in the past.

The third type, obviously European-inspired, is a tectiform
about 6 to 8 feet long, constructed from sheets of galvanized
iron. A ridge-pole about 3 feet 6 inches high is lashed between
two forked posts. Sheets of iron, which are laid against this at
an angle of 45 degrees, are secured with wire lashing and a piece
of iron bent into a vee-shaped ridge-plate. A sheet of iron closes
one end of the hut, while the other, generally the southern, is
open or partly closed. Earth is piled against the walls. At one end
of this iron "tent" a rectangular bough-shade may form a ver-
andah, under which the occupants escape from the almost intolerable heat of the hut.

Most shelters are rebuilt two or three times in a year, the
new sites usually being a few yards from the old, unless the house-
holders move to evade quarrels or join new friends. The initial
construction is so slipshod that, after the first few weeks, a constant process of makeshift renovation begins. Husband and wife,
often assisted by their children, undertake the initial building
and the subsequent repairs.

Although the various types of dwelling do not as a rule reflect
differences in the social statuses of the occupants, it is noticeable
that the iron tectiforms are most often built by younger men
who have had more contact with Europeans. They are more
common in the working men's camps and to this extent indirectly
reveal the presence of monetary incomes. A very few of the

Men acting the wild melon totemic ritual.

Gadjari ritual cycle. Senior novices supervise junior novices as they watch a revelatory totemic ritual. The clubs the men carry are used to discipline the youths.

A totemic ceremony involving the use of a string-cross. This refers to the bush banana totem.

Young man having his chest cicatrised with a flake of glass. The cuts follow the ochre guide-lines.

more affluent working men buy small canvas tents, which do not survive for long the rough handling given them.

On settlements N.A.B. also provides the people with a number of large huts, and it directs employers to do likewise on cattle-stations. Some huts are of galvanized iron, either prefabricated or built on the spot with bush-timber frames, and others are of mud-brick. The natives much prefer the latter, which are well-suited to the extreme temperatures of the desert. The occupants of the iron huts usually prefer to live outdoors. They build bough-shades outside the huts and use the latter chiefly as store-rooms for food, clothing and other gear. In wet or very cold weather, however, they welcome the protection of these huts, in which as many as nine or ten people and a dozen dogs may sleep huddled around a small fire.

Apart from the widows' and the bachelors' camps, each shelter is an individual dwelling, occupied by one family. Outsiders should not enter a shelter without an invitation (no matter how informal) from some member of the family. Although such invitations are freely extended to countrymen, even close kin would not enter a man's camp unless asked. Only children are thought to be unaware of this rule of etiquette, which is con-nected with the notion of personal "space" and with various kinship avoidances.

The occupants. Ideally, the residential unit should be a com-posite family, comprising a man, several wives and their unmar-ried daughters and uncircumcised sons, all of whom should share the one shelter. Many of the domestic units are in fact of this kind.

TABLE 8

Wives per married man (observed)

	Number of wives						Total men	Total wives	*Mean* wives per husband
	1	*2*	*3*	*4*	*5*	*6*			
Frequency	42	18	11	2	–	–	73	119	1·6

$$\frac{Number\ of\ composite\ families}{Number\ of\ families\ in\ sample} = 42\cdot5\ \text{per cent}$$

In theory, there is no limit to the lateral extension of the family; but in practice it is limited by the availability of eligible women and by the real difficulties that face a man who tries to control more than three or four wives simultaneously. Most of the married and single men with whom I discussed the matter said that two or three wives were enough for anyone; this number would provide adequate economic help and sexual variety for the husband, would bear him many children, and could be supervised comparatively easily.

The sample in Table 8 includes families from all four communities and from the three settlements; the husbands were of all ages. As the total population of the tribe is about 1400—about 300 families at the most—the sample of 73 families is statistically reliable, being about one quarter of the estimated universe for this variable. As a check on the accuracy of the figures for polygynous marriages, however, I abstracted another 175 cases from genealogies for analysis.

TABLE 9

Wives per married man (reported)

	Number of wives						Total men	Total wives	Mean wives per husband
	1	*2*	*3*	*4*	*5*	*6*			
Frequency	115	43	9	5	1	2	175	265	1·5

$$\frac{Number\ of\ polygynous\ husbands}{Number\ of\ husbands\ in\ sample} = 34·3 \text{ per cent}$$

The mean number of wives per husband is much the same in both samples, but the percentages of polygynists (42·5 and 34·3) differ significantly (chi squared $= 7·2$, df $= 1$, p $< ·01$). The difference probably reflects the tendency of people to underestimate the numbers of wives possessed by kinsmen whom they have not met for several years.

The nuclear families that form the residential family unit should be linked consanguineally through the mothers as well as through the father; ideally, co-wives should be actual or half-sisters, or parallel cousins. But, as men pointed out to me, this is not easily arranged. Even if a wife has several unmarried sisters, her husband may often be unable to marry any of them, because their father has ceremonial commitments that force him to give the girls in marriage to other men. An analysis of a sample of marriages confirms this opinion.

TABLE 10

The relationships of co-wives

Category	Frequency	Percentage
sisters	18	13·2
half-sisters	6	4·4
parallel cousins	4	2·9
doubtful: either full-sisters or half-sisters	17	12·5
	45	33
others	91	67
total	136	100

As the people are often reluctant to talk of dead kinsfolk, the figures in Table 10 probably understate the true frequency of polygynous unions. This, however, should affect sororal and non-sororal unions equally. The "doubtful" category comprises instances where this reluctance made it difficult for me to ascertain whether actual or half-sisters were involved. The distinction is unimportant in Walbiri eyes. Allowing for such sources of error, it is clear from the sample that polygyny as such is a more important determinant of family composition than is sororal polygyny.

All the family units I observed included only a man, his wife or wives and their own or adopted children; these were the only people who regularly shared the one dwelling. But informants asserted that the household occasionally includes other relatives. A man may take into his camp his old widowed mother, father, father's father or wife's father—people towards whom he has strong ties of affection and obligation. Even so, he continues to seek some young person to whom he can marry his aged dependent.

The regular operation of the levirate and the allocation of young wives to old men, however, generally ensure that old people have young spouses to care for them until they die; and the Walbiri recognize the element of social insurance in these usages. As a result, it is rare for the household to include more than the parent and child generation-levels. And when the people describe the families of several men as sharing "one camp", they imply only that the families reside close to each other in separate shelters and that the members, especially the men, often eat, hunt and gossip together. The men may be related in various ways, for instance, as father and son, brothers, brothers-in-law, and so on.

Other factors also limit the size of the residential family or household. By the time girls are 10 or 12 years old, they have usually left their families of orientation to join their husbands. Widows live, often with their young children, in the women's camp during the mourning period and, like married daughters, eat only occasional meals at their parents' camp. Once boys are circumcised, they spend less time in their parents' camps and more in the bachelors' camps; by the time they are aged 16 to 18 they rarely sleep or eat with the parents.

TABLE 11
Households in the Hooker Creek camp, 1953

Residential family unit	Number of members				
	Husband	Wife	Son	Daughter	Total
No. 1	1	3	4	2	10
No. 2	1	3	3	2	9
No. 3	1	2	4	1	8
No. 4	1	2	2	3	8
No. 5	1	3	2	1	7
No. 6	1	4	–	2	7
No. 7	1	2	1	3	7
No. 8	1	2	1	2	6
No. 9	1	1	2	2	6
No. 10	1	1	2	2	6
No. 11	1	3	1	–	5
No. 12	1	1	2	–	4
No. 13	1	1	1	1	4
No. 14	1	1	–	1	3
No. 15	1	2	–	–	3
No. 16	1	1	1	–	3
No. 17	1	2	–	–	3
No. 18	1	1	1	–	3
No. 19	1	2	–	–	3
No. 20	1	2	–	–	3
No. 21	1	2	–	–	3
No. 22	1	1	–	–	2
No. 23	1	1	–	–	2
No. 24	1	1	–	–	2

| Residential family unit | Number of members | | | | |
	Husband	Wife	Son	Daughter	Total
No. 25	1	1	–	–	2
No. 26	1	1	–	–	2
No. 27	1	1	–	–	2
No. 28	1	1	–	–	2
No. 29	1	1	–	–	2
No. 30	1	1	–	–	2
No. 31	1	1	–	–	2
No. 32	1	1	–	–	2
No. 33	1	1	–	–	2
No. 34	1	1	–	–	2
No. 35	1	1	–	–	2
No. 36	1	1	–	–	2
No. 37	1	1	–	–	2
Total members 37	57	27	22		143
Mean members 1	1·5	0·7	0·6		3·9
Standard deviation					2·35
Standard error of mean					·39
t at 1% level					2·72
degrees of freedom					36
fiducial limits at 1% level					±1·06

Widows' camp	Widow	Son	Daughter	Total
No. 1	5	–	1	6
No. 2	4	–	–	4
Total	9	–	1	10

Bachelors' camp	Bachelor	Total
No. 1	14	14

Grand total	Males	Females	Total
15 years and over	50	61	111
Under 15 years	28	28	56
Total	78	89	167

The family has, of course, other functions besides that of pro-viding shelter for all or some of its members. Thus, although it is recognized that some men are likely to initiate sexual liaisons with certain extra-familial relatives, the overt norm in sexual relationships is that men should copulate only with their wives, and reproduction should occur only within the family. Illegiti-mate births are strongly deplored. However, the social relation-ships into which family members enter to fulfil other functions of the group are not necessarily bounded by the current limits of the family as a household, nor do they involve only past and present members of the household.

It is true that family members consume much of the food they gather and use many of the objects they manufacture; but they distribute a significant quantity of these things to relatives outside the family in return for other goods and services. Educative, as well as economic, functions are also generalized beyond the family and through the kinship system. Thus young girls receive domestic and ritual training not only from their mothers but also from married elder sisters and mothers' mothers. Boys derive much of their knowledge of kinship organization from the patient teaching of their mothers' fathers; they learn hunting and fighting techniques as much from uncles and brothers-in-law as from fathers and elder brothers. The sister's husband, the mother's mother's brother, and the classificatory sister's son take a larger part in disciplining a youth than do his father or brother.

It is significant that economic and educative functions are in a sense correlative. All giving, whether of material commodities, wives, ritual aid, or religious knowledge, involves the return of counter-gifts. In this respect, the people tend to minimize the distinction between duty and privilege. The forms of giving that role-expectations define are generally taken to be privileges as much as obligations. Most men of my acquaintance genuinely desired to meet their commitments to each other and went to considerable trouble to ensure that they did so. Although calculated self-interest was doubtless an important factor in some situations, there was also present on most occasions the implicit value or ideal of being a Walbiri in good standing with his fellows. And the "decent" Walbiri welcomes the opportunity to act with propriety, for his behaviour then confirms his own high opinion of himself.

The kinship system. The Walbiri kinship system is of the Aranda type: four primary lines of descent are distinguished in the second ascending generation, five generation-levels are specified, and the preferred marriage is with the classificatory "mother's mother's brother's daughter's daughter" (vide Elkin, 1954, p. 67; Radcliffe Brown, 1930, p. 50). The two diagrams, 1 and 2, in which relatives are represented by initial letters and classificatory relatives by inverted commas, indicate the distinction made between actual and classificatory relatives within certain categories—a distinction that is of particular significance in social situations such as cult initiation and betrothal.

Overlapping families of orientation' and procreation are important structural elements in the system, which in some respects is an elaboration of the prototypic relationships that exist within the conjugal family. At the same time, the system can be viewed as a structure of intersecting matri- and patri-lines of descent (vide Diagram 3). Indeed, perceptive Walbiri men talk about it in very much these terms. The interstices of the lattice-work of descent lines are the loci of a series of social relationships that express important rights and duties connected with circumcision, subincision, ritual guardianship, and the disposal of women in marriage. These further reinforce the structure which, ideally, is comparatively rigid. The patri- and matri-lines are in turn components of the patri- and matri-moieties and are articulated with the subsection system.

In theory, the structure can extend indefinitely in time (that is, vertically and diagonally) and in space (that is, laterally); but in practice there are limits to this extension, chiefly the absence of written records and the presence of physical obstacles to communication. This structure, however, as it is summarized in Diagram 3, provides a framework within which to analyse the norms of Walbiri social behaviour.

Before I begin this task, I shall comment on the kinship terminology itself. It is of the bifurcate merging type that recognizes sex differences in the categories of primary relatives, while generally ignoring collaterality as a distinguishing criterion among most categories of kin (vide Murdock, 1949, p. 141). Some relatives are also characterized in terms of their relative age or seniority to the speaker, and of their sex as such.

Despite the presence of such potential barriers to the classificatory tendencies of the terminology, there are no denotative terms. All terms appear to be elementary, although in practice some are combined to form descriptive phrases. Thus, *maliri* is a classificatory "mother's mother's brother's son" who is also a possible wife's mother's brother; ŋ*amini* is a mother's brother. *Maliri-ŋamini-bia*, the mother's mother's brother's son who resembles a "mother's brother", is the actual mother's mother's brother's son who cannot also be a wife's mother's brother. Any term, apart from such descriptive phrases, may be used indifferently in address or reference, the former being indicated by the appropriate possessive pronoun.

In addition to the full-scale system of terminology, there is what seems to be a short-hand system of terms of reference only. It is distinct from the first and in fact is not often used. The rules are simple enough—the speaker applies a particular term to a person according to the actual or classificatory relationship of that person's spouse to the speaker. Some of the categories are so broad, however, that they are confusing to anyone who lacks full knowledge of the context of the conversation in which they appear.

Thus, a man refers to the spouses of:

> M.F., m.m.; M.M.B., m.f.sr.; F.M.B., f.f.sr.; Sr.H., sr.; M.B.S., m.m.b.s.d.; M.M.B.S.S., m.b.d.; D.S., sr.d.d.; Sr.D.S., d.d.; Sr.S.S., s.d. as *margari-njanu*
> F.F., f.m.; B., w.sr.; S.S., sr.s.d. as *gali-njanu*
> F., m.; M.B., f.sr. as *ŋabudju-njanu*
> D.H., d. as *galjagalja-njanu*
> S., s.w. as *jabili-njanu*
> W.F., w.m.; Sr.S., sr.s.w. as *maŋga-njanu*
> W.M.B., w.f.sr.; Sr.D.H., sr.d. as *ŋaŋgari-njanu*

There also exists a set of manual signs that indicate kinship relationships. Although all adults know the signs, they use them as terms of reference only in certain situations (Meggitt, 1954).

THE STRUCTURE OF
WALBIRI KINSHIP

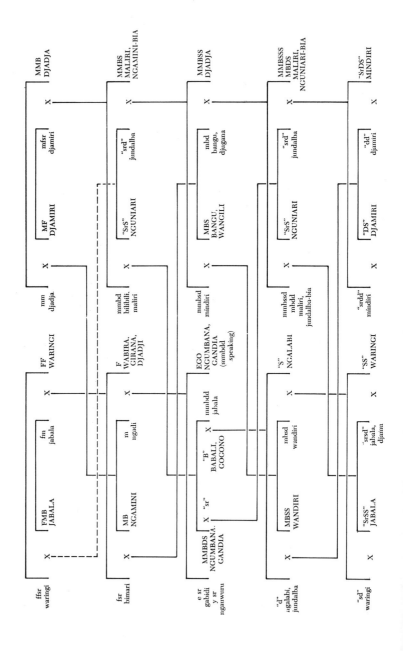

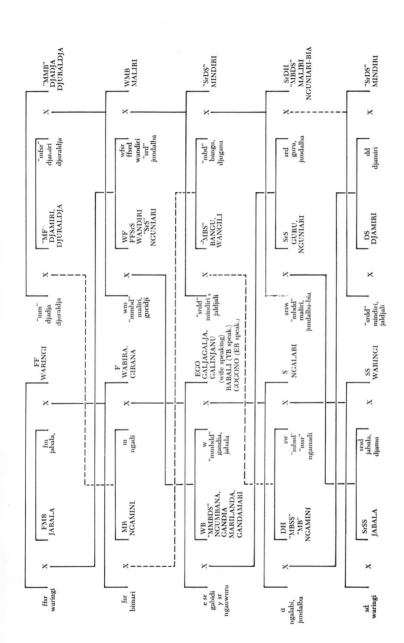

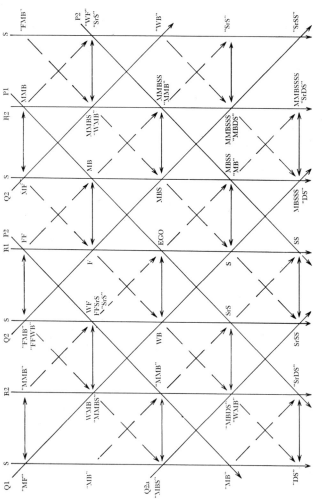

Diagram 3. *The structure of Walbiri kinship*

Remarks:

a. To simplify the diagram, I have indicated only males.

b. ↓ = (lodge) patrilines of descent.

c. R.S = patrimoieties.

d. ✕ = matrilines of descent.

e. P.Q = matrimoieties.

f. ⤢ = direction of circumcision-relationship and the giving of daughters in marriage.

g. ↔ = ritual guardianship and exchange of sisters in marriage.

h. R1 = EGO's (lodge) patriline.

i. P1 = EGO's matriline = WB's marriage line = "MBS" alternative marriage line.

j. Q1 = EGO's marriage line = WB's matriline.

k. Q2a = EGO's alternative marriage matriline = "MBS" matriline.

l. Ideally, the structure extends indefinitely in all directions.

CHAPTER VII

INTRAFAMILIAL RELATIONSHIPS

Husband—wife. A man should find his wife among the women who are his classificatory mother's mother's brother's daughter's daughters ("m.m.b.d.d."), that is, among women who are counted as his second cousins. Such a woman is at the same time his "sr.s.d." or his actual or classificatory f.f.sr.s.d., while he is her "M.M.B.D.S." and also her "S.S." or her actual or classificatory F.F.Sr.S.S. He calls his wife *gandia* if she is his "sr.s.d.", and *jabala* if she is his f.f.sr.s.d.; she calls him *galjagalja* and *galinjanu,* whether he is her "S.S." or her F.F.Sr.S.S. They may also call each other by the pidgin-English term *bandji.*

People who are actual m.m.b.d.d. and M.M.B.D.S. (*jabala* and ŋum*bana*) may not marry, however, for they are thought to be too closely related and too much like siblings. Each shares the maternal spirit of his or her own M.M.B., a man who in many respects is regarded as a kind of elder brother.

The reciprocal terms *gandia*, etc., and *galjagalja*, etc., also apply to people who are not actual spouses; but the referents are distinguished in terms of sentiments and behaviour as follows:

(a) actual spouses;
(b) parallel (same-sex) siblings, half-siblings and cousins of actual spouses, who because of sororal polygyny and the levirate are likely potential spouses; and spouses of parallel siblings, half-siblings and cousins who are also likely potential spouses;
(c) spouses of near parallel "siblings" (especially countrymen), and near parallel "siblings" (countrymen) of spouses, who are also likely potential spouses;
(d) spouses of near parallel "siblings" and parallel "siblings" of spouses who are not countrymen but are still potential, if less likely, spouses.
(e) spouses of parallel "siblings" and parallel "siblings" of spouses who are non-Walbiri and are thus unlikely potential spouses.

Failing a suitable "m.m.b.d.d.", a man may marry a "m.b.d." cross-cousin) who is not also his actual f.sr.d. His own m.b.d. and f.sr.d. are "too close" to be his wives; they are like his "half-sisters" and intercourse with them would be incestuous. Spouses who are "cross-cousins" usually address each other by that term but may also use the pidgin term *bandji*.

Permanent cohabitation with women in other kinship categories is rare and is strongly deplored as an incestuous relationship. Jural marriage with them is consequently impossible.

TABLE 12

Adherence to the marriage rules

Kinship category of the woman		Number of cases	Percentage
Preferred union with: "m.m.b.d.d."		566	91·6
Alternative union with: "m.b.d."		26	4·2
Prohibited union with:			
"m."	9		
"m.m."	8		
"sr.d."	3		
"w.m."	2		
"sr."	1		
"m.f.sr."	1		
"d.d."	1		
		25	4·2
Total		617	100·0

Following Radcliffe Brown (1950, p. 11) we may distinguish among the affective, conventional and jural aspects of the marital relationship. Although these divisions are by no means absolute, they are convenient for expository purposes.

Marriage following elopement or adult courtship is uncommon among the Walbiri, and a young man has little say in the choice of his wife. Nevertheless, there is usually a strong bond of affection between spouses of long standing, which is overtly displayed in a number of situations.

The patent distress of a man whose own wife is ill, for instance, differs markedly from the conventional expressions of grief he utters when classificatory "wives" are ill. He asks the help of everyone who could possibly ameliorate her condition—medicine-men, her sisters and (through them) her mother, even Europeans. Then, having done all he can, he withdraws to ponder the probable cause of her sickness. Other people respect his solitude; they risk abuse, even physical violence, should they approach him uninvited. If his wife recovers, his relief is unbounded. He watches over her during the convalescence and ensures that various of her female relatives are present to care for her. If the woman dies, his observance of the prescribed rules of mourning exhibits an emotional intensity and scrupulousness that the behaviour of other mourners generally lacks. Even the members of his own family hesitate to approach him during this period.

A woman is similarly affected when her husband falls sick, and she rarely leaves his side until he recovers. I have often seen women spend hours at a time massaging husbands who had rheumatism or lumbago or embracing and consoling them when they had headaches, toothaches, influenza and the like. Should the man die, his widow, during the mourning period, practically ceases to be a member of the society.

Paddy Djabaldjari, aged about 60, had married the widow, Brassy nagamara, some years before when he was a widower. The couple lived at Hooker Creek, but their children by earlier marriages were widely scattered. Brassy, also aged about 60, was blind and liable to painful attacks of rheumatism and dyspepsia. Paddy not only visited the sickbay several times a week to obtain medicines for her but also fetched firewood and water and prepared food for her daily. Rather than leave her to depend on the perfunctory attention of other women, he declined frequent invitations to go hunting—an activity he greatly enjoyed. When he had to spend several weeks in the bush to participate in the Gadjari rituals, he walked the seven miles to his camp every second day to see how his wife was faring.

He told me that, although he wanted to spend some time with his oldest son at Gordon Downs (150 miles away) before he was too old to travel, he would not leave Brassy on her own. Nor would he marry a second wife. This would have certain advantages, he said, for a younger woman could not only care for Brassy but could also provide the sexual attraction that the latter lacked. But he knew Brassy did not wish to share his favours with another woman, and he did not relish the bickering that might follow. He would, therefore, continue to look after her himself and seek his sexual pleasures in casual affairs with other men's wives.

This sort of attitude is common among couples who have

been married for some years, and the presence of children strengthens it.

Liddy nagamara, aged about 26, was the senior wife of Alec djabaldjari, aged about 40, by whom she had three children. On several occasions, when discussing married life with my wife, she said that once she may have thought of taking a lover, but now she was too fond of Alec to consider it. He was more or less faithful to her; he provided for her and the children, and he was a kind and affectionate father to them. She would not leave him for any other man.

Lucy nagamara, aged about 20 and the youngest of the three wives of Wally djabaldjari, aged about 60, expressed much the same views, which in her case were put to the test. A younger "brother" of Wally offered to exchange one of his wives, aged about 28, for Lucy. Wally left the decision to Lucy. She indignantly rejected the suggestion and indeed appeared hurt that Wally had allowed the matter to be raised.

Despite the prevalence of such sentiments, domestic quarrels often occur. Some disputes arise *de novo* from trivial circumstances, as when a wife fails to prepare a meal or a husband jokes with another woman, but many are the culmination of a series of minor misdeeds. The wife who nags too often is struck across the jaw with the flat side of a boomerang or is beaten on the back and thighs with a heavy shield; the husband who habitually consumes food intended for the children can expect a salvo of abuse, an attack with a digging-stick, or even, as I have seen, his bough-shade to be burned down about his ears. Nevertheless, no matter who is in the wrong, the wife usually receives the worst of the argument.

Occasionally couples are encountered whose personalities are mutually antipathetic. If they are childless, they separate eventually and remarry, with public approval; but, if they have children, close relatives press them to remain married at least until the children approach puberty.

Most features of the marital relationship that are apparently mere matters of etiquette also express its jural aspects. Spouses may discuss sexual subjects when alone but should avoid such topics when both are in company with other people. Reference to genital organs and copulation is then made only by euphemisms or manual signs. If the audience includes only close kin or friends, however, spouses may indulge in mildly obscene humour. Heavy-handed sexual joking is common in all-male groups. A man's extra-marital affairs, even the size of his penis, can provide material for sharp witticisms in his presence, provided he is normally on good terms with the speaker; but it is ill-mannered, and indeed dangerous, to mention his wife in the jokes.

Walbiri men are notably uxorious, but even they marvelled at the sexual vigour of Louis djuburula, who by the age of about 40 had had five wives at various times. At this time he had three, who were from 12 to 30 years old. He would often slip away from ceremonies, card games, or casual conversations in order to copulate with the women, and as he left he would mutter that he was off to his camp for a meal. His departure was marked by sly grins and comments such as: "Of course he is hungry—hungry for coitus!" "He eats all the time, but see how thin he is. That's because he only eats his wives' vulvas!" But the remarks were never made until he was well out of ear-shot.

I never saw other relatives of a woman take offence at slighting references to her sexual activities, but such sneers were in any case rarely made in the presence of her own parents or siblings.

Ginger djabangari, aged about 55, had a wife, Marcie nambidjimba, aged about 22, who copulated energetically with most of her "cross-cousins" and "husband's brothers" in the Hooker Creek camp. Her insatiable appetite and blatant approach were the subject of many jokes made openly in the presence of her "brothers", "fathers", "sons" and "uncles", none of whom was upset by the humour. But if Ginger joined the group, the conversation was at once dropped. Even though he was well aware of Marcie's promiscuity and knew that everyone else discussed it, nobody dared to mention it to him.

Spouses usually copulate only at night in the privacy of their own shelters, for they would be deeply shamed if anyone observed this behaviour. As with people of the same sex, there is no taboo on their seeing each other's genitals. But a person should not expose himself in mixed company, particularly if the spouse is also present. The action would "shame" the onlookers; it would cause them to think about the married couple's sexual relationship, and the couple would be aware of their thoughts. This sort of modesty seems to have developed since the people began wearing clothes in the presence of Europeans. In the past they generally went naked or wore tiny and inadequate pubic tassels.

In some circumstances, the deliberate exposure of the genitals to people of the opposite sex is not merely a breach of etiquette but is also a vile insult to the offender's spouse.

> Yarry djabangari, aged about 40, had two wives and five children. He was devoted to the children and whenever they were involved in a misadventure he angrily berated and thrashed the wife who, he thought, had failed to look after them properly. His beatings became so frequent that the junior wife, Polly nambidjimba, decided to leave him. She moved to the widows' camp and for several days ignored his orders to return home. Yarry thereupon stormed naked through all the camps, waving his boomerangs and swearing obscenely at Polly. Onlookers were deeply shocked and withdrew to avoid witnessing Polly's humiliation. Yarry trailed her to her hiding-place, raped her, and then thrashed her. Thoroughly cowed, she went back to his camp. Other men criticized his behaviour among themselves, but none of Polly's close kin present in the camp came forward to avenge the insult. Yarry's size, rage and demonstrated fighting ability had intimidated the men, while at the same time Polly's declared intention of leaving him permanently had cost her their sympathy.

Spouses should not swear at each other. Although this prohibition is a rule of etiquette, it is also intended to protect jural rights. The people are aware that swearing usually leads to blows, and often to bloodshed. A woman's abusing her husband, however, is felt to be more culpable than the converse, for her action is also an attack on the basic stereotype of male superiority. It positively forces the husband to reply with physical violence.

> Willy djangala, aged about 30, was playing poker with a group of men when his wife appeared at a distance and berated him for some slight, real or fancied. He said nothing, although his expression became thunderous, and the other men ostentatiously ignored the woman's outcry. She then began to swear obscenely at him. Willy immediately seized a boomerang,

strode across without a word and felled her with several powerful blows to the head. Without a backward glance, he returned and took up his game. The other men exchanged winks but kept silent. Willy drew me aside afterwards and said, "I had to hit her. A woman cannot swear at an initiated man and order him about as though he were a child!"

Radcliffe Brown (1950, p. 11) has asserted that the jural aspect of kinship relations is as much concerned with rights and duties supported by moral and religious sanctions as with those maintained by legal sanctions, in the narrower "juridical" sense. The statement may be accepted provisionally at this point; but I doubt whether the jural aspect of Walbiri kinship relations can also be analysed adequately merely by making his distinction between *jus in personam* and *jus in rem*. These people, who have a minimum of tangible property, not only display little interest in its ownership or acquisition as such, but are also generally reluctant to equate persons with property (Maine, 1936, p. 152).

In almost all situations, what appear superficially to be possessive rights are essentially claims and privileges exercised by one (social) person in respect of another. I use the term "social person" in order to emphasize that an individual occupies several statuses simultaneously, each of which is associated with role-expectations that define various claims, privileges and duties he has towards other people. The terms "claim", "duty", and "privilege" have here the following meanings (Hoebel, 1954, chap. 4; Gluckman, 1955, p. 167):

> One person has a claim on another when he can demand specific services from the latter, whose duty it is to provide them. The performance of the service may involve incidentally the provision of material goods, but these are valued chiefly as visible symbols of the service and hence of the claim. Thus, an elaborate set of rules governs the distribution of hair-string among the Walbiri. As the recipients themselves make string to give to others, the distribution achieves no direct economic end. Instead, it symbolizes the personal claims that the recipients have on the donors in respect of various ritual, educative and sexual services.
>
> A person has a privilege when he can act in a specific manner in relation to another person whose duty it is to permit him to behave thus. It is a husband's privilege, for instance, to wound the man who elopes with his wife, for the enticement

has interrupted his personal claims on the wife's services. In theory, the lover should submit quietly, although in practice he rarely does so. The woman's kin have the privilege of punishing her, for her misdeed has jeopardized their personal claims on certain of the husband's services. This division of privilege makes it clear that the husband does not have simple possessive rights over the woman.

The term "rights" denotes briefly claims and privileges.

Thus, when a woman marries, her parents and close maternal kinsmen surrender to her husband certain personal claims on her services, but they retain the privilege of ensuring that she meets her obligations to him. At the same time, the husband assumes duties towards the woman (and her subsequent off-spring) and towards her maternal kin. The latter also have the privilege of enjoining him to discharge these duties.

In this society the sexual division of labour is clearly marked. The men hunt game, the women gather vegetable-foods and the smaller forms of wild life. The women also prepare most of the food, collect firewood, carry water, and care for the young children. The people assert that, in respect of these activities, each spouse has a claim on the other's services, both on his (or her) own behalf and on behalf of their children. If either fails to honour the obligation, the other is entitled to penalize the offender. A man should always berate his wife for such short-comings (although he should not swear at her) and he may occasionally beat her. But, if he strikes her too often or too heavily, or sheds her blood, her father should upbraid him. In the absence of the father, her brothers should intervene; failing them, her mother's brother is her protector. If none of these men is in the camp, the equivalent classificatory, but not distantly related, kinsmen should take her part. In theory, the woman may call on any of her countrymen in these kinship categories to protect her from injury, but in practice she can confidently rely only on the help of actual kinsmen.

A married woman who frequently neglects her domestic duties may also be reprimanded by her mother. Should the warning prove ineffective, her father, elder brother, or mother's brother may beat her. Usually, such punishment causes her to mend her ways for a time; if it does not, her husband is entitled to repudiate her. He can send her to her parents or, in their absence, to live

Danny djungarai—medicine-man and ritual leader. The scars on his thighs are from wounds self-inflicted in mourning.

Mess-hall at Warrabri settlement.

Part of the plant of stock-horses on a cattle-station, being brought in ready for the mustering season.

Roping a beast in the stock-yard.

in the widows' camp until she remarries. Few men would take such drastic action, however, for the woman's father is in no way bound to replace her with another daughter. Indeed, he might easily be angered by the severity of the son-in-law's punishment and come to blows with him.

The man who fails to provide enough food for his wife and children should be taken to task by his affines. Ideally, their public criticism should shame him into better behaviour; if it does not, they would hesitate to force a quarrel with him merely for such reasons. This would indirectly attack the conventional belief in male superiority; and most men are more concerned to maintain male solidarity than to redress the wrongs done to women. Nevertheless, a man who offended persistently might have his wife taken from him by her family and given to another man. I never heard of any actual cases of this.

In short, although husband and wife have in theory reciprocal claims on each other's economic services, there is often in fact marked inequality. The rights of the wife, both in the satisfaction of her just claims on her husband and in the rejection of his unjust demands, may be seriously infringed.

A similar state of affairs exists with regard to the care of young children. Paternal and maternal neglect or harshness should be equally culpable and liable to reprimand by the children's maternal kin. In practice, however, the negligent father (who is indeed rare) receives little more than scoldings from his wife and diffuse censure from the rest of the camp. The negligent mother, on the other hand, is sure to be beaten by her husband and very probably by her own mother as well.

In the past, a woman had no claim on the implements, weapons, and decorative and ritual objects that her husband made, or acquired in exchange, for his own use or for other men's use. A man similarly had no claim on the implements and decorative objects that his wife made, or acquired in exchange, for her own use or for the use of other women. Each could dispose of surplus articles made for him (or her) by the other, in order to meet kinship obligations. Neither, however, was entitled to dispose of the objects necessary for the efficient maintenance of the household without consulting the other. Each spouse had his or her own dogs, which could be given away freely. A couple

contributed equally to building the family shelter, but the husband determined where it was to be situated and when it was
to be renovated or rebuilt, abandoned or destroyed. There were
no individual or family possessive rights over tracts of land or
waterholes.

The introduction of money and European commodities has
made little difference to these property rules. The few horses,
camels and donkeys belong to the men, as does the necessary
harness. The purchaser of an article can now dispose of it freely,
and the spouse has no right to it. As few women are employed
by Europeans, men control most of the introduced commodities
and the little ready money that are in the camps. Some of them,
however, fearful of the lure of poker and two-up, give their cash
to their wives for safekeeping.

Spouses are expected to protect each other from the verbal
and physical attacks of outsiders. This ideal seems to me to aim
at the defence of the personal claims that each has on the other's
services. It might perhaps be argued that in this case the spouse
is merely a possession to be shielded from injury, or that each
spouse is concerned to safeguard his or her own social status and
self-esteem, of which the partner is thought to be an extension;
but I doubt that the people would think in these terms.

A person whose own spouse is attacked may often retaliate by
falling upon the aggressor's spouse as well. Thus, when one man
is struck by another, the victim's wife first tries to belabour the
assailant from the rear with a club; if she is prevented, she is
likely to turn on his wife. Although women are not positively
enjoined to assist their husbands in this way, they are usually
quick to do so. Such subsidiary engagements are often far more
sanguinary than are the quarrels in which they originated, and
in a matter of minutes they may transform a half-hearted alter-
cation between two men into a wild brawl that involves half the
camp.

Men frequently told me that many disputes among them would
end with only an exchange of insults were it not for the wives'
urging them to violence, and the development of most fights
that I saw certainly supported this statement. Husbands generally try to keep out of quarrels that begin among women. This
is a sensible precaution, for, as I have observed, the women

frequently sink their differences and join forces to attack any man who intervenes. Sometimes, however, a man whose wife is in the wrong in a dispute drags her from the mêlée before the weakness of her case exposes her to serious injury.

There had long been bad blood between Doris nagamara, the strapping young wife of Jack djabaldjari, and Beryl nagamara, the usually eventempered wife of Alec djabaldjari, and the women often quarrelled violently over trifles. The two men, who were good friends although not countrymen, kept out of these disputes. One day, an argument between the women flared into a bitter fight with clubs. As the two were evenly matched in strength and skill, the onlookers did not intervene; but, just as Chloe nagamara, Doris' close friend, arrived, Doris suffered a severe scalp wound. Swinging an enormous club, Chloe ran to her aid, and the pair were rapidly reducing Beryl to impotent screams when Clarry djabaldjari, Chloe's husband and Alec's half-brother, appeared. Energetically using the flat of a boomerang, he flogged Chloe the 400 yards back to their camp and furiously berated her for "double-banking" his brother's wife. Elsewhere in the camp, Jack and Alec elaborately ignored the affair.

A man immediately retaliates when another attacks his wife, and this is his duty rather than his privilege. Indeed, some of the angriest Walbiri I have seen were those whose wives and children had been injured in this way.

Wagulgari djungarai, the 15-year-old son of Wally djabaldjari, was a spastic and probably also a high-grade moron. A persistent thief, he was considered by everyone in the camp except his father to be a dangerous nuisance. One afternoon, he entered the camp of Paddy djuburula and tried to steal the tomahawk of Paddy's wife, Maudie nabanangga. She struck him with a billet of firewood and he ran away. Next morning, when Paddy was absent, Wagulgari seized the same tomahawk and hit Maudie between the eyes with the back of it. Hearing her screams, Paddy arrived in time to see Wagulgari fleeing. Grabbing a bundle of weapons, Paddy chased him through the camps, hurling spears, boomerangs and finally his shield at him. Only Paddy's blind rage and Wagulgari's extraordinary nimbleness saved the youth from being speared in the back. When old Wally, Wagulgari's father, came shouting from his camp, ready to spear Paddy, other men intervened to protect Paddy, whose actions, they all told me, were completely justified.

Marriage, with its accompanying exchanges, confers on people personal claims on their spouses' services in reproduction. All the Walbiri I encountered, except a few at Phillip Creek, wanted large families. Many stated explicitly that the satisfaction of this desire is the most important reason for marrying. Women rarely try to procure abortions (except, I suspect, at Phillip Creek), and most men and women consider the intention to be thoroughly reprehensible. It is the duty of a woman's kin, especially her mother, to thrash her for such an offence. Her husband may also upbraid and beat her.

Only a mild stigma of "laziness" attaches to childless couples. There seems to be no notion of female barrenness or of male sterility, and the absence of children is attributed mainly to the failure of the *guruwari* to enter the woman. This condition is not caused by any moral fault or ritual pollution. Rather, it is regarded as a regrettable indication of the imperfect control that humans have over dreamtime beings. The *guruwari* can be stimulated to act but cannot be directed or coerced into entering a specific animal or person. The selection of a particular individual is taken to be largely a matter of chance.

In consequence, childlessness is not a sufficient ground for divorce and this negation is in turn supported by the presence of polygyny, adoption and a classificatory kinship system. A couple who remain childless after several years are the objects of general sympathy, and the wife's kinsmen may try to arrange the marriage of a second woman (preferably a close "sister" of the first) to the man. But he has no automatic claims on them in this respect; it is merely their privilege to help him. If the only suitable girls are already bespoken by younger men, especially by bachelors, the husband cannot over-ride the claims of these men. He may collaborate, however, with his affines to negotiate with one of the men in order to receive the latter's betrothed as a wife. In return he relinquishes his claim to a subsequent daughter of his wife's father.

Such arrangements need delicate handling and may easily collapse. Thus, the younger man, having released his betrothed, is likely to change his mind and demand her return; or the original husband may revive his old claim to his "wife's sister" when she is ready to marry the younger man. The outcome is often a bloody fight. But, whatever steps are taken to provide the childless man with an extra wife, the arrangement is thought to benefit his original wife equally. She will also be a "mother" to children borne by the second wife and will share in their rearing and in the economic exchanges consequent on their initiation, betrothal, etc., as well as in the maternal prestige that accrues from such events.

A couple with several children may offer one to a close (generally an actual or half-) brother of the husband, or to a close sister of the wife, who is still childless after five or six years of marriage. I encountered only one instance.

A man claims as his own any child his wife bears to a lover, and he should treat it exactly as he would his own offspring. Although her misconduct has not in effect diminished his rights to her reproductive services, it has infringed his claims on her sexual services and has injured his self-esteem. He is therefore entitled to berate and beat his wife, and so are her own mother, father and brothers. I doubt that many men in this situation would bother to distinguish carefully between the infringements of their claims on reproductive and on sexual services. On the other hand, outsiders discussing the affair do occasionally make a rough distinction along these lines.

The punishment of the lover is largely in the hands of the husband, whose affines may also assist him. It is thought that the offender is further penalized by having no rights to the child he has sired. There is almost no way of knowing how many Walbiri children are conceived in adultery. Women, fearing the anger of their husbands, are reticent about their own amatory exploits, and their assertions about other women are at best guesses. I knew of only two instances at Hooker Creek, both of which were regarded seriously by everyone in the camp.

Kenny djabaldjari, aged about 48, had two nagamara wives, the younger of whom, Molly, he had acquired through the levirate. He had little affection for Molly and, when she left him to live with Bulbul djabaldjari, aged about 50, he merely "growled" at Bulbul. After enduring Bulbul's brutality for some months, however, she begged Kenny to take her back, and somewhat reluctantly he did so. Bulbul then publicly challenged Kenny to fight for the woman; but, as public opinion solidly supported Kenny, Bulbul's 18-year-old son intervened. Clem disarmed his father and broke his spears. Bulbul did not resist but said that he was prepared to let the matter rest. He approached Kenny in a friendly manner as if to embrace him. Kenny, essentially a simple soul, relaxed his guard and received a razor-slash across the forehead. Incensed, he knocked Bulbul unconscious with a bundle of boomerangs. Bulbul, who had been secure in his fighting reputation, was badly shaken by this defeat and dropped the quarrel in earnest.

Some months later Molly bore a son, her first child, which everyone assumed to be Bulbul's progeny. Kenny said nothing and raised the boy as his own. Mother and child later became seriously ill, and the infant died while they were being taken to Darwin. It was months before Molly returned, still ailing. She remained in Kenny's camp, but he had little to do with her. Doubtless aggravated by this indifference, Molly's condition became worse and she was again sent to Darwin for medical treatment.

Soon after she returned to Hooker Creek the second time, the whole camp moved into the bush for the Gadjari rituals. While Molly was gathering food with other women one day, she went into premature labour. (The women all denied that this was the result of an abortion, and there is no reason to doubt them.) To judge from their description, she miscarried twins. Word flew round the camp that, instead of being pale like new-born Walbiri babies, they were "black, like salt-water [Darwin] babies".

Kenny was residing in the men's ceremonial camp. When he heard of the "black babies", he went to the general camp and angrily accused Molly of adultery with Darwin men. He then publicly repudiated her and told her to live in the widows' camp. He did not attempt to beat her and, as she had no close kin at Hooker Creek, nobody else tried to punish her physically. Men with whom I discussed the matter praised the restrained way in which Kenny had treated the situation.

The other incident, however, had a more sanguinary outcome.

Ginger djabangari had two wives, Marcie and Liddy nambi-djimba, who were actual sisters. For some months the women had been involved in a liaison with two bachelors, Willy and Johnny djabangari, who were not Ginger's countrymen. Ginger knew this but, because of Marcie's poor reputation, was in no hurry to make an issue of it. Eventually Liddy became pregnant, so retired to the bush one day, where Marcie helped her procure an abortion. Somehow the news reached the camp and some well-meaning friends told Ginger, not only of the abortion, but also of the names of the women's lovers. This forced him to take action. He enlisted the support of several countrymen who were close brothers of his wives and then attacked the two women and their lovers. He speared Johnny through the knee and Liddy through the arm; Willy he stabbed in the back with a long knife, and only European intervention prevented him from cutting Marcie's throat. At the same time his djambidjimba countrymen thrashed all four of the offenders with clubs and boomerangs.

Liddy and Johnny were sent to Darwin for medical attention. There they declared themselves to be married. When the news reached Hooker Creek, all Ginger's countrymen agreed that he had no alternative but to spear Johnny again on his return. Liddy, who had already been punished adequately by the original spearing, would merely be thrashed.

When I left Hooker Creek, the couple were avoiding Walbiri camps and had last been heard of working at Pine Creek. Unless Johnny relinquished Liddy, he would be involved in disputes whenever he met Ginger's countrymen, for everyone now regarded the situation as one of elopement.

In this society elopements may occur in three sorts of circumstances. In the first, a girl who is betrothed but not yet married runs away with another man. I did not encounter any instances of this; but men asserted that the girl's youth and "silliness" would be taken into account and her enticer blamed as her abductor. Similarly, the young widow of an old man might cut short the prescribed mourning period and elope to avoid marrying another old man to whom she is promised through the levirate. Once again, most of the blame falls on her lover. Although she is thought to be old enough to know better, her kinsmen view with sympathy her desire for a young husband. This was indeed the reaction in the one instance I observed.

In both situations, the intended husband should try to recover the woman with the help of her maternal kin. If the fugitives are overtaken, the husband and the woman's kinsmen beat her, and he and his brothers belabour her lover. Sometimes they also punish him with a token spear-thrust in the thigh or the calf. But, should the couple evade capture and reach the country of another community, they may be confident that the feelings of the offended men will soon cool.

In the third form of elopement a man entices a woman from her husband's camp. This is a serious offence. Normally, a woman shuts her eyes to the casual extra-marital affairs of her own daughter or daughter's daughter, but she intervenes if the liaison looks like becoming permanent. Should her arguments, vituperation and blows prove ineffective, the matter becomes one for the girl's own father, brothers, mother's brother and mother's mother's brother to handle. The last is involved because he is also the "mother's father" of the girl's husband and one of the "bosses" of his "marriage line". The men admonish and, if necessary, thrash the girl. The husband warns his wife's lover to stay away from her and often backs the order with force.

Should the couple elope, the wife's kinsmen and the husband and his close agnates are obliged to follow them. Other close kin of both the spouses may join the pursuit, to ensure not only that the offending man receives his deserts but also that the wife is not seriously injured. The aggrieved husband and his agnates should thrash the enticer and spear him, although not fatally. The wife should also be beaten by her brothers and then speared lightly in the thigh, so that she will "sit down quietly" in her husband's camp. Some men said that the husband could spear his wife, but most disagreed with this. They asserted that his action would certainly lead to a fight with his wife's father. Thus, the woman's relatives retain certain privileges over her and should defend them from infringement by the husband. But when elopements actually take place and tempers become heated, the rules governing the administration of punishment are often ignored.

Some years ago, Paddy djabaldjari lived at Birrindudu station. Also in the camp was Ned djungarai, the son of Paddy's late elder brother. Ned's djangala wife was a "real larrikin" who had a succession of lovers. Moreover, she had illicitly acquired certain ritual knowledge about which she gossiped in the camp. Several men, including Paddy, told her father to punish her, but he was "too lazy and weak" to act. Eventually, Jim Tulum djuburula, who was her "M.M.B." and Paddy's close "Sr.S.", enticed her to live permanently with him. When her father still did nothing, a party of Ned's older agnates, including Paddy, attacked Tulum and the woman. Tulum was severely wounded. In the mêlée the nangala "ran into" a boomerang that Paddy had aimed at Tulum and was killed. As a result, Paddy spent four or five years in jail at Alice Springs.

Not only Paddy, but all the men with whom I discussed the affair, insisted that he was most unlucky, for he was merely trying to injure Tulum and not the woman. Everyone blamed her death and Paddy's jail sentence on her father's failure to discipline her.

An eloping couple who, in such circumstances, flee to another country are safe from physical attack while they reside there. But the man cannot live in exile for long; his desire to be with his own countrymen and to participate in his own lodge rituals draws him home. Nevertheless, he knows that, sooner or later after his return, the aggrieved husband and the latter's close agnates will force a quarrel with him. Whether this is a formal duel with knives or an informal brawl, he does not, if he is wise, try too strenuously to win. In theory, once the husband has shed the offender's blood, the matter is settled. The lover may retain the woman, who, in the eyes of the community, is now legally his wife—provided she is of an appropriate kinship category.

In fact, however, the offender may expect her former husband to take every opportunity to stir up trouble for him. But, such is Walbiri stubbornness, a man who has acquired a woman in this way will face any disputes rather than surrender her. He relies on his own fighting ability and on the aid of his close brothers to carry him through. Moreover, having paid in blood for the woman, he counts on the support of public opinion in the quarrels.

A woman who runs away from her husband is usually able to carry only her youngest child with her. Indeed, should an arduous journey be likely, she may leave all the children in the care of her "sisters". The energy with which her husband prosecutes the chase depends to some extent on her decision. If the woman takes none of the children and he has other wives to rear them, he may make only a token gesture of pursuing the fugitives. A man who entices a woman tries, therefore, to dissuade her from bringing any of her children with her.

The people could not recall any instance of a married man's eloping with another woman; and it was their opinion that only an insane man would thus jeopardize his own marriage. His wife would not accompany him on such a flight; she would be too affronted and too sensible of her children's welfare. Instead, she would take the children and live with her parents, who would soon arrange for another man to marry her and acquire the children. Sometimes, however, a married man becomes involved with an unmarried woman who is neither his "m.m.b.d.d." nor his "m.b.d."—that is, she is a woman he may not marry legally. If he brings her to live in his camp, his wife may return with her children to her parents.

> Gagalala djabaldjari gave his daughter, Annie nungarai, in marriage to Bob djangala. Bob soon acquired a reputation as a larrikin, always pursuing forbidden women, and the marriage was unhappy. When Annie was in her twenties and still childless, Bob installed his latest mistress, a "mother's mother", in their camp. Annie at once returned to Gagalala, who some months later gave her to Abe djangala, his close "M.B.S.S." Annie looked with favour on Abe and the couple are still married today.

A man who behaves in this way need not be physically attacked by his wife's kinsmen, although this sometimes happens. Generally, his loss of wife and children is considered to be sufficient punishment. Any other disputes arising out of his relationship with the forbidden mistress are most likely to concern a different group of people, in particular her actual and potential husbands.

The people, as a rule, consider it wrong for young children to be parted from their mothers. Consequently, whether or not a divorce is followed by the remarriage of the couple, the woman retains children younger than about five or six years. Her next husband raises them as his own. The ex-husband usually disputes her right to take the older children. Public opinion supports him in this, especially with regard to his sons; but there is no suggestion that his claim is simply based on his payments of brideprice. Rather, the arrangement is one of balancing practical against sentimental considerations—it is a matter of equity.

The woman is best fitted to care for infants; the man should not be denied the pleasure and privilege of guiding his sons through their later ritual education. He should also be allowed to retain daughters approaching marriageable age so that he may fulfil previous ceremonial commitments. The lack of elaborate rules determining the allocation of children in separations, or prescribing indemnification for their loss, is compatible with the absence of permanent residential groups that stress unilineal descent and also with the paucity of heritable property. The patrilines are localized only for ritual reference, while the matrilines are significant chiefly as "marriage lines" that have no residential connotations.

The people believe that the marriage tie and the rights of spouses should be protected from injury wherever possible. Permanent, stable unions are the ideal, for these ensure that not only will more children be conceived but also that the children will be reared properly—that is, as good Walbiri. Separations and divorces are in fact comparatively rare. At Hooker Creek, only two couples had founded their marriages on what were technically elopements; in one case the young woman had already lived apart from her ex-husband for some years, and in the other the man had enticed a young widow who did not wish to marry an older man allotted to her through the levirate. Similarly, in the time I was there only two divorces occurred. Analysis of genealogical evidence also reveals that the Walbiri divorce-rate is much lower than that in a number of native societies.

TABLE 13

Walbiri divorce-rates

Number of marriages terminated by death	119	A
Number of marriages terminated by divorce or permanent separation	31	B
Number of marriages extant	250	C
Total number of marriages in the sample	400	D

Ratios

B/D	B/C	B/A&B
7·7%	12·4%	20·7%

My observations also suggest that the norm of long-term unions is generally achieved. Many spouses have lived together for 20 years or more. That marriages rarely exceed this length is due largely to the practice of betrothing young girls to men who are much older than they. Most women may expect to be widowed after 20 to 25 years of marriage.

The stability of marriage is also supported to some extent by the custom of wife-exchange, which enables married people legally and amicably to satisfy their desires for sexual variety. The practice is not so common today, perhaps because some people are aware of the strong European disapproval. I observed only one instance, although I heard of several others. Normally, the exchange is arranged by close brothers who frequently hunt and camp together, and it is meant to last a month or two at most. The men discuss the matter privately and informally, then announce their decision to their wives. If the wives selected, or their co-wives, object greatly, the matter is dropped. A man should not force his wife into the situation, although sometimes he grumbles at her until she agrees. Usually, however, the women co-operate willingly, as they can in this way please their husbands and enjoy themselves. Children conceived during this period belong to their mothers' husbands.

The exchange is held to concern only the two men and their wives; the kinsmen of the women have no voice in it. But, although the wives should have some say in the affair, the practice nonetheless reflects the general superiority of men's privileges over women's. Only men may initiate an exchange. The husband of a woman who suggested it would at once accuse her of wishing to continue an adulterous affair with his brother.

Despite the presence of safeguards to the stability of marriage, there is a high incidence of casual adultery, in which the double standard of morality for the sexes is very clearly revealed. Male adultery is regarded with complacency and some amusement by most men, except of course the cuckolds themselves, and the stress on masculine solidarity is quite apparent. But all men roundly condemn female adultery as a shameful business. I have never heard the men, in their frequent discussions of the subject, admit the incompatibility of the two attitudes.

There exists a set of explicitly-stated conventions that govern men's behaviour in extra-marital affairs. A married man may court his single and married female "cross-cousins"—that is, women who are his potential, although alternative, wives; but intercourse with his actual cross-cousins is regarded as incestuous. Should no "cross-cousin" be available or interested, he pursues the wives of his "brothers"—women who are also potential wives for him. He should not try to seduce the wives of his own or close brothers, however, because fights between these men are strongly deplored. Opinions are generally divided on the propriety of copulating with women other than "cross-cousins" and "brothers' wives". Some men assert that, as it is forbidden to marry such women, it is also wrong to seduce them; but others, usually younger men, regard this sort of misconduct as rather dashing.

Having selected a suitable woman, the man performs love-magic rituals privately in the bush to engage her affections. As he already has reason to believe she is interested in him, he can confidently rely on the magic to sway her. (If it does not work, he simply assumes another man has anticipated him.) The adulterer then arranges to meet the woman secretly in the bush, where they spend an hour or two together. I was told that lovers fearful of discovery often lean against a tree and copulate in a standing position, so that they may flee the moment they hear someone nearby.

These adulteries must be carried out with the greatest discretion, not only in order to escape immediate detection by the woman's husband but also to avoid offending public opinion. The man who parades his mistress or flaunts his affairs quickly diverts male sympathy to the cuckold.

Although Bulbul djabaldjari had three wives, he devoted much time and energy to the pursuit of other women. On this occasion, he was involved in a liaison with the promiscuous Marcie nambidjimba, his "m.b.d.". As men recalled his recent affair with Molly nagamara, they passed acid comments on his current behaviour. However, nothing was said to Marcie's husband, Ginger, who was clearly aware of the situation. One afternoon, Bulbul's youngest wife, Margaret nagamara, surprised Bulbul and Marcie *in flagrante delicto* in Bulbul's own shelter. She upbraided him for "shaming" her in this way and then struck Marcie several times. Bulbul at once speared her in the thigh and abused her roundly. The noise attracted Ginger, who began to beat Marcie until Abe djangala, Marcie's "father", sent him spinning from a powerful blow with a club. This quite incapacitated Ginger, who could only look on while Abe thrashed Marcie.

Meanwhile, Margaret's own father, William djuburula (aged about 60), attacked Bulbul with a boomerang. He landed some telling blows but was no match for the younger man. Seeing William receive the worst of the fight, his "younger brothers" and countrymen, Paddy and Charlie djuburula, came to his aid. Bulbul was now in desperate straits, so Clem djungarai, his own son, and Windy and Larry djungarai, his "sons", tackled the two younger djuburula with clubs and boomerangs. Windy split open Paddy's scalp but had his fingers broken in return. Bulbul's own brothers, who had disapproved of his behaviour, would not help him. Eventually a group of Ginger's countrymen managed to break up the fight, which now no longer concerned them, and separated the combatants long enough for tempers to cool.

In the discussions that followed, I was repeatedly told, even by Bulbul's own brothers, that he had behaved abominably. By copulating with Marcie in his own camp, he had insulted all his wives and their kinsmen. Nevertheless, the men added, Margaret should have known better than to berate Bulbul in front of Marcie. He was bound to retaliate in order to maintain his prestige. She should have gone at once to her father with her complaint and let him gather relatives to punish Bulbul.

Many women resent the operation of the double standard. Some cannot understand why they should be more heavily penalized for adultery than are their husbands; others cannot see why, when they themselves try to remain chaste, their husbands can fornicate with impunity. As public expression of their grievances merely antagonizes their husbands, the women adopt other courses of action. Virtuous wives become insufferably so and privately nag at their husbands almost without pause. Anyone who has heard a Walbiri woman nag will readily appreciate the effectiveness of her technique.

Adulterous wives generally combine in a conspiracy of silence, so that their husbands are uncertain of what is occurring in their absences. But female solidarity is a rather brittle bond, and a woman never knows when some minor dispute with another woman will lead to tale-bearing. The women have also adopted masculine conventions in their own love-affairs and, by covert signs and the performance of love-magic, encourage male "cross-cousins" to approach them.

As a man's own behaviour informs him that at least some women welcome opportunities for adultery, he can never be entirely sure of his own wife's fidelity. Even if she is virtuous (and many are), she uses his uncertainty as a weapon to keep him more often in his own camp. This doubt is also reflected in the men's reluctance to leave their wives behind when offered employment with Europeans. Occasionally, a man who has a wife too old or unattractive to invite seduction places her in the care of a close (preferably an actual) brother, or of his wife's father or brother, while he is absent. But if the terms of employment demand that he leave behind a young and attractive wife, with or without guardians, he is unlikely to accept the job.

It was impossible in the circumstances to estimate accurately the incidence of adultery among the Walbiri. To judge from their remarks to my wife and myself and from observed situations, most of them probably commit adultery several times during early married life, while for a few it is a pastime to be pursued on all occasions. The presence of children, however, with the responsibility that their care entails and the consequent strengthening of affective bonds between the spouses, tends to reduce the frequency of extra-marital affairs among people who have been long married.

> Annie nungarai was gathering food in the bush when Jim Tulum djuburula (her "cross-cousin") suggested that they "play" together. She indignantly rebuffed him and called loudly for her husband, Abe. By the time Abe reached her, Tulum had disappeared. Abe praised Annie's presence of mind, took her back to her camp, and then went off on his own business. When he returned just before dusk, he saw Tulum sitting in his own camp nearby. Abe, who is a powerful man, at once seized him by the throat and dealt him a tremendous buffet on the jaw that knocked Tulum flat on his back in his own camp-fire. He warned Tulum that the punishment would be repeated if Annie was molested again. Abe's use of his fists as weapons and his comparative restraint in this situation were explicit attempts to emulate European practices. Normally a Walbiri would never fight with his bare hands, nor would he treat a potential adulterer so casually.

Old men in particular are likely to suspect the fidelity of young wives—and their suspicions are often warranted. Although these men are remarkably virile, and copulate regularly with their young wives, the latter often prefer the embraces of the handsome young men who swagger around the camps in ten-gallon hats, gaudy shirts and high-heeled boots.

Billy djambidjimba, aged about 55, had two wives, the younger being Margie nabangari, aged about 22. For months she had engaged in an affair with Norman djambidjimba, a bachelor aged about 25. Norman told me that he and Margie were truly fond of each other and would marry if only he could devise some way to detach her from Billy without too much difficulty. Billy eventually learned of the affair and attacked Norman with a spear. The latter did not try to defend himself and was slightly wounded in the foot. But, because he had not concealed his intentions, public opinion was against him and he could not risk removing Margie from Billy's camp. They were still lovers when I left Hooker Creek; and I was later told at Yuendumu that Billy had speared Norman again, whereupon Norman declared that he would still court Margie.

I have discussed in detail the significant affective, conventional and jural features of the marital relationship—treating both the ideal norms and the deviations from them—and indicated the high value placed on stable unions. The emphasis given in this account to the sexual and reproductive aspects of marriage reflects the great importance that the Walbiri themselves attribute to them. Ideally, reproduction exclusively concerns jurally-recognized spouses, and in fact little latitude about this norm is permitted. Extra-marital intercourse is regarded somewhat more tolerantly, provided it does not endanger the marriages of the people concerned.

Economic and educative activities, on the other hand, are not specifically tied to the marriage relationship, and a comprehensive body of rules regulates them in the context of social interaction with other relatives. The rights and duties of spouses in these respects seem self-evident to most Walbiri. They assume that a man, for instance, does not need his economic obligations towards his wife and children rigidly defined and policed. Reason and affection transform such duties into privileges, so that role-behaviour is more likely to exceed than to fall short of role-expectations. My own observations suggest that this assumption is generally valid.

Co-wives. Co-wives, that is, women simultaneously married to the one man, fall into four main categories.

(a) They may be actual or half-sisters, who address each other as *gabidi* (elder sister) and *ŋauwuru* (younger sister). This situation is not often encountered.

(b) They may be parallel cousins, who address each other as *gabidi* (senior "sister") and *ŋauwuru* (junior "sister"). This situation is not often encountered and in practice is not distinguished from (a).

(c) They may be "sisters", although not necessarily members of the one community, and they address each other as *gabidi* (senior "sister") and *ŋauwuru* (junior "sister"). This is the most common relationship.

(d) They may be reciprocally "m.m.b.s.d."—that is, one is the "m.b.d." of the husband and the other is his "m.m.b.d.d."—and they address each other as *jaldjali*. This is unusual.

If a man cohabits with a woman not in categories (a) to (d), she and his legal wives address each other by the kinship terms appropriate to their actual relationships.

Although the people are aware that disputes occasionally occur between co-wives, they believe the women should live together in relative harmony. Consequently, simultaneous sororal polygyny is approved, for actual or close sisters are thought to be less likely to quarrel. My observations revealed that most co-wives do in fact live together amicably and that a strong bond unites them. Simple affection is one element of this tie, which seems also to be based on a common solidarity of the women arising from the shared, intimate knowledge of the husband's foibles, faults and virtues, and reinforced by the shared responsibility of rearing his children.

The attitude is a more intense form of the tenuous solidarity that most women display in the face of assertions of male superiority. Between co-wives the bond is most clearly expressed when one defends the other from the verbal or physical attacks of the husband, or lies to conceal the other's omissions or misconduct. Such behaviour is neither a duty nor an explicit convention; it follows from friendship. Nevertheless, relations between close sisters are not necessarily smoother than those between unrelated co-wives. The sisters may exhibit a greater affection, but (perhaps because of this) the quarrels that do occur are often very bitter.

Liddy nagamara had a deep affection for her husband, Alec, despite the difference of 15 years in their ages; but, after they had been married for 10 years, Alec took Liddy's half-sister, Beryl nagamara, as his second wife. Liddy begrudged the attention shown to the newcomer and eventually insisted that Alec no longer sleep with Beryl. She also threatened to beat Beryl if Alec did not accede to her wishes. Alec, easy-going and fond of both women, pretended to agree; and thereafter Liddy shared his shelter every night, while Beryl slept in a shelter nearby. Beryl made no complaint, for Alec copulated with her in secret in the bush each day. Liddy came to hear of this and taxed Alec. To avoid a quarrel, he denied the allegation.

Unfortunately for Alec, Beryl's pregnancy was soon apparent. Liddy again tackled him and he, foolishly, offered more denials. At this Liddy dropped the matter; but, the evening after Beryl's baby was born, she announced loudly that Alec must have been cuckolded, for he had assured her he had not copulated with Beryl. No husband could suffer this imputation in silence, and Alec was forced to inform the audience (by now numerous and amused) that the child was certainly his. At this admission, Liddy attacked Beryl and the baby with a digging-stick, but other women shepherded her from Beryl's camp. She then belaboured Alec, who tried to retaliate with a knife. Only the intervention of onlookers prevented bloodshed.

By then quite incensed, Liddy swore at Alec at great length, displaying a virtuosity never before observed among Hooker Creek women. Her vituperation was so devastating that Alec packed up his swag and camped for the next three days with the bachelors. All the men discussed Liddy's performance with the greatest admiration, although they hastened to point out to me how shocking it was for a woman to swear like that at her husband.

Having vented her feelings, Liddy made no more attacks on Beryl, but relations between them remained tense for weeks. When Liddy was later confined, however, Beryl voluntarily assisted during the birth and afterwards. Her cheerful forbearance impressed Liddy, and from that time on the two were friendly. Nevertheless, Liddy continued to demand most of Alec's attentions.

A woman should not demand services from her husband or be granted privileges by him (other than those due to her age or seniority), to the detriment of the claims of her co-wives. Relations among co-wives are not as elaborately organized as, for instance, those in some African societies; instead, they are loosely defined in terms of an equitable distribution of the husband's services. He should not show discrimination in the allocation of the food he provides, although in practice very old wives are sometimes fed less well than their juniors. Some men are not always scrupulous in ensuring that younger wives attend to all the needs of old and infirm or blind women.

A man should distribute his sexual favours without bias among his wives; but it is accepted that a comparatively old woman is no longer sexually active and, therefore, need not share her husband's bed. She still eats in his camp and helps to care for her junior co-wives' infants, although usually she sleeps in a separate shelter nearby. Old wives also spend much time in the widows' camp gossiping with their coevals. Nevertheless, men do not discard wives who are sexually inactive, and the women retain jural claims over their husbands. Still more effective is the affection, usually deep, that has developed between them through the years. A man may sometimes appear careless of the rights of an old wife but he never fails to defend her from insult and injury.

A man is usually most attentive to his latest wife and sleeps with her to the exclusion of the other women for the first few months. After a reasonable time, however, this partiality should cease, and the sexually active co-wives should also share his attentions and his bed. I could discover no explicit system of rostering co-wives. The usual practice seems to be that the wife currently in possession of the husband's swag vacates it at the onset of her monthly period and is replaced by a co-wife. The out-going wife sleeps either in the widows' camp, in the old wife's shelter, or in a shelter that has been constructed for this purpose near the husband's camp. The second wife in turn occupies the husband's bed until she menstruates. Similarly, a woman whose pregnancy is advanced should give up her place in the swag in favour of her co-wife. A man who has only one wife, however, is likely to copulate regularly with her until a few weeks before the birth of her child.

I observed little friction among co-wives over the allocation of these rights, but on occasions quarrels were noisy and sanguinary. Finally, a man should not discriminate among the children of his various wives, and I saw no evidence of such prejudice.

Sporadic infringements of the rights of co-wives by the husband are rarely penalized. The offended wife can do little more than berate him. There is nothing of the African notion that the violations are valid grounds for divorce, and the injured wife is not indemnified in any way. A woman may ask her father or brothers to admonish her husband if he is a persistent offender, but they would hesitate to dictate the course of his sexual habits. The criticism would derogate from male dignity and prestige. The injured woman's mother can sometimes exert pressure on the co-wife who shares in the offence and induce her to recognize the claims of the latter's "sister".

The duties owed to each other by co-wives are defined as "tuition from the elder, service from the younger". When a man takes a girl into his camp to "grow her up" as a second wife, the senior wife treats her very much as a daughter. She continues her education in the techniques of gathering and preparing food, sexual relations and infant nurture. The older woman disciplines the girl, shields her from the advances of other men, and instructs her in those features of ritual life that are open to women. In return, the girl shows affection and some respect for the senior wife, undertakes the tedious fetching of firewood and water, and tends to the needs of the younger children. It is believed that "close" sororal polygyny is especially advantageous in this respect, as the bond between sisters makes for more patient teaching and more willing service.

Co-wives should also share the food they gather equitably among themselves and their children, and this usually happens in fact. Although each woman ultimately has the right of disposal over the implements, clothes and decorative objects that she herself has made, in practice co-wives share all their possessions freely.

Jim Tulum djuburula, aged about 35, had two wives, Nelly nabanangga, aged about 14, and Liddy nungarai, aged about 45. Liddy should not have been in Tulum's camp. Although she was of the correct subsection, she was not his "m.b.d." and possible alternate wife but was his "m.f.sr." and therefore the appropriate alternative wife for his djuburula "father's father".

In 1953 Polly nambidjimba bore Bessie nabanangga and Tulum asked Yarry djabangari, Bessie's father, and Silent djambidjimba, Bessie's mother's brother, to betroth the baby to him. Both agreed, and the betrothal was publicly announced when Bessie was about three months old. Bessie was, however, the actual daughter's daughter of Liddy, Tulum's senior wife, which made the latter the wife's mother's mother of Tulum—a woman he should avoid.

When I expressed surprise that this betrothal was permitted, men told me that it was a neat solution to an awkward problem. As a woman and her d.d. should always be close friends, Liddy was now assured of affectionate care in her old age, while Bessie would be trained by a sympathetic and patient mentor. It also seemed that the betrothal would "legalize" the union between Tulum and Liddy, so that it ceased to be "wrong" and would become merely a breach of good taste. I am sure that Tulum was alive to this possibility when he asked for Bessie's hand.

Most of the people believe that polygyny benefits the wives as much as the husbands. A few younger women, however, are reluctant to share their husbands with co-wives and, by nagging and being generally obstructive, sometimes dissuade the men from making second marriages. Usually, they achieve a postponement only for as long as they remain sexually attractive.

Kenny djabaldjari betrothed his daughter Margaret nungarai to his countryman, Abe djangala, who was already married to Annie nungarai. When Margaret was old enough to live with Abe, Annie objected to the marriage. She was fond of Abe and jealous of her position as sole wife. Abe, equally fond of Annie and wary of her active tongue, gave in; and Margaret went instead to his young brother, Freddy. Later, Abe negotiated with Alec djabaldjari for the latter's daughter, Elizabeth nungarai. As the time approached for Elizabeth to enter Abe's camp, Annie again objected; but Abe this time stated firmly that he intended to receive the girl. Recognizing Abe's determination, Annie decided that she liked Elizabeth and made no more objections.

I encountered a few young men who said that monogamy is to be preferred to polygyny. They were aware that most Europeans would rather employ monogamous Aborigines, for the Europeans regard these as being more moral and less likely to be involved in camp brawls over the disposal of women. Nevertheless, I doubt that the men's attitudes will long survive the extensive example of polygyny before them or the desire for extra comforts that develops with advancing age, especially when more wives are actually offered to them.

As most men are indifferent to European opinions of their marital practices, as well as to incipient emancipist aspirations among the very few wage-earning women, it seems clear that polygyny will die hard in this society.

CHAPTER VIII

INTRAFAMILIAL RELATIONSHIPS (Continued)

Father–children. The kinship term *wabira* applies to all men regarded as "father". They may include:

(a) The actual father, father's brother and half-brother, and the F.F.B.S., all of whom may also be called *djadji* or *girana*.
(b) The mother's husband who is also "M.M.B.S." and *maliri*. The terms *wabira* and *bimari*, father's sister, are also extended to include his close brothers and sisters.
(c) The "fathers" who are countrymen but are not included in (a).
(d) All other Walbiri who are "fathers".
(e) All non-Walbiri who are "fathers".

A man's children are his *ŋalabi*, son, and *jundalba*, daughter. The latter is also referred to as *ŋalabi* in contexts where the fact of her sex is unimportant. Considerations of genealogical and geographical distance implied in (a) to (e) also apply to the categorization of children, and indeed to all kin. Qualifiers may also be affixed to possessive pronouns or to the kinship terms themselves to indicate own or "close" relatives.

The Walbiri today recognize the fact of physiological paternity, as those in the past also seem to have done; but the significant link between a man and his children is still thought to be spiritual. Although he has only a limited control over the allocation of the children's conception-dreamings, the father determines their lodge-dreaming. His sons are initiated into his cult-lodge and thereby share a common lodge-spirit or -dreaming with him. His daughters are not initiated in this way, but he and his sons hold the same lodge-spirit in trust for them. This intimate tie between a man and his children essentially expresses common membership in a patrilineal descent grouping.

Father–son. The marked affective bond between father and son, which develops early in the boy's infancy and persists until death, is manifested in many situations. Until they are initiated, boys are indulged by their fathers to an extent rarely observed in our own society. Only on two occasions did I see a man strike a young son; and the mother who tries even mild and warranted castigation of the boy usually incurs her husband's displeasure.

During their first three or four years, boys delight in accompanying their fathers around the camp, walking hand-in-hand with them or riding on their shoulders. A man receives favourable comments on his son's physique, temperament, or intelligence with obvious pride and pleasure. Although the youngsters do not attend totemic ceremonies, they often sit with their fathers when the latter discuss ritual matters in all-male company; it is thought that the boys are too young to understand these conversations. But, if the child becomes fretful, the father makes little attempt to pacify him and quickly returns to the camp to hand him over to his mother.

After the boy is aged five or six, he roams the bush with other lads, and his father sees little of him by day. Men spend much time cutting up damaged boomerangs to make throwing-sticks for their sons to use on these jaunts; and the boys display remarkable accuracy in killing small birds and lizards with the weapons. They now learn which flora and smaller game provide the best foods, they develop their tracking skills and acquire an intimate knowledge of the bush for 10 miles or so around the camp. During this period, men take little part in educating or disciplining their sons, whose behaviour towards them often reflects this lack of control.

Bulbul djabaldjari was playing poker with a circle of men. His son Peter, aged about 9, was at first content to watch the game quietly. But he tired of this and began grabbing at the playing-cards dealt to his father. Bulbul bore this behaviour with good-humour for some time and rebuked several men who told Peter to leave. Eventually his own patience wore thin, and he asked Peter to bring some water from the bore, about 800 yards away. Peter ignored the request and, seizing some of the articles forming Bulbul's stake, withdrew some distance to play with them. Bulbul again asked him to bring the water. Within a few minutes Bulbul was literally dancing with rage as he shouted at the boy. Peter, silent and unconcerned, sat and played. Bulbul then went for the water himself. He did not chastise the boy in any way. When I commented on this, other men saw nothing unusual in the behaviour of either person. On a number of occasions I observed men with young sons tolerate such frustrations without striking the boys.

The following situation clearly illustrates the strength of paternal affection.

Wagulgari djungarai, the 15-year-old son of old Wally djabaldjari, was often in trouble, much of it serious and of his own making; and Wally was inevitably drawn into fights in which he received painful injuries. Nevertheless, he always stood by his son and defended his character. When it was suggested that Wagulgari would have to be removed from the camp, Wally voluntarily took him and the rest of the family into the bush, where they camped alone for long periods. This regard for his son cut Wally off from much social intercourse with old friends and, more important, prevented him from participating in several major rituals.

Men who have been separated from their fathers or sons for some time make great efforts to visit them, no matter how long the journey.

Paddy djuburula, married and aged about 35, had not seen his father for three or four years. The old man was then living at Haast's Bluff, and Paddy often told me of his desire to visit him before he died. Eventually, Paddy decided to travel in the mail 'plane from Hooker Creek to Yuendumu, walk to Haast's Bluff and back to Yuendumu (about 150 miles), then return by road to Hooker Creek, via Alice Springs and Newcastle Waters. He winced when I told him of the cost of the air-fare but said that he would simply have to work until he had enough money. Although Paddy had no liking for steady work, within three months he was in the 'plane bound for Yuendumu.

Such expressions of affection, which could easily be multiplied, are compatible with the absence of formal etiquette and the relaxed relationship that exists between men and their adult sons. Mild joking, including obscenities, is allowed, but it never develops into physical horseplay. No matter what the provocation, they should not swear at each other.

Until the son is fully adult—that is, until he is betrothed—
he owes his father few duties, whereas the latter has definite
obligations towards him and privileges in respect of him. A
man should protect his son and share food with him, and his
affines may reprimand him if he neglects to do so. If the boy
falls ill, the father obtains the services of a medicine-man and
supervises the treatment. He expresses his sorrow by refusing
to attend religious rituals until his son recovers.

Although a man rarely chastises his son, he should do so if
the lad is involved in sexual misconduct. Even then, he would
prefer to delegate the punishment to the offender's elder brother.
I encountered only one instance of such misbehaviour, and everyone agreed that young lads rarely engage in heterosexual escap-
ades.

As the boy approaches puberty, it is his father's privilege to
consent formally to his pre-initiation seclusion. But if the father
repeatedly refuses his consent (and this is most unlikely), the
elder brother, father's father and M.M.B. tell the "sister's husband" of the boy to take him into seclusion without more ado.
The father must then ensure that the novice is furnished with
food and water during this period. A man has few other duties
at the time of his son's circumcision; the most important is the
making of the sacred string-cross that symbolizes the lodge-
dreaming.

The father contributes the major part of the gift of food,
weapons and hair-string that a youth must make to his circumciser on return from seclusion. He also helps to teach his son
the fundamentals of the indigenous technology and the fighting
and hunting techniques, while sharing in his religious education,
which now begins in earnest. During the period of religious
training, a youth shows much more respect for his father than
before, for he knows that all the initiated men strongly support
the latter's control over him. He is eligible to attend the first
cycle of Gadjari or Big Sunday revelatory ceremonies that is
held following his circumcision, but his father's permission
should be sought before he is secluded for these rituals.

In February 1954 the "bosses" of the Hooker Creek Gadjari
decided it was time to seclude the circumcised youths in
readiness for the rituals. One night the guardians ("sisters'

husbands") took the lads to a camp prepared in the bush, where they saw the first episode of the cycle. Next morning Yarry djabangari stormed through the general camp, swearing and brandishing his boomerangs. His son Francis, aged about 13, had been secluded without his consent. The men assembled near the novices' camp that afternoon, awaiting the arrival of Yarry, who had threatened to take Francis home. As Yarry approached, they prudently dispersed into smaller groups, forming less obvious targets for spears and boomerangs.

Yarry repeated his threats, then harangued the Gadjari bosses. Abe djangala, their countryman and spokesman, admitted that the men who carried off Francis without notice were at fault; but, he said, nothing could now be done. The boy had already seen the first ritual, and the "line" of ceremonies must be followed without interruption. After a long and violent argument, in which he hurled boomerangs at a number of opponents, Yarry won his point. To avoid more quarrels on or near the ceremonial grounds (a serious offence), the bosses reluctantly returned all the novices to their parents' camps. Nine days later the novices' camp was reformed. Yarry now made no objection to Francis' joining it.

Throughout the Big Sunday, the novices' fathers instruct them and ensure that they are supplied with food. This is prepared by the mothers, then given by the fathers to the guardians to hand to the youths. At the same time, the lads receive their first formal tuition in throwing boomerangs at human targets, and the fathers spend hours carefully making scaled-down boomerangs for this purpose. The desire of men to have sons in whom they can take a pride, and whom they can instruct during such revelatory rituals, is reflected in the practice of temporary cross-adoption of close (preferably own) brothers' sons.

Alec djabaldjari had only one son, Edward, aged about 3. His elder brother, Bulbul, had several subincised sons and one, Lindsay, who had recently been circumcised. Alec approached Bulbul before the Big Sunday and, pointing out that Bulbul had already enjoyed guiding three sons through the ritual, asked that he might "look out for" Lindsay for the next few months. Bulbul agreed, and Alec and his wife took over all the obligations that would normally have been met by the boy's own parents. In return, Alec had to promise that Bulbul could "look out for" young Edward when it was his turn to enter the Big Sunday.

A man's consent should be asked before his son is subincised at the age of 17 or so. Following this operation, the young man may accompany his father to rehearsals of Gadjari singing; and he learns the songs by sitting between the father's legs and "hearing the sacred words from the boomerangs", which are beaten in time to the singing. By this time, he rarely visits his parents' camp but spends his days with his coevals in the bachelors' camp. This potential disruption of the father-son tie, however, is counteracted by the young man's growing recognition of his place in his father's cult-lodge, in whose ceremonies and lore he is slowly being permitted a greater share.

At any time after his subincision the young man may be publicly betrothed, and his father formally witnesses this event. The latter also contributes substantially to the gift of hair-string, weapons, and meat that the son sends to the father and mother's brother of the girl. Betrothal marks the point at which a man is no longer exempt from normal kinship obligations. He is now mature enough to act as circumciser to young lads. His father can claim his assistance in fights, and only a very negligent son would refuse this aid. Not only does he now have to meet extra-familial economic claims, but he is also expected to help his father materially, especially by sharing game with him.

Fathers and sons who are countrymen borrow each other's possessions freely. Neither should refuse to give the other any article he desires, and I have seen men meet such demands on dozens of occasions. The requests should, however, be kept within reasonable limits. Thus, a man who has several spears parts with some of them willingly; but, should he have only one, his son or father should not ask for it. If he is asked, the man usually gives the single article to an actual or close father or son, but he refuses distant "fathers" and "sons".

This sharing of possessions has developed a new characteristic where gambling is concerned. Older men, unsure of themselves in these alien games, call on their sons for help. They supply most of the stake, and the sons contribute skill and knowledge of the rules. The winnings are shared equally.

At the death of his father or of a son approaching manhood, a man wails in a prescribed fashion and gashes his thighs deeply. He takes no other active part in the funerary ceremonies. He merely wails in a perfunctory manner when distant "fathers" and "sons" die.

Father—daughter. Men see less of their daughters than they do of their sons. Unmarried girls spend most of their time in the company of their mothers and other female relatives; marriage then takes them to new residences and often to other communities. Nevertheless, men have a strong affection for their daughters, which usually persists after the latter marry.

Men may often be observed nursing and fondling their infant daughters. They like to deck them out with combs and bangles, and some go to great trouble to obtain small pearlshell pendants to hang round the girls' necks. (These shells are imported from the Kimberley coast.) The intermittent meetings of married women with their fathers are also marked by an easy familiarity that exhibits no obvious signs of filial respect. Mild joking may occur, provided it does not involve any obscenity.

The claims of a young girl on her father concern his provision of protection and food. He calls in a medicine-man to cure her illnesses and abstains from ritual activities until she recovers. If the girl is taken to a settlement sick-bay, he spends hours by her side, comforting her. The father has little to do with her early education, however; this is the province of the mother.

The mother's brother and M.M.B. of the girl consult her father in the matter of her betrothal, but they may over-ride his objections to their choice of a particular spouse. The father, as a rule, does not attend the public ceremony of betrothal; he is grieved by the thought that his daughter must eventually leave his camp. From the time of her betrothal until she marries, her father protects her from the attentions of other men. He also punishes her if she is detected in sexual play with uninitiated boys and ensures that the latter are beaten by their fathers.

When the girl is between eight and twelve years old, her betrothed claims her. Her father must surrender her; but he does so with a show of reluctance, reminding the young man of his duties towards his new wife. A man who has not acted as a circumciser for some years may have a daughter not already committed to marry a particular person. The father may postpone her betrothal for some years, simply to keep her as an assistant and companion for her mother. Or he may wish to have the girl on hand to offer to some man in return for aid in a serious dispute.

While they were at Yuendumu, Wally djabaldjari and his sister's husband, Jack djagamara, were allies in a series of disputes that involved a homicide. Knowing that reprisals were likely, they offered Jack's daughter, Julie, then about 10 years old, to a djabanangga man in return for a promise of aid in future fights. This man, however, did not honour his agreement in the next fight that occurred, so Jack declared the betrothal to be at an end. Other men criticized Jack's action. They stated that betrothal should be an unconditional arrangement and should lead automatically to marriage.

When Jack later moved to Hooker Creek, he took Julie with him. As he still feared repercussions from the earlier disputes, he offered the girl on the same terms to Peter djabanangga of Wave Hill. Peter was already married and refused to be entangled in Jack's quarrels. He suggested that Julie be offered to his "young brother", Robber djabanangga, who accepted the betrothal.

About a year afterwards, Robber arrived from Wave Hill and asked for Julie in marriage, guaranteeing to let her visit her mother at Hooker Creek frequently. Although Jack had had no cause to call on Robber for fighting aid, he handed the girl over without argument to avoid public disapproval of a second default. At the same time, he offered another young daughter to Peter in return for help in disputes, but Peter again declined.

A man has certain obligations towards his daughter after her marriage, especially if she still resides in his community. He should continue to protect her from insult and injury, especially from maltreatment by her husband. But, if the father is very old or living far from her, she cannot expect always to be treated justly in this respect.

Margie nabangari, the younger wife of Billy djambidjimba, was the daughter of Peter djabanangga of Wave Hill. During a visit to Hooker Creek Peter told me he was worried about Margie's increasing blindness (actually the result of trachoma). He was sure that an enemy was "singing" her. Peter several times berated Billy for not seeking out the sorcerer, and he said he would leave a son at Hooker Creek to ensure that Billy looked after Margie better. He also criticized Billy's failure to shield her from the attentions of her lover, Norman djambi-djimba. On an earlier visit to Hooker Creek, Peter had threatened to spear Norman—a warning that Billy should have issued. When Norman heard that Peter was coming again to Hooker Creek, he suddenly discovered urgent matters to discuss with relatives at Yuendumu, 200 miles away.

Although women are not obliged to give their fathers physical aid in brawls, they are expected to defend the men's reputations from insult. Occasionally a woman employs violence to this end.

Lame Lila nambidjimba, a widow aged about 50, told many people in the course of her persistent gossiping that Abe djangala, her countryman and "brother's son", was involved with a mistress. Neither Abe nor his wife paid attention to this canard, but Marcie nambidjimba, Abe's countrywoman and close "daughter", was angered by it. She attacked Lila with a club and split open her head. Next day, Lila's countrywoman and "young sister", Maggie nambidjimba, assaulted Marcie, and both women received split heads. No men intervened in the fights.

People everywhere asserted that sexual intercourse with an actual or a close classificatory daughter was unheard of. Nor were they coherent about the punishment to be meted out in the event, other than to state that somebody would have to be killed. Copulation with a distant "daughter" is deplored but does sometimes occur. It is treated like any other adultery. Cohabitation with a distant "daughter" is forbidden, and no instances appeared among the prohibited unions that I recorded in genealogies.

When a woman dies, her fathers (actual and classificatory) wail in the prescribed manner but take little part in the mortuary ceremonies. Women wail and gash their heads at the deaths of their close fathers, but they merely wail when distant "fathers" die.

Mother—children. All women regarded as mother are called ŋadi, but they are distinguished behaviourally and attitudinally in terms of their genealogical and geographical distance from the speaker. Behaviour towards one's own mother, own mother's sister (whether or not she is the mother's co-wife) and own mother's co-wife (whether or not she is the mother's sister) forms a unitary complex that differs in intensity and quality from behaviour towards any other women called "mother". The latter, who may include a man's own daughter-in-law, are also called ŋamadi. If a man marries his "m.b.d.", she and her brothers are wandiri, "f.f.sr.d. & S.", to his children, but they may also be called ŋadi and ŋamini, "mother's brother", respectively. A woman either distinguishes between her children as ŋuniari, son, and jundalba, daughter, or refers to them as guru, irrespective of sex.

The people stress the physiological link that exists between women and their children, but they also recognize a spiritual bond between them. The latter derives from the beliefs that, first, the child's conception-dreaming enters the mother in order to animate the foetus, and, second, that all members of a matri-line share a vaguely defined and impersonal spirit that the child automatically acquires while in its mother's womb. The latter notion has none of the ritual elaboration that characterizes attitudes towards lodge patri-spirits.

Mother—son. The Walbiri regard a woman's love for her son as one of the most intense and enduring affective attitudes there is. It often excuses behaviour that in other people would be considered outrageous.

For the first nine or ten months of its life, the child is carried everywhere in a wooden trough slung from the mother's shoulder and is never out of her sight. Whenever it cries, the mother simply pushes her pendulous breast towards its mouth. Although in some respects maternal care is haphazard (little attention being paid to personal cleanliness or the presence of flies), the woman lavishes affection on the baby. She constantly fondles it, runs her lips over its body, blows gently on it, and keeps up a flow of "baby-talk". Other women, whatever their kinship category, also treat the child with great tenderness.

Later, the infant rides on its mother's shoulder and is rarely separated from her for more than a few minutes at a time. The woman follows no feeding schedules but suckles the child when-ever it cries. Meanwhile solid food, ranging from damper soaked in black tea to half-cooked lizards and boiled beef-fat, is already being introduced into its diet, and the child is always offered small portions of its mother's own food.

Once a boy is able to walk freely, however, he spends much time with his father around the camp; and by the time he is five or six years old he joins the gang of older boys, returning home only for meals and to sleep at night. Up till this time, his mother provides some of his education, including practical hints on food-gathering and the elucidation of kinship terminology. She occasionally scolds him and strikes him lightly for minor misdemeanours. But, once he mixes with the other boys, she sees him too irregularly to be able to continue this training. Nevertheless, she remains ready to defend him from the attacks of outsiders.

The strong affection that the boy develops for his mother during his formative years persists throughout his life, and it carries over to a large extent to the mother's sisters. A woman whose adolescent or married son is away working for Europeans feels his absence deeply. Without any apparent stimulus, she often bursts into shrill keening and gouges her scalp with a digging-stick. She has thought of her son and is "sorry" for him. This behaviour, as far as I could judge, expresses genuine grief. Women also wail for sons who are ill, and a night rarely passes without the camp being disturbed by these eerie cries.

A woman is not formally consulted when her young son is to be secluded in readiness for circumcision, and her permission is not asked. But throughout the relevant ceremonies her status is carefully defined and she has an important role to play. There is symbolic recognition that the lad's impending ordeal and removal from her care grieve her deeply, and she (with her daughters and her husband's sisters) is allowed ritual privileges denied other women.

The youth also takes public and formal leave of his mother before being secluded for the later Gadjari or Big Sunday ceremonies. During this seclusion, she prepares each day the veget-able-food and tea that her husband gives to him. Every night she joins the mothers of the other novices in making the ritual calls that help to protect the lads from supernatural dangers. At the conclusion of the Big Sunday, the guardians of the youth present him to his mother, so that she may see he is unharmed.

The youth now moves to the bachelors' camp and only occasionally eats and sleeps with his parents. He may still exercise claims over his mother for food and protection, but she has little to do with his education or discipline. As yet she has few claims over his services; he considers it beneath his dignity as a male to assist her with domestic tasks, and the game he catches is generally consumed in the bachelors' camp.

On the day her son is subincised, a woman asks any female relative who possesses a steady hand to cicatrize her chest. The cuts, usually one or two in number and three or four inches long, are a mark of her sorrow at the pain the son is experiencing. The woman later witnesses the public betrothal of her son, a ceremony that indicates his acceptance of a man's obligations and prerogatives. He begins now to repay his mother's earlier care and kindness, especially by giving her choice cuts from game he kills, such as the ribs of a kangaroo or the tail of a goanna. If he is employed by Europeans, he buys her an occasional gift, such as a length of dress-material or a housewife. He also takes her part in quarrels.

Clarry djabaldjari and his wife Chloe were building a new shelter. Maggie nambidjimba, the young wife of elderly Budda djabaldjari, was helping them, for she was a close friend of Chloe. Budda, who was always unreasonably suspicious of Maggie's fidelity, was obviously brooding over this "proof" of her interest in Clarry. Suddenly he rushed over and struck her across the neck with a boomerang. Maggie lay unconscious for several hours. Even Budda's close brothers protested at his action, and Albert djabanangga, Maggie's countryman and close "son", threatened to spear Budda.

Women are also concerned to defend the reputations and persons of their adult sons.

Jim Tulum djuburula objected when Paddy djuburula, his distant "brother", publicly teased Nellie nabanangga, Tulum's young wife. An argument followed, in which Liddy nungarai, Tulum's senior wife, attacked Paddy with a digging-stick. Big Polly nabaldjari, a countrywoman and close mother of Paddy, at once belaboured Liddy with a club, wounding her severely about the head and face. Tulum did not intervene in the fight.

Sexual intercourse with an actual or close classificatory mother is regarded as incestuous, and people knew of no instances of this behaviour. Copulation with distant "mothers", however, must occur relatively often, for of the 23 forbidden unions I recorded nine involved cohabitation of "mothers" and "sons". Although such liaisons may be thought to provide a substitute satisfaction of incestuous wishes directed at actual mothers, a more prosaic explanation may also be considered. A man's "mother" may also be his daughter-in-law, in which case he has opportunities to initiate an affair with her.

At the death of her adult son, a woman singes off her pubic hair and cuts off her head-hair, gouges her scalp and sears the wound with a firestick, then wails for days. If the deceased is a child, she neither singes the pubic hair nor burns the scalp; she merely wails for distant "sons" and, occasionally, gashes her scalp. Men wail at the deaths of their mothers, whether close or distant.

Mother—daughter. This relationship is also characterized by a strong and lasting affection that is reinforced by the daughter's later recognition of the women's community of interests as members of a more or less solidary group coping with men's vagaries. Women feel deeply the wrench of parting with daughters who go to live in other communities when married, and years afterwards they still mourn the girls' absence. Complete informality at all times marks the intercourse of mother and daughter; they may discuss sexual topics freely.

A woman treats her infant daughter with the same loving care that she displays towards a son of the same age. Before the girl is betrothed, which generally occurs during this period of her life, her father discusses the matter with the mother, whom he informs of his deliberations with the girl's matriline. Although the mother has no right to veto decisions made by the men, she is sometimes able to sway their judgment if she dislikes the son-in-law they have chosen. She does not attend the actual betrothal ceremony, for women must avoid their sons-in-law on all occasions. Until the girl marries, she rarely leaves her mother's side. Her tuition and discipline largely fall to her mother. Although the mother's co-wives should also help in these matters, the mother rarely welcomes their interference.

Della nagamara, the two-years-old daughter of Millie nabanangga, misbehaved in her mother's absence. Minnie nabanangga, a younger co-wife of Millie, slapped the child several times and berated her. Hearing the cries, Millie rushed to the camp. She took in the situation at a glance and struck Minnie on the head with a heavy club. The husband later upbraided Millie for being too free with her blows, but he confided to me that he could not really blame her for defending her child.

A girl accompanies her mother on the daily search for food and firewood, during which she learns what foods to gather, where to find them, and what techniques to use. In the camp, she learns how to prepare foods. As her knowledge and strength increase, she becomes a valuable domestic assistant to her mother and takes over many of the more time-consuming activities, such as carrying water and caring for the infants.

As well as showing the girl how to use a digging-stick, the mother instructs her in the conventional fighting techniques of women, using a light stick in place of the club. She also teaches her the basic dance-steps that women employ at circumcision ceremonies and in the *djarada* and *jauwalju* dancing. This constant association not only enables a woman to protect her daughter from injury by outsiders but also to dissuade her from sexual misbehaviour. If the girl falls ill, her mother tends her carefully.

When the girl's betrothed asks her father and mother's brother for her in marriage, the father tells the mother to send her to her new home. A woman is always upset at the loss of her daughter, even though the initial separation may only be for a few nights. The girl returns several times to her mother's camp after staying with her husband for longer and longer periods. Finally she settles permanently with him. If the girl resides in her mother's community or settlement, she visits her almost daily for the first few years after she marries, and the mother is usually asked to act as midwife at the birth of each child.

A woman who marries out of her own community generally brings her first-born home to show to her mother, a visit that also allows the latter to discover whether the daughter has been ill-treated or not. Women who are unable to visit regularly their mothers or their married daughters often send them small gifts in the care of travelling Walbiri. Such exchanges also speed the circulation of commodities through the society, but the women are simply concerned with the goodwill they engender.

Clarry djabaldjari and his wife, Chloe nagamara, had walked from Wave Hill to Hooker Creek. Chloe brought a dress and a housewife for Nancy nabaldjari as a gift from Nancy's foster-mother and three dresses for Biddy nabangari from Biddy's own mother. A few days later the hawker, who had been visiting Hooker Creek, set off for Top Spring, via Wave Hill. He took with him as employees Biddy, her co-wife Mary and her husband Paddy. Biddy purchased several yards of dress material from the hawker to take as a gift to her mother, while Nancy gave her a dress, a length of dress material, cigarettes, soap, sewing cotton and needles to give to Nancy's foster-mother.

A woman's behaviour at the death of a daughter is the same as that at the death of a son, except that she takes charge of the daughter's personal possessions. Women wail, cut off their hair and gouge their scalps when their mothers die.

Siblings. The terms *babali*, senior or elder brother, *gogono*, junior or younger brother, *gabidi*, senior or elder sister, and *ŋauwuru*, junior or younger sister, are applied without reference to the speaker's sex to:

(a) actual siblings;
(b) uterine and seminal half-siblings;
(c) parallel cousins;
(d) distant "parallel cousins" who are countrymen; these are "close" siblings;
(e) distant "parallel cousins" who are not countrymen; these are "distant" siblings;
(f) members of the one subsection, whether or not Walbiri, in contexts where the usual distinctions among the generation levels represented are insignificant.

Strictly speaking, the terms reflect the actual order of birth only among the children of the one woman. When the children of two women use the terms, they apply them on the basis of the relative seniority of their mothers, irrespective of the relative seniority of their fathers; and the women's seniority depends in turn on the relative seniority of their own mothers, and so on. Thus, if a man *A* marries a woman *a*, and his younger brother *B* marries her "elder sister" *b*, all the children of *B* and *b* are the senior siblings of all the children of *A* and *a*. The distinction between elder and senior and between young and junior siblings is not directly paralleled by any behavioural or attitudinal differences other than those indicative of increasing genealogical distance from the speaker. A person calls his half-siblings who are born of a parental "cross-cousin" marriage by their normal kin-terms, as "f.f.sr.d." and "M.M.B.S." children.

Brothers. The relationship between Walbiri brothers nicely exemplifies the operation of the principle of sibling unity, and the people themselves stress both the desirability and the prevalence of fraternal solidarity and substitution. The general belief that close brothers, as lodge-mates, share a common patri-spirit reinforces this attitude. Furthermore, if the men have the one mother, or mothers who are sisters, they also share a common matri-spirit. These putative connections create a peculiarly intimate bond, which is even more pronounced between close brothers who have been circumcised during the one series of ceremonies. These men should camp together whenever possible, rendering mutual aid in most everyday activities, and they should never fight.

Nevertheless, fraternal affection appears to me to differ significantly in quality from the affection between a man and his son. Although the brothers may be close friends, they are still potential sexual rivals; and there seems in their intercourse to be always an element of distrust. This tension may also reflect, perhaps, earlier childhood rivalries. Thus, although the people did not remark on such matters, I often noticed that small boys were intensely jealous of maternal attention paid to their newborn siblings. However that may be, fraternal hostility does exist; and, despite the strong social pressure on brothers to suppress it, it occasionally breaks through violently—a fact that is also expressed in some of the myths.

The informal relations of early childhood extend into adult life, and brothers treat each other with considerable familiarity.

They often joke together, and the humour may lead to obscene horse-play, such as the simulation of sodomy. But the men should never swear at each other.

Until a boy is ready for circumcision, he has few explicit claims on his adult brothers, but from this time the elder brother has a series of clearly-defined duties to perform. He supervises the ritual guardians of his younger brother and may accompany them on the pre-circumcision tour to other communities. He prepares the place where the circumcision is to be carried out. Throughout the rituals, he reassures his younger brother, instructs him and subjects him to moral exhortations. He should kill the circumciser if the boy is mutilated during the operation.

After the boy's return from seclusion, his elder brother contributes towards the gift made to the circumciser. In subsequent revelatory ceremonies, including the Big Sunday, he helps his father to instruct the youth and also joins the M.M.B. in teaching him how to quiver ritually. He also gives his younger brother his own arm-blood to drink in order to strengthen him. Meanwhile, in everyday life, the elder brother continues to look to the youth's discipline, an obligation that his father is usually eager to evade.

> When Clem djungarai was assisting the settlement super-intendent to move some equipment, Clem's young brother, Lindsay, aged about 14, offered to help. It was later discovered that Lindsay had stolen several small articles. The super-intendent gave the boy's father, Bulbul, the choice of chastising Lindsay himself or of turning him over to the superintendent for punishment. Bulbul would not agree to the latter course, but he shirked the former. He delegated the task to Clem, who thrashed Lindsay far more severely than his father would have done.

A man also joins with his father in teaching a young brother the techniques of hunting, fighting and implement-making. He usually witnesses the betrothal of the young man and contributes towards the bride-price. If two brothers have been circumcised by the one "sister's son" or "F.F.Sr.S.", the elder has a prior claim to the circumciser's first two daughters as wives—"he bars the track of his younger brother". He can, however, relinquish his claim to the girls in favour of the latter. A man whose betrothed or wife has eloped turns first to his close brothers for help in the pursuit and punishment of the enticer.

Brothers may exchange wives for short periods; and a man who goes away to work may leave his wife in his brother's care. In return for feeding and protecting her, the custodian is entitled to sleep with her. A ceremonial messenger from another community or tribe should be allowed access to the wife of one of his "brothers" among the hosts, provided that both the "brother" himself and the woman's mother's brother are first consulted. If a man has no daughter to give in marriage to a man he previously circumcised, he has the right to ask his own brother to provide a substitute daughter. Close brothers may temporarily cross-adopt each other's young sons and guide them through important ceremonies.

Brothers should support each other in disputes and usually do so, unless one of them has outraged public opinion or broken some important law. Even then, there is a tacit expectation that, right or wrong, the brothers will act as one. The withdrawal of fraternal help is an emphatic public statement of the moral weakness of the offender's position.

Alec II djabaldjari, aged about 38, was married to his "m.b.d.", Topsy nambidjimba, aged about 40. In the past Alec's boorishness had not only lost him many friends but also his original betrothed. The girl's father had refused to entrust her to a man of Alec's uncertain temper, and other important relatives had supported his decision. After several years of enforced bachelorhood, which did little to improve his temper, Alec acquired Topsy as his mistress. As her promiscuity was already a by-word, her jural husband, Clarry djabaldjari, was prepared to relinquish her to Alec, his half-brother. Clarry in turn soon married his own mistress. Everyone agreed that Alec and Topsy were ideally matched, and no more was said.

Within a few years Alec had tired of Topsy (who was incredibly ugly), and he became involved with a young widow. When the widow married another man, Alec announced that he wanted a "straight" wife to replace Topsy, who as his "m.b.d." was only "half-straight". As there were no single "m.m.b.d.d." available, he demanded Doris nagamara, the attractive young wife of his distant "elder brother", Jack djabaldjari, on the grounds that she had once been his mistress. Everyone in the camp dismissed the assertion and the claim as farcical. Some days later, Alec, armed with a varied array of weapons, came to Jack's camp to take Doris by force. Jack, also armed, stood his ground. When Alec attacked him, a dozen men protected him with their shields, and the frustrated Alec retired, still demanding Doris. During the incident his actual brothers, Bulbul and Alec I, stood aside and called on him to give up his foolishness, while his half-brother, Clarry, actively defended Jack.

Alec stormed around the camp for some nights, shouting that he would seize Doris. He caught Jack unawares one morning and split his head with a club and cut open his shoulder with a knife. In the ensuing fight, Jack wounded Alec deeply in the upper arm with a knife, and the latter nearly bled to death. Nevertheless, Alec's own brothers again stood by and watched. They would not directly help Jack, but they refused to be identified with Alec's impossible behaviour.

A man publicly accused at a ceremonial gathering of a serious offence may try to place his penis in the hand of an actual or classificatory brother. If the latter permits this, he undertakes to plead for the accused and, should the plea fail, to fight beside him. The brother, however, cannot be forced to accept such a responsibility.

The brothers of a dead man, as members of his matriline and matrimoiety, have important duties to perform in the depilation and exposure of his corpse on a tree-platform. They also wail in mourning but do not gash their thighs, for the wounds would interfere with their mortuary tasks. A year or so after the inhumation, the elder brother discusses the disposal of the widows with their kinsmen. Normally, the women are offered first to the deceased's own younger brother, but this man is bound by convention to reject them—their presence would re-animate his grief for the dead man. They are then offered in turn to more distant "younger brothers", until one is found who may accept the widows without feeling unduly sorry for the deceased. Long after the death has been avenged, people refrain from mentioning the dead man's conception-dreaming in the presence of his close brothers lest the latter's sorrow find an outlet in aggression directed at the perpetrator of the solecism.

Brother—sister. Brothers and sisters generally remain on affectionate terms throughout their lives. They do not have to avoid each other in daily activities, and their intercourse displays a relaxed familiarity. They should not swear at each other, however, nor indulge in any horseplay.

Girls help their mothers to care for young brothers in infancy, but, once the latter are old enough to join in the usual boys' pastimes, their sisters see little of them. The two do not activate any specific rights and duties in respect of each other until the girl is married and the lad is circumcised. Thus, a woman, together with her mother, provides food for her young brother during his seclusion. She also has a prominent role in the circumcision dancing and, in certain parts of the ceremonies, carries the boy from place to place on her shoulders. During the subsequent Big Sunday ceremonies, the sister joins the mothers in making the ritual calls intended to protect the novices. When a youth is subincised, his close sisters may have their chests cicatrized in sympathy.

A woman takes no direct part in her brother's betrothal, but she is involved by implication. In theory a man receives a wife partly to compensate for his parents' loss of daughters to his future wife's brothers, who are also his sisters' husbands. This sort of transaction is sometimes called in anthropological literature "brother-sister exchange". Among the Walbiri, however, it is not a simple transfer of sisters between two men. The women are in the custody of their own fathers, mothers' brothers, and M.M.B., and the brothers usually have little say in their disposal in marriage.

Sexual intercourse with close sisters is regarded as incestuous, and I heard of no instances. The two cases of long-term cohabitation of men with distant "sisters" that I discovered were strongly reprehended by everyone.

For some years Barney djabaldjari had lived with a nabaldjari "sister" whom he had enticed from her husband. As a result, he could not reside permanently in a Walbiri camp. As soon as he settled in one camp, the djagamara men present, who were the potential husbands of the woman, forced quarrels on him. They would continue to do so until life became intolerable for him, and he would have to move to another locality. Nevertheless, Barney refused to surrender the woman, even though this action would have halted the disputes. At first his close brothers used to help him in the fights, but now they no longer did so. They told me his stubbornness had alienated their sympathy.

Married and single women wail for brothers who are sick or wounded. The elder brother of an unmarried girl who falls ill may anticipate her father by calling in a medicine-man to cure her. He also shares with his parents the duty of protecting her from other men's advances.

> After rain had flooded Hooker Creek, the younger women went swimming together daily. Among them was Julie naburula, the close younger sister of Paddy djuburula and the "cross-cousin" of Clem djungarai. Paddy accused Clem of taking advantage of the women's activities to seduce Julie. Julie's father, Jack djagamara, also upbraided Clem and Julie, who was already betrothed. Neither man, however, attacked Clem physically, for there was no definite evidence that he had copulated with the girl.

A man undertaking a long journey may leave his wife in the care of her married daughter or his married brother, but the woman's own elder brother should also be concerned with her moral and physical welfare during the husband's absence. Sometimes the brother closes his eyes to her sexual affairs, but usually he reprimands her. A man also shares the responsibility of safeguarding his sister's marital rights.

> Jack djagamara, aged about 60, had two wives, Netta and Big Polly nabaldjari. The latter, aged about 50, was the younger sister of old Wally djabaldjari. In the widows' camp lived Lizzie nabaldjari, aged about 50, whose old husband had been removed permanently to the Darwin lazarette. Some months after the leper's departure, Jack began an affair with Lizzie, whom he wished to marry. He did not tell his own wives of his intentions, but the women soon learned of his actions.
>
> Netta was complaisant; but Big Polly was incensed. Jack should have consulted her, as senior wife, and, in any case, she wanted no more co-wives. For some hours Jack and Polly argued loudly; then, losing her temper, she struck him shrewdly

across the knees with a heavy club. To the surprise of the amused audience, Jack retaliated only with obscene curses. Meanwhile, gossips had told Wally of the dispute and he appeared, threatening to spear Jack. Jack shouted and waved boomerangs in return, then withdrew from the camp. He did not, however, make any more advances to Lizzie.

A woman is expected to defend her brother from insult and may use force to do so. Should two brothers quarrel over a woman, especially a mistress, their sisters are likely to belabour her, for she has caused the dissension. Although a man often gives food to his mother to share with his unmarried sisters, he is not directly involved in economic relations with a married sister. He should always give her his hair-cuttings, however, to pass on to her husband, who spins the hair into string for ritual use. A man releases a widowed sister from her period of mourning silence by "opening her mouth" with food, and he discusses with his M.M.B. her disposal in marriage. When his sister dies, he cuts off her hair and places her body on a tree-platform. A woman cuts her hair, gouges her scalp, and wails at the death of a brother.

Sisters. The significant aspects of this relationship have already been touched on in the discussion of the intercourse of co-wives.

Although people speak often of the solidarity and affection that sisters should display, the fact that the women are often rivals for the favours of one man means that a latent hostility may exist between the women. Sororal polygyny more frequently exacerbates than emolliates these feelings. Nevertheless, sisters usually treat each other in friendly fashion in everyday life, and their behaviour exhibits no formality.

A young girl looks to her elder sister, as well as to her mother, for domestic training and tuition in dancing and fighting. The right of the elder sister to discipline the younger continues into adult life. Thus, a married woman who takes a lover may expect her elder sister to castigate her. A woman also prefers to call on her close sister to act as her midwife.

At the death of her sister, the woman wails and gashes her head as a mark of sorrow.

CHAPTER IX

EXTRAFAMILIAL RELATIONSHIPS

Father's sister—brother's children. The term *bimari* applies
to all women regarded as father's sister, whatever their genealogical distance from the speaker. Such women are the preferred
wives of men counted as mother's brother. If the mother's brother
has married his "m.b.d.", the latter, who is the *maliri* ("m.m.b.d.")
of the speaker, is often referred to as *bimari-bia,* "the woman who
is like a father's sister".

A woman refers to all persons regarded as her brother's
children by the term *ŋalabi.* They are further distinguished as
ŋalabi, brother's son, and *jundalba,* brother's daughter. If the
woman's brother has married his "m.b.d.", his children are the
aunt's *maliri,* but they may also be referred to as her *ŋalabi-bia*
and *jundalba-bia.*

Although a woman displays great affection for her close
brothers' children, she has little to do with more distant
"nephews" and "nieces". Indeed, the relationship has significance
only where close kinsfolk or countrymen are concerned.

An actual or close father's sister is a member of the father's
own patriline and is indirectly connected with his cult-lodge.
He and his father are custodians of the lodge-dreaming on her
behalf. Her brother's children owe her no special respect,
however, other than that normally due to a member of a higher
generation-level; and she has no disciplinary powers over them.
The informal help that she gives her brother's wife to educate
the latter's daughter is offered simply for reasons of friendship
and affection. Occasionally she acts as midwife for a close
brother's daughter.

In the ceremonies that accompany circumcision, the father's
sister of the boy has a well-defined role, one that obviously
derives from her agnatic connection with his lodge. Thus, the
senior aunts may see certain sacred objects revealed during the
rites, whereas all other women must cover their eyes at these
times. When her brother's son is subincised, a woman has her

chest cicatrized as a sign that she grieves for him in his "trouble".

A man may marry, as a second choice, the daughter of a distant "father's sister", especially one who is a member of another community. He must then always avoid the individual "father's sister" who is his mother-in-law, as well as all "m.m.b.d.", who are still his potential mothers-in-law. He need not avoid other "father's sisters", however, even if they are his wife's mother's sisters. The existence of this rule of mother-in-law avoidance partly determines the prohibition on marrying the daughters of an actual father's sister. But, in any case, this aunt is thought to be so close to the father that her children are often referred to as half-siblings. Sexual intercourse with these true cross-cousins or with an actual or classificatory father's sister is regarded as incestuous, and I have no record of its occurrence.

A woman wails and gashes her head at the death of the child of a close brother but merely wails for distant "brothers' children". A man wails when his father's sister dies and his sister wails and gashes her head.

Mother's brother—sister's children. The term ŋamini refers to all men considered to be mother's brothers, but a distinction is made among the actual or close mother's brother, the "mother's brother" who is also a wife's father, and the "mother's brother" who may also be a daughter's husband. The last two relationships will be discussed under the heading of wife's father—daughter's husband. The children of a man's sister are his *guru* and include ŋuniari, sister's son, and *jundalba*, sister's daughter. The actual or close sister's son is distinguished from the "sister's son" who may be wife's father or son-in-law.

The mother's brother is the preferred husband of the father's sister; but, if she has married her "M.B.S.", the latter remains the *wandiri*, F.F.Sr.S., of the speaker. Similarly, if a man's sister has married her "M.B.S.", her children are the brother's *wandiri*.

Mother's brother—sister's son. A man takes a deep interest in his close sister's sons, and the affection he feels for his sister clearly extends to her children. The latter are also members of the man's matriline and share his matri-spirit. A young boy, however, has no specific claims on his mother's brother, nor is he disciplined by the uncle. Any social or technical education he receives is informal.

The uncle is closely concerned with the circumcision of his sister's son. He consults with the father and father's father when it is decided to seclude the boy, although I doubt that his opinions here carry the weight of those of the other men. During the rites, close mother's brothers are prominent on the circumcision ground and assist the fathers to make the hair-string cross that symbolizes the novice's lodge. The mother's brother also confers with the lad's father on the choice of the circumciser. They consider such factors as the matriline to which the man belongs, his age, and the likelihood of his having eligible daughters when the initiate is ready to marry. The mother's brother helps later to pay the circumciser.

The father, mother's brother and M.M.B. of a young man decide when he may ask to be formally betrothed to his circumciser's daughter (or sister's daughter), and the uncle may carry the request to the girl's kinsmen. He contributes towards the bride-price paid at the betrothal, which ceremony he witnesses, and again at the marriage. Once the young man is betrothed, he shows his gratitude for all his mother's brother has done by sending him portions of the larger game he kills. Such gifts are bigger and more frequent when the uncle is old or widowed. The nephew also supports his close mother's brother in all fights and may even substitute for him in formal duels if he is old.

A man mourns when his mother's brother or sister's son is wounded or dies. The senior mother's brother supervises the distribution of the dead man's possessions among the other mother's brothers who are of the deceased's matriline and community. He should also initiate the expeditions or the sorcery undertaken to avenge the death of his sister's son.

In short, no situation that significantly concerns a man (living or dead) should proceed until all his close mother's brothers are present. Some of the uncle's importance clearly derives from his capacity to represent the mother of the nephew in situations normally closed to women. Nevertheless, ordinary daily intercourse between adult mother's brothers and sister's sons is informal, with no obvious displays of respect by the junior men. Sexual joking is common, although I never observed any physical horseplay. The strength of the bond between the two men is well illustrated by the following:

> By Walbiri standards, Jim Tulum djuburula was a man of little worth. Not the least of his misdemeanours was his attempt to elope with the daughter-in-law of Paddy djabaldjari. Nevertheless, the two men always seemed to be on good terms afterwards at Hooker Creek. When I remarked on this to Paddy, he replied, "Yes, Tulum is a larrikin, a man who is no good at all. He is always in trouble with women. But I can't quarrel with him; I have to like him, for he is my boy, my close sister's son!"

Mother's brother—sister's daughter. In some respects this relationship parallels that of a man with his sister's son; but he and his niece are not thought to be "mates" in the way that uncle and nephew are. Although he has little face-to-face contact with her, however, his rights and duties in respect of her are defined early in her infancy. As a member of her matriline, he is correlatively a member of her future husband's "marriage line". The uncle, together with his own sister's husband and his own mother's brother, is consulted by the young man's kinsmen when it is time to betroth the niece. He carries the baby girl to the young man and places her on the latter's thigh; he publicly announces the betrothal, then returns her to her parents. He shares equally with his own sister's husband the bride-price handed over at the betrothal and at the marriage of the girl. With his sister's husband and sister's son, he is responsible for protecting her rights in marriage. In return, the niece, throughout her adult life, gives her hair-cuttings to her mother to pass on to the mother's brother. He spins the hair into string, which he retains for ritual use.

Sexual intercourse with a sister's daughter is incestuous, but I recorded two instances of long-term cohabitation with distant "sister's daughters". Both were greatly deplored.

A woman wails and gashes her head for a dead mother's brother, and a man wails for a dead sister's daughter. The senior mother's brother shares the dead woman's possessions among the close mothers of her matriline and community, and he organizes the avenging of her death.

Father's father—son's children; father's father's sisters—brother's son's children. The term *wariŋi* refers to all persons regarded as father's father and f.f.sr., to all regarded as son's children by a man, and to all regarded as brother's son's children by a woman. Normally, the f.f.sr. is also f.m.b.w., the S.S. is "Sr.S.D.H.", the s.d. is "sr.s.s.w.", the B.S.S. is "S.D.H.", and the b.s.d. is "s.s.w."

The use of the one term for all these relatives, who are members of the one subsection, reflects the equivalence of alternate generation-levels. Father's father and f.f.sr. are thought to be like senior siblings, and son's children like junior siblings, an attitude reinforced by the fact that the men involved are generally all members of the one cult-lodge and share the same patri-spirit. Indeed, for everyday purposes, few people bother to specify the generation-levels of their distant *wariŋi*, especially those of other communities or settlements; they are all "siblings". Membership in the one subsection facilitates this identification but is not the primary determinant.

A woman has little to do with her brother's son's children. She treats them with affection when they are young and helps their mother to care for them; but her chief concern is for her own daughter's children. Occasionally her personal name is shared by an actual b.s.d. By the time her brother's son's children grow up, she is usually too old for them to be interested in her. But, if she is still active when her B.S.S. is circumcised, she has much the same ceremonial role as has his father's sister.

Men wail at the death of a close f.f.sr.; women wail and gash their heads for close f.f.sr. and B.S. children.

The father's father has limited contact with his son's daughter, towards whom he displays mild affection. But he stands in a clearly-defined relationship with his son's son, for he is leader of the latter's cult-lodge. When the boy is sufficiently developed, physically and mentally, to bear the rigours of the circumcision ritual and to appreciate some of its significance, his father's father discusses with the boy's M.M.B. and F.M.B. the desirability of circumcising him in the next ceremonial season. He then informs the boy's father and mother's brother of the decision.

During the ceremonies an active father's father may perform many of the duties usu₂ lly carried out by the lad's elder brother; but an old man merely watches and gives advice. The father's father contributes meat to the payment of the circumciser. He also advises on the youth's subincision, and he gives hair-string to his own son to hand on to the son's son as part of the bride-price at betrothal. Meanwhile, he shares with the youth's father and elder brother the duty of teaching him the traditional crafts (generally those of a sedentary kind, such as spinning hair-string) and of explaining totemic rituals to him.

Before circumcision, the boy behaves towards his father's father much as he does towards an elder brother, except that he expects more kindness and less discipline from the old man. Afterwards, however, this affectionate familiarity is tempered by his recognition that his father's father is a ritual leader of his patriline and lodge. The youth now pays him a certain amount of respect, more than he displays to any other relative. Joking is mild and restricted, and physical horseplay very rarely occurs. On the other hand, the basic notion that the father's father is an "elder brother" persists, uncomplicated by the covert hostility that may exist between real brothers.

Although a man and his father's father are of the one sub-section, they do not compete for the same women as wives, for the selection of wives is determined by considerations of genea-logical connection and generation-level. Occasionally a man tries to seduce the wife of a "father's father", but, even allowing for the discrepant ages of the "father's father" and "father's mother", the latter is rarely young enough to attract her "son's son" sexually. I did not hear of any permanent unions of this sort.

At the death of a father's father or son's son, a man behaves as he would when his brother dies—he cuts the corpse's hair, places the body on a tree-platform, and so on.

Father's mother—son's children; father's mother's brother—sister's son's children. All people regarded as father's mother and F.M.B., as well as a man's Sr.S. children and a woman's son's children, are *jabala*. Generally, the F.M.B. is also the

DIAGRAM 4

The jabala relationships

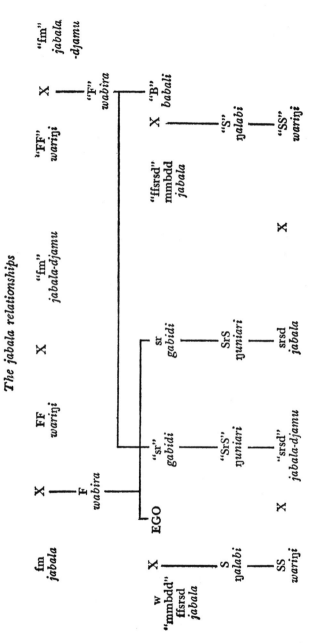

F.F.Sr.H., the Sr.S.S. is the "S.D.H.", the sr.s.d. is the "s.s.w.", the S.S. is the "B.S.D.H.", and the s.d. is the "b.s.s.w." All these relatives are of the one subsection and of alternate generation-levels.

A man also calls *jabala* his own m.m.b.d.d., with whom he is forbidden to copulate, and his own f.f.sr.s.d., who may at the same time be his classificatory "m.m.b.d.d." and hence his preferred wife. It is thought that he need not separate in terminology these female cognates either from each other or from his own father's mother, for he knows his exact consanguineal connection with each. On the other hand, he should distinguish both his classificatory "f.m." and "sr.s.d." from other female *jabala*, despite the fact that all the women belong to one subsection. The first two he calls *jabala-djamu* to indicate that, although they are possible sexual partners for him, ideally they are the proper wives for his father's father and son's son respectively. The frequent occurrence of intercommunity marriages probably made it necessary to differentiate these women from the eligible "m.m.b.d.d."

The father's mother, like the f.f.sr., chiefly concerns herself with her own daughter's children and has little to do with her son's children. She may, however, share her personal name with a close son's daughter. Similarly, the F.M.B. may give his name to a Sr.S.S.; but, apart from this, his relations with the latter are significant in a few ceremonial activities. As the F.M.B. is likely to have been either the ritual guardian or ward of the father's father in the past, he attracts some of the respect that a youth normally shows to the father's father. He often leads the decorating of his Sr.S.S. for the latter's lodge ceremonies and may construct the temporary ritual objects used in these. Secular intercourse between the two men is quite informal.

Mother's father—daughter's children; mother's father's sister —brother's daughter's children. All people regarded as mother's father and m.f.sr. are *djamiri*, as are a man's daughter's children and a woman's brother's daughter's children. Normally, the m.f.sr. is also the m.m.b.w., the D.S. is the "Sr.D.D.H.", the d.d. is the "sr.d.s.w.", the B.D.S. is the "D.D.H.", and the b.d.d. is the "d.s.w." All these are members of the one subsection and of alternate generation-levels relative to the speaker.

Children have few contacts with their own m.f.sr., although she may occasionally share her personal name with a b.d.d. A young boy, however, is often in the company of his own or a close mother's father. The child is not only likely to take the latter's personal name, but he also acquires much of his knowledge of kinship terms and behaviour from the old man. A man may often be seen nursing an infant daughter's son and carefully pointing out various relatives as he describes their reciprocal rights and duties. The grandfather displays an affectionate patience throughout the teaching. He never punishes the boy for inattention or ignorance, although he may employ mild ridicule to correct an error.

A boy's mother's father has no direct say in the former's seclusion and circumcision; but, as he is interested in the boy's welfare, he is usually included in discussions held by the father's father, F.M.B. and M.M.B. After the lad returns from seclusion, his mother's father spends much time teaching him crafts and hunting techniques. Intercourse between adult daughter's sons and mother's fathers exhibits an affectionate familiarity and involves joking that is often most obscene by Walbiri standards. The relationship of a man with his daughter's daughter is not clearly defined. Affection is the keynote, but he does not instruct her in any way.

Although "m.f.sr." and "d.d." are of the same subsection as a man's "m.b.d.", he should not marry either woman. Nevertheless, in the absence of eligible "m.m.b.d.d." and "m.b.d.", such unions are sometimes permitted. They are thought to be in poor taste, but they are regarded as jural marriages and not merely as long-term liaisons. People justify their occurrence by pointing out that such women are the appropriate alternative wives for the man's father's father and son's son, who are the same as his senior and junior brothers. As he may wed the ex-wife or widow of his "brother", his marriage with the potential wife of a kind of "half-brother" is also allowable.

As the preferred wife ("m.m.b.d.d.") is also a "m.f.sr.d.d.", certain "m.f.sr." are significant as a man's actual w.m.m. They are in his "marriage lines" (that is, the matrilines of his wives) and he therefore refers to them as *djuraldja* and avoids them almost as carefully as he does his wife's mother. Marriage with this "m.f.sr." is most improper, yet I knew of one man (Jim Tulum djuburula) who married his "m.f.sr." and, later, her daughter's daughter, thus making the first wife his own *djuraldja*. Men justified his action at the time, but it did nothing to enhance his social reputation.

The "mother's father" who is also the W.M.M.B. is similarly a man's *djuraldja*. He is treated circumspectly, for he shares with the wife's father and mother's brother the right to dispose of the woman.

Before a boy is circumcised or his sister is betrothed, his marriage lines are more or less implicit in the kinship structure— almost any "mother's father" who is not his M.M.H. is a potential W.M.M.B. But once the boy's father and mother's brother decide on his circumciser (usually but not always his F.F.Sr.S. or "Sr.S."), his marriage line is fixed in a particular "mother's father's" matriline. As close sororal polygyny is not common, a man may marry into several different marriage lines. Furthermore, a close ritual link exists between the "mother's father" who is the wife's M.M.B. and the "M.F.Sr.H." who is the husband's "M.M.B." Therefore the latter and his sister, a "mother's mother" who is at the same time a "m.f.w.", are also *djuraldja*. Conversely, a girl's "mother's father" is indirectly important to her because he, and his own wife's brother (her "M.M.B."), are *djuraldja* to her future husband. Thus, a man's wife's brother's matriline is his own marriage line, and his own matriline is the marriage line of the brother-in-law. In the same way, a man becomes *djuraldja* to the "Sr.D.S." who marries the former's own daughter's daughter.

If a boy is circumcised by his "sister's son", which is common, the circumciser is the "daughter's son" of the boy's father. The fact of the circumcision and subsequent betrothal makes little difference to the relationship between the two men, except that the boy's father cannot be *djuraldja* to the circumciser. They do not have to avoid each other as, for instance, the novice's father and the circumciser do among the Aluridja of the Musgrave Ranges (vide Elkin, 1940).

A woman wails at the death of her mother's father, m.f.sr., or her b.d. child; a man wails for his m.f.sr. and daughter's daughter and may gash his thighs when his close mother's father or adult daughter's son dies.

Mother's mother—daughter's children; mother's mother's brother—sister's daughter's children. All M.M.B. and m.m. are *djadja*, but the "M.M.B." and "m.m." who become W.M.F. and w.m.f.sr. are also *djuraldja*. All daughter's children of a woman and all sister's daughter's children of a man are *mindiri*. Generation-levels here are distinguished by the use of two terms to indicate the importance of the M.M.B. in a man's ceremonial life and in a woman's marriage. The actual or close mother's mother and M.M.B. are "bosses" of a person's matriline and share one spirit with that person, the mother and the mother's brother. They are therefore regarded as senior "half-siblings" of the *mindiri*. Consequently, sexual intercourse with an actual or close m.m.b.d.d. or M.M.B.D.S. is incestuous and marriage is impossible. But, at the same time, the close relationship with the M.M.B. justifies alternative marriage with a "m.b.d.", for she is the potential wife of the man's M.M.B., who is his "half-brother".

The mother's mother is thought to be much like a mother, albeit one who is less likely to punish her children. Indeed, women commonly try to prevent their own daughters from chastising the daughters' children.

> Danny djungarai had a daughter Gladys, aged about two, by his wife Maggie nangala and a son Richard, aged about two, by his wife Mona nangala. One day Gladys attacked Richard, and Maggie slapped her lightly in the presence of Big Maggie nabangari, Maggie's own mother. Big Maggie at once split open Maggie's scalp with a digging-stick. When Lady nangala, Maggie's half-sister, heard of this, she belaboured Big Maggie with a club. By the time the amused onlookers separated the women, Big Maggie's head was split, her knee bruised, and her wrist broken.

People are aware of the prevalence of this sort of behaviour, and they often remark on the domestic difficulties that follow when a woman interferes with the discipline of her daughter's children. Her action is rarely condemned, however, for a woman is expected to feel great affection for her grand-daughter.

A young girl usually shares the personal name of her mother's mother, who takes the initiative in offering it. As a woman is *djuraldja* to the future husband of her close daughter's daughter, she is kept acquainted with the arrangements made for the girl's betrothal; but she plays no other part in the affair. Before the girl marries, her mother's mother shares with the mother and elder sister in her domestic training, but afterwards the two women see less of each other. Nevertheless, they remain good friends and may joke freely and obscenely with each other.

The woman treats her infant daughter's son much as she does a young daughter's daughter. She has little to do with him in later years, however, and their behaviour is not sharply defined in terms of rights and duties. When the boy is formally separated from the women before being secluded for the Gadjari rituals, a close mother's mother may substitute for his absent mother and provide him with food. When he is subincised, she may be cicatrized in sympathy.

Relations between a boy and his distant "mother's mothers" are tenuous. Even if a particular "mother's mother" has become his *djuraldja*, he has little contact with her. Nevertheless, seven of the forbidden unions that I recorded involved these women. A Freudian analyst might perhaps argue that such women are selected as mistresses because, in terms of the prevailing social structure, they are obvious mother-substitutes.

Although a man has few face-to-face dealings with his sr.d.d., he is a key relative in her betrothal. He maintains a watching brief over her interests in marriage and should join with her father, brother and mother's brother to enforce her just claims on her husband's services and to ensure that she in turn discharges her obligations to her husband. Old age may restrict his participation to the mere giving of advice, but he must be consulted in these matters. The classificatory "M.M.B." has less significance in a woman's life, even if he is her *djuraldja*, for a woman has little or no say in the choice of her husband.

A man is closely linked with his Sr.D.S. During the latter's infancy, the M.M.B. is an affectionate friend, although he has less to do with the boy's education than does the mother's father. He may sometimes share his personal name with the boy. As a member of the lad's patrimoiety, the M.M.B. should be informed by the father's father and the F.M.B. when they decide to seclude the novice before circumcision. During the ceremonies, he may act as an "elder brother", instructing, exhorting and reassuring the boy.

Two djabanangga boys at Hooker Creek were to be circumcised during the one set of ceremonies. At the time there were only two djabanangga men in the camp to act as the elder brothers of the novices. A few weeks before the event, however, Clem djungarai, a "M.M.B." of the boys, returned from a droving trip. The appropriate kinsmen of the lads (largely at the urging of Clem's father) then decided that Clem should take the place of the younger djabanangga man as the novices' "elder brother". The reasons they gave for the choice were: Clem, who was about 18, needed the experience, for his own younger brother was soon to be circumcised; the selection would be a pleasant gesture to welcome home a young man well-liked by his elders; and, finally, Clem was a fairly close "M.M.B." of the boys.

The actual M.M.B. contributes meat to the payment of the circumciser, and he also donates weapons to the bride-price at the youth's betrothal, a ceremony he should witness. He shares with the father and elder brother the duty of explaining to the youth the significance of the post-circumcision ceremonies and, with the elder brother, gives him arm-blood to drink during the Gadjari seclusion. The M.M.B. also joins with the elder brother to teach the youth how to quiver ritually and how to clap boomerangs to accompany Gadjari singing. A classificatory, but not an actual, M.M.B. is often chosen to be one of the ritual friends that a boy acquires at the time of circumcision. Another "M.M.B.", especially if he is already *djuraldja* to the lad, may be his subinciser and may also cicatrize his chest afterwards.

Once betrothed, the young man sends occasional gifts of meat (especially of emu or kangaroo) to his close M.M.B., in return for his ritual services, and to his *djuraldja* "M.M.B.", in return for the latter's offering of a sr.d.d. as a future wife. He supports his close M.M.B. in disputes, as he would a brother; but he is also expected to dissuade him from hasty action that might endanger the latter's life. In quarrels at Hooker Creek, for instance, I often saw armed M.M.B. hovering at the disputants' elbows, saying little but standing ready to fight for their men or to remove them as circumstances demanded.

The half-brothers Donny and Yarry djabangari usually camped together in friendly fashion. One afternoon, however, one of Donny's young sons hit Yarry's child. The mothers of both children intervened and were soon involved in a scuffle with digging-sticks. Donny came to his wife's aid, striking her opponent several times. Yarry at once attacked Donny, and the two men, both tall and powerfully built, engaged in a vicious fight. Donny speared Yarry in the arm, but had his head split open with a club in return. Younger men, chiefly their brothers-in-law, separated them, but the quarrel quickly flared up again. Donny felled Yarry with a club, splitting his head in several places. Throughout the affray, the "M.M.B." of the combatants were quite at a loss. As they could not attack the assailants of their Sr.D.S. in the approved manner, they ran about the camp, wailing, swearing and brandishing weapons. Everyone was thoroughly upset by the quarrel, which clearly revealed the difficulties created when close brothers fought each other.

Men wail and may gash their thighs when a close M.M.B. or adult Sr.D.S. dies. The gashing is obligatory at the death of a "M.M.B." or "Sr.D.S." who was a ritual friend. After the death of his close Sr.D.S., a man confers with the deceased's elder brother and with members of the matriline of the dead man's widow on her disposal in marriage. The men also wail when a close mother's mother or sr.d.d. dies, but they do not for a "mother's mother" or "sr.d.d." who is not a *djuraldja*. Women cry and gash their heads at the death of a close M.M.B., mother's mother and daughter's child but merely wail for classificatory relatives.

Wife's mother—daughter's husband; wife's mother's brother—sister's daughter's husband. The wife's mother is occasionally *bimari*, "father's sister", and the W.M.B. *wabira*, "father". The daughter's husband (woman speaking) is then ŋ*alabi*, "brother's son", and the Sr.D.H. (man speaking) is ŋ*alabi*, "son", although both may also be called *wabira*. But normally the wife's mother and W.M.B. are a man's *maliri* "m.m.b.d." and "M.M.B.S." Other relatives are also *maliri*, a usage that may be confusing unless certain distinctions are noted.

(a) The wife's mother who is *maliri* is also *guridji* (= a hollow wooden shield) and *gadjin* (= shame); her brother is *maliri-djuraldja* (= the *maliri* associated with a marriage line).

(b) The actual m.m.b.d., who may not be wife's mother, is *maliri* and *bilibili* (a hollow wooden scoop); her brother is *maliri-ŋaminibia* (= the *maliri* who is like a mother's brother).

(c) The daughter's husband (woman speaking) who is "M.B.D.S." is *maliri* and *gadjin*. His W.M.B. calls him *maliri-ŋuniari-bia* (the *maliri* who is like a sister's son). The d.h.sr. (woman speaking) who is "m.b.d.d." may also be son's wife. She is *maliri* to her husband's mother and *maliri-jundalba-bia* to her H.M.B. They are *maliri* to her, and she may also refer to the former as *guridji*.

(d) The actual m.b.d. children are *maliri-jundalba-bia* and *ŋuniari-bia*, especially to their M.M.B.S., who is *maliri-ŋaminibia* to them.

(e) A man who marries his "cross-cousin" has children who are his "m.b.d." children. He calls them *maliri-jundalba-bia* and *-ŋalabi-bia*.

Young boys have little reason to distinguish between their actual and classificatory m.m.b.d., whom they regard as a kind of m.f.sr. However, by the time the boy is nine or ten years old he has learned that all the "m.m.b.d." are potential mothers-in-law, women to be scrupulously avoided after he is circumcised. As a result, he tends to avoid them long before he is secluded.

By the time the boy goes into seclusion, interested people have some idea of the matriline into which he will later marry. The "m.m.b.d." likely to become his *djuraldja* give vegetable-food to his mother to send to him while he is secluded. During the circumcision ceremonies the close mothers of the novice give fire-sticks to such "m.m.b.d." to carry when they dance; the "m.m.b.d." not involved in this way are called *widji* to distinguish them.

Generalized mother-in-law avoidance is evident at these ceremonies, which bring the whole camp or community together. Every woman is bound to have an actual or potential son-in-law ("m.b.d.s.") among the men. All the men therefore face in one

DIAGRAM 5

The maliri relationships

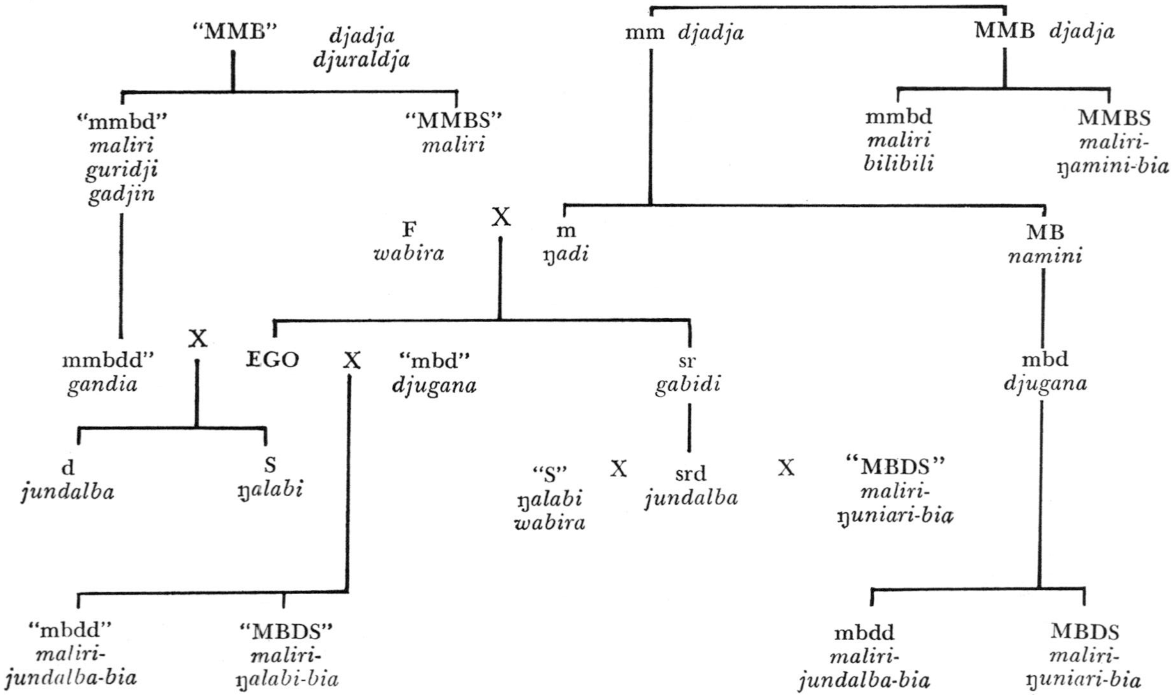

direction while they sing, and the women dance in a group behind them.

Once he is circumcised, the lad cannot approach, speak to, or deliberately look at any "m.m.b.d." He rarely refers to the women in conversation and then only by using their subsection name or the term *gadjin* (shame). Although he may mention their conception-dreamings in other contexts, he should not employ these to identify the women; however, he exhibits no other special attitudes or behaviour towards the dreamings. Every Walbiri is trained to recognize the foot-prints of each of his fellows, and, whenever a man espies those of his own wife's mother, he carefully erases them with his foot.

No matter how old a man is, none of these restrictions is ever relaxed. A man who inadvertently comes face-to-face with a "m.m.b.d." must turn and run away, even if he is a grey-bearded elder and she an infant just able to walk. If the man thus encounters his own wife's mother, he later gives his wife a piece of meat to take to her to expunge the shame he feels; but he need not do so where other "m.m.b.d." are concerned.

The ban on intercourse with mothers-in-law is one of the strongest taboos operating in Walbiri society, and I have never seen any of the accompanying rules broken. Nevertheless, I was told of three instances of men's cohabiting with "m.m.b.d." who were potential mothers-in-law. All were alleged to have involved Walbiri residing with non-Walbiri communities (at Waterloo, Birrindudu and Wave Hill), groups in which, according to the Walbiri, the old marriage laws were fast breaking down.

The Walbiri continue to avoid mothers-in-law despite countervailing European pressures that often force "m.m.b.d." and "m.b.d.s." into close contact. If both are riding in a motor-truck, the men stand facing the front and the women sit facing the back. A man who has to enter a building where women are working will not do so without first announcing his identity and then waiting for the "m.m.b.d." to leave.

On government settlements that I visited, the superintendent supervised the distribution of rations but native workers actually handed out the food. Only men handled the men's rations at Hooker Creek and Yuendumu, and women the women's rations. At Phillip Creek, however, men had to give out all the rations;

consequently each was bound to encounter some "m.m.b.d." in the process. Usually, such women sidled up to the distribution table with heads averted. They held their ration-bags as far from their bodies as possible, so that loose rations could be poured into the bags without any direct physical contact between man and woman. Tinned rations that were handed to other women were thrown to the ground to be picked up by the "m.m.b.d." No words were exchanged.

The people dealt with such situations by regarding them as "government business" and therefore outside Walbiri moral requirements. By carefully divorcing these anomalies from everyday, "tribal" activities, in which the old laws must be followed, the people were able to preserve the mother-in-law taboo.

Thus, I was considered to be a member of the djuburula subsection, and my wife was a nabanangga; we stood in particular kin-relationships to all the residents of the Hooker Creek camp. Nevertheless, I was not expected to avoid any "m.m.b.d.", nor my wife any "m.b.d.s." Our allocation to kinship categories was largely a matter of courtesy; in the last analysis we were thought to be amenable only to the Whitefellow law, which was seen as very different from the Walbiri law. Similarly, when a Bathurst Island man was given a Walbiri wife during his stay at Hooker Creek, he was told he need avoid only those women who were his close mothers-in-law. As an alien, "he had his own law", so a compromise was reached.

Despite the strength of mother-in-law avoidance, a man still has significant, albeit indirect, contacts with his own wife's mother. He should frequently give his wife meat to hand on to her mother, who in return may send him gifts of vegetable-food. The man always takes an interest in her welfare and relies on her children to inform him of her activities.

Judy nungarai, a widow aged about 50, was the mother of Silent djambidjimba and the mother's sister of Polly nambidjimba. When Silent's arm was broken by a boomerang in a fight, he was sent to Darwin to have it reset. Judy had behaved oddly from the time of the fight, but after Silent went away she became obviously insane. She gibbered and tore up her clothes, drank her own urine and gashed herself severely, attacked children with sticks, and burned down other people's shelters. Altogether, the picture seemed to be one of involutional melancholia precipitated by a stress situation. A few relatives connected her behaviour with Silent's absence; but most simply regarded her as a lunatic whose condition had been caused by the sorcery of an unknown enemy.

Eventually Judy became such a nuisance that she was leg-roped to a shady tree for some days, and her close daughter Polly kept her supplied with food, water and words of comfort. She was released when she appeared to have become quiet, but she disappeared from the camp on the same morning. Polly's husband, Yarry djabangari, was greatly alarmed by the news. He at once led a search party and tracked her to the Seven Miles Bore, where she was found naked and exhausted by the heat. She wandered off again a few days later, and Yarry once more took the initiative in recovering her.

A man who marries a "cross-cousin" avoids not only all his "m.m.b.d." but also the "father's sister" who is his actual wife's mother. Although his behaviour in respect of her parallels that towards a wife's mother who is "m.m.b.d.", it seems to lack the emotional quality of the latter. The difference may, perhaps, be due to the fact that a man acquires a "m.m.b.d." as a mother-in-law when he is young, whereas he is unlikely to marry a "f.sr.d." until he is sure he cannot obtain the "m.m.b.d.d." who is a preferred wife.

When a man dies, his wife's mother, whether she is "father's sister" or "m.m.b.d.", singes her pubic hair and cuts off her head-hair, gouges her scalp, and sears the wound with a firestick. A man merely wails for a dead mother-in-law.

During a boy's early years, his "M.M.B.S." is not a significant relative; but, once the choice of his circumciser establishes the identity of the lad's *djuraldja* or marriage line, the "M.M.B.S." who will be his W.M.B. stands in a clearly-defined relationship with him.

Although the future wife's father is the first choice as the cir-cumciser, the W.M.B. may perform the operation. Sometimes he joins with the wife's brothers and "sister's sons" to form the circumcision table. The W.M.B. is often chosen to be the boy's *jualbiri*—that member of the boy's marriage line who ensures that the circumciser later gives the lad a wife. The *jualbiri* also cuts the youth's hair during the post-circumcision seclusion and becomes his bond-friend; thereafter, the two should never quar-rel. A "M.M.B.S." who is W.M.B. or *djuraldja* may subincise the youth and, afterwards, cicatrize his chest. He receives gifts for both services. In the past, he usually performed the nose-piercing operation.

In the absence of a girl's father and M.M.B., her mother's brother takes sole responsibility for betrothing her to his "F.Sr.D.S.", a privilege not granted to any other kinsmen of hers. Thus, the "M.M.B.S." who is a potential W.M.B. has a position of strength in the marriage line of his future Sr.D.H. The people recognize this and say that young men should always remember it in their dealings with their "M.M.B.S."

At the public ceremony of betrothal, the W.M.B. places the girl on the young man's thigh and reminds him of his obligations to her and her kinsmen. He shares the two instalments of bride-price with the girl's father and is closely involved in protecting her interests in marriage. Yet, although a man is in a sense always indebted to his W.M.B. for the wife he receives, he displays no obvious respect for him in their secular relations. Instead, the two men are "mates", who may joke together obscenely and indulge in horseplay.

At the death of his close W.M.B. or Sr.D.H., a man wails and may gash his thighs in mourning. He also has the privilege of having the deceased's conception-totem painted on his own back as a mark of affectionate sorrow.

Husband's mother—son's wife; husband's mother's brother—sister's son's wife. The husband's mother may occasionally be *bimari*, "father's sister", and the H.M.B. *wabira*, "father"; both the son's wife (woman speaking), who is also "brother's daughter", and the sr.s.w. (man speaking), who is also "daughter", are then called *jundalba*. Normally, however, the husband's mother is *maliri*, "m.m.b.d.", as is the H.M.B. or "M.M.B.S."; son's wife and sr.s.w. are then also *maliri*, "m.b.d. children". The distinction between these relatives and others called *maliri* has already been discussed under the heading of wife's mother and daughter's husband.

Little need be said about these relationships. A woman does not have to avoid any "m.m.b.d.", whether actual husband's mother or not, nor the "father's sister" who is her mother-in-law. She has no explicit obligations towards the women, and their contacts appear to display merely casual friendliness. A young girl on first entering her husband's camp is likely to receive helpful advice from his mother, but the mother-in-law is not bound to assist her. The two women may occasionally exchange small gifts. I observed very few instances of women's interfering in the domestic affairs of their married sons.

A woman regards her H.M.B. or "M.M.B.S." as a kind of "mother's brother" and does not have to avoid him. In effect, her behaviour is the converse of that of her brother in this respect. He must avoid his "m.m.b.d." but not his "m.b.d.d."; his sister must avoid her "M.B.D.S." but not her "M.M.B.S." There is no other specification of her relationship with her H.M.B. The fact that the "m.m.b.d." and the "M.M.B.S." are both in her *djuraldja* or marriage line has not the same significance for a woman as it has for a man.

At the death of her husband's mother, H.M.B., or son's wife, a woman wails and gashes her head. A man wails at the death of a close sr.s.w.

Wife's father—daughter's husband; wife's father's sister—brother's daughter's husband. The wife's father may sometimes be ŋamini, "mother's brother", who is also "F.Sr.H.", and w.f.sr., ŋadi, "mother"; the daughter's husband or B.D.H. is then ŋuniari, "son" or "sister's son" respectively. More often, the father-in-law and his sister are actual or classificatory F.F.Sr. children, *wandiri*; the same name is given to the daughter's husband or B.D.H., who is actual or classificatory M.B.S.S. Just as frequently, however, the wife's father is ŋuniari, "sister's son", and the w.f.sr. is *jundalba*, "sister's daughter"; in this case the daughter's husband or B.D.H. is ŋamini, "mother's brother".

The distinction between fathers-in-law who are *wandiri* and those who are ŋuniari roughly reflects the difference between intra- and inter-community marriage. That is to say, *wandiri*, like father's fathers, are more likely to be clearly recognized within the community. Just as other "father's fathers" tend to be identified with "elder brothers", men of the same subsection and of alternate generation-levels, so other "F.F.Sr.S." merge with "Sr.S."

The "mother's brother" generally becomes a wife's father

only as a second choice, and the relationship between him and his son-in-law is not as sharply defined as it is between a daughter's husband and the preferred types of father-in-law. A man is likely to be mature before he decides to marry a "m.b.d.", and he negotiates privately with her father and mother's brother for their consent. Once he hands over bride-price, the union is regarded as a jural marriage; but it lacks the ritual, emotional and "temporal" background of the ideal marriage with a "m.m.b.d.d." There is no such distinction between marriages with f.f.sr.s.d. and with "sr.s.d.", for both are alliances with women who are also "m.m.b.d.d."

A young boy's dealings with his F.F.Sr.S. and his "sister's son" are informal and friendly. At this stage the men have no explicit duties or privileges in respect of him; but eventually he learns that one or more of them will be his circumciser and father-in-law, and this knowledge colours his attitudes towards them. His first specific claim over such men is expressed during his pre-circumcision grand tour. The boy and his ritual guardians visit as many communities as possible. Although he is still in seclusion, at each locality he comes under the temporary care of various "sister's sons", who are obliged to feed him and also give him hair-string to take home to his father. (For the rest of this section, "sister's son" will also refer to F.F.Sr.S.)

The boy's kinsmen choose the particular "sister's sons" who are to circumcise him; these may number from one to three men. Although only one actually performs the operation, the others also have the right to become the lad's fathers-in-law. Other "sister's sons" may be asked to act as the boy's *jualbiri* and ensure that his future wife's father hands over the bride. On emerging from seclusion, the lad, helped by certain kinsmen, makes a gift to the "sister's son" who circumcised him. For months afterwards he treats this man with circumspection and, indeed, tries to avoid him. The wife's father may also subincise the youth, and occasionally he performs the operations of cicatrization and nose-piercing. He should receive gifts for all these services.

When the time comes for the public betrothal of his daughter, the "sister's son" does not witness the ceremony, for he feels the loss of his child. Nevertheless, his wife's brother brings him his share of the bride-price. If at that time he has no daughter to surrender, he must make a gift to his future son-in-law as an earnest of good faith and then commission the other "sister's sons" who are the latter's *jualbiri* to find another girl to give him. One of these men may, if he wishes, provide his own daughter as a substitute and receive the bride-price in return.

Following the betrothal, the girl's father receives frequent gifts of meat from the future son-in-law and expects to be fed whenever he visits the latter's camp. Although the daughter's husband is not obliged to offer help in disputes, he usually does so, and he wails if the wife's father is wounded. After the marriage, the father-in-law maintains a close interest in his daughter's fortunes, and he should safeguard her claims on her husband. A man whose wife's father is old and widowed should assist him freely with food and assure that he is cared for when ill. The failure of a son-in-law to meet these commitments leaves him open to strong criticism from other "mother's brothers" of the old man.

Timothy djagamara left Yuendumu to work at Alice Springs, taking his nabaldjari wife with him. In his absence his wife's father, Jim djungarai, died at Yuendumu. When Timothy returned home, his elder brothers, Jumbo and Loomie djagamara, came from Mount Doreen to accuse him of neglecting the old man. Timothy denied the charge, stating that he had cared for Jim for months before going to Alice Springs. It seemed clear that the two elder brothers were seeking an excuse to force a quarrel on Timothy, who had fought with Jumbo some years before over the disposal of another nabaldjari woman. Indeed, the younger man had gone to Alice Springs chiefly to avoid more disputes.

The elder brothers were determined to press the matter, however, so a formal duel with knives was arranged. Loomie acted as Jumbo's second, and Tommy djabangari, Jumbo's own wife's brother, seconded Timothy. Hitler djuburula, the M.B.S. of old Jim, was referee. Jumbo was given first blow and sliced open Timothy's shoulder. This should have ended the duel, but the incensed Timothy struck at Jumbo. Hitler tried to restrain him, and the deflected knife severed an artery in Jumbo's upper arm. Jumbo quickly bled to death.

Most people agreed that Timothy could not be blamed and that Jumbo and Loomie had themselves caused all the trouble. The important point, however, is that the latter thought that by charging Timothy with the neglect of his father-in-law they could justify their actions to the rest of the camp.

In everyday activities, a man behaves towards his son-in-law much as he does towards a sister's son. The men are usually on good terms and often exchange obscene jokes. Men wail when a father-in-law or a son-in-law dies.

A man has little to do with his w.f.sr., and I could not discover any explicit rules governing the relationship between them.

Husband's father—son's wife; husband's father's sister—brother's son's wife. The husband's father may be ŋamini, "mother's brother", or wandiri, F.F.Sr.S., or ŋuniari, "son". The h.f.sr. may be ŋadi, "mother", or wandiri, f.f.sr.d., or jundalba, "daughter". The son's wife or b.s.w. may be jundalba, "daughter" or "sister's daughter", or wandiri, m.b.s.d., or ŋamadi, "mother".

These relationships may be discussed very briefly. A young girl rarely sees her future father-in-law or h.f.sr. In later years she has more contact with the former, and their intercourse is one of easy friendship. Mild sexual joking is permissible. Although a man does not have any definite disciplinary rights over his son's wife, he is usually quick to apprise his son of any adverse gossip he hears concerning the woman. In effect he appoints himself an informal guardian of his son's rights in marriage, but the kinsmen of the girl would certainly dispute his actions if he tried directly to discipline her.

Wife's brother—sister's husband. Brothers-in-law may occasionally be reciprocal "M.B.S." and "F.Sr.S."; they call each other wangili or bangu, "cross-cousin", or they may use the reciprocal "brother-in-law" terms marilanda and gandamari. The latter terms, which have apparently come from the East Kimberleys, do not imply relative seniority or specify any classificatory genealogical connections.

More frequently, brothers-in-law are reciprocally "M.M.B.D.S." They may call each other marilanda or gandamari; but their proper titles are ŋumbana, senior brother-in-law, and gandia, junior brother-in-law. Actual M.M.B.D.S. also call each other ŋumbana and gandia. Relative age does not determine the allocation of the terms. Instead, ŋumbana is the man whose own father was the "mother's father" of the actual father of the other, who is gandia.

I cannot see, however, how this rule operates for two "M.M.B.D.S." who are also reciprocal F.F.Sr.S.S., for their fathers must be cross-cousins. The people themselves could not clarify the matter for me; they simply asserted that a particular man was ŋumbana to the other's gandia because the two had always called each other by these titles. I can only assume that the really significant factor in such cases is the relative seniority of the men's mothers—the mother of ŋumbana is "mother's mother" to the mother of gandia. This arrangement would be compatible with the rule that the relative seniority of "siblings" depends on the relative seniority of their mothers. Nevertheless, it is possible that men simply inherit the titles from their fathers' fathers, who similarly acquired them.

The Walbiri ascribe considerable social and ritual significance to the brother-in-law relationship. When a boy's physical development indicates he is old enough to be circumcised, his sister's husband should point this out to his kinsmen, who place the lad in seclusion under the supervision of one or two close sister's husbands. These men are preferably, but not necessarily, members of his future wife's matriline. They care for his material needs but, being of the opposite patrimoiety, do not instruct him in ceremonial matters. The guardians should provide the hair-string used by the lad's father and mother's brother to manufacture the string-cross that symbolizes his cult lodge. At the conclusion of the post-circumcision seclusion, the sister's husband tells the jualbiri that it is time for them to cut the boy's hair, which is given to the sister's husband. This initiates a lifelong series of exchanges of hair between the brothers-in-law; and at various times during the circumcision and Gadjari seclusion the sister's husband rubs his own arm-blood into the lad's head to promote the growth of hair.

The brother-in-law is the youth's guardian throughout the Gadjari ceremonies and sleeps beside him every night. He also gives him the food supplied by the father and mother, some of which he keeps for himself. At the beginning of the Gadjari seclusion, the sister's husband has formally taken the novice from the latter's mother; at the conclusion of the rituals he decorates the youth with totemic patterns and skeins of hair-string, then returns him formally to the mother. The youth's father keeps the hair-string on his behalf.

A sister's husband may support the lad at the revelatory ceremonies that follow circumcision, but, as a member of the opposite patrimoiety, he may not explain their significance to him. He is his brother-in-law's guardian once again during the subincision rituals, and he is usually chosen to be the operator in nose-piercing, a service for which the youth's father repays him with gifts. The sister's husband is also an alternative choice to the W.M.B. as a cicatrizer. He takes no active part in the betrothal of his wife's brother, but, as the men are reciprocally *djuraldja*, he is interested in seeing the affair proceed without hindrance. The young man now sends his sister's husband occasional gifts of meat.

The relationship established between brothers-in-law when the junior is circumcised extends into adult ritual activity. Thus, a man has the privilege of supervising the decoration of his brother-in-law when the latter participates in increase and revelatory ceremonies. Indeed, at Phillip Creek only the brothers-in-law could contribute the arm-blood used in the ritual decoration of the actors, a convention that appears to be of Warramunga origin. Men also tend to call on the services of medicinemen who are their "brothers-in-law" rather than of those in other kinship categories; but I could not discover any explicit rule to this effect.

Although there is no formal constraint on the everyday behaviour of brothers-in-law, joking tends to be mild. The men are expected to be close friends and in fact they often camp and hunt together.

Men wail and gash their thighs at the death of a close brother-in-law, but they merely wail for more distant relatives.

Husband's sister—brother's wife. Sisters-in-law are usually *mandari*, "m.m.b.d.d." but sometimes they are *djugana*, "cross-cousins". Actual m.m.b.d.d., *jabala*, cannot be sisters-in-law.

The relations between distant "sisters-in-law" are friendly but tenuous. But actual sisters-in-law, especially if both have married young, may be thrown into continuing, close contact, from which there often develops a strong relationship involving mutual assistance and friendship. The women may exchange small gifts, and sometimes they act as midwives for each other. An older woman is likely to be concerned with the social reputation of her brother's wife, whom she is ready to upbraid or even assault if the latter engages in extra-marital affairs. The husbands try to keep out of such disputes.

Cross-cousins. The term *bangu*, mother's brother's or father's sister's child, is used reciprocally by all actual or classificatory cross-cousins; they are further distinguished as *wangili*, male cross-cousin, and *djugana*, female cross-cousin.

A person regards the children of an actual or close mother's brother or father's sister as a kind of sibling, their parents share matrispirits with his parents. Sexual intercourse with such close cross-cousins is therefore incestuous, and I heard of no instances of this. The children of a classificatory "mother's brother" or "father's sister", however, are possible alternative spouses, and "cross-cousin" marriages comprised four per cent of all the unions I recorded.

The people gave several reasons for the occurrence of these marriages, each of which involved a manipulation of the notion of sibling equivalence. Thus, a man's "m.b.d." is the preferred wife for his M.M.B., who, because he shares one matrispirit with this man, is the same as an elder brother. As the man may, through the levirate, marry the ex-wife of a "brother", he may with some propriety marry the potential wife of the M.M.B. Similarly, the man may, through the operation of sororal polygyny, marry the "sister" of his wife. As his "m.b.d." is like a sister to his "m.m.b.d.d.", the preferred wife, he may occasionally marry the former as well.

No formal rules govern the behaviour of "cross-cousins" in childhood. But, eventually, the camp gossip and quarrels inform children that distant "cross-cousins" are the people most likely to be involved in extramarital sexual liaisons. As a result, by the time most youths reach late adolescence they have initiated casual and tentative affairs with their young "m.b.d."

In the absence of a suitable "sister's son" or "M.M.B.S.", a boy may be circumcised by a "M.B.S.", who later provides his own m.m.b.s.d. or f.f.sr.d.d. as the young man's wife. That is to say, the circumciser's father's father, who is the lad's "mother's father", becomes the head of the latter's marriage line. If the "M.B.S." cannot give his own f.f.sr.d.d. to the young man, he may offer him a younger sister as an alternative. A "M.B.S." is frequently chosen to be a ritual friend of a newly-circumcised boy and occasionally he becomes his *jualbiri*. Although he may support the novice at subsequent ceremonies in the absence of the latter's elder brother or brother-in-law, he does not give him religious instruction. The "M.B.S." may substitute for the W.M.B. as the youth's cicatrizer and he may also pierce his nose. He often performs the subincision operation.

Intercourse between men who are cross-cousins is informal and is marked by frequent obscene joking. Men and women who are "cross-cousins", however, do not mix freely in everyday life, lest other people take their friendliness to indicate that they are lovers—which indeed they may well be. A man never feels at ease when he knows his wife is in close association with her "M.B.S."

Men wail and gash their thighs at the death of a M.B.S., and they wail when a m.b.d. dies. Women wail and gash their heads at the deaths of cross-cousins.

This completes the survey of the chief dyadic relationships within the kinship system. I have treated the relations between spouses in some detail, for these are in some respects self-contained. Other relationships, such as parent-child, father-in-law and son-in-law, and mother's brother—sister's son, will need to be re-examined as they interlock in important social situations, notably those of betrothal, initiation and death. Similarly, some data presented above will have to be re-assembled to facilitate the analysis of the inter-connections of subsections, patrilines and patrimoieties, matrilines and matrimoieties.

CHAPTER X

THE SUBSECTION SYSTEM

The names of the Walbiri subsections are cognate with those of sections and subsections of tribes that are distributed from the Kimberleys to Alice Springs and from Musgrave Range to the Gulf of Carpentaria.

TABLE 14

Walbiri subsection names

(UPPER CASE = male term; lower case = female term;
X = preferred marriage; arrow = maternal descent.)

(I base these tables on my own field-work and on published and unpublished reports by Spencer and Gillen, Elkin, Fry, Kaberry and Berndt.)

The Walbiri at Phillip Creek also use another set of subsection terms in connection with young people, terms probably borrowed from the neighbouring Yanmadjari tribe.

The Walbiri are aware that their own terms resemble those of other tribes and that similar terms may be differently arranged in the various systems; but they do not try to account for these facts. Moreover, although there are detailed myths relating the origins of circumcision, subincision, the Gadjari cycle, etc., which are generally known by initiates, few men could recount analogous myths concerning the origin of subsections. The accounts that I did obtain were unusually brief.

At Phillip Creek, for instance, I learned that the important ibis totem at Renner Springs (Bunarabanda) long ago told the

TABLE 15

Male subsection and section names among other tribes

Djauan	Yangman	Mudbara		Yangman	Djauan
bading	yuwangari	djangari	djambidjina	tabidjin	warmut
balyeri	iwalyeri	djaljeri	djimara	yanmira	kamarang
kangila	yangala	djangala	djimidja	imitja	bulain
waitban	yurwela	djulama	djanama	uwanai	ngaritj

Karadjari	East Kimberley	Gurindji		East Kimberley	Karadjari
paldjeri	djangeri	djangari	djambidjina	djambin	karimba
	djoalyi	djaljiri	djabada	djakera	
burung	djangala	djangala	djimidja	djungera	panaka
	djuru	djulama	djanama	djoan	

South Aranda	North Aranda	Warramunga		North Aranda	South Aranda
pultara	appungerta	thapungarti	tjambin	anbitjana	kamara
	pultara	thapaltjeri	thakomara	kamara	
purula	ungalla	thungalla	thunguri	uknaria	pananga
	purula	thupila	thapanunga	pananga	

Ooldea	Pintubi	Luritja		Pintubi	Ooldea
burong	purunga	tapangarti	tambitjina	purukula	karimara
	{ panaka / ipaka }	tapaltjari	takamara		
panaka		tangala	tjungarai	tararu	dararu
		taparula	tapananga		

TABLE 16

Phillip Creek subsection terms

Phillip Creek		Yanmadjari	
DJABAIJADI	ngambidjagudu	DJABA:RI	ngambidja
ngambaiadi	DJAMBIRILGA	ngamba:di	DJAMBULGA
DJABALJI	wadjala	DJABALJA	wadjila
naljiri	DJAGARA	ngaljiri	DJAGARA
DJANGALI	ngabida	DJANGALI	ngambugulu
nanggala	DJUGADAI	nganggala	DJUGUDAI
DJULAMA	ngamara	DJULAMA	ngamana
ngambula	DJANAMA	ngambula	DJANAMA

Walbiri (sic) that, when men died, they died "completely". The sun, moon and rain dreamings, however, contradicted the ibis. They said that, just as they themselves reappeared regularly, so the Walbiri would always return after death—that is, dead people would be reincarnated in the form of the guruwari spirit-entities. The rain dreaming from Walabanba, near Bullocky Soak, then "gave" the subsection system to the Walbiri, saying that this too "never finished", for it enabled subsections to cycle continuously through the generations. The myth seems to be Warramunga-inspired; but it is of interest that the Lunga of the eastern Kimberleys believe that the rainbow-snake gave them subsections (Kaberry, 1937, p. 441).

Hooker Creek Walbiri, on the other hand, simply said that in the dreamtime the eaglehawk allocated four subsections to one set of alternate generation-levels, and the pink cockatoo gave four to the other generation-levels. Repeated questioning of the men elicited no more details; they did not know the circumstances of the birds' actions and did not appear to be at all interested in the matter.

The apparent absence of a Walbiri generic term for subsections and for the subsection system may well be connected with this paucity of mythological material. The people always refer to the subsections by the Territory-wide pidgin term "skins".

The list of terms in Table 15 suggests that the Walbiri received subsections during a general diffusion of the system from the Kimberley coast to the borders of Queensland and South Australia. Comparison of these and other sets of section and subsection terms confirms the supposition beyond doubt and indicates that the Walbiri probably borrowed the typical section system first. The evidence supports the hypothesis that both were acquired comparatively recently from the north or northwest.

Spencer and Gillen (1899, p. 90) reported the presence in 1896 of subsections among the northern and south-eastern Walbiri, groupings that were then still in the process of acceptance by the southern Aranda. Evidence from other areas has also demonstrated how quickly these systems can spread. Thus, in less than 20 years subsections crossed the Roper River and reached peoples more than 100 miles to the north in Arnhem Land (Spencer, 1914; Warner, 1937). Similarly, in 1931 the natives around Mount Margaret (Western Australia) were experimenting with a newly-acquired section system (Elkin, 1940, p. 295); by 1941 the same system had been adopted by Aborigines at Ooldea (South Australia) over 500 miles to the east, who were not yet sure of the "proper" way to interpret the categories (Berndt, 1945). This system also spread north to the Pintubi at Mount Leibig, where in 1932 Fry observed that the people were not only wrestling with the novel section groupings but were also trying to correlate these with the neighbouring Walbiri subsection system (Fry, 1934, p. 473).

Evidence of this sort strongly suggests that the diffusion of subsections in the central desert followed hard on the spread of sections. It is probable that the Walbiri received the section system no more than a century ago and subsections 20 or 30 years later. But, whatever dates are eventually allotted to these events, we may say that, compared with many other elements in their culture, the people have not possessed subsections for long.

Elkin (personal communication), on the basis of his field-work in northern and north-western Australia, has suggested that considerations of social prestige have importantly determined the speed of diffusion of sections and subsections. Aborigines, he says, dislike admitting that a neighbouring tribe possesses social groupings or categories that they themselves lack, even though the elements in question are functionally redundant in their own society. Stanner (1936, p. 186) has also remarked on this attitude among the Murinbata of Port Keats. My own acquaintance with the Walbiri supports the proposition; for instance, I often heard men speak contemptuously of the Pintubi, who even yet have not fully grasped the principles underlying subsection affiliation.

Indeed, it is difficult to see what other motive than a desire to keep up with their neighbours could have impelled the Walbiri to adopt these new systems. They apparently possessed already such "section-like" phenomena as double-unilineal descent groupings, merged and named alternate generation-levels, and preferred marriage with a type of cross-cousin; and the existing kinship structure could perform all the important functions apparently mediated by the section and subsection systems. Thus, subsections today are still to a large extent functionally superfluous, as the people themselves are aware.

Basically, they regard subsections as a summary expression of social relationships that may sometimes be practically useful but just as often is dangerously ambiguous. When important questions arise concerning, for instance, the disposal of a woman in marriage, the selection of a circumciser, the avenging of a death, or the organization of a revelatory ceremony, specific genealogical connections and local community affiliations constitute the approved frame of reference within which decisions are made. Subsection membership as such is irrelevant, for it does not make the fine discriminations among people that are considered significant in such situations.

The most obvious feature of the subsections is their application as terms of address or reference for people of both sexes. (A man even addresses his dogs by the subsection term appropriate to his own children.) The relevant kinship terms or conception-dreamings are invoked, however, to distinguish among people of one subsection. If it is desired to single out from other members of a subsection a person who has spent much time with another tribe, the people may also use that tribe's version of his subsection name. Thus, a Walbiri djabanangga man from Wave Hill is called djanama (Gurindji); a djagamara man from Teatree is djagara (Yanmadjari). The Walbiri also recognize the practical utility of subsection terms as behavioural signposts in casual intercourse with members of other tribes; but they prefer to deal with such people on an individual kinship basis when the contacts are prolonged, as by European employment or by inter-marriage.

Men at Hooker Creek also frequently used an additional set of relative terms, which, they said, had been borrowed from the Waringari tribe to the west:

Subsection	Term	Subsection	Term
A1 (EGO)	—	B1 (W.B.)	*ngagunju*
A2 (M.M.B.)	*wadu*	B2 (M.F.)	*ngagunju*
C1 (Sr.S.)	*wari-wari*	D1 (W.M.B.)	*binbin*
C2 (M.B.)	*wari-wari*	D2 (F., S.)	*wari-wari*

The terms were usually uttered as ejaculations to underline an amusing (especially obscene), exaggerated, or inept remark. The term chosen might indicate either the original speaker's subsection relationship to the interjector, or the interjector's relationship to a person being discussed. I could discover no other reason for using the terms, at least one of which, *wari-wari*, is common throughout the Kimberley tribes.

The subsections employ only 16 terms (8 male, 8 female) to summarize the 26 basic, named kinship categories, which in fact extend to 36 by the addition of affinal or consanguineal qualifiers. In the following table, the allocation of the speaker to subsection A1 is arbitrary, and to simplify presentation the table is set out from a man's point of view. The capital letters in brackets refer to matrimoicty (P,Q), patrimoiety (R,S) and generation-level (T,U) affiliation.

Inspection of such a table indicates clearly that subsections are essentially a summary of kin terms, rather than of modes of behaviour. Thus a man refers to his wife's mother and his s.s.w.m. by the one subsection term, but he does not behave towards both women in anything like the same manner; although both his mother's father and his W.M.M.B. are in the one subsection, he behaves towards them in different ways. Some anthropologists, however, seem to have misinterpreted the significance of this subsection terminological classification. Lawrence, for instance, when criticizing Radcliffe Brown's analysis of sections and subsections, has said that "a kinship term, though expressing a person-to-person relationship, is applicable to a group of people, just as is a class name" (1937, p. 337). He then assumes that the Aborigines' classification of individuals by kin terms is therefore no different from that by subsection terms, and, on the basis of this false identification, he concludes that subsections, and not genealogical connections, are the important regulators of marriage. Murdock (1949, p. 51) agrees with him.

TABLE 17

The kinship composition of Walbiri subsections

Subsection	Members	Subsection	Members
A1 (PRT)	B, sr, FBS&d, FF, ffsr, SS, sd.	B1 (QST)	MMBDS&d, w, WB, SrH, FMB, fm, SrSS.
A2 (PRT)	MMBSS&d, MMB, mm, WMF, wmfsr, SrDS&d.	B2 (QST)	MBS&d, w, MF, mfsr, WMMB, wmm, DS&d.
C1 (PSU)	FFSrS&d, WF, wfsr, SrS&d.	D1 (QRU)	MMBS&d, WMB, wm.
C2 (PSU)	MB, m, DH, sw, WF, wfsr.	D2 (QRU)	F, fsr, S, d, wm.

Now, when a Walbiri refers to a classificatory "father's father" as his "distant elder brother", he implies that the man is genealogically a "brother" of the speaker's own father's father, no matter how remote the connection may be or how far apart the two men reside. He may no longer be able to trace all the intervening links (because, for instance, of name taboos following deaths), but he is sure that at one time they existed in fact—otherwise he would not have been taught to call that man "father's father". The latter must be an actual parallel cousin ("brother") of an actual parallel cousin (and so on) of the speaker's own father's father. Moreover, the father's father is in many ways like an elder brother to the speaker: the men are members of the one cult-lodge and share the one patrispirit, which they both call "father"; the elder behaves as an elder brother does in the ceremonies accompanying the circumcision of the younger man; the men are also in merged alternate generation-levels. As the father's father and son's son behave towards each other very much as do elder and younger brother, they, naturally enough, often refer to each other as "brother". (Similarly, the f.f.sr. and her b.s.d., being the sisters of these men, are "like elder and younger sister".) The "father's father", being a "brother" of the father's father, occupies, from the son's son's point of view, the same relative position in the kinship structure; consequently he also is "like an elder brother".

The only persons that a man calls by his own subsection name are his actual and classificatory father's father, f.f.sr., son's children, and elder and younger siblings, all of whom are, on genealogical and quasi-genealogical grounds, his "siblings". Consequently, as the people themselves point out, the members of any subsection are, with respect to each other, "siblings", although they are not necessarily regarded as such by non-members. This ascription of "siblinghood" is not, as Lawrence (1937, p. 324) has implied, an "artificial" extension by class names of patrilineal kinship beyond the "patriclan". That the particular classificatory relatives are not a man's "siblings" simply because they are members of his subsection becomes obvious when it is remembered that any such relatives are "siblings", including those non-Walbiri who either have no subsections at all or arrange them in different systems.

Moreover, in terms of Lawrence's assumptions, we would expect a man to refer to all the women of his wife's subsection as "wife", for she regards them as her "siblings". In fact, he does not do this; it is important for him to remember that he cannot marry either his "w.f.f.sr." or his "w.b.s.d.", as they are of the wrong generation-level and kinship category for him. Similarly, he cannot marry the m.m.b.d.d. in that subsection, even though his wife calls them "sister"; although they are of the correct generation-level for him, they are genealogically "too close". Subsection membership has nothing to do with this discrimination. Thus, when the Bathurst Island man visited Hooker Creek, he was not simply allocated to the djangala subsection and given any nungarai as a wife. Instead, he was regarded as the elder brother of his sponsor, who was his junior and happened to be a djangala, and was offered a particular "m.m.b.d.d." whom his sponsor could have married. It is clear, then, that the Walbiri do not view the "classification" of relatives in the same way as they regard the "classification" of subsection members.

In order to support my contention that, in making important decisions, the people think in terms of genealogy and community and not of subsection affiliation, I shall present a detailed case-history of the behaviour involved in a dispute over the disposal of two women in marriage.

Malu djagamara died when his son, Louis djuburula, was a lad, and Minyana, Malu's brother and Ngalia countryman, acted as Louis' foster-father. Romeo djuburula, Minyana's son, and Louis became close friends and often camped and hunted together. They worked at the Hatches Creek wolfram mines during the war years and moved to Yuendumu in 1946.

Louis had been circumcised by a "sister's son" and countryman, the djabangari father (now dead) of Polly and Yma nabanangga, who had given him Polly (a "m.m.b.d.d.") to "grow up" as a wife. Later, Louis negotiated with another "sister's son" and countryman, the djabangari father of Milly nabanangga, and received her as his second wife. Then Polly's father gave him Yma as a third wife, but, as Romeo had not yet received a wife from his own circumciser, another djabangari "sister's son" and countryman, Louis charitably handed Yma on to him. Soon afterwards, Romeo acquired Minnie nabanangga, the wife due to him, but also retained Yma. Finally, Louis arranged with Minora djabangari, Milly's father's brother, to receive Elizabeth nabanangga as another wife. Elizabeth was the daughter of Minora's wife, Ruby nambidjimba, by a previous husband who was the father's brother of Polly. During the time Romeo and Louis had camped and worked together, they had often exchanged wives temporarily.

In 1949 or 1950 Romeo became insane and was taken from Yuendumu to the Alice Springs hospital for observation and treatment. He returned to Yuendumu some months later, apparently cured. Louis told me that Romeo had several times before behaved similarly, and his description of Romeo's behaviour was of a manic-depressive syndrome. In 1952 Louis and Romeo and their five wives were in the large party of Walbiri sent to

Hooker Creek. Within a few months Romeo again lapsed into a depressed state, which culminated during Easter 1953 in a violent outburst. He assaulted several men for no apparent reason and, when placed under restraint, attempted to commit suicide. He was sent to the Darwin hospital and, following a diagnosis of insanity, was taken to Alice Springs. When Romeo left Hooker Creek, Louis brought Yma and Minnie into his own camp and treated them as his own wives. At the time, he and other interested men asserted that he did this solely to protect the women, whom he would relinquish when Romeo came back.

By May 1953, however, some of the men were ready to accept the superintendent's statement that Romeo was unlikely to return—a contingency that would radically alter the status of his wives. If he had withdrawn permanently from the society, he was "dead" and his "widows" would have to remarry. Louis would have none of this view; Romeo had come back before, he said, and would do so again. Although fraternal affection partly determined Louis' attitude, he also knew he could not admit openly that Romeo was "dead", for the levirate would then operate to his disadvantage. A widow should be given to the deceased's "junior brother", and Louis was Romeo's senior brother. Moreover, in the people's eyes, Louis was Romeo's own brother; and a man should not accept his own brother's widows lest their presence revive the keen grief he must feel for the dead man.

Soon most of Louis' countrymen overtly opposed his keeping the two women. Although some were genuinely concerned at his flouting convention, others simply envied him his five wives. Not even the old men, they said, had more than three wives each. Yarry djabangari, a junior half-brother of Milly's late father and of Minora, the step-father of Polly, Yma and Elizabeth, became the informal leader of Louis' critics. They not only included the countrymen who hoped to marry the women in question but also those who simply wanted to see fair play.

Two men in particular stood to gain if Louis relinquished Romeo's wives. Paddy djuburula, a countryman and distant junior brother of Louis, was the "M.M.B.D.S." of Yma and Minnie. Although he had a wife, she was much older than he and was an economic dependant rather than an asset to him;

he therefore needed another wife. Charlie djuburula, the junior half-brother of Romeo, was a bachelor whose betrothed was only three years old. Although in theory he was too closely related to Romeo to receive one of the women, the men who wished to embarrass Louis were ready to overlook this obstacle. Indeed, Yarry soon devised a plan to meet the problem. He demanded that Louis give up his youngest wife, 12-years-old Elizabeth, who, he argued, was really too immature for sexual intercourse; her services were thus unnecessary to a man with four adult wives. If Louis surrendered Elizabeth, no stigma of widowhood would bar her from either Charlie and Paddy, and he could then retain Yma and Minnie. But Louis stubbornly refused to accept this compromise, and he and Yarry came to blows.

Already I had been told repeatedly that the whole affair legitimately concerned only the Ngalia people in the camp. Members of other communities had no rights in the dispute, for none of them was in any way a "marriage boss" of the two women. Thus, neither old Danny djungarai, their distant Waneiga "M.M.B.", nor Ginger djabangari, their distant Waneiga "father", could dictate their disposal. Yarry djabangari, on the other hand, was in a strong position. Not only was he both a countryman and a close father of the disputed women (being a half-brother of their step-father), but his own wife's brother, Silent djambidjimba, was also their close mother's brother; that is to say, Yarry had married into their matriline. This gave him an advantage over his own half-brother, Donny, whose wives came from a different matriline, and even over old Mick, the women's step-father's brother. Moreover, Mick lacked the personal drive necessary to maintain pressure on Louis and would have been no match for him in a fight.

Yarry's status had been clearly indicated in an earlier and unrelated quarrel. Wagulgari djungarai had assaulted Yma when she reprimanded him for stealing food from Louis' camp. Yarry had defended her and thrashed Wagulgari, with no assistance from either Donny or Mick. Wagulgari's father, Wally djabaldjari, had in turn attacked Yarry, splitting his head and breaking one of his fingers. Yarry then split old Wally's head open and left him badly shaken. This fight accounted for Wally's vacillation in the subsequent arguments over the women.

Silent, the uncle of Yma and Minnie, was not a forceful person, although his quietness could be deceptive; despite his status as close mother's brother, he was content to let Yarry do most of the shouting. Two other young men, Norman and Long Jim djambidjimba, were not of the women's matriline but were involved as their countrymen and fairly close "mother's brothers". Windy and Larry djungarai were also concerned, but only as countrymen; although they were "M.M.B.", they were of another matriline. Jack djagamara and his wife's brother, Wally djabaldjari, were countrymen and the close "father" and "mother's brother" respectively of the disputing djuburula men.

Meanwhile another dispute had broken out in the camp. Windy djungarai, who was married to his "m.b.d.", Kitty naburula, tired of her constant nagging and announced that he would take a second wife, his widowed "m.m.b.d.d.", Joan nangala. Two of the latter's co-widows had already been given to old Danny djungarai, the countryman and "brother" of their late husband; but Joan had remained for about nine months in the widows' camp, during which time Windy had occasionally slept with her. A few men grumbled at Windy's announcement, for he was not a countryman of the dead djungarai man, but most approved the proposed marriage. They knew that Joan had previously been the mistress of her distant "son", Alec II djabaldjari, and they were now anxious to see her safely married to a suitable "M.M.B.D.S."

A few days after Louis and Yarry had fought for the first time, the hawker paid a visit to Hooker Creek. He wished to engage a married couple to work for him at Top Springs, so Kitty, seeing an opportunity to separate Windy from Joan, applied for the job. She had already asserted publicly that Joan had been performing sorcery to make her ill and that she feared to remain in the camp. But, despite her appeals, Windy refused to go with the hawker. Hurt and indignant, Kitty took her child and moved to the widows' camp. Next day, when Windy again told her that he intended to marry Joan, Kitty upbraided him and belaboured Joan with a club. Alec II, angered by the loss of his ex-mistress, also joined in and split open Joan's head.

Throughout this dispute, Kitty's comments indicated that, as Windy's "m.b.d.", she felt her marital status to be quite insecure. She was merely an "alternative" wife, and she feared that public opinion would support Windy's desire for a "preferred" wife or "m.m.b.d.d." A temporary reconciliation followed Kitty's fight with Joan, chiefly because Windy did not wish his little daughter, Topsy, to live in the widows' camp. He brought Kitty back to his camp and offered to postpone making a decision about Joan. But, within a fortnight, he was once more sleeping with Joan; and the two women fought again. Joan received a broken finger and Kitty a split head. Kitty moved to the widows' camp, and Joan entered Windy's camp as his wife. A few days later, Jack djagamara and Wally djabaldjari, the countrymen and close father and mother's brother respectively of Kitty, gave her in marriage to Comedy djabanangga, her unmarried "M.M.B.D.S." and countryman. Kitty's daughter went with her.

This rearrangement of women again focused public attention on the wives of Louis djuburula. Kitty was a close sister and countrywoman of Charlie djuburula and, when she married Comedy, Charlie asked for one of Comedy's close sisters in return —in particular, he wanted Louis' wife, Milly, with whom he had had an affair in the past. He could not have made a more unfortunate choice. Milly was not only Louis' favourite wife but was also the mother of his only child, Della, on whom he doted. Louis naturally rejected Charlie's demand and, when Charlie threatened to spear Louis, Milly's "fathers", Yarry and Donny djabangari, intervened to warn him off. Although they privately sympathized with Charlie, they could not openly support his show of force nor his selection of the only mother among Louis' wives. Indeed, Milly herself did not wish to join Charlie. When she said so, Netta, the wife of Jack djagamara and the close mother of Charlie, at once attacked her for not favouring Charlie. She broke Milly's hand and received a split head in return. Alec II promptly took advantage of the general confusion to thrash his ex-mistress, Joan, once more to punish her for deserting him. Windy retaliated but did him no serious harm.

An uneasy peace followed the fights. Kitty several times stated that she wished to return to Windy. Although Comedy was a handsome and dignified young man, kind and attentive to Kitty and her daughter, and was also her "proper" husband, Kitty found the ties of her earlier marriage were still strong. Her "marriage bosses", however, ordered her to remain with Comedy. Windy in any case was now satisfied with the taciturn Joan and had no desire to listen again to Kitty's nagging. Occasionally old Danny djungarai, who had acquired both of Joan's co-widows, made a disturbance by ordering Windy to hand Joan over to him; but, as Danny was too old to support his unreasonable demands with force, Windy simply ignored the outbursts.

By now Louis had openly claimed Yma and Minnie as his jural wives and asserted that he would not surrender them. Consequently, many men who had earlier regarded Romeo as dead now hoped that he would return and spear Louis for his presumption. Then in August Louis made a move nicely calculated to detach at least one man from the ranks of his opponents. In the widows' camp dwelt Rosie naburula, whose husband had gone to Yuendumu and left her and her seven-years-old daughter, Florrie, temporarily under the protection of her close brother, Louis. Florrie was already betrothed to Silent, the mother's brother of Yma and Minnie, so Louis (quite legitimately) urged Rosie to send the girl to Silent at once. By thus anticipating Silent's request, Louis hoped to place him under a debt of gratitude and gain his support in the dispute. His action did in fact keep Silent more or less neutral in the interminable discussions still in progress.

At this stage of the dispute, Louis was advancing a number of arguments to justify his retention of the two women:

(a) When Romeo had been removed, he had freely "given" the women to Louis. (As Romeo was insane and under restraint for several days before his departure, this seems improbable.)

(b) Wally and Larry, the women's countrymen, had advised Louis to keep the women. (Wally had certainly done so, just as he had pressed Yarry to act against Louis. Disliking both men, he was ready to say anything that would keep the quarrel alive. His close son, Larry, half-heartedly supported Louis, for he had not forgiven Yarry's earlier attack on old Wally.)

(c) The women's close mother's brothers had told Louis to retain the women. (This was true; Silent was under an obligation to Louis, while both Norman and Long Jim disapproved of the frequency with which Yarry beat his own wives, who were their close sisters.)

(*d*) Mick, a close father of the women, had supported Louis' claim. (Unfortunately for Louis, Mick's opinions varied with his audiences, and he had just as readily assured Yarry that Louis had no right to the women.)

(*e*) Louis and Romeo had regularly exchanged wives in the past. (This fact was simply irrelevant to the question of the permanent disposal of the women.)

(*f*) Yma had once been Louis' own wife and he had given her freely to Romeo. (For most men, this was the strongest basis of Louis' claim.)

Yarry, as the spokesman for the opposition, put forward a number of counter arguments:

(*a*) If Romeo was "dead", Louis was obviously too close a brother to receive the women through the levirate. (Most men agreed that this was an important consideration.)

(*b*) If Romeo was not "dead", his wives should live chastely in the widows' camp until he returned. (This was Yarry's own re-interpretation of customary procedure to meet a novel situation; few men accepted it.)

(*c*) As it seemed unlikely that Romeo would return, the women should be given to his "younger brothers", Charlie and Paddy, who were in need of active, adult wives. (This was also a strong argument.)

(*d*) The opinions of Silent, Norman and Long Jim had no force, for there were closer mother's brothers of the women living at Yuendumu. (Yarry was on shaky ground here. Not only was Silent a very close uncle, but also, in the absence of any actual mother's brothers, all three men did have the right to discuss the women's disposal.)

(*e*) As close fathers, Yarry and Donny had as much authority over the women as did Mick and Minora. (This was true of Yarry, but not of Donny.)

(*f*) Irrespective of all other considerations, Louis should not have had five wives; this was too many for any man.

Many of the men were by this time wearying of the dispute, and Yarry feared that he would lose their tacit support. So, to revive their interest, he personally took the quarrel to Louis. After a noisy argument that lasted all one night, Yarry challenged him to a public duel. Onlookers were unsure what Yarry hoped to achieve by this; but they all agreed that, whoever won, Yarry could not in clear conscience pursue his vendetta if he wounded Louis. Louis was eager to capitalize on Yarry's tactical error and next day came heavily armed to one side of the general camp. Yarry, similarly armed, appeared at the other side.

All the women and children had been sent away; the other men sat talking in the middle of the camp and ostentatiously ignored the combatants. After a pregnant silence, Yarry burst into a long tirade, in which he touched on Louis' sexual habits and immoral behaviour, while he extolled the purity of his own motives. Louis replied in similar vein but with a humour that drew chuckles from the audience. As Yarry's anger mounted, everyone took cover. He then hurled boomerangs at Louis and narrowly missed him. Quick to put Yarry at a disadvantage, Louis did not retaliate; but his distant "mother's brother", slow-witted Jimmy djabaldjari, marred the effect of this shrewd self-restraint by throwing a boomerang at Yarry and hitting Alec I djabaldjari in error. Incensed, Alec returned the blow, and everyone was swept into the confused brawl that erupted.

Louis' moderation on this occasion had gained him some sympathy, but his stubborn determination to keep five wives still galled many men. Yarry realized that, although he had lost ground by demanding the abortive duel, he could still exert a certain amount of pressure on Louis. The general attitude in the camp now was that Louis should relinquish one of his wives, so that public opinion would prevent Yarry from carrying on the dispute.

Meanwhile, Louis was having domestic troubles. Emboldened by his general unpopularity, Charlie, Paddy and Jim Tulum djuburula took every opportunity to copulate with his wives— Charlie with Milly, Paddy with Minnie, and Jim with Yma. Louis could not watch all the women simultaneously and, as he knew what was afoot, he daily grew more morose. The fact that everyone was aware of the situation and did not trouble to hide their smiles added to his discomfort. Moreover, Yma and Minnie had been growing less willing to be members of a group of five co-wives, so that Louis' uncertain temper simply increased their desire to find other husbands.

Up to this point, none of the men in the dispute had bothered to consult the opinions of the women concerned; such an action would have been foreign to the accepted way of arranging marriages. Consequently, the next episode in the chain of events startled everyone. The five wives of Louis simply took up their swags and moved to the widows' camp, announcing that they were tired of the whole affair and would remain with the widows until they had decided what they wanted to do. All the men were quite at a loss, for, as they told me ruefully, this sort of thing had never happened before. Indeed, they saw the "revolt" as a direct attack on male prestige. Had there been no European authority present to shield the women, the latter would have been thrashed into submission; but, as it was, all the men, even including Yarry, found themselves supporting Louis' attempts to induce the women to return to his camp.

Within a few days, however, the rebels' solidarity had weakened to the extent that Polly and Elizabeth visited Louis' camp to cook his food and to sleep with him. The other three women, having lovers, were content to remain in the widows' camp. Wally and Mick then urged Louis to give up Milly and, if necessssary, Minnie, while they tried to persuade Yma to rejoin him. Louis flatly refused to do this; he wanted his daughter, Della, to return with Milly. He seemed also to place greater reliance on the efficacy of the love-magic he was performing in the bush than on the success of human intervention.

It was now October, and public attention was diverted from Louis' problems by the preparations for the opening ceremonies connected with the circumcision of two djabanangga boys, the sons of Yarry and Mick. As all the djuburula men concerned in the dispute over the women were the close "sister's husbands" of the novices, they were deeply involved in these ceremonies and had little opportunity for argument. Indeed, quarrelling would have been most improper in these circumstances, a fact that the ritual "bosses" of the boys clearly had in mind when they organized the lads' seclusion.

By the time the circumcision ceremonies had concluded, all of Louis' wives were again residing in his camp, although three of them still met their lovers regularly in the bush. Louis began one inconclusive fight with Jim Tulum over the latter's association with Yma, but, deciding that three half-loaves were better than none, he did not go on with the matter. A few days later, however, when Yma returned from another tryst with Tulum (who was then tailing cattle), she was savagely beaten by Big Polly, the wife of Romeo's father's brother, Jack djagamara. Big Polly asserted that Romeo would one day come home; until then Yma and Minnie should live chastely in the widows' camp. Yma was badly knocked about in this encounter; but Louis took no overt action. Instead, he slipped into the camp of the absent Tulum and seduced the latter's young wife, Nellie, who was also his "m.m.b.d.d." A noisy argument followed when Tulum learned of this, but he did not attack Louis. He considered his liaison with Yma to be adequate compensation.

Shortly after this affair, Milly discovered that she was pregnant. Although everyone in the camp was sure that Charlie was the father, Louis, desirous of more children, said nothing. Childless Polly, who had generally stood by Louis in his troubles, envied Milly's good fortune and was angered by Louis' complacent acceptance of the situation. She therefore thrashed Milly with a club and, when Louis intervened, turned on him and broke his forearm. He made very little fuss about his injury, for he did not wish to antagonize Polly further. But, from then on, she spent more time in the widows' camp than she did with Louis.

In November a working party that included Paddy djuburula camped for several weeks at the Seven Miles Bore to cut fence-posts. In its absence Louis at last decided he could no longer tolerate his unhappy domestic arrangements. He publicly withdrew his claim to Minnie and sent her to live in the widows' camp. Charlie djuburula, who now realized that he had little hope of detaching Milly permanently from Louis, promptly severed his association with her and made Minnie his mistress. At the same time he announced that he wished to marry Minnie. While Yarry, Donny, Mick, Silent and the other interested men were debating his request, Paddy returned from the bore. He was furious when he found that he had been forestalled, and he kept up a running argument with Charlie for days. This culminated in a bloody duel with knives.

Yarry, as a close father of the disputed woman, intervened on Paddy's behalf, for he had borne a grudge against Charlie for some time. Charlie had been a ritual guardian during the recent seclusion of Yarry's son, and it was strongly suspected that he had practised sodomy with the boy. As definite evidence was lacking, Yarry had simply berated Charlie, whose mother's brother, Wally djabaldjari, had also beaten him with a boomerang. Now, when Paddy and Charlie began to fight, Yarry tried to spear the latter. Silent, Minnie's close mother's brother and Charlie's friend, protected Charlie from Yarry, whereupon Comedy, Yarry's close son, broke Silent's arm with a boomerang. All the countrymen then joined in the fight—including Rosie and Kitty naburula, who split open Minnie's head as punishment for causing trouble between their close brothers.

Charlie and Paddy, meanwhile, had hacked each other's back and shoulders to ribbons, until both had collapsed, exhausted. As each had drawn blood in great quantities, their dispute was ended; so they sat peacefully side by side and watched the rest of their countrymen brawl around them. The genuineness of their reconciliation was indicated later when Paddy publicly supported Charlie's demand for Minnie. Yarry then did not oppose the request; he regarded his vendetta with Louis as more important than his grudge against Charlie. Within a month, Minnie was installed in Charlie's camp as his wife.

Louis had carefully kept out of these quarrels, and his next action was to negotiate with old William djuburula for a temporary exchange of wives. Polly, who objected to being one of four co-wives, had been spending more time in the widows' camp. This was largely a matter of principle with her, for she had no lover. Louis, therefore, suggested that she live with William for a few weeks. In his camp she would be one of only two co-wives. Polly agreed, and William gave Louis his senior wife, Melba, in return. In this way Louis made it unlikely that Polly's discontent would lead her to take a lover, but at the same time he retained his jural claim on her. In addition, he acquired the dubious privilege of sleeping with Melba, who, by Walbiri standards, was extraordinarily ugly. The arrangement lasted for about three weeks, when Polly said she wanted to return to Louis. I do not know whether Louis counted on Polly's revulsion from the older man sending her back to him and not to the widows' camp, but I suspect that he did. He was a very shrewd man.

By January 1954 a position had been reached that was unchanged when I left Hooker Creek in March. Kitty and Comedy, Windy and Joan, and Charlie and Minnie were legally married. Milly and Elizabeth resided with Louis and had no lovers. Polly, also without a lover, alternated between Louis' camp and that of the widows, despite his attempts to induce her to remain with him permanently. Yma lived in Louis' camp, but she continued her covert association with Jim Tulum. Louis knew of this, and the two men frequently quarrelled. All the countrymen of Louis who had previously busied themselves with his affairs now elaborately ignored his problems. Having forced him to relinquish one of the women, they were content to let matters rest for a time. But I have no doubt that, using the same technique of attrition, they later managed to detach either Polly or Yma from his menage.

This history has several interesting aspects. It clearly illustrates the virtual absence of private life in an Aboriginal community and indicates how mechanisms of social control operate when a person flouts convention but does not transgress basic laws. Louis' countrymen were not aiming to punish him formally; they merely wished to bring him back into line with the group. Notice how the chain of events appeared to trail off inconclusively. This was precisely what Louis' critics desired, for it left the way open for them to renew the pressure on him whenever they chose to do so. None wanted a cut-and-dried settlement of the dispute.

But what is most to the point here is the demonstration of the way in which the Walbiri take genealogical connection and community affiliation to be the significant determinants of the exercise of authority in general and of marriage arrangements in particular. Kinship provides the framework within which wives are selected and, in conjunction with community membership, defines the people who have the right to allocate specific women as those wives. Thus, throughout the protracted and complicated manoeuvrings I have just described, none of the protagonists tried to justify his actions by invoking subsection affiliation, nor were any of the relevant rules and conventions ever formulated in such terms.

The disposal of the women was disputed because they were the "m.m.b.d.d." of certain men, not because they were of the nabanangga subsection. Other men claimed authority over them because they were close fathers and mother's brothers, as well as countrymen, of the women, not because they were djabangari or djambidjimba. For the same reasons, outsiders, who themselves included djabangari and djambidjimba, regarded the men's claims as valid. Contrary to Lawrence's assertions (1937, p. 339), the people did not consider "the distinction between control of marriage by kinship and control by section or subsection" to be "secondary or trifling".

It is true that, in casual conversation, men may employ subsection terminology to summarize marriage rules and kinship connections. They often do so when talking to Europeans, who, they assume, are too stupid to understand finer discriminations. But, if they speak in this way to other Aborigines, they know that their audience is aware of the qualifications implicit in this usage, qualifications that are immediately made explicit when a difference of opinion arises. Thus, a man may characterize marriage rules in the following terms: djangala gives nambidjimba to djabangari, and their children are djabanangga; djabangari gives nabanangga to djuburula, and their children are djagamara; and so on. Should nambidjimba go to another "skin" than djabangari, her children remain djabanangga, for their father is "thrown away".

On closer enquiry, however, the men always rephrase the statement in genealogical terms: a man should give his *jundalba* (daughter) to her "proper" husband *galjagalja* ("M.M.B.D.S."), and her children are her own father's *djamiri* (daughter's children). Should the *jundalba* cohabit with another man, her children are still her father's *djamiri*. If, for instance, the woman has a son by her *maliri* ("M.M.B.S."), her father calls the boy *djamiri* and not *maliri* ("M.M.B.S.S.S."), she calls the boy ŋuniari (son) and not *mindiri* ("M.M.B.S.S."), and the genitor calls him *jabala* ("M.B.D.D.S.") and not ŋalabi (son). That is to say, the convention that the father is "thrown away" when determining subsection affiliation is for the Walbiri simply an expression of the basic rule that the mother is an unequivocal point of reference in the kinship system. In the same way, relative seniority is ascribed to "siblings" and to "brothers-in-law" in terms of the relative seniority of their mothers.

The rule is never set aside for purely social reasons, although it may be ignored on rare occasions for ritual purposes. The allocation of subsection and kinship terms to all the Walbiri half-castes whom I encountered, for instance, always "followed the mother". On the other hand, if a man contracts an improper union, so that his son is born into the opposite patrimoiety, the men of the father's patriline may alter the boy's subsection and kinship category in order to bring him back into his father's patrimoiety and make him eligible to participate in the father's dreaming ceremonies.

The matrimoieties formed by the combination of subsections further summarize marriage rules and kinship categories, and they bring together a set of matrilines into one matrimoiety and their reciprocal marriage matrilines into the other. The Walbiri are aware that maternal descent cycles regularly through the subsections comprising each matrimoiety, and they consider this to be an interesting but not particularly significant feature of the system. Men at Hooker Creek sometimes drew diagrams in the sand for me and pointed out the matricycles, likening them to the revolution of the vanes on the settlement windmill. Using the same diagrams, they also demonstrated how subsections may form patrimoieties and how patrimoiety affiliation oscillates between the matrimoieties.

The combination of couples of subsections to make up patrimoieties, however, has significance for the men, for it summarizes in a fairly univocal manner their system of classificatory totemism. This differs from the subsection totemism observed, for instance, in the Kimberleys and along the Daly River (Kaberry, 1937, p. 440; Elkin, 1933, p. 96), where particular dreamings are associated solely with each subsection. The Walbiri dreamings are linked primarily with cult-lodges, each of which includes men of two subsections; the one couple of subsections comprises men of several patrilodges and is therefore associated with a number of dreamings.

Behind these arrangements there is again the notion of genealogical connection. A man shares in the kangaroo or the goanna dreaming not merely because he is a djabaldjari, but because his father was a member of that lodge. A djabangari man may participate in these rituals not only because he is in the same patrimoiety, but because he is a M.M.B. and hence "like an elder brother" to some of the actors.

This relationship with cult-lodges gives Walbiri subsections an indirect local reference. Certain localities "belong to" the dreamings of particular lodges within a pair of subsections; but this is a spiritual and not a residential tie. That is to say, unlike the Aranda situation (Spencer and Gillen, 1927, I, p. 354), the couples of subsections are not associated with individual "hordes" and their territories; instead, all the subsections are represented in each of the four local communities. Moreover, as the smaller bands within the community were unstable in size, composition and duration, no consistent relation between these groups and subsections could exist.

Thus, kinship and community provide the framework within which the Walbiri make significant decisions. Subsections summarize these relationships among people and totems and also articulate with them; but, like all summaries, they cannot furnish the basis for the fine discriminations that are required in the solution of important problems.

CHAPTER XI

MOIETIES AND DESCENT LINES

The Walbiri kinship system constitutes a matrix of interconnected statuses, whose correlative roles define the norms to which observed social behaviour more or less conforms. The matrix, however, is not homogeneous. Within it people single out certain statuses as being especially significant and group these in various ways to make subsidiary frameworks, or descent lines, that orient specific sorts of behaviour.

These groupings are in turn aggregated to form more inclusive structural units, the moieties, which also channel behaviour in definite directions. Subsections stand mediately between these two kinds of groupings and derive much of their significance from articulation with them.

Grouped alternate generation-levels. The people believe that subsections were allocated to the two groups of alternate generation-levels as follows: djabangari-djabaldjari-djambidjimba-djagamara by the wedge-tailed eagle, and djangala-djuburula-djungarai-djabanangga by the pink cockatoo. The birds are now the dreamings of the endogamous moieties thus formed, and the relationship between the birds and the moieties is one of classificatory totemism. Neither bird is a prized food, but each is valued for its feathers. Men may kill their own moiety bird, and the moieties *per se* do not perform rituals to maintain the supply of the birds. This is the task of the appropriate patrilodges—of certain djabangari-djabanangga men for the eagle and of djabaldjari-djungarai men for the cockatoo.

Thus, the relationship between totemite and totem in the case of alternate generation-levels is very different from that between lodge member and lodge-dreaming, or that between a person and his conception-dreaming. (It is analogous to the position among the Wolmeri of the Kimberleys, where birds represent the endogamous moieties created by the rainbow-snake; vide Kaberry, 1939, p. 196.)

The Walbiri, like the Pidjandjara to the south, possess reciprocal terms for the moieties comprising the alternate generation-levels. A man refers to all members of his own moiety as *jalbaru-gulaŋu*, "equivalent status—belonging to"; *jalbaru* is also a male term of address and reference for age-mates. Members of the opposite moiety are *ŋauwu-gulaŋu* or *guiju-gari*, "flesh-having". The terms are never used in address; indeed, they are rarely used at all. (Kaberry, 1937, p. 441, observed that the Wolmeri refer to members of the one endogamous moiety as "mates"; Elkin, 1939, p. 212, has noted that a term meaning "your flesh" refers to the opposite endogamous moiety in many South Australian tribes.)

In everyday life the moieties rarely operate as a basis for distinguishing groups of people. Camps, for instance, are not laid out on these lines. Although the existence of the moiety division is compatible with the prohibition on cross-generation marriage, it is never invoked as a criterion of classification in discussions of marriage. Unlike some of their neighbours (vide Kaberry, 1935, p. 38; Elkin, 1937, p. 293; 1939, p. 212; Berndt and Johnston, 1942, p. 192), the Walbiri do not apportion burial and mourning duties in these terms. Rain-making ceremonies do not reflect the groupings. The moiety division may perhaps be implicitly expressed during circumcision ceremonies, when the novice's father, father's sister, mother, and mother's brother are collectively referred to as *julbaru*; but these people do not act as a group. Occasionally, when I commented on the affection displayed between, say, a man and his daughter's son, I was told that this was proper, for they were *jalbaru-gulaŋu*, members of the one endogamous moiety; but no other reason was given for the statement.

The chief function of the endogamous moieties appears to concern the allocation of roles in the few ceremonial activities that are peculiar to women—in particular, in the secret *djarada* and *jauwulju* dancing of the Ngalia women at Yuendumu and Mount Doreen. I did not witness these dances, and it is possible that the moiety division has more ramifications than those indicated by the women who discussed the matter with me. (Kaberry, 1939, p. 175 has reported a similar arrangement of women's rituals in the eastern Kimberleys, and Berndt, 1950, has described women's ceremonial activities in a neighbouring area.)

Ngalia women of each moiety possess in common a collection of decorative patterns, which they paint on their bodies for the dances. Some of these designs I have seen worn at circumcision ceremonies by the mothers, sisters and future mothers-in-law of the novices; they related to such dreamings as rain, whistling duck and rock-wallaby. It is the duty of an informally elected female leader to superintend the women of the opposite moiety as they paint the patterns in ochres and grease on the dancers of her own moiety; to be an efficient superviser, she must have memorized all the patterns belonging to her own moiety.

Apparently the moiety "boss woman" is chosen on the basis of her maturity, knowledge of the designs, songs and dances, her organizing ability and her forceful personality. When the current leader is too old or feeble to maintain her position, she nominates her successor, to whom she passes on all her knowledge. My female informants obviously thought that the ritual leaders and duties of the men were similarly apportioned between the endogamous moieties, although in fact they are not.

I could discover no other social behaviour in which these moieties figured as principles of grouping, and there is no evidence to suggest that, in the past, they were any more significant.

Matrimoieties and matrilines. Men often ended a discussion of marriage rules by saying to me that such arrangements were, or expressed, *magunda* and that this accounted for the names borne by the exogamous matrimoieties. A man calls the members of his own matrimoiety *wiarba* or *gundawaŋu,* and those of the opposite matrimoiety *guluwaŋu, gundaŋga,* or *magundawanu.*

It is not easy to translate these terms briefly. The key to their meaning, however, lies in the use of the one term, *gunda-djari,* "to be ashamed", in connection with behaviour towards the mother-in-law as well as with that towards circumcisers, subincisers and ritual friends. This notion of "shame" is most important in Walbiri attitudes.

A youth must avoid his circumciser or subinciser until the ban on their association is formally removed. Should he encounter the operator before then, he would be ashamed and fearful—not only because he was in the presence of the man who had ritually "killed" him, but also because the meeting violated the law. Indeed, I never saw this rule of avoidance broken.

Similarly, a man should never fight with a ritual friend, whether he is *bilarli* or *jualbiri*, and he should always try to halt a fight in which the friend is involved. Consequently, a man who sees the blood of a ritual friend is ashamed and remorseful; he has failed to follow the law and to protect his mate from injury. The strength of this feeling is clearly apparent, even to outsiders.

When Jack and Alec II djabaldjari fought over Doris nagamara, Jack's ritual friend and countryman, Abe djangala, was unable to reach the scene of the fight in time to prevent Jack from being badly wounded, so he retired to the other side of the camp to mourn. He scrupulously avoided Jack on the next day, for, as he told me, he could not bear to look on Jack's wounds. But, on the following day, Jack was forced to discuss an important ceremonial matter with Abe. The conversation, which the men conducted over a distance of 15 to 20 feet, was terminated as quickly as was compatible with intelligibility. Both men kept their heads averted, and Abe, as the junior, obviously suffered agonies of embarrassment. He literally could not stand still but sidled away from Jack until, at the last words, he fairly ran to rejoin the other men. His distress was so patent that I forbore to discuss the matter for some time. When at last I did so, Abe repeatedly referred to the shame he had felt on seeing the congealed blood that still adhered to Jack's wounds.

I soon learned that a man reacts affectively in the same way to a chance encounter with his wife's mother, who is in fact referred to as *gadjin*, or "shame". Not only does the contact in itself distress him, but he is also fearful and remorseful, for he has broken a fundamental rule of avoidance. Similar feelings, although of reduced intensity, are caused by meetings with classificatory "mothers-in-law". I could well understand, then, why an old man would literally jump in the air and flee when he came across a "wife's mother", no matter how young she was.

We can now better comprehend the reciprocal matrimoiety names. A man's opposite matrimoiety includes his actual and classificatory mothers-in-law. It is therefore *gunda-ŋga*, "the location of shame", or *magunda-wanu*, "the origin of shame". His own matrimoiety, by contrast, is *magunda-waŋu*, "lacking shame". The opposite moiety is also called *gulu-waŋu*, "without anger"; the man should remain on good terms with his wife's matrikin, for they gave him the woman and, in some circumstances, could take her back again. The term *wiarba* is used only rarely in reference to the man's own matrimoiety, and its relevance is not clear to me. In everyday usage, it is also an expression of sorrow or sympathy; applied to the speaker's matrimoiety, it may perhaps refer indirectly to the duties of the members at the death of a fellow.

Men employ *gundaŋga*, the term most often heard, to refer to all members of the opposite matrimoiety, but as a term of address for the men only. Moreover, it is rarely used in address outside "joking" situations. Thus, if a man is engaged in a friendly scuffle with one of the other matrimoiety, or makes mock attacks on him with weapons, men of the latter's moiety laugh and shout, *gundaŋga! guluwaŋu!*—that is, "he is of your wife's matrimoiety, so do not lose your temper!" Although the women know of all these terms, they do not use them.

At first sight, this evidence might suggest that the matrimoieties and, by implication, the subsections are the important regulators of marriage; but further observation and questioning reveal that the matrilines within matrimoieties are much more significant. As the men themselves put it: whereas the opposite matrimoiety is *magunda* for a man, his wife's own matriline is *magundawanu djuŋa*, "the true source of shame", for it is his *djuraldja* or marriage line.

The people who make up a matriline share a common spirit. Although, like a lodge patrispirit, it is called *bilirba*, the matrispirit does not represent any particular natural species or object and has no other title to distinguish it from the spirits shared by members of other matrilines. It is regarded as a non-material, pallid, tiny "child" that resides either in a woman's uterus or behind her navel. When she is pregnant, a part of her matrispirit transfers to the foetus, where it becomes a double of the parent spirit. A man's matrispirit is located in his kidney-fat.

At death, the spirit becomes a *manbaraba*, an ethereal, pale ghost, whose features resemble those of its previous owner. It hovers near the tree-platform that supports the corpse until the death is avenged. It then dissipates.

Despite the absence of an identifying name, the matrispirit of each matriline is thought to be distinct from the others; there is no general matrispirit or totem belonging to the matrimoiety as a whole.

The possession of a common matrispirit is given as a reason for prohibiting marriage with one's own m.b.d. or m.m.b.d.d. A man's mother's brother and M.M.B. share the one spirit with him and his mother, and they are therefore "too close" to provide wives for him. The mother's brother so resembles the mother that his daughter is like a half-sibling; the M.M.B. is the same as an elder brother, so that his daughter's daughter is like one's own daughter's daughter.

The Walbiri theory of matrispirits resembles in some ways the secular, matriclan, ŋulu totemism that Stanner (1936, p. 196) observed diffusing from the Mudbura to the Murinbata of Port Keats. In Walbiri the word ŋulu means "vegetable seed", but I did not hear it used in connection with conception or with matrispirits. Moreover, the northern ŋulu totems are natural species; the Walbiri matrispirits are not. On the other hand, Stanner reported that Murinbata men owe assistance and friendship to ŋulu clansmen; the Walbiri stress the solidarity of the matriline at the betrothal or death of a member. The Murinbata postulate a physical similarity among ŋulu clansmen; the Walbiri take possession of one matrispirit to explain observed physical and temperamental likenesses between a woman and her children. It seems possible, then, that the Walbiri belief in matrispirits is historically connected with the ŋulu beliefs of the neighbouring Mudbara, Djingili and Warramunga.

It is difficult to estimate the average number of individuals comprising a matriline that a set of siblings regards as distinct from other such lines. The matrilines do not constitute easily identified local units. As marriages were made between the communities as well as within them, in the past the personnel of a man's matriline might be scattered through the whole tribal area and were likely to act as a group only during circumcision ceremonies, in disputes over betrothal or marriage, and at the death of an adult member.

Nowadays, the population movements that have followed the establishment of widely separated settlements make it even more difficult for the members of a matriline to assemble on such occasions. Consequently, I could not make accurate counts of the people who should have been present at these gatherings. I was forced to rely to a large extent on statements from informants as to who should have participated, and I found that a person could rarely number accurately in their absence all the members of his matriline.

In ordinary discussion and in everyday behaviour, little distinction is made between the members of a man's matriline and all his maternal kin who are also countrymen; but, when the matriline functions on significant occasions, it is singled out as a separate group, whose collateral limits tend to be set at the range of the matrilateral parallel cousins of the central figure —it includes his "close siblings". The restriction on size is connected with the shallow time-depth of known genealogies (five generations at most), which in turn is partly determined by the people's deep-seated reluctance to refer to dead relatives.

Thus, men were rarely sure of details of genealogy in their grandparents' generation-level, and they often had difficulty in distinguishing the m.m.sr. descendants from those of close "m.m.sr." In particular situations, however, the matriline tends to be defined as the group that includes the M.M.B., mother's mother, mother's mother's children, m.m.d. children, m.m.d.d. children and the m.m.d.d.d. children.

The fact that matrispirits lack individual names also facilitates continual fission of matrilines; there is no distinctive symbol to function as a permanent record of previous matriline affiliation. We might expect, therefore, that matrilines would be small; and the average membership does tend to be about 30 or less. Of these people, only about 10 (the M.M.B., mother's brothers, M.Sr.S., and brothers) are of particular social significance to a mature man. This figure agrees with the "ideal" accounts I received of activities related to death, inquest and revenge, and to circumcisions and betrothals in pre-settlement days.

About 40 or so distinct matrilines can be referred to actual people within the tribe; there are the lines of a man's own M.M.B., mother's father, father's father, and F.M.B., and those of separate sets of "M.M.B.", "mother's fathers", "father's fathers", and "F.M.B." As only the matrilines of a man's "mother's fathers" are potential wife-givers, his choice of spouses is necessarily limited.

The people summarily state the role of the matriline in marriage as follows: "the M.M.B. should control a person's betrothal." Thus, although a boy's father and father's father are concerned in sanctioning his circumcision and subsequent initiation into their cult-lodge, his M.M.B. not only has a voice in this discussion (being of the same patrimoiety) but also advises the lad's father and mother's brother on the selection of a circumciser and, consequently, on the choice of the matriline of the boy's future wife. Similarly, although a girl's father has an important role in her betrothal (for he must meet his own obligations as a circumciser), he may not ignore the opinions of her mother's brother and M.M.B. As one man expressed the relationship to me: "the father and father's father have authority over the boy in the lodge (*banba*) line. The M.M.B. and mother's brother have authority in his betrothal, and his lodge line should be content with the latter's decision. One line supervises the dreaming matters; the other superintends the betrothal matters. This division makes quarrelling unlikely."

A woman's own matriline is, in effect, of the greatest significance to her, for its men actively give her in marriage and protect her rights thereafter. Although her father is also concerned, it is as an individual, apart from his own matri- or patri-line. Conversely, a man is more concerned with the matriline from which he receives a wife, for it should ensure that he honours his obligations to her. This matriline the man calls *djuraldja*, but as the woman's father also has a say in her betrothal, he too, is referred to by this term.

At first sight there appear to be only four matrilines of descent in the kinship structure that are terminologically recognized in the second ascending generation—those of the father's mother, mother's mother, f.f.sr., and m.f.sr. In fact, however, the matriline of the mother's father is clearly distinguished both in terminology and behaviour from that of the "mother's father" who is also the wife's M.M.B. Thus, there are five types of matrilines of descent. Correlatively, there is a fifth patriline discriminated in addition to those obviously descending from the father's father, mother's father, F.M.B., and M.M.B.—that of the "M.M.B." who is also the wife's mother's father.

The discussion in anthropological journals of the kinship system of the Murngin peoples of Arnhem Land has shown that there the three matri- and patri-lines descending from the father's father, mother's father (who is also the F.M.B.), and M.M.B. are extended by a clear distinction between the mother's father and the wife's M.M.B. (vide Elkin, 1953, and Berndt, 1955, for the relevant references). Much earlier, Elkin (1954, p. 77) had pointed out that the Karadjeri of the Kimberleys, who like the Murngin have preferred matrilateral cross-cousin marriage, also recognize a fourth line, that of the W.M.M.B., in addition to those of the father's father, mother's father, and M.M.B.

An analogous arrangement is found among the Arabana of South Australia. Spencer and Gillen (1899, p. 59) had noted that these people distinguished terminologically three lines of descent in the second ascending generation—those of the mother's father, father's father (who is also M.M.B.), and F.M.B. Elkin (1938, p. 438) later confirmed this but also demonstrated that the F.F.S. is in fact separated from the M.M.B.S. who is W.M.B.; that is, an extra line of descent appears in the first ascending generation.

Thus, in all four societies (including that of the Walbiri), the importance of specifying in genealogical terms the status of desirable affines is reflected in the recognition of extra lines of descent in the kinship system. It seems likely that a re-examination of the systems of other Australian tribes will reveal similar arrangements.

In a structural sense, intermarriage between a pair of Walbiri matrilines involves the men in an exchange of "sisters" (although the wife one man receives may in fact be his sr.h.m.sr.d. and not his sr.h.sr.). That is to say, a man and his wife's brother (who is his sister's husband) are reciprocally *djuraldja*; the former's W.M.M.B. is also his "mother's father", just as his M.M.B. is the "mother's father" of the latter.

Diagram 6 illustrates the way in which the operation of circumcision, ritual guardianship and betrothal bind intersecting reciprocal marriage lines together. The asymmetry of the diagram is intentional. A man's descending matriline is of significance to him in that he becomes *djuraldja* to the "daughter's son" who marries his own sr.d.d. His own *djuraldja* line (his wife's brother's matriline) is less important to him below the point of intersection created by his own or his sibling's marriage. He is concerned with

DIAGRAM 6

Intermarriage between Walbiri matrilines

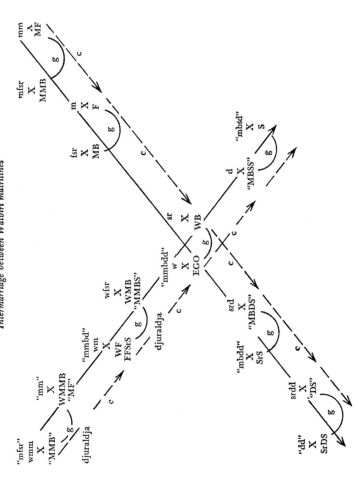

the marriage of his own daughter, but in this he is *djuraldja* to the "M.B.S.S." only by an extension of the title from his own wife's brother. As well as showing how the "exchange of sisters in marriage" expresses the intersection of matrilines, the diagram also makes it clear that actual "niece exchange" (which is practized in some tribes) cannot occur among the Walbiri. A man could repay his W.M.B. for the gift of the latter's niece only by inducing a "wife's brother" to provide a daughter as wife for the W.M.B., or by giving his own sister's daughter to a "W.M.B." who is also a "son's son" of the actual W.M.B.

Usually, a man's marriage lines are implicit in the kinship structure until a wife is selected for him. But, if his sister is already betrothed to a "M.M.B.D.S.", or if his elder brother has married a "m.m.b.d.d.", that particular "m.m.b.d." matriline *ipso facto* becomes a *djuraldja* line on which he has a tacit claim for a wife. Although he is expected to marry into this matriline, he is not forced to do so. Indeed, even if his circumciser was the actual father-in-law of his sister or his elder brother, that man might not have a daughter to give him. The young man may then negotiate with another "wife's father" and "W.M.B." for a bride and so marry into a different *djuraldja* line from that of his sibling. His own circumciser might be able to offer him a daughter later, but he need not accept her.

Thus, in theory, a man may create as many *djuraldja* lines for himself as he has wives but, in practice, he marries into only one or two matrilines. I have pointed out in an earlier chapter that marriages with the wife's sister, half-sister, and parallel cousin comprise about 30 per cent of polygynous unions.

The arrangement of the matrilines precludes the development of a tradition of intermarriage between certain lines. A pair of matrilines can intersect only once in time, when people of the one generation may become spouses and siblings-in-law. On the other hand, the kinship structure permits continual association of particular pairs of patrilines in marriage. A man who wished to renew the link between his lodge line and that of his sister's husband and erstwhile ritual guardian might invite the circumciser of his son's son to come from his own matriline; the young man's wife's brother would then be a F.M.B.S.S. who is F.F.Sr.S.S. The son's son could later arrange for his own W.B.S.S. to be the sister's husband of his own son's son. A man's *djuraldja* matriline would thus be predetermined, even without his siblings' first marrying into it.

Although such arrangements are by no means common and, indeed, are rarely mentioned, their existence is compatible with the fact that the ideal wife is not merely a classificatory "m.m.b.d.d." but is the "m.m.b.d.d." who is also a f.f.sr.s.d.—a specification that considerably limits the number of potential *djuraldja* matrilines a man may possess. The other "m.m.b.d.d.", who are also "sr.s.d.", are in this sense second-preference wives— although still more desired than "m.b.d.", whom I call alternative wives. It may be noted in passing that consistent adherence to such a marriage rule produces what might be regarded as 16 unnamed sub-subsections.

Despite this ideal distinction between fathers-in-law who are F.F.Sr.S. and those who are merely "sister's sons", analysis of a sample of 100 marriages reveals that in fact "sister's sons" out-number actual and classificatory "F.F.Sr.S."

TABLE 18

The kinship category of the wife's father

	"FFSrS"	"SrS"	"MB"	"MF"	"MMBS"	Total
First marriage	21	27	10	2	1	61
Subsequent marriage	8	30	1	–	–	39
Total	29	57	11	2	1	100

chi squared (FFSrS,SrS) $= 5 \cdot 27$, df $= 1$, p $= \cdot 02$

The explanation of this apparent anomaly is as follows: a man's father's father is like an elder brother and the f.f.sr. like an elder sister; hence the F.F.Sr.S. is an "E.Sr.S." Thus, as the preferred father-in-law is a kind of "sister's son", the usual "sister's son" may also be a father-in-law, especially if he belongs to another community. Men are less concerned to distinguish between such distant "F.F.Sr.S." and "sister's sons"; indeed, both could be members of the one patriline and lodge or of the one matriline, a possibility that facilitates their identification.

As we might expect on these grounds, the fathers-in-law that men acquire after their initial marriages tend to be "sister's sons" rather than F.F.Sr.S. (phi coefficient of association $= \cdot 24$). Men are more likely to take subsequent wives from other communities and from "sister's sons", for they are by then old enough to travel about and negotiate privately for the women. Moreover, subsection affiliation may well have some effect here, as the F.F.Sr.S. and the "sister's son" are in the one subsection. Given the tendency for the two kin categories to be merged as a result of the general practice of stressing quasi-fraternal resemblances, the fact of common subsection membership may aid the assimilation.

In a later chapter I shall give a detailed account of the distribution of social duties when a person dies; but here it may be noted that the allocation of roles is largely in terms of matriline and matrimoiety affiliation. (Elkin, 1937, p. 280, and 1938, pp. 50, 74, has described a similar division of funerary activities among the Dieri, Piladapa, Yantruwanta and neighbouring tribes in South Australia.)

Although the members of a matriline may be said to be linked by ceremonial ties when they act at the death of a fellow, the people themselves do not regard these bonds as having the ritual significance of those between members of a patriline. The distinction they make is primarily between social and cult affiliations, between flesh and spirit. A Walbiri man does not inherit ritual objects, knowledge, or status through his matriline. There is, for instance, nothing like the *maduka* totemism of the Dieri and Southern Aranda, wherein a man acquires special privileges in his mother's brother's cult-lodge (Elkin, 1954, p. 150). The ritual interest that the M.M.B. takes in a youth during circumcision and the accompanying ceremonies is connected with his status as an "elder brother"—that is, as a quasi-agnate. An elder brother should help the father and father's father to establish the lad's ritual status, for they are members of the one patrilodge. The M.M.B. may substitute for the elder brother and instruct the youth, because they are both of the same patrimoiety; in this respect, matrimoiety affiliation is irrelevant. Moreover, the interaction has none of the formality of the M.M.B.–Sr.D.S. relationship that Berndt (1955) has described for the tribes of eastern Arnhem Land.

The lack of emphasis on ritual ties among the members has important consequences for the character of the matriline. It is not a localized descent group; indeed, the members need not even reside in the one community country. They differ from the men of a patriline in that they do not assemble regularly to perform ceremonies.

The matriline is in certain respects a corporate group, but it is organized on a contingent basis. That is to say, it functions corporately only at irregular intervals to deal with the betrothals and deaths of its members. Now, Leach, in his analysis of matrilateral cross-cousin marriage, has suggested that "the corporate group of persons who have the most decisive say in bringing about an arranged marriage is always a group of resident males . . . in practice, membership of such groups is defined by descent as well as residence" (1951, p. 24). Stated thus, the generalization does not hold for the Walbiri, among whom marriages may be arranged by men who do not normally reside together but assemble in order to deal with the matter. I suspect, too, that this arrangement exists in other desert tribes, such as the Pintubi, Aluridja and Aranda.

In view of the shallow time-depth and the relative imprecision of definition of these dispersed sets of matrikin, I have hesitated to speak of matrilineages, preferring instead to use the neutral term "matriline". The latter conveys better the implication that what is involved is ideally a descent line, which is not the nucleus of a localized descent group. Moreover, it would be misleading to regard a Walbiri matriline as being "a single legal personality" of the kind, for instance, that some African lineages are (vide Fortes, 1953, p. 25). A person also possesses significant ritual, jural and political statuses apart from those he acquires as a member of a matriline; and the men of a matriline are not necessarily "jurally equal" in the eyes of outsiders. Thus, a man considers his own father and a distant "father", who are of two different matrilines, to be more nearly equivalent in ritual and jural status than are a "father" and a "M.B.S." who are of the same matriline.

Summary. In the previous chapter I said that although subsection affiliation may appear to be the significant determinant of marriage arrangements, closer observation reveals that it is entirely secondary to considerations of genealogical connection. Analogously, whereas the casual remarks of the people might suggest that matrimoiety affiliation alone orients behaviour in betrothal and death, in fact the structural units primarily concerned are the matrilines. And, in turn, specific genealogical relationships single out the particular matriline that is selected to deal with a given betrothal or death.

I also demonstrated the way in which the preoccupation with the definition of the genealogical status of affines involves terminological and behavioural recognition of an additional matriline of descent in the kinship structure. This parallels the discrimination of supernumerary descent lines among the Karadjeri and Murngin tribes. Finally, I indicated that, contrary to Leach's hypothesis, the men who are corporately involved in arranging a marriage need not form a localized descent group. Among the Walbiri, the dispersed matrikin who are required to handle the betrothal or death of a fellow member of the matriline assemble only as the situation arises.

CHAPTER XII

MOIETIES AND DESCENT LINES (Continued)

Patrimoieties and patrilines. On the basis of their encounter with a few Walbiri men who were visiting the Warramunga, Spencer and Gillen (1904, p. 102) asserted that the Walbiri patri-moieties had the same names as the Warramunga patrimoieties —that is, the djabangari-djabanangga-djabaldjari-djungarai sub-sections were called the *uluuru* patrimoiety, and the djambi-djimba-djangala-djagamara-djuburula subsections the *kingilli* moiety. I could not confirm this statement. Instead, I found that the patrimoieties, like the matrimoieties and the merged alter-nate generation-levels, have no absolute titles but are referred to by reciprocal terms.

A man refers to the members of his own patrimoiety as *gira* and to those of the opposite moiety as *gurunulu*. These are not terms of address. The term *gira* means "the fathers and sons"; and the totems that a man calls "father" also belong to his own patrimoiety. The usual pidgin translation of *gira* is "the bosses" —the custodians of the patrimoiety dreamings, the men who per-form the ceremonies to increase these totemic species. The term *gurunulu* may have two meanings: *gurunu-lu*, "those who give the arm-blood for ritual decorations", or *guru-nulu*, "those who may not act in a particular ritual". Phillip Creek men prefer the former translation, Hooker Creek and Yuendumu men the latter.

The choices reflect slightly varying definitions of ritual duties. The Phillip Creek men assert that the donors of arm-blood for a ceremony should not only be members of the opposite patrimoiety to the actors but should also be the close brothers-in-law of the latter. This convention has probably been adopted from the Warramunga at Phillip Creek, who say that ideally the actor's father-in-law should give the arm-blood (vide Spencer and Gillen, 1904, p. 597). In any case, the men themselves often ignored the rule during the *gadjiga* initiation ceremonies that I witnessed at Phillip Creek.

The Walbiri at Hooker Creek and Yuendumu declare that

provision of arm-blood has nothing to do with patrimoiety definition; any initiated man may give blood to decorate the actors,
including the actors themselves. My observations of ceremonies
performed at Hooker Creek confirmed this statement; of the 53
donations of arm-blood that I noted, 26 were by men of the
actors' patrimoieties. The few instances I saw at Yuendumu were
also in line with this.

On this evidence I take the second meaning of *guruŋulu*, those
who may not perform the ritual, to be basic and the first to be
a Warramunga innovation. The usual pidgin translation is apt
—"the working boys", those who make preparations for other
men's ceremonies.

The structural relationship of patrilines to patrimoieties
parallels that of matrilines to matrimoieties; but the people do
not distinguish as sharply between the former as they do between
the latter. The subsections, which are functionally important in
classificatory totemism, form an intermediate category, so that
the relationship involves the patriline, the father-son couple of
subsections or semi-patrimoiety, and the patrimoiety.

Patrimoiety affiliation is in many respects of considerable significance to men for, despite the qualifications imposed by actual
genealogical connection and community membership, many of
the rules governing ritual behaviour are defined in patrimoiety
terms. The practical requirements of ceremonial preparation
and performance are an important factor here. When two or
three actors are to participate in an increase or revelatory ritual,
a dozen or so men have to work for some hours in order to
assemble and prepare the necessary materials, construct the temporary ritual objects and decorate the actors. Were these tasks to
be confined to a few kinsmen of the lodge members performing
the rite, the affair would be inordinately protracted.

Similarly, the ceremonies themselves sometimes require more
initiated men as actors than the relevant lodge can supply. Other
men of that patrimoiety must be called on if the rituals are to be
performed in the prescribed manner. This shortage of man-power
is not the result of abnormal conditions following European
contact; because of the small size of the patrilodges, the situation
has always existed.

The patrilines of descent in the kinship structure are, terminologically speaking, only of five kinds—those of actual and classificatory father's fathers, mother's fathers, and F.M.B., of M.M.B., and of "M.M.B." who are also W.M.F. Of these, a man regards his own father's father's patriline as the most significant, for it provides all or most of the personnel of his dreaming-lodge. Some other lodges comprise men of several distinct "father's father" patrilines, and a man may speak of them all as his *banba* or lodge-ceremony line. But this term properly refers only to his own father's father's patriline, which forms his own lodge; he distinguishes this patriline from all others included in his father-son couple of subsections.

A man similarly discriminates the members of his own F.M.B. patriline from all other men of the various "F.M.B." patrilines, for the F.M.B. was once the ritual guardian or ward of the father's father and attracts some of the respect due to the latter. Ideally, the agnates of the F.M.B. have first claim on certain ceremonial privileges over the man and his father's father but, in their absence, men of other "F.M.B." lodges exercise the claim. The patrilines of the M.M.B. and the various "M.M.B." are fairly important, for their lodges may participate in the man's own lodge ceremonies. The mother's father's patriline includes the mother's brother who was the ritual guardian or ward of the man's father. When the father replaces the father's father as a lodge leader, the mother's brother's patriline tends to assume some of the privileges previously exercised by the F.M.B. patriline.

As the men of a patriline share lodge-dreamings that are more or less geographically localized and refer to particular species, one might expect the identification of patriline membership to be a fairly simple matter. Probably it was in the past; nowadays, however, redistribution of people on settlements and cattle-stations makes it difficult for an outsider to determine the average number of individuals whom a man recognizes in his own patriline. The best estimate I can make is that the patriline is comparable in size with the matriline and has about 30 to 35 members at a given time. About 10 of these are initiated men in the corresponding lodge. Altogether, there are probably about 40 distinct patrilines.

I have recorded over 150 Walbiri dreamings (and there are

doubtless more), all associated with specific localities or tracks. As there are obviously not this many patrilines or lodges, some arrangement must be made to preserve the myths and ritual designs of the additional dreamings and to perform the increase and revelatory ceremonies. The solution of the problem suggests that, in some respects, Walbiri cult totemism resembles that of the Aranda (vide Strehlow, 1947, p. 139, who clarifies the remarks of Spencer and Gillen, 1899, p. 153).

Thus, Waneiga men of the rain lodge whose local reference is to the Gulbulunu waterholes are also the custodians of the neighbouring and related fire, crimson chat and whistling duck dreamings. Ngalia men of the *jaribiri* snake lodge, which is connected with the paintings in Ngama cave near Mount Eclipse, are also custodians of the dingo and rock-wallaby dreamings whose tracks intersect at the cave. Some dreamings, then, such as rain, *jaribiri* snake, eagle-hawk, the two kangaroos, *Acacia coriacea*, the initiated men, and women's digging-stick, are ritually important enough to identify lodges. Many others that are associated geographically, classificatorily, or mythologically with them also come under the care of those lodges, so that the number of lodge-groups is much less than the number of dreamings.

In a sample of 80 initiates of all communities, for instance, only 16 different totems were nominated as lodge-dreamings. This suggests that some 30 or 40 separate lodges exist, which agrees with my estimate of 40 distinct patrilines for the tribe.

Normally, a lad is initiated into his father's lodge at the time of circumcision. Boys all witness much the same collection of rituals during their pre-circumcision seclusion, chiefly a sequence of dramatized episodes from the myth of the two kangaroos; and the overall structure and content of the actual circumcision ceremonies are everywhere the same. The crucial difference on each occasion lies in the string-cross that symbolizes the particular lodge. Although the crosses are all made in the same way and conform to a type, the designs depicted on their faces vary; each lodge-dreaming has its own pattern.

When the boy's father and mother's brother make the cross and "sing" the pattern, it becomes charged with the dreaming essence of the lodge; it absorbs part of the lodge-spirit, *bilirba*.

This spirit is not quite the same thing as the *guruwari* spirit-entity that becomes a person's conception-dreaming. The eagle-hawk *bilirba*, for instance, is the concentrated expression of all the eagle-hawk *guruwari* existing in all the eagle-hawk dreaming-sites in the country of a community. Merely by being, it asserts the "facts" that the original eagle-hawk dreaming deposited these *guruwari* in the dreamtime, that today they still animate embryonic eagle-hawks and human beings, and that lodge members are so intimately related to the eagle-hawk spirit (as distinct from its *guruwari*) that they can perform the rituals necessary to maintain the supply and vigour of the *guruwari*.

Thus, when the elder brother presses the lad against the lodge pattern on the string-cross, some of the lodge *bilirba* enters him. As this has already happened to the elder brother, father, father's brother, father's father, etc., all of them share the one lodge-dreaming or patrispirit. They all call the dreaming "father" and are therefore spiritual "brothers". When each lodge member dies, his share of the patrispirit returns to the lodge dreaming-sites to be reincorporated in the generalized lodge-spirit.

The structural implications of the popular theories of matri- and patri-spirits are clear. Possession of each spirit betokens membership in a category or grouping of social persons, and the two kinds of grouping have more or less complementary secular and ritual functions in Walbiri society. The beliefs may be regarded as symbolic expressions of a principle of complementary filiation. Moreover, the distinction that the people make between lodge-spirit and conception-dreaming is reflected in the fact that possession of a particular conception-dreaming is not a prerequisite for entry into the lodge of the same name. I rarely encountered men who had the same lodge- and conception-dreamings, or even conception-dreamings that were in any way related to their lodges. The two attributes are quite distinct.

In short, patrilineal descent is the main determinant of lodge membership, which by inference also involves community affiliation. A boy is initiated into the lodge of his patriline, and this is almost always connected with a dreaming located somewhere in his own community country.

The beliefs concerning the inter-relations of patri-, matri-, and conception-spirits or -dreamings also constitute a crude theory of personality for the natives. Possession of a common matrispirit, which later becomes a person's ghost, *manbaraba*, explains the similarities of appearance and temperament among maternal kin. The shared patrispirit functions similarly in respect of the men of a lodge or patriline. Moreover, the patri-spirit has a mobile manifestation in the form of a tiny, non-material lizard, *ŋuwa*, that resides in a man's left shoulder. The creature occasionally walks about during the man's waking state and returns to warn him of impending trouble or of distant events concerning him; that is, its actions account for premonitions. The conception-dreaming is thought to link the owner's personality with a definite dreaming-locality and, inasmuch as other members of his patri- and matri-line may not share this dreaming, it accounts for his distinct individuality. When the person dreams, the conception-dreaming in the shape of a natural species or object (in this manifestation called *djuŋguru*) travels about, untrammelled by space or time. It may meet the ghosts of dead relatives, and it also brings back information and warnings to its host.

Spencer and Gillen asserted that Ilpirra (southern Walbiri) men would eat only sparingly of their (conception?) totems, whereas Walpari (northern Walbiri) men would not kill or eat their (lodge?) totems (1899, p. 202; 1904, p. 166). I expected, therefore, to find extensive, ritually-inspired dietary restrictions among the people.

In fact, I did not encounter any instances of Walbiri abstaining from killing or eating their conception-dreamings, and my repeated questioning merely elicited surprised comments that men would be stupid not to eat such foods when available. A few Phillip Creek men said that they had adopted the Warra-munga rule that a person whose conception-totem was emu could eat the bird only when someone else killed it; but I could not discover any other rules of this sort. If such restrictions did exist in the tribe fifty years ago, it seems to me highly unlikely that no trace of them would exist today—especially when most other important ritual prohibitions are still in force.

I can only assume that, as Spencer and Gillen had little first-hand contact with the Walbiri, they mistakenly attributed to these natives cultural elements current among the Aranda. (There was, incidentally, also no evidence of the taboos that they reported on a man's killing or eating his mother-in-law's conception-totem.)

Similarly, I did not observe any instances of men refusing to kill or eat their lodge-dreamings. Occasionally a man would express sorrow, in a half-joking fashion, when he ate a bird or animal he called "father"—that is, a creature associated with any lodge in his own patrimoiety. The usual comment, accompanied by winks and smiles, was: "What a pity—I am eating my poor father! I am so sorry for him!" The only other explicit rule that I learned concerned men of the Gulbulunu rain lodge. They may not drink water from Gululba rockhole unless a man of the opposite patrimoiety gives it to them; nor may they eat game killed near this site, lest the rain-snake become angry and refuse to co-operate in the rain-making rituals. Everyone I questioned, however, said that no other lodges or dreaming-sites are subject to similar restrictions.

The people generally distinguish among six main types of magico-religious songs and dramatization:

(*a*) *djarada* and *jauwalju*: performed privately by women.

(*b*) *ilbindji*: love-magic rituals performed by men or by women, either singly and privately, or in small groups.

(*c*) *bulaba*: performed in the camp by men but witnessed by everyone; these entertainments include introduced *waranggan* dancing from the north.

(*d*) *banba*: lodge increase and revelatory ceremonies performed by men and completely closed to women.

(*e*) *maliara*: although essentially *banba* ceremonies, their incorporation into the Gadjari cycle enhances their ritual significance.

(*f*) *buarilba*: Gadjari ceremonies, which are secret and extremely important.

The women of a patriline are not initiated into the corresponding lodge and may never learn the songs and ceremonies performed by the men of the lodge. The ritual objects, such as bullroarers and incised boards, belonging to the lodge are also carefully hidden from the women, who know little or nothing of the particular myths and dogma in the custody of the lodge. Only a very few older and inquisitive women have any idea of the nature of the lodge and its place in the structure of the society, information they have coaxed from loquacious husbands.

Indeed, most women my wife and I encountered had no desire to know anything at all about the men's ritual activities. They assumed that I would never reveal any ritual knowledge to my wife; nor did they ever question her about such matters. These were men's affairs, which were best avoided by women who wished to remain safe from injury and trouble. The men in turn made it clear to them that they would punish severely any woman who pried.

Despite the sharp separation of women from the secret life, men often said that their sisters and daughters possessed the same patrispirits as themselves. What the statement really meant was that the men were also custodians of patrispirits on behalf of their female agnates. A man's patrispirit, like his matrispirit and conception-dreaming, is an essential part of him, an element of his social personality. A woman's personality does not include this component, which is one reason why men and women differ temperamentally and behaviourally. The people assume, however, that a man's participation in his lodge ceremonies and his understanding of its mysteries ultimately benefit the women of his patriline. This is not seen as simple utilitarian advantage, whereby the men's performance of increase rituals assures the women of food supplies.

More important is the notion that the lodge has a specific role in maintaining the integration and balance of man, society and nature, and that women also share in the social euphoria that results from the lodge members' playing their appointed parts. A man exercises his patrispirit for his sisters' and daughters' spiritual, as well as economic, welfare. Thus, such women are thought to "have that patrispirit". One consequence of this belief is the allocation to the elder sister, father's sister, and f.f.sr. of a novice definite and significant duties in the public ceremonies that precede his circumcision and initiation into the lodge, whose spirit the women already, in a sense, possess.

It will be convenient at this point to summarize some of the remarks I have made. The Walbiri distinguish terminologically among five basic patrilines of descent in their kinship system, which, in this respect, are structural categories with no local connotation. From the individual's point of view, however, they represent the principle on which the personnel of actual groups of people are recruited. Each patriline provides the members of an associated cult- or dreaming-lodge, through which it establishes an indirect local reference.

Fortes, in his analysis of African unilineal descent groups, suggested that "unilineal descent groups are not of significance among peoples who live in small groups, depend on a rudimentary technology and have little durable property" (1953, p. 24). Berndt has taken issue with Fortes on this proposition. He argues that, among the Wulamba of Arnhem Land, patrilineages are important social units, and he asks "whether corporate descent groups of a unilineal nature are common in Australia" (1955, p. 102). I shall now examine the Walbiri patrilines in the light of this query.

Although the patriline has a local reference in that its lodge is ritually linked with identifiable dreaming-sites, it is not in itself a local, residential group; the members do not exclusively occupy a defined territory. Nevertheless, the men of a patriline generally live (or did so in the recent past) scattered about the country of one community, and, as there is no rule of community exogamy, some of the women of the patriline also remain in the same country after marriage. Despite the wide dispersal of family units during much of the year, the degree of localization of the patriline is sufficient for the men to maintain fairly frequent face-to-face contacts and to act as a corporate group. Unlike the men of a matriline, they do not meet sporadically to deal with more or less unpredictable events but gather together regularly to perform revelatory and increase ceremonies and to assist other lodges in such affairs. Indeed, before European settlement changed the pattern of local organization, the meetings often took place at specific dreaming-sites that were the spiritual foci of the lodge's activities. Today, the rituals still refer indirectly to such localities.

The primary aim of the men of a patriline is assembly for ritual purposes. This has several implications. Although the patrilines exhibit only a limited time-depth in genealogical recollection, there is nevertheless a firm belief (that is probably fallacious) in their temporal continuity. In the form of lodges, they are the contemporary human expressions of the dreamings. The dreamings themselves are by definition timeless and, as long as they exist, the lodges must also survive to preserve and to activate the relevant myths and dogma.

Such (putative) endurance is also visibly symbolized for the natives by the indestructible dreaming-sites. Thus Yarungganyi (Mount Hardy) has always been the locality of the ŋarga (initiated-men) dreaming. The people believe that, as the mountain is immutable, the dreaming will always exist there; consequently, the custodial lodge must, in the nature of things, remain to play its role, and there must always be a patriline present that provides the lodge members. Whenever I pursued the question of who would take over the duties of an extinct lodge, the only answers I received were bewildered stares. The men simply could not believe that a lodge might disappear completely, and there was obviously no explicit provision made for this eventuality. (Of course, patrilines must die out occasionally, and I assume that, when this happens, another lodge of the same patrimoiety and community as the extinct group acts informally as caretaker of the latter's dreamings, which in time it incorporates into its own set of dreamings.)

Each dreaming, moreover, occupies a definite place in the overall unity of man and nature, and its lodge has an homologous status in the total system of lodges and dreamings; the patrilines thus have complementary ritual functions in maintaining the whole socio-religious framework. On the one hand, they significantly reinforce the local organization epitomized by the community; on the other, they are important elements in the categorical system of classificatory totemism that is also supported by the patrimoieties and subsections.

A patriline also possesses an internal pattern of authority, which is closely bound up with the distribution of lodge members through the generation-levels. The elders make the important decisions concerning corporate lodge activities and, in doing so, exercise considerable control over their juniors, who have a subordinate ritual status. Such authority, however, is generally defined in terms of the ultimate dreamtime laws and is normally limited to ceremonial situations; the older men can rarely employ their power to their own advantage in secular affairs. The basic sanction upholding their authority within the lodge is the threat of keeping back ritual knowledge, without which the younger men cannot become full social persons.

The patrilines are particularly concerned in the transmission of such ritual knowledge; incorporeal valuables, such as dreaming myths, ceremonies, songs and decorative patterns, are regarded as an important part of the group's heritage. The current members of the associated lodge not only enjoy the benefit of this intangible property but also hold it in trust for future members, as well as for their female agnates. Similarly, the lodge group possesses material property in the form of bullroarers and incised boards; these are also seen as symbols of the lodge's corporate identity, which must be passed on to the future members.

The fact that the senior men of the lodge are its joint spokesmen in ceremonial matters doubtless facilitates the recognition by outsiders of the group as a corporate unit, an attitude reinforced by the members' own assertions that they are all "brothers" in spirit. But we should not press this identification too far and assume that, *ipso facto,* the lodge men regard themselves as jurally equal on all occasions, or that others view them as such. It is true that a man's patriline affiliation largely determines his ritual status *vis à vis* outsiders, and this in turn defines some of his jural rights and duties. Thus, lodge members are potentially interchangeable when a novice has to be instructed, or when the desecrators of ritual objects have to be punished. Such merging of identities, however, does not extend into other fields of social activity, such as the arranging of betrothals or the avenging of deaths. A man who calls the yam dreaming his "mother's father", for instance, does not in nonritual contexts treat all the men of the yam lodge as his "mother's fathers". Some of them may be so in fact; but others may be his mother's brothers and M.B.S., with whom he has different jural relations.

Although patrilines are *de facto* exogamous units, this characteristic is in a sense incidental or derived. The prescriptive

marriage rules, as we have seen, are defined primarily in genealogical terms. A man may marry only two categories of women:
his "m.m.b.d.d." and, as an alternative choice, his "m.b.d."
Matriline affiliation has a bearing on this selection, for the
actual m.m.b.d.d. and m.b.d. are forbidden as spouses, on the
grounds that a man shares the matrispirit of his M.M.B. and
mother's brother. The prohibition might therefore be viewed
as an indirect reflection of matriline exogamy. Patriline affiliation, however, does not function in this way. A man may, indeed
should, marry the "m.m.b.d.d." who is also his f.f.sr.s.d. Although
he should not marry the "m.b.d." who is also his actual f.sr.d.
this proscription is based as much on her sharing his father's
matrispirit as on her mother's quasi-ritual tie with him.

A patriline corporately administers little utilitarian property
and is not an economic unit in the usual sense of the term.
Nevertheless, the lodge ceremonies are in part aimed at maintaining food-supplies, and they help to validate the community's
claim to the products of its own territory. Neither the patriline
nor its associated lodge "owns" a defined tract of land on which
its members reside or hunt to the exclusion of other people;
but, when all the ritual relationships between lodges and
dreaming-sites are summed, they constitute in part the community's title to its country and to the resources of that region.

Thus, although the patriline is not the "primary political
association" within the tribe, it may be involved in indicating a
person's political status (for what that is worth among Walbiri),
because lodge and community affiliation are commonly related.
That is to say, a man's political status depends ultimately on
whether he is a Ngalia, Lander, Walmalla, or Waneiga countryman. His ritual status refers to his membership not merely of,
say, a rain lodge but of a rain lodge belonging to a particular
community. Lodge, and hence patriline, membership may be
an index of community affiliation and, indirectly, of political
status.

The discussion of the characteristics of the Walbiri patriline
demonstrates that, despite its small size and the ritual orientation of most of its functions, it is a social unit of great significance in this tribe of nomads, who lack durable property and
possess only a rudimentary technology. It is true that the puta-

tive genealogy of the descent group is limited in depth and span, and that there appears to be a continual process of group fission, which goes on unremarked by the people. They regard the patriline, or more particularly its associated lodge, as an enduring corporation that administers property which, although mainly intangible, nevertheless has great social value. Membership of a patriline has important consequences for an individual in a variety of situations, not all of which are specifically ritualized. In short, it may be argued that, allowing for differences in scale and cultural emphasis, the patriline possesses formal features and exercises material functions that are analogous to many of those of patrilineal descent groups in societies elsewhere—for instance, in communities of sedentary horticulturalists in parts of New Guinea.

Berndt's analysis (1955) of patrilineages in north-eastern Arnhem Land has indicated clearly their structural significance in that area. If small-scale, corporate unilineal descent groups exist in societies as widely separated as the Wulamba and the Walbiri, we might expect to find that they are also important in other Aboriginal tribes, especially as the range of variation of cultural, demographic and ecological factors is by no means extensive from one region to another.

As this is not the place for a survey of all the Australian tribes, I shall merely point out that re-interpretation of evidence already available supports my view. The description of the Warramunga given by Spencer and Gillen (1904), despite its imperfections, suggests that corporate patrilineages were a feature of the social structure; Strehlow's account (1947) of Aranda cult-organization reveals that the "clans" there resembled Walbiri patrilines; and Elkin (1932), p. 312; 1933, p. 452) refers to patrilineal descent groups among the Ungarinyin of the north-western Kimberleys that were certainly corporate units with ritual, kinship, economic and jural functions.

So far I have discussed the inter-relations of patriline, lodge and community; I still have to show how patrilines articulate with the subsections and the patrimoieties.

Subsections are involved chiefly in the system of classificatory totemism, a system that extends to include the lodges and, hence, the patrilines. Normally, all the members of a man's patriline belong to the one father-son couple of subsections, which I shall call A1-D2, and to which also belong all the people of the parallel "father's fathers'" patrilines. All these patrilines together make up a semi-patrimoiety of the tribe. Similarly, all the members of the man's M.M.B. patriline and its parallel "M.M.B." patrilines are included in the other father-son couple of subsections, A2-D1. These together form the remaining half of the patrimoiety, the whole of which comprises the subsections A1-D2-A2-D1.

The classification of dreamings in subsection terms seems to have developed from this sort of arrangement. A man regards the dreamings of his own and parallel "father's fathers'" lodges as "father". All the men of the A1-D2 couple call all these dreamings "father", and they are, therefore, thought to be A1-D2 dreamings. In the same way, the dreamings called "father" by A2-D1 men are A2-D1 dreamings. As the A1 and D2 men are severally related to the A2 and D1 men as actual or classificatory M.M.B. or Sr.D.S., the A1-D2 dreamings are "M.M.B." to the A2-D1 men and the A2-D1 dreamings are "M.M.B." to the A1-D2 men. Every dreaming of the man's patrimoiety is either his "father" or his "M.M.B.", and, analogously, all dreamings of the opposite patrimoiety are either his "mother's father" or his "wife's brother".

The allocation of dreamings among the subsections has thus apparently followed simply from genealogical considerations. Granted that a man may call a dreaming "father", the rest of the classification follows automatically.

Community affiliations, however, cut across this structural pattern. Countrymen in a particular lodge are without question the true custodians of the associated dreaming; next to them in authority stand their countrymen of other lodges of the same father-son couple of subsections. The remaining extra-community patrilines of the semi-patrimoiety follow, then the patrilines of the complementary semi-patrimoiety within the community. Finally, there are the extra-community patrilines of the complementary semi-patrimoiety.

The constant association of dreaming-lodges with particular father-son couples of subsections depends of the people's regular adherence to the preferred marriage rule, and, as we have seen,

DIAGRAM 7

The interrelations of patriline, subsection and totem

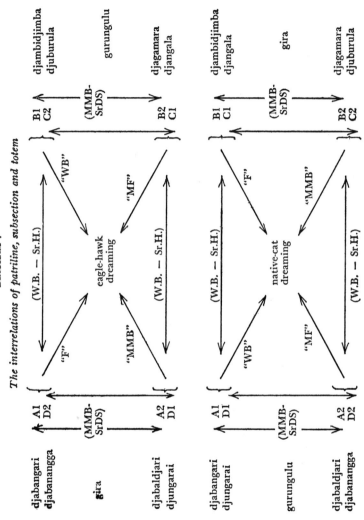

91 per cent of marriages in fact conform to this ideal. Nevertheless, occasional anomalies in lodge affiliations are met, which appear to result from alternative "cross-cousin" marriages made in the past. Thus, one important Waneiga yam dreaming and its lodge are djabangari-djabanangga; but at Hooker Creek three members of the lodge were djabaldjari men. An earlier A1 or D2 man in the lodge had married a "m.b.d.", so that his son, as a "M.B.D.S.", was a member of the A2 or D1 subsection. Being of the same patrimoiety as his father, the son was, however, initiated into the former's lodge; that is to say, in this ritual context, genealogical connection with the father may occasionally over-ride that with the mother in determining group affiliation.

Usually, the daughter of an alternative or prohibited union is simply regarded as her mother's child and enters the appropriate subsection, whatever its patrimoiety relationship to her father. But rather than let the son of an alternative or a prohibited union fall into his mother's patrimoiety, the men of the father's patriline may call the boy the "younger brother" of the father and later receive him into the latter's lodge. I recorded two instances of this. (It is possible that the relatively large proportion of forbidden unions I noted which involved "mothers" and "sons" was due to the fact that the sons born to them would be "younger brothers" of their own fathers and therefore eligible to join the fathers' lodges.)

Although the few "cross-cousin" marriages that occur (5 per cent of the total) have little immediate effect on the subsection statuses or lodges and dreamings, they must eventually cause some lodges to alter their affiliations. Presumably the changes are too gradual to be readily apparent, for I met few men who realized their significance. I found no explicit procedure whereby a man who married his "m.b.d." arranged later for his son to marry the latter's "m.b.d." and thus bring the lodge-subsection relationship back to normal.

Rain-making powers and techniques are inherited patrilineally, and only a few men connected with the two djambi-djimba-djangala rain lodges possess them. The people assert that, while not all members of these lodges are *ipso facto* rain-makers, all rain-makers must belong to the lodges. Paddy djambidjimba and his seminal half-brother, Billy, were members of one of the lodges and, like their late father, were rain-makers. Paddy had no children of his own, but some years before, his senior wife, who was his "m.b.d.", had adopted the young son of her own sister. Paddy treated James as his own son; and he told me that the lad, although a djuburula of the complementary semi-patrimoiety to Paddy, would not only be initiated into Paddy's rain lodge but would also receive his rain-making powers. When I remarked that Paddy himself had often told me that only certain djambidjimba-djangala men could be rain-makers, he would not admit there was any inconsistency in his statements. Thus, if Paddy had his way (and nobody seemed likely to prevent him), djuburula-djagamara men would become rain-makers, ritually related to the djambidjimba-djangala rain-site at Gulbulunu.

The following history also exemplifies the desire of men to have their sons join their own lodges.

A Ngalia djangala man at the Bungalow settlement had married a Djingili tribeswoman, a nabanangga widow from Newcastle Waters who was his "m.b.d." She had already had a nagamara daughter by her late husband. At the Bungalow she bore two daughters and a son to the djangala man. Instead of regarding them as his "m.b.d.d.", nagamara, and "M.B.D.S.", djagamara, respectively, he insisted that they were his daughters, nambidjimba, and son, djambidjimba. He allotted his own conception-dreaming, which was rain, to all three and arranged for the boy to be initiated later into his own rain-lodge.

Facts of this sort indicate that, although we may draw neat diagrams to illustrate the ideal relations existing among persons, patrilines, lodges, subsections and patrimoieties, the real-life situations are not necessarily as rigidly structured as the diagrams suggest. The deviations from the norms that occasionally occur do not greatly perturb the people, and eventually the anomalous case is fitted into the framework. Such discrepancies, moreover, are not a recent product of social disorganization following European contact; the very complexity of Walbiri social structure made it inevitable that there would always be some individuals who could not, or would not, follow all the rules.

Although religious dogma and authority are phrased primarily in terms of membership of patrilines and their associated lodges, the actual performances of the rituals are to a large extent organized on a patrimoiety basis. Moreover, a further distinction must here be made among the kinds of ceremonies involved.

Public entertainments, including those of the imported *waranggan* type, have only an indirect connection with lodges. One performed at Hooker Creek, for instance, dramatized the exploits of a famous djangala rain-maker, now dead. As he had been the close "father" of Billy and Paddy djambidjimba, they were the individual custodians of the legend, the songs, and the symbolic patterns worn by the actors; such (recently acquired) knowledge was to remain in their patriline but not as lodge property. The central theme of the ceremonies, which involved mime and dance, was the hero's journey from Wave Hill to Nganggarida, near Haast's Bluff, and back—a distance of about 800 miles. Sixteen men (of six subsections and three communities) enacted eight important episodes on consecutive nights. Some of the energetic young men, who wished to impress the women in the large audience, danced as often as six times each. Men of all subsections and of various lodges undertook the lengthy preparations each day. Lodge and patrimoiety affiliations were not considered, but Billy, as an "owner" of the cycle, had always to be present to supervise the men. This sort of arrangement is typical of the *bulaba* public ceremonies.

Although the allocation of duties and privileges during the secret increase and revelatory rituals is more obviously on the basis of lodge and community affiliations, it tends for practical reasons to become an alignment in patrimoiety terms, which during the Gadjari or Big Sunday cycle of ceremonies is even more noticeable. Thus, the principles of selection of participants and assistants vary according to the sorts of ceremonies performed and the number of initiated men available to act.

No sharp distinction can be drawn between the increase and the revelatory ceremonies that lodges perform. Whereas those accompanied by the retouching of rock-paintings are clearly intended to increase directly a natural species, all lodge dramatizations indirectly have this effect no matter where they take place. For instance, although the kangaroo ceremonies that occur before circumcision are primarily revelatory and intended to educate the novices, they also affect the numbers of kangaroos everywhere in Walbiri country.

It is worth noting here that the term "increase", although commonly used in the literature in relation to such rituals, is not strictly accurate. The participants are simply concerned to maintain the supplies of natural species at their usual level, to support the normal order of nature. Thus, rain ceremonies are not performed until late spring, when the first heavy cumulonimbus clouds appear in the north-west. The men do not believe that they can force the rain to fall at any time of the year; instead, they try to ensure that it will come in the appropriate season. Similarly, rituals connected with slow-maturing fruits as those of *Acacia coriacea* do not as a rule take place until long after the rain has fallen. Yams, however, flourish all year round, so that there is no special season for their ceremonies.

The general notion of the maintenance of a natural or, rather, a dreamtime order extends to human beings. The ceremonies not only facilitate the entry of *guruwari* catalysts into natural species so that they will reproduce themselves; they also sustain the vigour and health of those people who possess the particular conception-dreamings as part of their personalities. Men often told me that, when they knew the ceremonies pertaining to their own conception-dreamings were being performed, they felt happy and strong, because the actors were "working for them".

Correlatively, most increase ceremonies (I retain the term for its venerable associations) are also revelatory; circumcised youths are usually brought to witness them and have their significance explained. Men of the youth's patriline or patrimoiety should make the explanations, even if they are of the opposite patrimoiety to the dreaming in question. This arrangement expresses the general norm that the giving of religious instruction is the duty of agnates.

When it is time to enact a particular dreaming ceremony, men of the opposite patrimoiety request the lodge members to undertake the performance. (This is also the practice of the Warramunga; vide Spencer and Gillen, 1904, p. 197.) Ideally, a senior man of the lodge is asked by his sister's husband, preferably one who has been his circumcision ward or his guardian, to prepare for the occasion. He tells the men of his lodge and others of that patrimoiety; and they all assemble in the bush, hidden from the women, and "sing the line of the dreaming".

A line may include from 100 to 500 separate songs recounting the travels and exploits of the dreaming-creature, and it should be sung in the temporal-geographical order laid down in the myth. If a misplaced song "breaks the line", the singers should start the cycle again. In fact, although I heard some lines dozens of times, I did not hear one sung twice in precisely the same order, and I rarely saw the singers begin anew after an error. Moreover, a man's personal name is generally a phrase from such a song. When a song is reached that contains the name of a man recently dead, it must be dropped from the line—a requirement that often throws the singers into great confusion.

The song may be reintroduced into the line after a few years, but I am sure that it rarely reappears in the same position or form as before. As the songs are the chief mnemonic aids to the correct presentation of myth and ritual, their rejection is an important mechanism in the gradual alteration of the content of the religion.

Once the men of the patrimoiety of the dreaming, the "masters", begin to sing its line, none may break off until the cycle (or a discrete section of it) is concluded. The singing, which continues for four or five hours before the actual ceremony, is as important as the ceremony itself, for it prepares the actors for their participation in the dreamtime. The songs have virtue and strength and are actively dangerous to uninitiated people; they should be sung downwind from the general camp, lest the women distinguish the words and fall ill—a convention that clearly helps to keep the women ignorant of ritual matters.

Meanwhile, men of the opposite patrimoiety, the "working men", prepare the materials necessary for the actors' decorations. Men at Hooker Creek and Yuendumu interpret this rule to mean that they must collect the vegetable- and bird-down and at least begin to make it ready by pounding it and colouring it with powdered red-ochre and limestone. As these tasks are time-consuming, men of the actors' patrimoiety are also expected to help in the later stages. The Phillip Creek Walbiri, however, follow the Warramunga rule that only the actors being decorated may be present during the working men's activities; other men of the patrimoiety must stay apart from them and sing the lodge songs.

A number of lodge ceremonies demand the manipulation or wearing of temporary ritual objects, usually wooden frames padded with leaves, bound with hair-string and decorated with coloured down stuck on with arm-blood. Some represent goannas, snakes, kangaroos' tails, heroes' hearts and the like; others are conventionalized single- or double-armed string-crosses, or decorated posts. They should always be made by the working-men patrimoiety, concealed from the masters; and the makers should use their own arm-blood to decorate them. I never saw this rule broken. (The manufacture of circumcision string-crosses follows a different convention.) In some ceremonies, small stone bullroarers are employed, and the working men apply fresh ochre patterns to them for each occasion.

While the working men toil, they also sing the relevant lodge songs to impart the dreaming essence of the lodge to the objects, which they later hand over formally to the masters. This concealment of the working men from the masters was the only explicit spatial separation of the patrimoieties that I discovered in lodge ceremonies.

A few rituals require the making of elaborate ground-paintings of blood and coloured down, similar in execution and appearance to those of the Warramunga (vide Spencer and Gillen, 1904). They are in effect maps of dreaming-countries, and the actors kneel on them when performing the rituals. Anyone may contribute the arm-blood that is used, but only the working men, supervised by the lodge masters, do the painting, which may take five or six hours to complete.

The working men, sometimes helped by the masters, use boomerangs to clear the ground on which a lodge ceremony is to be enacted. The orientation depends on factors of shade and terrain, not on the directions of dreamtime sites and journeys, and the area is determined by the type of performance intended. In "free" ceremonies the actors run, dance and mime over a space of several hundred square yards; in "fixed" ceremonies they kneel, mime and shuffle about in a circular or rectangular clearing of three or four square yards. The free action generally imitates the behaviour of dreamtime heroes, the fixed that of dreamtime animals, plants and the like.

During the preliminary singing, all the masters, whether

actors or not, have their heads and upper torsos smeared with fat (beef, emu, or kangaroo) and powdered red-ochre—usually, but not always, by the working men. The people explicitly associate red-ochre with blood, health and strength; they also use it as body insulation against heat or cold and as protection from the myriad flies that plague the camp.

The actors are then decorated with designs relevant to the dreaming incident to be dramatized. The outlines are first painted in blood with bold sweeps of a leaf-brush and then filled in with down or charcoal. Except at Phillip Creek, any initiated man may provide the arm-blood. Working men, especially the brothers-in-law of the actors, should apply the patterns, guided by the lodge members, but other men sometimes assist. Throughout the painting, all the men "sing the line" of the dreaming. (The equation of working men with decorators is more carefully observed during the Big Sunday rituals.) Should the decorations include the conical or mushroom-shaped head-dresses that are made by binding a base of leaves with 40 or 50 yards of hair-string, the working men build these directly onto the actors' heads.

The nucleus of the actors is drawn as a rule from the lodge associated with the dreaming; they may invite other initiated men of the same patrimoiety to join them—but never men of the opposite patrimoiety. Depending on the ceremony, there may be from one to 20 actors.

TABLE 19

The observance of patrimoiety ceremonial divisions, Hooker Creek, 1953-4

	Patrimoiety affiliation of the person		
	Same as dreaming	Opposite to dreaming	
Category	being enacted	being enacted	Total
Actors	68	–	68
Assistants:			
decorators of actors	42	59	101
makers of head-dresses	2	36	38
removers of head-dresses	–	38	38
Total	112	133	245

chi squared (actors, assistants) = 112·32, df = 1, p $\angle$ ·01
phi coefficient of association = ·67

When all is ready for the ceremony, men give a long, high-pitched shout, fluttering the palm of the hand in front of the mouth, to call the recently circumcised and subincised youths from the camp. The cry, heard only on ritual occasions, may be uttered by any initiated men at the behest of the lodge seniors. Sometimes the youths are gathered before the decoration of the actors is completed; accompanied by a guardian (usually the brother-in-law of one lad), they sit about 50 yards from the clearing, where they cannot easily see the details of the preparations. This is done so that they may hear the sacred songs at greater length. The youths may not approach the clearing until the actors are in position and all the older men are assembled; then each lad stands before his father, elder brother, M.M.B., or sister's husband, who embraces him throughout the ritual.

The actors in free performances usually emerge from hiding-places in the trees and for four or five minutes dance and mime a meandering course back to the group; a working man accompanies their actions with intermittent club-beats on a shield. There is no singing. In fixed performances, everyone crowds around the actors who kneel in a small clearing. To the accompaniment of rhythmical boomerang-clapping, singing and grunting, the actors shuffle about—imitating the dreamtime beings making the tracks and creeks. Sometimes they move at a rapid tempo to a rocking, four/four beat; at other times the miming is much slower and more deliberate. The fixed dramatizations last from five to ten minutes, by the end of which time the actors are quite spent.

Each youth then steps forward at his guardian's command and firmly presses the actors' shoulders, rubbing off some of the down in order to acquire its virtue. The guardian explains the meaning of the ceremony before sending the lad back to the camp. When temporary objects, such as figures of goannas or snakes, have been used in the ritual, the youth before leaving lies on top of one of the working men, and another strikes him heavily across the stomach several times with the sacred object; he tells the novice that he has now eaten freely of this food and will not need to eat so much in the future. (Spencer and Gillen, 1899, p. 172, reported a similar practice among the Aranda.)

When there are no novices present at a ceremony, the working men halt the performance by pressing the actors' shoulders. In either case, they must remove the actors' head-dresses and dismantle them, retaining the hair-string which they had contributed. Sometimes an actor removes his own body-decorations with the aid of other masters; but this should be done by working men, who carefully salvage the down for renovation and future use.

Three or four lodge ceremonies may be enacted by both patrimoieties in the one day; and the preparations by contiguous groups of men may over-lap in time. Often the consequent cacophony of conflicting songs develops into good-humoured, competitive singing between the patrimoieties. Sunset marks the end of the performances. Gathering their materials, the men return to the main camp, joking and gossiping as they go.

Such ritual occasions should not be disturbed by argument or ill-feeling, and offenders would risk punishment by the demons' "singing" them or stealing their spirits (Meggitt, 1955a, p. 393). I saw only two men violate this rule during lodge ceremonies, whose participants generally manifest great good-humour. Recognition of the sacred character of the activity does not prevent the men from laughing, joking and enjoying themselves. Audiences are quick to commend well-executed performances and to offer pungent advice to the few incompetent actors. Although the men would receive the criticism with hostility in secular matters, they take it in good part during the ceremonies. In short, the occasions are text-book exemplifications of the effects of social euphoria and "we-feeling".

The Walbiri at Phillip Creek say that, after the ceremonies, the working men of the opposite patrimoiety should present game to the lodge members in return for performing the rituals that have benefited everyone, and I have seen this happen there. At Yuendumu and Hooker Creek such gifts are not made. But, when initiated men of either patrimoiety are escorted to an important dreaming-site, such as Ngama cave, to learn the significance of the rock-paintings or the bullroarers, they should later give meat to the men of the associated lodge as payment for the tuition. Other men of neighbouring lodges of the opposite patrimoiety, who have to retouch these paintings annually to maintain the species, are regarded as permanent custodians of the site; they too should attend any revelation of the paintings to outsiders and share the meat given to the lodge masters.

The Gadjari or Big Sunday complex of rituals (which includes many that are typical lodge ceremonies in other respects) has apparently developed from an amalgamation of the non-Walbiri Kunapipi fertility cult with the Walbiri cycle of the dreaming of the two *mamandabari* heroes. The Waneiga, who first received the alien elements from the north, are the acknowledged authorities on these matters and the *mamandabari* lodge in effect comprises all the initiated Waneiga of the djabangari-djabanangga-djabaldjari-djungarai patrimoiety. All these men call the dreaming "father", for it is considered too important to be confined to one patriline or even to one semi-patrimoiety. Men of that patrimoiety who live in other communities also regard it as "father", but they have little say in organizing the rituals. Although, in theory, some are the custodians of the sections of the long dreaming-track that pass through their own community countries, they defer in practice to the greater knowledge of the Waneiga.

The distribution of ritual duties during the annual performance of the Gadjari markedly reflects patrimoiety alignment. The ceremonies occur over a period of weeks on a secret clearing (*ganala*) in the bush, which is made and kept in repair by men of the workers' patrimoiety. Once the ceremonies begin, men must follow the "line" of the myth without interruption, and none may return to the general camp until the end is reached. The working men erect a bough-shelter nearby, under which they prepare the down, ochre, hair-string, etc., that are needed for each dramatization. The masters (all the men of the patrimoiety of the particular dreaming) sing under another bough-shade. When the tasks are completed, everyone moves to the sacred clearing. Whenever the masters enter this clearing to sing or to watch rituals, they must sit cross-legged and concentrate on the performance. The working men, supervised by Waneiga elders, decorate the actors, using the arm-blood of any initiated men.

New *mamandabari* body-patterns are still appearing as men dream of novel designs to symbolize the various incidents and sites recorded in the myth. Normally, men of the master patrimoiety create them and, although the individual dreamer receives credit for a pattern that is generally accepted, the pattern itself belongs to all his countrymen in that patrimoiety. Sometimes men of the opposite patrimoiety dream of new Gadjari designs, but they must give them to their sisters' husbands or sisters' sons to keep.

At Phillip Creek, when Walbiri join with Warramunga and Walmanba tribesmen in *mandiwala* or *gadjiga* circumcision ceremonies, an actor may wear any dreaming-pattern lent by his mother's brother or sister's son. This does not occur among other Walbiri either in lodge or Gadjari rituals; a man may wear only patterns of his own patrimoiety. Moreover, a young man wearing a pattern for the first time in the Big Sunday must ask the permission of his elder brother to do so, lest a quarrel follow.

A few ceremonies that occur in the Gadjari refer to lodge-dreamings of the working men's patrimoiety. These men perform them and are decorated by the master patrimoiety. Some of these ceremonies are connected only indirectly with the "true Gadjari line"; therefore, they may not be enacted on the sacred clearing itself but take place nearby.

The usual patrimoiety rules determine the manufacture of Gadjari head-dresses and temporary ritual objects. Bull-roarers also play an important part in these ceremonies, and additional rules define their handling.

The Walbiri make seven main types of sacred wooden objects intended as permanent ritual symbols.

(*a*) *jarandalba*—these boards, made of tough acacia wood, resemble the Kimberley *pirmal* and the Pidjandjara *inma*. Of 23 that I measured, the average length was 58 inches, the breadth 4·5 inches, and the thickness ·75 inch; they are not meant to be swung as bullroarers. The boards are almost exclusively related to circumcision ceremonies. The incised pattern of scrolls, arcs, circles and spirals indicates a specific dreaming, and only men of the patrimoiety opposite to that dreaming may make the board. When the boards are not in use, the makers (and not the lodge masters) hide them and regularly rub them with grease and red-ochre; they should know where the objects are at all times. The custodians should seize any woman or outsider who steals, damages, or merely sees the board and hack the offender to death with its sharp edges.

(*b*) *djabanba*—these bullroarers, made of acacia wood, are swung with a doubled hair-string about 8 feet long. Of 13 measured, the mean length was 29 inches, the breadth 4 inches, and the thickness ·5 inch. The low-pitched drone is audible for a mile or more. Although the incised patterns may symbolize a variety of dreamings, the objects are primarily Gadjari paraphernalia. Only men of the workers' patrimoiety may make them; they should also guard these very sacred boards and use them to kill intruders.

A man working alone may not make either a type (*a*) or type (*b*) board; this is a task for at least two men forming a team. If one man successfully made the object, it is believed that others of his patrimoiety would become insanely envious and use sorcery to acquire his skill. I have never seen the convention flouted, which seems to me to ensure that designs will be applied with little variation.

(*c*) *mana-baganu*—of 5 measured, the mean length was 6·5 inches, the breadth ·75 inch, and the thickness ·125 inch; (*d*) *mandagi*—of 6 measured, the average length was 8·5 inches, the breadth 1 inch, and the thickness ·125 inch. The two types look very similar, and men appear to distinguish them only in terms of their size.

The objects, made of acacia wood, are attached to about 3 feet of hair-string, which is affixed to a thin wand about 30 inches long. Whipped rather than swung, they emit eerie screams audible for about half a mile. Both are connected with the Gadjari cycle and bear only *mamandabari*-hero patterns. Men say they are the "elder sisters" of the *djabanba* bullroarers (*b*), which form a less sacred category. Men of the workers' patrimoiety make and care for them. The custodians should kill anyone who desecrates the object by stabbing him (or her) under the collar-bone or in the throat with its sharp-pointed end.

(*e*) *jaŋarindji*—of 7 measured, the mean length was 18 inches, the breadth 3 inches, and the thickness ·375 inch; (*f*) *gunamanu*—of 3 measured, the average length was 19 inches, the breadth 3 inches, and the thickness ·375 inch. Both types, made of acacia or eucalyptus wood, are much alike, and I believe that only the makers can tell which is which.

The bullroarers are swung with about 8 feet of hair-string in the same way as is the *djabanba*, but the sound is more high-pitched. Each bears a dreaming pattern and is used in associated lodge ceremonies. A man of the opposite patri-moiety may make the object on his own without fear of sorcery. He should guard it thereafter and kill a thief or intruder by thrusting the board down the culprit's throat.

(g) *windilburu*—of 4 measured, the mean length was 15 inches, the breadth 2·5 inches, and the thickness ·25 inch. Made of acacia or eucalyptus wood, it is swung like a *djabanba* and emits a soft drone. When a boy is to be cir-cumcised, his mother's brother makes a *windilburu* bearing the pattern of the lad's conception-dreaming. The novice should contemplate this during his seclusion.

The *djabanba, mandagi* and *mana-baganu* bullroarers appear often in the Gadjari ceremonies. Men of the master patri-moiety select men of the opposite patrimoiety to care for the objects during this period. The working men keep them greased and ochred and ensure that they are strung ready for swinging at a moment's notice. They may have to swing the bullroarers a dozen times or more a day at the request of the masters. The senior Gadjari master is the only other man who shares this great privilege of swinging the boards; if anybody else tried to do so, the men of his patrimoiety would ridicule his pre-tensions to authority.

Senior men of the master patrimoiety select the ceremonial messengers who travel to other communities or tribes to invite outsiders to attend the Big Sunday. The masters decorate the backs of the messengers with *mamandabari* patterns outlined in red-ochre on grease. The working men bring the *djabanba* bullroarers from their hiding places, and the masters select two or three for the messengers to carry. They choose *djabanba* that are not required for ceremonies—those which are ill-made or produce little sound. Possession of the bullroarers verifies the status of the messengers and guarantees their safe-conduct through alien territories.

The working men place each of the selected *djabanba* on the knees of each of the masters in turn and ask if it is the bull-roarer to be sent to such-and-such a group. The senior masters pass the bullroarers on to the messengers with final instructions and then tell them to depart. When the messengers reach their destination, they at once contact senior men of the master patrimoiety there. They take these men out of sight and earshot of the main camp to deliver their messages, and they hand over the *djabanba* without formality. The messengers leave within a day or two and return home ahead of the people they have invited, who bring several of their own *djabanba* as gifts for the hosts.

Meanwhile, in the hosts' territory, men of the opposite patrimoiety, the working men, dig the large ŋ*angaru* pit in which the Gadjari novices are to be placed (so that other working men may hurl *djindjimirinba* firesticks over their heads), and they also make the tall, decorated *gumagu* posts, which they will later shake continuously for an entire night in one of the rituals. Throughout the Big Sunday period, these men have to carry out many tasks, which in theory prevent them from collecting their own food. Consequently, the master patrimoiety should do this for them. Nowadays, the issue of rations makes this problem less pressing, and the masters actually contribute little food to the workers.

When visitors from other communities attend the Gadjari, masters among the hosts should also feed members of the opposite patrimoiety among the strangers for the first few days, until the visiting masters are ready to fulfil this obligation. In expectation of this aid, the visiting working men bring gifts of hair-string, ochre and weapons for the local masters. On arrival they place the goods in a row about a mile or so from the hosts' camp, and the local masters parallel these articles with a row of food-stuffs. The local working men allocate the food to the visiting working men, while simultaneously the visiting masters distribute the counter-gifts among the local masters. Despite the availability of European food today, these exchanges still take place.

During a performance of the Gadjari cycle at Hooker Creek, I was camped on the *ganala* clearing with the men for some weeks and was able to observe how onerous and time-consuming were the ritual duties of the working men's patrimoiety. Whereas the masters could spend long hours dozing and gossiping between ceremonies, the working men always had some tasks on hand. Few demanded hard physical labour, but they all required the expenditure of energy and attention at a time of the year when the high temperatures and excessive humidity made any sort of concentrated thought an effort.

As one djangala man said to me, while pounding vegetable-down in readiness for a ceremony, "This Big Sunday is a really important affair, and we working men must toil hard to follow the line properly. I want to meet all my commitments fully—but why should all (sic!) the Gadjari rituals belong to the other patrimoiety? Why should the masters sleep all day while we work? We have big rituals, such as those of the rain-dreaming, which are just as sacred. Why cannot we be the masters for a while and let those others be the working men?" As I watched the sweat stream down his face, I sympathized with him.

The Walbiri attach an enormous importance to ritual matters. Because of the functional significance of patrilines and patrimoieties in ritual life, my discussion of these units has necessarily been detailed. The patrilines provide the personnel for the lodges that co-operate to support the totemic system, and the patrimoieties classify the dreamings included in the system. As the dreamtime is ultimately the source of the social groups and their titles to the country, the patrilines and lodges indirectly sustain themselves jurally, politically and religiously by their own activities.

CHAPTER XIII

GRADATIONS OF AGE AND MATURITY

The individual Walbiri progresses through a series of stages that may loosely be called age-grades, although, as in most Australian societies, age in itself means little to the native. He classifies people in terms of physiological maturation and observed capacities, and on this basis he places them in successive, named social or ritual statuses. In general, the terms he uses refer merely to membership of broad categories; their main purpose is to relate a particular person to a class of people, without necessarily implying that the members act together in solidary groups. Nevertheless, the terms, most of which may be used in address and reference, are consistent indices of the kinds of behaviour and attitudes expected from their referents and exhibited towards them.

The Walbiri refer to themselves in general as *jaba*, "people", a term that may also include other Blackfellows, as distinct from White- and Yellow-fellows. Children are *jabarandji*, of which those younger than about three or four years are simply *wida*, "the small ones", a usage reflecting the uniform behaviour of adults towards infants of both sexes. From this age onward, however, boys spend more time together, whereas girls remain with their mothers. Although the girls do not have to work hard when accompanying women on food-gathering expeditions or when residing in the camp, they receive responsibilities earlier than do the boys, who devote their days to playing and wandering through the bush near the camp. Girls at this stage are *nalali*, a term that may also apply to girls from birth to puberty, and the boys are *murgu* or *bubu-gari*, "those with foreskins". Both must observe minor dietary restrictions; thus, they may not eat the highly-prized bustard or the echidna.

When a boy goes into pre-circumcision seclusion, at about the age of 12, he is *burunjuŋu*, "the hidden one". During the seclusion period he makes his grand tour of other community countries and is then called *malulu*. This term, or its cognates, is current from the Kimberley coast to Arnhem Land in the north and Ooldea in the south; but the Walbiri derive it from the kangaroo (*malu*) ceremonies that the lad sees while secluded. After his circumcision the boy is called *juguru* or *bubu-waŋu*, "lacking a foreskin". He now receives formal tuition in the manufacture and use of weapons, in hunting techniques and in religious dogma; he must scrupulously avoid his mothers-in-law.

Soon after circumcision, he sees his first Gadjari rituals, which include *maliara* dreaming-ceremonies. Strictly speaking, the term *maliara* also denotes only those men who have actually participated in a completed cycle of Gadjari rituals, but it may be applied loosely to any circumcised youth who is seeing the Gadjari for the first time (and even to the anthropologist who attends all the ceremonies). Variants of the term *maliara* are also found from the east Kimberleys to the Finke River.

A youth is subincised when he is about 16 or 17 years old—when his moustache is becoming noticeable—and is then called *bara-banda*, "he who has a subincision wound" (the term *bara* is also known from the Kimberleys to the Finke). By this time he lives chiefly in the bachelors' camp, *jambiri*, in company with males whose ages range from about 14 to about 25 years. They have no formally-appointed camp leader; but the older bachelors naturally organize most activities and give sporadic and friendly moral and technological instruction to their juniors. A man remains *bara-banda* until he dies.

As long as a subincised man is unmarried, he is called *jambiri-wanu*, "he of the bachelors' camp", and the men bearing this title tend to form a solidary group rather than a mere category. They see themselves as a group covertly opposed to the married men who control the women they desire. In turn the older men with young wives usually regard the bachelors as larrikins, whose immoral behaviour endangers the marriages of others; and indeed they often have good reason to be anxious.

Men are generally betrothed by the age of 19 or 20, but they rarely receive their wives for another six or seven years. They then become *jubugara*, "married men", a title they retain until death. No specific term distinguishes married men with children from those without, nor is there any formal lifting of food taboos or other restrictions to mark the achievement of the status of husband or father.

Gradually the older men come to regard the married man as ŋarga, a term that has several nuances. Basically it implies that the man's opinions on most important matters are now worth consideration. As a husband, he can talk knowledgeably about the vagaries of women; as a father, he appreciates the obligations entailed in having children; as a hunter, he knows the country and can provide adequately for his dependants; as a craftsman, he can make ritual, as well as secular, objects; as an initiated member of a lodge, he may make suggestions concerning the performance of lodge ceremonies. He is becoming a full social person.

But the elders still do not accept a man fully in all these capacities, especially that of lodge member, until he is about 40 or so. That is to say, although a man has seen all the ceremonies and ritual objects by the age of about 30, he does not as a rule understand the religious significance of all of them; and he continues to acquire this knowledge slowly from his seniors, until he is an old man and is competent to teach others.

A man usually attains his highest social (as distinct from ritual) status between the ages of 40 and 55 years. Not only is he still active enough to hunt and fight effectively and to control several wives, but he has also acquired considerable social poise and ritual information. By the age of about 60, however, he is regarded as bulga, "old man", or lailai, "grey-haired man", a fate that no man I knew accepted with equanimity. By and large, being old has few advantages apart from that of ritual recognition. The old men in each community or, nowadays, on each settlement tend to form a clique and spend their time in gossip and in deploring the lax moral standards of the young. Very few attain 65 years, and a man who passes this age is in effect already socially "dead"—his physical death is not avenged and his corpse is not given the dignity of exposure on a tree-platform.

A woman's life-cycle is divided into fewer named stages. The prepubescent girl who is married remains nalali until her breasts form, when she becomes djabinba. Although the occurrence of the menarche (generally at the age of about 14) indicates her transition to womanhood, it occasions little comment and no formal rituals. She is now called *maraguda*, "mature woman", or *ganda*. Strictly speaking, the latter term denotes only women who have borne children. After the menopause a woman is called *mil-gari*, "one who has an eye", a term whose use reflects the incidence of blindness (chiefly due to trachoma) among older people. The old women also constitute cliques, generally centred on the widows' camps which are hotbeds of gossip.

TABLE 20

The named stages in the individual's life-cycle

Approximate age	Male term	Stage	Female term	Stage
1-3	*wida*	infancy	*wida*	infancy
3-12	*murgu*	childhood	*nalali*	childhood
12-13	*burunjuŋu*	seclusion		
	malulu	on tour		
13-16	*juguru*	circumcised	*djabinba*	pubescent
14	*maliara*	Gadjari novice		
16 plus	*barabanda*	subincised	*maraguda*	mature
18-25	*jambiriwanu*	bachelor	*ganda*	child-bearing
25 plus	*jubugara*	married		
40 plus	*narga*	mature	*milgari*	aged
60 plus	*bulga*	aged		

Table 20 reveals that the Walbiri allocate such status terms on much the same bases as do other Australian tribes, for instance, the Ooldea Pidjandjara, the Aranda, the Murngin, and the Unambal of the Kimberleys (vide Berndt, 1945, p. 85; Spencer and Gillen, 1899, p. 212; Warner, 1937, p. 125; Hernandez, 1941, p. 122). They make in effect a cross-classification as they take physical development, marital condition, and ritual status as the criteria for the allocation of individuals into certain categories. Most of the other societies I have mentioned, however, use a wider range of terms and make finer discriminations. In particular, the Walbiri possess nothing like the highly elaborated systems of the coastal Kimberley tribes, such as the Bard and Karadjari, wherein a man passes through as many as nine graded ritual statuses (vide Elkin, 1936; Piddington, 1932b; Worms, 1938).

In addition to the general categorization I have just described, Walbiri men also employ a system of relative age-grading, which expresses the great importance they attach to circumcision and its concomitant ceremonies in establishing male status. All the men who have been circumcised in the same ceremonial season, irrespective of their community affiliations, are *jalbaru*. This term appears also in *jalbaru-gulaŋu*, "those who are members of the one group of merged alternate generation-levels", and its basic connotation is "those of equivalent status". Such *jalbaru* are likely, too, to enter the Gadjari together and to be subincised in the one season.

Sometimes, however, the automatic ascription of each lad to a set of *jalbaru* is upset. For instance, a boy may have been living on a cattle-station at the time he should have been circumcised, and his father may have been unable to arrange for the operation to be performed until two or three years after the appropriate season. This places the lad in an anomalous position. He is thought to be too old to enter the age-set comprising the other boys who are circumcised at the same time as he is initiated, but he cannot be identified with the age-set formed in the season when he should have been circumcised. Men say that to do so would negate the whole rationale of the system, for the *jalbaru* are men who have shared a significant ritual experience. In effect, then, the lad has no age-grade at all, and his condition is cited as a reason for avoiding any postponement of circumcision beyond the proper time. Nevertheless, my acquaintance with the few youths who were in this position convinced me that they do not suffer any practical disabilities as a result.

Despite the fact that the allocation of youths into age-grades is public knowledge, men are often unsure of the precise membership of age-sets temporally distant from their own. In particular, young men tend to lump together into one set all the old men of a community or settlement, whereas these regard themselves as members of several sets. The younger men at Hooker Creek, for instance, recognized 13 grades ranging from the most junior, which included three boys circumcised in the summer of 1953-4, to the most senior, recently vacated by a very old leper. But six of the older men, who they thought formed one set, actually made up three separate sets. Although the women are also aware of the existence of men's age-grades, they know little of the details of their composition and are not interested in them.

A man may refer to all age-grades earlier than his own as *gambaru-wanu,* "those who go before", and to all later grades as *biraŋili-wanu,* "those who come after"; but he uses the ordinary kinship and subsection terminology when speaking of the individual members of the associated age-sets. When dealing with men of his own age-set, however, he may employ self-reciprocal terms of address and reference that relate specifically to age-set status. Normally, these terms are not often heard around the camp; but at Hooker Creek I noticed that, for some weeks after my inquiries into the subject, the younger men used them constantly.

TABLE 21

Terms of address and reference used by age-mates

Kinship category	Term	Kinship category	Term
F.F./S.S.	*liŋgiminimini*	E.B./Y.B.	*gidjidji (-djara)*
F./S.	{ *wabiraminimini* *wabiralga*	M.B./Sr.S. W.F./D.H. }	{ *lambanilga* *lambanu*
W.M.B./Sr.D.H.	{ *wadjamanilga* *wadaminilaŋu*	M.M.B./Sr.D.S.	{ *bilbililga* *bilbilira*
F.M.B./Sr.S.S. W.B./Sr.H. }	{ *malgarilga* *malgarira*	M.F./D.S. M.B.S./F.Sr.S. }	{ *ŋamaralga* *ŋamarara*

The terminology is obviously arranged on subsection lines (thus *ŋamarara* refers to "mother's father", "M.B.S." and "daughter's son"); strictly speaking, each term (apart from those for F.F./S.S. and E.B./Y.B.) simply denotes "man of such-and-such a subsection who is my age-mate". This suggests that the system originally came from the north or north-west, an hypothesis supported by the presence of the term *lambanu* for "father-in-law". From Katherine to the east Kimberley region, *lambara* is a common term for wife's father.

Some men find it amusing that others who are roughly their coevals are also their classificatory "grandfathers" or "grandchildren"; other men, however, feel that this is somehow illogical and even vaguely annoying, and they prefer to use the age-grade instead of the kin terms in order to indicate equivalence of social status in various contexts.

By and large, the sets of *jalbaru* age-mates do not form solidary groups in later life. It is true that lads circumcised in the same season usually spend their seclusion-period together in a single camp in the bush, and the attitudes of mutual regard that develop at this time doubtless persist, if only in a latent state. The youths have shared a remarkable experience and will do so again during the Gadjari rituals. But, when they are back in the general camp, they are simply members of the loosely-organized class of bachelors. From this they pass into the less cohesive category of married men and afterwards into the rather more solidary group of old men. Through the years their common bond as age-mates assumes less and less significance, until, as my questioning of middle-aged and old men revealed, it becomes merely a topic of reminiscence. The fact that a man is a member of a particular age-set rarely determines his actions in specific social situations.

An exception should be made, however, of the special category of age-mates known as *baŋandja*. This usually includes actual or close brothers who were circumcised, not only in the same season, but also at the one ceremony on the one ceremonial ground. The men are expected to remain close friends, camping and hunting together and exchanging wives; they must never quarrel. Moreover, they should not call to each other by name across the camp. This prohibition does not refer only to personal dreaming-names (for no man would use these in public) but to kinship, age-grade and subsection terms as well. The people do not attempt to explain this restriction.

During my sojourns with the Walbiri I observed only one dispute in which young men explicitly organized themselves as a group on the basis of age-set membership—an event unusual enough to warrant a detailed description of the circumstances.

The djungarai father of Lucy nabaldjari gave her in marriage to Jumbo djagamara, whom he had previously circumcised; and she lived with Jumbo for some time at the Granites and Mount Doreen. His disposition was so unpleasant, however, that, like several of his earlier wives, she left him. She resided with relatives at Yuendumu, then soon afterwards, when she was aged about 17 or 18, she moved to Hooker Creek, where she lived in the widows' camp.

Lucy had no close kinsmen at Hooker Creek; but her classificatory "fathers", "mother's brothers" and "M.M.B." who were her countrymen decided that she was still Jumbo's wife and did not try to give her to another man. Before long she became the mistress of Long Jimmy djambidjimba, an unmarried "M.B.S." aged about 23. The couple were discreet about their affair, so that, although everybody in the camp knew of it, they raised no objections. Later, Jimmy prevailed on a close friend, Abe djangala, who was Lucy's "mother's brother" and countryman, to approve of their marriage. Abe knew that he would have to tread warily in this matter. He therefore waited until a party of younger people, married and single, went on an extended hunting trip, in which he and his wife, Annie, and Jimmy and Lucy joined. Rightly judging that these companions would sympathize with young lovers, he announced that, as far as he was concerned, Jimmy and Lucy were married; and the couple camped together openly for the rest of the trip.

When the party was ready to return, one man went ahead to the main camp to break the news of the "marriage". At once all the men gathered to discuss the affair. This was one of the few times that I saw a general assembly convene for secular reasons. The debate was typically Walbiri—each man had already decided his stand and no amount of argument could move him from it. Most agreed that, although it was inconvenient to have an unattached young woman in the camp, Lucy was still Jumbo's wife and would have to leave Jimmy.

The rest of the hunting party arrived next morning. Abe went quickly to his shelter, where he remained without talking to anyone. Lucy, Jimmy and his seven age-mates (who included men of five subsections and three communities) stayed on the outskirts of the camp for some hours. Meanwhile. a group of seven of the older djabaldjari men armed themselves and congregated in the camp, shouting threats and obscenities at Jimmy and their "sister", Lucy.

Eventually the young men formed a hollow square around Jimmy and Lucy and walked slowly through the camp towards Abe's shelter. They used their shields and clubs to beat off the djabaldjari men, who kept trying to attack the offending couple with knives, clubs and spears. Some of the older nabaldjari women also joined in, swinging clubs at their "sister" who had disgraced herself. Suffering only gashed and bruised hands and arms, the defending party reached Abe's shelter, where a number of young women, led by Abe's wife, quickly surrounded Lucy. The young men then slipped away from the camp.

The presence of so many women effectively prevented the djabaldjari men from continuing their attacks on Lucy, for some of the women were their "mothers-in-law". They had to retreat to the other side of the camp. Jimmy and his age-mates met them there, and a confused brawl followed, in which nobody was seriously injured. The outcome was that the djabaldjari, presented with an accomplished fact, reluctantly approved the new union, and no more was heard of the matter.

I later asked Jimmy how he had managed to attract such a variety of relatives to his cause. He said he had simply appealed to the sympathy of the young men and reminded them that they were his age-mates. I am sure that their desire to score off the older, married men greatly facilitated his task. In a few years, however, there would be little likelihood that the same men would submerge kinship obligations to age-mate ties in other affrays.

CHAPTER XIV

GOVERNMENT AND LAW

Government. The Walbiri regard themselves as one people, who share a common culture and occupy a continuous territory with definite boundaries. They are aware that certain of their social groupings, such as subsection and moiety divisions, extend beyond these boundaries into other tribes, and they know that neighbouring Aborigines also possess the same framework of religious beliefs; nevertheless they assert that they have always been a people distinct from others, that they have never been members of any wider confederation or "nation" of contiguous tribes.

They say that in general they were not responsible to other Aborigines for their behaviour, although they realized that some actions, such as inter-tribal raids or violations of the secrecy of inter-tribal religious rituals, could invite retaliation. Concomitantly, they claimed the right to defend themselves from injury by non-Walbiri.

Men might describe such disputes as if they occurred between "the Walbiri" and, say, "those Waringari", but in fact the quarrels did not involve concerted tribal action. Similarly, when "we, the Walbiri", acquired new kangaroo myths and rituals from "those Bidjabidja", neither tribe as a unit initiated the transaction. It was a matter for particular cult-lodges to arrange. In short, the tribe as a whole did not function as a political or administrative entity. There were no tribal leaders, headmen, or chiefs; nor was there any controlling or ruling class of old or important men whose power extended through the society.

Although the Walbiri population was relatively small, the great size of the tribal territory and the difficult terrain combined with the subsistence pattern to limit the frequency of actual or surrogate inter-personal communications involving the entire tribe. Thus, if a sudden danger threatened or an emergency arose, the people as a whole could not learn of it in time to assemble in force to meet it; component groups simply had to take independent action as best they could. Moreover, none of the regular ceremonial gatherings brought together all the tribe at the one time, for there was no camp-site that could provide enough food and water to support a thousand people for more than a day or two. Instead, the normal pattern of inter-action was such that people who usually lived in localities as widely separated as, say, the Lander Creek and Vaughan Springs had no contacts with each other for nine or ten months of the year. If food was scarce as a result of poor seasons, they might not meet for two or three years at a time.

The subsections, patrimoieties and matrimoieties, which ex-tended through the tribe, likewise did not form distinct political units. They were not territorially-based and solidary groups with economic functions; rather, they defined (as they still do) broad categories of people, within which action groups could be speci-fied in terms of other criteria. The members of a subsection or a moiety did not all act together as a group, either *vis à vis* other Walbiri or in dealings with non-Walbiri. As I indicated earlier, community affiliation cut across these formal categories.

The four localized communities that made up the tribe were the largest groups with political and administrative functions. Although they were linked together by ties of friendship, mar-riage and ritual obligation and possessed the same laws and customs, each was nevertheless autonomous in its everyday affairs. The community was the largest unit that could be said to have "a corporate title to all the territory normally occupied by (its) resident members" (vide Oliver and Miller, 1955, p. 119) and to constitute an active group and not merely a social cate-gory. I did not, however, discover any myths directly or sym-bolically expressing separate origins or identities of the com-munities. Most myths indirectly imply that community inter-dependence is necessary for the maintenance of the totemic system, whereas their dramatization in ritual reflects the separa-tion of the communities.

Community affiliation depended primarily on birth (or, more strictly, conception) and subsequent residence in the territory occupied by the community and totemically associated with it. There were no ceremonies that facilitated the conversion of non-members into members. The fact of residence in itself gave only economic, and not ritual, rights to immigrants. Thus, a person living in the country of the spouse's community had free access to the available food supplies. On the other hand, although the host group would invite men of other communities to participate in religious ceremonies and, as a matter of courtesy, would consult them on these matters, the outsiders had no authority to make decisions. Today, this attitude extends to settlement membership.

> Peter djabanangga, a Waneiga Walbiri, was an important Gadjari leader at Wave Hill. In 1954 he paid a long visit to Hooker Creek to put his sons through the Gadjari ceremonies. His Waneiga countrymen, who included the local Gadjari leaders, welcomed him warmly. They included him in their discussions of plans for the rituals and often asked for his opinions. But I never saw them follow Peter's suggestions when these differed from their own, and Peter never volunteered advice unasked, except on matters directly concerning the Wave Hill Walbiri. On one occasion, he confided to me that the Hooker Creek leaders had erred badly in beginning the ceremonies while two men and their families were absent on a hunting trip. Everyone should be present for the Big Sunday, he said, so that "they would all think in the same way with the same head, and not in different ways". He also told me he could not make this criticism openly; even though he was a member of the master patrimoiety and had acted in the ceremonies, he was still only a visitor with no right to interfere in local affairs.

I have mentioned in previous chapters the chief activities that involved community-wide participation. In the good seasons, when particular localities could support large numbers of people, the whole community camped together in close face-to-face contact. The men commonly engaged in large-scale and highly-organized hunts, which involved firing the desert scrub to drive game into predetermined positions where hunters were stationed. The women went out daily in large parties to gather food and firewood. At night the men acted in ceremonies attended by all the camp. These dramatizations, like mediaeval European mystery plays, provided instruction, edification and entertainment for the young and (to judge from their performance on settlements today) they must have clearly expressed group solidarity. Serious religious ceremonies and initiation rites also took place on these occasions, activities in which all the community members had specified roles.

People of neighbouring communities were invited to participate in the ceremonies, but they could not direct their performance. Awareness of community unity and independence was further reinforced at these times by adherence to the rule that each group camped apart and did not enter the others' dwellings without permission. The intercommunity betrothals that were initiated or finalized during these gatherings also stressed community affiliations—especially when disputes arose over the identities of the true marriage "bosses" of the girls.

Whereas in everyday life people apparently treated a long-term resident from another community (especially a wife) as a countryman, their actions at the death of the outsider revealed the fundamental difference in the latter's status. Classificatory kin of the appropriate categories might mourn and carry out the duties connected with the disposal of the corpse that close kin and countrymen normally undertook; but the avenging of the death still remained the prerogative of the deceased's own matriline and natal community. A messenger informed these people, notably the mother's brothers, of the death, and they came to participate in the inquest. Later, they organized the revenge expedition or performed sorcery to destroy the putative killer, who was generally located in another community. It is at this point that we approach most closely the notion of intercommunity warfare.

Walbiri society did not emphasize militarism—there was no class of permanent or professional warriors; there was no hierarchy of military command; and groups rarely engaged in wars of conquest. Every man was (and is still) a potential warrior, always armed and ready to defend his rights; but he was also an individualist, who preferred to fight independently. In some disputes kinship ties aligned men into opposed groups, and such a group may occasionally have comprised all the men of a community. But there were no military leaders, elected or hereditary, to plan tactics and ensure that others adopted the plans. Although some men were respected as capable and courageous fighters and their advice was valued, other men did not necess-

arily follow them. Moreover, the range of circumstances in which
fights occurred was in effect so limited that men knew and could
employ the most effective techniques without hesitation. This
is still true today, even of young bachelors.

There was in any case little reason for all-out warfare between
communities. Slavery was unknown; portable goods were few;
and the territory seized in a battle was virtually an embarrassment to the victors, whose spiritual ties were with other localities. Small-scale wars of conquest against other tribes occurred
occasionally, but I am sure that they differed only in degree
from intratribal and even intracommunity fights. Thus, the
attack on the Waringari that led to the occupation of the waterholes in the Tanami area involved only Waneiga men—a few
score at most; and I have no evidence that communities ever
entered into military alliances, either to oppose other Walbiri
communities or other tribes.

The fact that wrong-doers could often find refuge in another
community also indicates that the communities usually respected each other's boundaries; and indeed the punitive party was
likely to confine itself to performing sorcery at a distance. Nevertheless, attempts to avenge deaths sometimes led to incursions
into the territories of neighbouring communities or tribes. In
the former instance, the men of the revenge party in a sense
represented their community against another community and
went out with their countrymen's approval. But the raids and
counter-raids usually concerned only specified groups of kinsmen and could thus be kept within manageable limits; rarely
would the whole community arm. The members not directly involved often acted as informal referees; by inviting men of the
other community to visit them for ceremonies, they created
opportunities for the public settlement of grievances.

Naturally, even such restricted conflicts no longer occur, in
the face of European penal sanctions; and to some extent the
mingling of communities on cattle-stations and Government
settlements has removed the reasons for them. Although the
belief is still current that almost all deaths are basically "homi-
cides", men now seek to retaliate covertly through the performance of sorcery.

The procedures by which group action was initiated and guided to its intended goal seem to have been fairly rigidly standardized—as indeed they still are. What people do now should as far as possible duplicate what is believed to have been done in the dreamtime, for this provides the ultimate sanction for any activity. Of course, complete parallelism cannot often be achieved in fact. A comparison of a number of circumcision ceremonies that I saw revealed that various contingencies and obstacles resulted in divergences in detail from mythologically-prescribed norms. Also, the norms themselves slowly change in response to deviations in the role-behaviour of individuals.

But it is clear that the over-all structure of community action must have been markedly constant through time. The close correlation of some activities with the seasons doubtless contributed to this stability; recognition of climatic, floral and faunal cues regularly stimulated their performance. Enactment of the Gadjari ceremonial cycle, for instance, waited on the appropriate season of the year, as did the communal kangaroo hunts. Nowadays, seasonal periodicity is still an indirect stimulus to ceremonial and other activity, because it affects the economic enterprises of European employers; they usually have to suspend pastoral and transport operations in the summer wet season, and this enables Aborigines to gather for rituals.

Whatever the source of the stimulus to action, its significance was at once apparent to the community members, who had early learned to recognize it. Similarly, they generally knew without prompting what roles to adopt in the subsequent activities. Most of these expectations were (and are) defined in genealogical terms. Consequently, the people did not have to make *ad hoc* plans for action; the norms of the religious and kinship systems constituted an enduring master-plan, which met most contingencies and to which there were few approved alternatives.

Thus, although the actual communication of news of an emergency posed a real problem for the Walbiri (one partly solved by sending out messengers), the organization of effective responses did not. Once a person was aware of the situation, he

knew what to do about it. There was, therefore, little need for
secular leaders in the community. Some men, better acquainted
than others with certain rules, might be asked to expound them,
but such requests chiefly concerned religious dogma and ritual
behaviour. And it is only in this field that we observe an approxi-
mation to institutionalized leadership.

There were particular men, for instance, who were expected
to co-ordinate the activities of Gadjari participants, and their
status as "Big Sunday bosses" was specifically defined and more
or less permanent. Once a man was recognized as a Gadjari
organizer (and there was no explicit procedure of election),
he remained a leader of all such ceremonies in his community
until he died or became senile. But, unless he was an unusually
forceful man, his authority did not extend into secular affairs,
even in his own community.

A clique of four Waneiga men usually organized the Gadjari
activities at Hooker Creek. The eldest, Danny djungarai, was
chief co-ordinator. Although he was a man of wide ceremonial
experience, he did not in fact know as much about the Gadjari
details as did Ginger djabangari, another of the clique. Nevertheless, Danny, as the senior man present of the master patrimoiety, announced all the decisions made by the four men
and as a rule gave the actual instructions to the various participants. His high ritual status, however, did not extend
into non-ceremonial activities. I saw him try several times
to halt fights in the general camp, but only once did he
succeed. Similarly, his ritual status did not prevent men from
attacking him physically when they had legitimate complaints
to make about his everyday behaviour.

At Yuendumu, Minjana djagamara, the senior man of the
lodge responsible for the important dreamings at Ngama
cave, was greatly respected for his vast ritual knowledge and
was loved for his personal charm. A few years earlier, his
intelligence and energy had extended his ceremonial authority
into other spheres of community life; but by 1955 he was old
and blind and rarely stirred from his shelter. Men still consulted him on ritual matters, but he had little to say in everyday affairs. No other man had come to occupy the position
he once held. His son, Hitler djuburula, who was aged about
50, had a certain amount of influence in the camp, largely
because he was an adept manipulator of men and a formidable
fighter. He could not, however, use his considerable ritual

knowledge (acquired from Minjana) to enhance his own prestige as long as his father was alive. Nor would he automatically succeed to Minjana's former status when the old man died; he would have to achieve this position by displaying tact, intelligence and drive. The number of enemies he had acquired made it unlikely that he would ever succeed.

The medicine-men or "clever fellows" (of whom there could rarely have been more than four or five to a community) often possessed a degree of prestige within the community boundaries and occasionally beyond them. In other respects, however, the medicine-man was hardly to be distinguished from his countrymen. He might be married or single, and of any age above about 30 years. The exercise of his assumed curative, destructive and divinatory powers, either on his own or on other people's behalf, brought him no material rewards (vide Elkin, 1945). Normally, he directed his sorcery outside the local community, so that he had little direct power based on fear over his countrymen; but occasionally he could indirectly control the actions of these men by threatening to withhold curing aid from wrong-doers (Meggitt, 1955a, p. 393). This was not a common occurrence in the past, nor is it today. In general, whatever secular or ritual authority he possessed was acquired in the same way as that of other men in his community.

Although the members of the community conceded some of their fellows the right to co-ordinate certain activities, the ascription of authority to particular men on particular occasions depended largely on considerations of kinship status and, by extension, of descent-line and moiety affiliation. Thus, a man might lead a specific revenge expedition, or dispose of a certain woman in marriage, or direct the actors in one circumcision ceremony, because of his genealogical connection with the person to whom the situation primarily referred—the deceased, the bride, or the novice. On the next occasion of this sort, however, he might play only a minor role, being now in a different kinship category relative to the central figure.

Obviously, this frequent variation in the extent of the authority that an individual exercised from one situation to another militated against the emergence of a class of permanent leaders of community enterprises, of men who could regularly and legitimately direct group behaviour in several fields of action.

Moreover, there was no consistent correlation of social prestige with authority, with the accepted control over the actions of others. A man who had high prestige as a custodian of ritual knowledge was often a mere spectator in certain community activities, whereas a man of poor reputation could, because of the kinship statuses involved, be the currently active organizer.

As we have seen, a system of age-grading embraces all the males over the age of about 12 years. But this did not produce a hierarchy of social classes or culminate in a gerontocracy; there was no solidary group of old men who wielded political power throughout the tribe. It is true that, within each community (and nowadays in each settlement camp), the old men made up a common-interest group; but it was informally recruited and cut across by moiety and descent-line affiliations. In general, the group or clique possessed social prestige simply because its members had a longer, but not necessarily wider, experience, particularly in ritual matters, than did their juniors.

Mere longevity, however, did not make these elders the leaders of the community. Whatever *de facto* control they had over the actions of others simply derived from their ability to make suggestions based on first-hand knowledge of commonly-recurring situations; people were bound to follow this advice only when it was couched as a statement of dreamtime rules. Not only were the old men unable to command the services of others, except on the basis of accepted kinship and ritual rights and privileges; they were also obliged to fulfil the corresponding duties. Age gave no immunity from social obligation; at best, it received mildly sympathetic tolerance and respect. Indeed, the prestige accorded to knowledge acquired in old age was, to some extent, offset by the loss of prestige following the effects of age on hunting and fighting skills. Thus, in some contexts, a man attracted social prestige only as long as he could validate his status by actual performance.

In short, the community had no recognized political leaders, no formal hierarchy of government. People's behaviour in joint activities was initiated and guided largely by their own knowledge and acceptance of established norms. European contact has not greatly changed this pattern, although there is an increasing (but still informal) delegation of authority by Europeans to men who have acquired new skills and who can speak some English. These men tend to stand between the Europeans and the camp people, transmitting instructions to the latter, voicing their complaints, and explaining to the Europeans the problems faced by the camp.

So far, the men who have achieved this new status have not come into serious conflict with conservative Walbiri, partly because they themselves recognize the dangers of such a collision. They take care to maintain their positions in the indigenous kinship and ritual systems by scrupulously meeting their obligations and by displaying great energy in ceremonial affairs. Consequently, the members of the camp can continue to grant them prestige as "true Walbiri", while at the same time tacitly utilizing them as go-betweens in the new plural society. The demonstrable efficacy of this innovation may well facilitate the painless emergence of accepted political leaders, supported by a tradition of service to both Walbiri and Europeans.

Law. The absence of individuals or groups in Walbiri society with permanent and clearly-defined legislative and judicial functions does not mean that social interaction is chaotic. There are explicit social rules, which, by and large, everybody obeys; and the people freely characterize each other's behaviour insofar as it conforms to the rules or deviates from them. The totality of the rules expresses the law, *djugaruru,* a term that may be translated also as "the line" or "the straight or true way". Its basic connotation is of an established and morally-right order of behaviour (whether of planets or of people), from which there should be no divergence.

Walbiri law, then, is a body of jural rules and moral evaluations that specify: (*a*) the rights and duties (the role-expectations) associated with all the statuses in the society; (*b*) the manner in which reasonable occupants of the statuses should fulfil the expectations; and (*c*) the procedures to be followed when the expectations are not fulfilled.

Adherence to the law is itself a basic value, for this is thought to distinguish the Walbiri from all other people, who are consequently inferior. As the law originated in the dreamtime, it is beyond critical questioning and conscious change. The totemic philosophy asserts that man, society and nature are interdependent components of one system, whose source is the dreamtime; all are, therefore, amenable to the law, which is co-eval with the system. The law not only embraces ritual, economic, residential and kinship rules and conventions but also what we would call natural laws and technological rules. The care of sacred objects by the men of one patrimoiety, the sexual division of labour, the avoidance of mothers-in-law, the mating of bandicoots, the rising of the sun, and the use of fire-ploughs are all forms of behaviour that is lawful and proper—they are all *djugaruru*.

Although the people speak as if these observably different kinds of behaviour are fundamentally the same, they do in practice distinguish between, on the one hand, role-expectations and penal procedures and, on the other, the techniques or modes of role-fulfilment. Their division roughly parallels the traditional anthropological distinction between law and custom, in terms of the criterion of "the degree of compulsion exerted on the actor". For instance, a man's father- and brothers-in-law upbraid and sometimes attack him physically if he refuses to give meat to his wife. Other members of the community approve as legitimate their attempts to force him to adhere to the law. Moreover, the meat should come from game he has hunted himself; if, instead, he offers his wife meat given to him as a ritual payment for circumcising a boy, his behaviour is both unusual and improper. But his affines do not have the right to penalize him for this action, although they may ridicule his eccentricity. The difference between the two cases is that between offence and poor taste, between breaking a law and ignoring the customary way of meeting the law's requirements.

The relationship of the law to the behaviour of natural or non-human objects is somewhat different. The sun, the rain and the kangaroos, for instance, are also included in the social structure and have role-expectations to fulfil; but the problem of their failing to act lawfully rarely arises. The sun rises regularly, the rain falls eventually, and the kangaroos breed; their behaviour is thus rather more lawful than that of contemporary people. Men interested in religious dogma do, I think, take this characteristic to indicate that non-human beings are more under the control of dreamtime law than are ordinary people. There seems to be a none-too-explicit recognition of the operation of human free-will in daily affairs, which is correspondingly balanced by a lack of complete control over the actions of dreamtime noumena.

Despite this apparent anomaly (which, doubtless, most Walbiri rarely consider), men believe that all forms of behaviour are ultimately subject to dreamtime laws. Regularity, frequency, efficiency, and propriety are all expressions of normality—behaviour is predictable because it should be. Walbiri monism, like all monistic metaphysics, is inevitably moral, conservative and circular.

The people clearly had little difficulty in maintaining this conservatism before the coming of the Europeans. Their sociocultural and physical environment was then comparatively stable, and the range of events that men were likely to encounter was relatively limited. We do not know how the law developed to meet this reality; but, once it was formulated, the people had little reason to change it, especially as the putative basis of the stability of the cosmos, the dreamtime, was thought to be everpresent.

This is not to deny that some changes must have occurred; but, as innovations came either from within the group or from neighbouring groups that were very similar, they were likely to have been fully compatible with the existing framework, and the fiction of the immutability of the law could be maintained. Certainly, the people have no tradition that the law can be changed.

On the other hand, they do recognize that conventions or customary modes of behaviour alter. In the past, they were probably rarely forced to distinguish in this way between law and custom, as whatever new cultural element that was accepted from inside or outside the tribe could with little alteration be accommodated to the existing pattern of belief and usage. This was true, for instance, of the subsection system, the Gadjari cycle, and of subincision. But contact with Europeans has sharpened the distinction, and the most obvious changes have been in behaviour previously guided by convention rather than compulsion.

Men today may light fires with matches, smooth boomerangs with metal rasps, warm their bodies with clothing, circumcise their boys with razor-blades. Such innovations do not upset even the most conservative. Yet, although it is now unimportant whether a man acquires his meat by spearing a kangaroo or by collecting an issue of beef, public opinion still demands that he be penalized if he refuses to share it with his father-in-law. Men may substitute money for weapons in bride-price, but they must still give some kind of bride-price to complete a betrothal. Conventional ways of behaving may change as a result of European contact, but the laws have altered little to meet new problems. This immutability is related in part to the absence of any self-conscious legislative body among the Walbiri.

There is, moreover, an internal consistency in the law. I rarely observed disputes in which the jural norms themselves conflicted. What sometimes appeared to be disagreements of this sort were in fact usually pseudo-contradictions that arose because the disputants ignored, deliberately or unwittingly, the existence of qualifying or mitigating circumstances. Thus, the people assert that it is a crime for one Walbiri to kill another, unless the intended victim is demonstrably a homicide or has interfered with certain sacred objects; then it is the duty of specified persons to execute him. If a man has been killed for such an offence and his matrikin wish to avenge his death (their intention is itself unlawful), they may try to justify their actions by citing only the principal clause of the rule.

Ambiguity in the statement of a rule occasionally brings people into opposition, which they may resolve by appealing to equity. A widow, for instance, must not remarry until she has mourned for a decent period, lest her husband's ghost attack her. Although there is no explicit definition of this interval, it is generally taken to last for about 12 to 18 months. But, should the future husband of the widow be a bachelor or widower, he is likely to demand her within a few months, pointing in justification to the norm that every man should have a wife to care for him and to bear him children. The men of the woman's matriline may then decide that it would be equitable to redefine the mourning term to hasten her remarriage, and apparently the ghost concurs. At the same time, another man who hoped to marry the widow might insist, unsuccessfully, that she mourn for the full period. The notion of general equity may also enter to mitigate the unintended harshness of some rules.

Although a man may marry his "m.b.d." as an alternative to his "m.m.b.d.d.", he should not marry his "d.d.", who is of the same subsection as the "m.b.d." Nevertheless, the maternal kinsmen of young Maggie nambidjimba allowed her to marry her old "mother's father", Budda djabaldjari. They thought it unreasonable that the absence of suitable "m.m.b.d.d." and "m.b.d." should force a man of his age to live alone.

In general, however, there is little "uncertainty" or "flexibility" inherent in the basic jural norms (vide Gluckman, 1955, p. 291). The coherent cosmology of the dreamtime is reflected in unequivocal statements of what should or should not be done in particular situations. In the absence of formally-appointed judicial bodies equipped to expound the law, such simplicity has obvious advantages. It is also apparent in the summary assessment of guilty intent. Men argue that, as all intercourse among the people concerns "relatives", and as everyone has been taught the rules defining the relevant roles, a person cannot plead ignorance of the law in extenuation of misconduct. Every reasonable man knows that certain behaviour is unlawful and incurs definite penalties. If he has acted in this way, he must have placed present advantage above future punishment; he must have intended to break the law.

Some of the terms that describe human and other behaviour express this "legalistic psychology" (vide Gluckman, 1955, p. 153): *jidjaru*—true, factually correct; *walga*—false, factually incorrect, intended to deceive; *djuŋa*—proper, morally correct; *djuŋanigili*—behaving properly, law-abiding, expressing proper intentions, "straight", right-handed; *wiŋgi*—improper; *wiŋgigili* —behaving improperly, lawless, expressing improper intentions, "crooked".

The effective punishment of law-breakers involves the general acceptance of certain conditions by the public at large: (*a*) some person (or group) who is acquainted with the law must be accepted as competent to compare the alleged facts with the legal norm and to decide whether the behaviour in question is illicit; (*b*) some person conversant with the range of legal penalties current in the society must be accepted as competent to nominate the punishment due to the offender; (*c*) some person must be accepted as competent to administer the punishment, which should be sufficiently publicized to deter potential law-breakers;

and (d) some person must ensure that the offender and his kinsmen do not try to retaliate against the administrator of the legal punishment.

Every adult Walbiri at some time or other has the privilege of judging the behaviour of others; but only the older initiated men are competent to judge the whole range of problem-situations that are inherent in traditional social life. That is to say, although every person should know the legal norms governing his or her own statuses, only the initiated men are able to learn all the rules associated with all the statuses in the society. Thus, they should know not only how a man should behave towards his father-in-law, or a woman towards her daughter, but also how a lodge member should behave towards the sacred bull-roarers of his brother-in-law's lodge. Women and children are, and should be, ignorant of the last.

There are, therefore, some forms of behaviour whose illegality uninitiated people cannot assess, because they are not permitted to know of the situations or the relevant rules. Every person, however, is expected at least to have an opinion about any alleged transgression of any legal norms of which he is cognizant; and personal, veridical observation of the behaviour in question is not a necessary condition of his making a judgment.

I list in Table 22 the offences that are commonly recognized by the Walbiri; these are the forms of behaviour regarded as "unlawful". I have ranked them roughly in order of seriousness.

TABLE 22

Offences recognized by the Walbiri

A. *Offences of commission*
1. Unauthorized homicide (that is, not decreed as a punishment for another offence).
2. Sacrilege (that is, the unauthorized possession of sacred knowledge and objects and the unauthorized observation of sacred rituals).
3. Unauthorized sorcery (1. and 3. are not easily distinguished).
4. Incest (copulation with actual kin of certain categories).
5. Cohabitation with certain kin (usually classificatory relatives in the categories associated with 4.).
6. Abduction or enticement of women.
7. Adultery with certain kin (usually classificatory relatives in the categories associated with 5.).

8. Adultery with potential spouses (7. and 8. in effect cover all cases of fornication).
9. Unauthorized physical assault, not intended to be fatal.
10. Usurpation of ritual privileges or duties.
11. Theft and intentional destruction of another's property (exclusive of 2.).
12. Insult (including swearing, exposure of the genitals).

B. *Offences of omission*
1. Physical neglect of certain relatives.
2. Refusal to make gifts to certain relatives.
3. Refusal to educate certain relatives.

Partly as a result of the comparative stereotypy of most social behaviour (including that of offenders) and partly because of the limited number of possible offences, public opinion is rarely divided on the question of whether or not a person has broken the law. Such popular consensus, of course, does not always mean that he is in fact guilty; but miscarriages of justice appear to be uncommon. The people rarely permit considerations of intratribal social status to distort their interpretation of the law (except sometimes in the case of women). What is penalized on one occasion is unlikely to be condoned on another.

A Gadjari leader is not immune from punishment when he attacks another person for private reasons. A medicine-man who "sings" a faithless mistress is as guilty of intended homicide as is any other man who performs sorcery for personal advantage. Indeed, when a medicine-man "sings" an alleged killer in another community, his own countrymen do not justify his action simply in terms of the superior status of their group; they regard him as the agent of an impartial Walbiri law. It is true that an inquest on a death is likely to locate the culprit in another community, rather than in that of the deceased, and covert ethnocentrism may well determine this outcome; but in theory the putative killer could have been a local person, who would be punished in the same way as an outsider would be.

But, although the law should protect and punish all Walbiri without fear or favour, it tends to stop short at the borders of their territory. Thus, there is no penalty for the Walbiri who kills a member of another tribe, who cuckolds a non-Walbiri or abducts his wife. Such behaviour is by no means praiseworthy, but the people condone it.

Sacrilege, however, is a different matter. If, for instance, a Walbiri desecrates ritual objects belonging to the Yanmadjari tribe, the men of the Walbiri patrimoiety corresponding to that of the Yanmadjari custodians upbraid and even attack the offender. I was told that, should the Yanmadjari custodians pursue him into his own country, only his close kinsmen would stand by him. Other Walbiri would hesitate to save him from the punishment he deserved. That is to say, the law, where it concerns religious beliefs and activities, is to some extent international; neighbouring tribes share the same jural norms.

The variety of penalties recognized as appropriate to proven offences is as limited as the range of offences themselves. The paucity of material property clearly has a bearing here. At any rate, if the people cannot fine, bankrupt, or imprison an offender, they can do little else than berate, strike, or kill him. Ostracism, whether formal or informal, does not occur, probably because of the practical difficulties in attempting it in an Aboriginal camp. The notion of enforced, permanent exile is repugnant to the people. Exile would sever a man from his dreamings and prevent his participation in the dreamtime, and without his dreamings he would no longer be human.

In the following table, I have arranged the penalties roughly in order of their severity. The letters and figures in brackets refer to Table 22; they indicate offences for which the punishments are typical.

TABLE 23

The penalties faced by Walbiri law-breakers

1. Death—a. caused by a non-human agency (A2).
   b. caused by human sorcery (A1, possibly A3).
   c. caused by physical attack (A1, A2, possibly A3).
2. Insanity—caused by a non-human agency (A2).
3. Illness—caused by human sorcery (A1, A2, A3, A5, A6, A7, A8; B1, B2).
4. Wounding—attack with a spear or knife, intended to draw blood (A5, A6, A7, A8, A9, A10, A11).
5. Battery—attack with a club or boomerang (A6, A7, A8, A9, A10, A11, A12; B1, B2, B3).
6. Oral abuse—this accompanies all human punishments.
7. Ridicule—this is directed mainly at offences of omission.

When people are taught legal norms, they simultaneously learn of the punishments appropriate to their infraction; consequently, a person who is competent to judge whether certain behaviour transgresses a rule is also able to nominate the punishment due to the offender. It is at this point that considerations of community membership, kinship and friendship are likely to bias the individual's judgment.

The stated penalty is in effect the maximum that may follow the offence; and people sympathetic to the offender may plead for a lesser punishment. They do not deny his offence, for this is usually patent, but they argue *ad misericordiam* on his behalf, often successfully. Sometimes, however, people (even close relatives) demand that a persistent offender receive the heaviest penalty possible. Thus, a person's reputation, and not his present behaviour alone, may determine the treatment accorded him; very rarely, a chronic recidivist is killed for an offence that, in another man, would occasion a much lighter punishment.

The legal norms not only define the offence and its consequence but also nominate who should carry out the punishment. Community membership and genealogical connection are the basic criteria in this selection; and there is rarely any doubt about the identity and the acceptability of the person who should act. Thus, an inquest following a sudden death reveals (magically) the kinship category and the community affiliation of the putative killer; the law states specifically that the close mother's brothers of the deceased must ascertain the actual identity of the murderer and then kill him. If a man wounds his wife for some trifling delinquency, the law asserts that her father, brother, or mother's brother (but nobody else) should attack him.

In short, the people have little difficulty in discriminating between acceptable, authorized punishment of an offence and unauthorized injury inflicted for personal advantage. The clear definition of genealogical statuses and community affiliations facilitates this distinction.

Evidence of this sort suggests that transgressions of jural norms generally take the form of torts or private delicts (vide Radcliffe Brown, 1952, p. 12); one individual or group injures another, who directly or through a surrogate retaliates in a prescribed manner, while other people stand by to see fair play. Particular kinsmen and countrymen of the aggrieved person judge the offence and punish the offender, but to a large extent their actions are guided by public opinion, as expressed by people not directly involved in the dispute. There are, however, some misdeeds (those we might loosely term sacrilege) that are crimes or public delicts. The people regard them as attacks on the religious system itself, as undermining the bases of the law and the society as a whole. It is significant that their retribution is sometimes thought to follow automatically, without the intervention of other people.

During circumcision ceremonies held at night at Hooker Creek in 1953 some of the men wore the dangerously "strong" *landjulgari* dentalium shells, the sight of which is believed to be fatal to women. While the men were secretly arranging the shells in the bush near the ceremonial ground, little Biddy nabanangga, the daughter of Maggie nambidjimba, wandered away from the dancing women. Being a close "father's sister" of the novice, Maggie could not stop dancing, so her close "mother", widowed Maisie nungarai, set off to look for Biddy. Mistaking her path in the darkness, Maisie inadvertently stumbled on the men preparing the shells. Terrified, she said nothing but retired to the widows' camp.

Nobody had injured Maisie physically or performed sorcery against her; but within a few days she was insane and had wasted away to skin and bone. One morning the medicine-man was called to the widows' camp, where she lay apparently lifeless. He examined her and announced that she was dead. Relatives at once prepared her for burial. After another examination, however, my wife discovered that Maisie was still alive. Subsequent attention apparently counteracted the prevailing mental factors; the old woman rallied and was on her feet two days later. Nevertheless, she remained insane.

Men with whom I discussed the affair said that Maisie's "trouble" did not surprise them. She had broken an important dreamtime law, the automatic punishment for which should be death; everyone therefore expected her to die. The fact that she had seen the shells accidentally while acting like a good "mother" to help her "daughter" was irrelevant. She knew what she was doing; she knew the law; consequently, she must have intended to act in that way.

In practice, complete reliance on the supernatural punishment of sacrilegious behaviour seems to be relatively rare. Usually men of the patrimoiety who are custodians of the desecrated ritual objects are required to seek out the offender and kill him (or her), either by making a physical attack or by performing sorcery. The avengers are authorized executioners, who express the common will of all the men of the tribe. The transgression has injured not only the lodge to which the objects belong but also the whole tribe in its relationship with the dreamtime. In effect, all the initiated men judge the matter; and, although those who actually administer the punishment are chosen ultimately on a kinship and community basis, they act for and with the approval of all the men.

I did not learn of any actual cases of incest, that is, of sexual intercourse with close relatives in certain prohibited categories; but people's accounts of what should be done when incest is discovered indicated that there is no sharp distinction between private and public delicts. Some men regarded incest as a private offence that simply infringes the rights of the actual or potential spouses of the culprits. Their punishment, administered by the spouses and maternal kin of the offenders, should be that suitable to aggravated adultery. Other men saw incest as a prime offence against fundamental dreamtime law, a transgression that undermined the whole basis of marriage. If the culprits did not die at once as a result of supernatural intervention, their relatives should act as the representatives of tribal law and morality to punish them. This division of opinion is also reflected in myths that tell of incest which occurred in the dreamtime. I give two examples.

A rain-dreaming man, Munggudulu, who lived near Djabia-djabia in the dreamtime, continually pursued the wives of his "brothers", a habit that led him into many quarrels. One day, however, he seduced his own mother-in-law, a woman with whom intercourse was regarded as incestuous. He incurred no supernatural or automatic punishment; but when his father-in-law learned of the offence, he was so angry that he performed sorcery and "sang something into Munggudulu's body". Munggudulu pleaded with a medicine-man to remove the object and cure him, but the latter refused to help such a wrong-doer. Munggudulu then died in great pain.

A dreamtime man who lived near Wagulbu (Rock Hill) tried to seduce his own mother-in-law. Horrified, she rejected his advances. He was so overcome by lust that he raped her. His penis burst as soon as it entered her vulva, and he died at once. The place where his body entered the earth is now called Gulu ("penis-bone") rockhole.

The question of publicizing the punishments of offenders in order to deter potential law-breakers requires little discussion. There is almost no privacy in a Walbiri camp. Punishment must be meted out in the public gaze, and the observers are quick to point the moral to their juniors. This inevitable publicity may well be a significant factor determining the general conformity of the people to the more important jural rules. Not only does everyone actually see that wrong-doers usually suffer for their offences, but they also see that by and large law-abiding persons benefit from public approval in that the latter find it easier to acquire wives, ritual gifts and prestige.

Finally, I should mention that the plaintiff in a Walbiri dispute never seeks punitive damages, and there is no way in which the defendant may offer material compensation for a misdeed. But a recognized procedure exists whereby a man may compound symbolically for a serious offence.

When men from another community or tribe arrive for ceremonies, they usually first perform a penis-offering ritual with their hosts. Each visitor approaches each of the seated hosts in turn and lifts the latter's arm. He presses his penis against the host's hand, so that the subincised urethra is in full contact with the palm, and then draws the penis firmly along the hand. A man with a grievance against the visitor refuses to raise his hand for the ritual. At this sign of hostility, the visitor at once presents his penis to each of his classificatory "brothers" among the hosts. Should none of the "brothers" take it, the outsider must be ready to fight or to flee; he now knows that public opinion is solidly against him. But a "brother" who touches the visitor's penis consents to sponsor him and must stand and plead his case. If the appeal fails, he must also fight beside the outsider. In fact, if the visitor can find a sponsor in this way, he is likely to win his argument, for the "brother's" action indicates that many of the hosts tacitly support the outsider.

The aggrieved man among the hosts, however, may still be

unsatisfied and may demand blood. If the visitor has a son (either of his own or of a "brother") who is old enough to be circumcised or subincised, he places a stone knife on the shoulder of the angry man. This action nominates the man as the son's circumciser or subinciser, an obligation he cannot refuse, whatever his kinship relationship to the youth. He must, therefore, ritually "kill" the youth, who substitutes for the father, and he can no longer urge his quarrel on the outsider. But, unlike the usual circumciser, he does not have to find a wife for the youth afterwards.

The Walbiri assert that they acquired this ritual of penis-offering from the Pidjandjara to the south and in turn have taught it to the Mudbura, Gurindji and Malngjin to the north. The observations of Berndt (1945, p. 328) at Macumba (in South Australia) and Wave Hill confirm the Aborigines' statements.

CHAPTER XV

BETROTHAL, MARRIAGE AND CHILD-BIRTH

I have so far dealt mainly with the more general structural features of Walbiri society—the local divisions within the tribe, the statuses comprising the kinship system, the descent lines and moieties, the subsections and the age-grading systems. Finally, I discussed the distribution of authority within the tribe and the ways in which the jural norms are supported. I want now to examine in detail a number of recurring and institutionalized situations in order to demonstrate how the various social groupings and categories interact and how this orients people's behaviour. The situations I have chosen concern betrothal, marriage, child-birth, initiation and death.

Betrothal. There are three ways in which a man may legitimately acquire a wife—through the levirate, through private negotiation with the woman's kinsmen, and as a result of being circumcised by a man who becomes his father-in-law. In the first two there is no preliminary stage of betrothal, but I mention them here to clear the ground for discussion of the third.

A bachelor who constantly demands a wife from his *djuraldja* line (the wife's matriline of descent) may receive a woman through the operation of the junior levirate. The allocation of a widow in marriage is in the hands of her male matrikin, who consult with the elder brothers of her late husband. They offer her first to the actual younger brother of the deceased; but this is a mere formality. Ideally, he (and other genealogically close "younger brothers") should reject her, for her presence would re-animate the grief he feels for the dead man. Eventually, she should be given to a distant "younger brother" of her late husband, one who has not been so attached to the latter. A man does not have to hand over bride-price for a widow.

The figures in Table 24 (drawn from genealogies) indicate that the remarriage of widows tends in fact to conform to this ideal, which raises the problem of how to characterize it accurately. To refer simply to the levirate misses the point as far as the people are concerned. For them, subsections do not "make the levirate practically inevitable" (vide Murdock, 1949, p. 175); they go to some trouble to give the widow to a man who is not an actual or close brother of the deceased.

TABLE 24

Remarriage of Walbiri widows

Category of new husband	Frequency
Husband's brother	3
Husband's half-brother	1
Husband's father's brother's son	5
"Husband's brother"	50
Total	59

chi squared ("H.B.", others) $= 28 \cdot 5$, df $= 1$, p $\angle$ ·01

From the group of eligible "husband's brothers", the widow's matrikin are likely to select a bachelor as her new husband, especially one who has for some years pressed them to give him a wife. As the widow may well be nearing middle-age, sexually unattractive, unable to bear children, and of doubtful economic assistance, the young man in effect acquires a dependant rather than a wife. Older men are aware of this probability and see the marriage as a rather bitter joke played on the young man, one intended to teach him that he cannot bully or bustle his elders into favouring him.

Sometimes a man (married or single) privately approaches the father and mother's brother of a woman and asks for her in marriage. Even if he choses a prepubescent girl, there is no betrothal. Her parents, mother's brother and M.M.B. discuss the request informally. Provided the girl is not promised in any way to another man, they may accept bride-price from the suitor and tell him to take her into his camp as soon as he wishes. Normally, he does not hurry the transfer of the girl; if she is very young, he permits her to spend long periods with her mother. Nevertheless, the girl is regarded as his wife from the moment he hands over the bride-price. He need not make another gift when she comes to live permanently with him, although some men do so in order to consolidate their friendship with their new affines.

Marriages are not often arranged in this way. As most men have been circumcisers several times by the time they are middle-aged, they are unlikely to have young daughters who are not already committed to marry. Adult women free to be the subjects of negotiation are even more rare. The very few that I encountered had divorced husbands of poor reputation.

The ideal marriage arrangement, and indeed the most common, is that in which a man promises his daughter (as yet unborn) to the M.B.S.S. or the "mother's brother" whom he has circumcised. If, as occasionally happens, he has circumcised his "F.Sr.D.S." or his "F.Sr.S.", he should later find a sister's daughter or a w.m.b.d. for him. But, irrespective of the kinship status of the circumciser, a betrothal is essentially a union between two matrilines of descent. The circumcision ceremony is, among other things, a public indication that a particular matriline will later provide the lad with a wife. Other men, by acting as the boy's *jualbiri*, those who decorate him before the circumcision, guarantee that they will ensure that this matriline honours its obligation.

Ideally, a young man is betrothed to a "m.m.b.d.d." who was born when he was about 18 years old. There may be deviations from this norm, as when his elder brother has a prior claim on the same father-in-law; but generally care is taken to prevent a man from entering into too many marriage commitments simultaneously. Thus, the elder brother, father, mother's brother and M.M.B. of a candidate for circumcision prefer not to invite a man to perform the operation who already "owes" daughters to a number of youths. If it does happen that the circumciser has no daughter available when the time comes for betrothal, he must ask an actual or close brother who has married into his wife's matriline to provide a daughter. In return he surrenders to his brother the right to dispose in marriage a daughter subsequently born to him. Should his brothers be unable to help him, he may call on one of the *jualbiri* to give a daughter or a sister's daughter to the young man.

The public ceremony of betrothal occurs when the girl is between six and 18 months old. The father and maternal kinsmen of the young man decide that his *djuraldja* line (his future wife's matriline) must now meet its obligation, and one of the men warns the girl's father or mother's brother of this. Close cognates of the suitor help him to accumulate the bride-price. In the past this included such things as cooked meat (especially kangaroo and emu), pieces of red-ochre, skeins of hair-string, boomerangs, hunting and fighting spears, spear-throwers and softwood shields—articles readily available to all men in the society. Nowadays, clothes, cloth, blankets, and money are also acceptable.

> Larry djungarai gave £1, six blankets, six spears and eight boomerangs to the father of his first wife and £1 to her mother's brother. He gave £1 each to the father and mother's brother of his second wife (from another matriline).
>
> Robber djabanangga gave £1, two iron-headed spears, four skeins of hair-string and three pieces (about three yards) of calico to his wife's father and the same (less the money) to her mother's brother.
>
> Paddy djagamara gave £1 and several shirts, pairs of trousers, and pieces of calico to be shared equally by the father and mother's brother of his wife.

A close kinsmen of the young man advises the girl's mother's brother that the bride-price is on hand. The suitor sits near his father's shelter, with his parents, mother's brother and, occasionally, his elder brother. The bride-price lies in a heap at his side. The parents of the young girl wait with her in their own shelter, which is likely to be on the other side of the camp. Her mother's brother ascertains that both groups are ready and then carries the infant slowly through the general camp, telling everyone who asks where he is going. He places the girl on the right thigh of her betrothed and, as the young man gently holds her, announces the reason for his visit. He informs the young man that the child is his future wife, of whom he must take good care or answer to her matrikin for his negligence. (If the suitor is already married, for instance, through the operation of the levirate, the betrothal takes place at his own shelter. The girl's mother's brother then hands her first to the man's wife, who is normally her "elder sister", and she places the child on her husband's thigh. The mother's brother then makes a speech.)

As soon as the audience say that they understand and approve of his remarks, the mother's brother carries the child back to

her parents, telling them that everything has gone forward satis-
factorily. He returns for the bride-price, which he shares with
the girl's father in accordance with the donors' instructions. The
parents and the mother's brother of the child eat the cooked
meat without more ado. Later, her father gives some of his own
portion of the bride-price articles to his adult sons, and the
mother's brother gives part of his to the M.M.B.

A few days later, the girl's mother prepares a return gift of
cooked vegetable-food, usually several unleavened and stodgy
cakes made of ground grass-seed, which the mother's brother
carries to the young man. The latter shares the food with all
those who contributed to his bride-price. The direction of this
exchange of gifts is strictly defined; a woman would not eat
vegetable-food sent by her son-in-law, and he would not accept
cooked meat from her. (Elkin has reported the existence of a
similar rule among the Pidjandjara; 1940, p. 344.) Henceforth,
the man makes occasional gifts of meat to the girl's parents
and mother's brother and feeds these men whenever they visit
him. His mother-in-law need not send him more vegetable-food.

The Walbiri regard betrothal as a significant event, and they
confirm the new relationship formally and publicly. In this
respect, they differ from many of the peoples who surround
them, such as the Pidjandjara, Warramunga, Daly River and
east Kimberley tribes (vide Berndt, 1945, pp. 111, 116; Elkin,
1940, p. 342; Spencer and Gillen, 1904, p. 602; Stanner, 1934,
p. 459; Kaberry, 1939, p. 77). The Aranda, however, celebrate
a betrothal with a public ceremony (vide Spencer and Gillen,
1899, p. 558).

Marriage. A bachelor sees little of his future wife during
the seven or eight years following his betrothal, even if both are
members of the same community. The girl is always in the
company of her mother or her mother's mother, women whom
he must scrupulously avoid. But a man who is already married
encourages his wife to invite his betrothed to visit her occasionally, so that the two may become better acquainted.

When a man thinks his betrothed is old enough to leave her
mother—that is, when she is about eight or nine years old—he
privately asks her father and mother's brother to send her to
his shelter. The men instruct the girl's mother accordingly, and

the girl joins her husband without any formality. Her father and mother's brother simply tell onlookers that the betrothal is consummated. At first the girl stays only two or three nights with her husband and then returns to live with her mother for a week or two. Gradually she spends longer periods in his camp until, within about three months, she resides there permanently.

Shortly after receiving his wife, the man informally hands over some meat and other articles to her father and mother's brother. He provides the gift himself, which is smaller than that made at the time of betrothal. (If the couple belong to different communities, the man usually comes to the girl's country in order to marry her. The same procedure is followed; and, after about six months, they go to live with the man's community.)

The statement that there is no wedding ceremony requires comment. The people regard the initial removal of the girl to her husband's dwelling at his request as the termination of the betrothal and the beginning of the marriage. Her walking through the camp to join the man constitutes the public statement of the fact. There is no additional, formal behaviour on the part of the relatives of either the husband or the wife, for instance, analogous with that which Berndt (1945, p. 116) has observed among the Pidjandjara or Kaberry (1939, p. 94) among the East Kimberley tribes.

Spencer and Gillen have asserted that, among all the tribes of the central desert, it was usual when a pubescent girl married for certain kinsmen to deflower her manually and to copulate with her (1899, p. 92). Moreover, there is some evidence that in inland Aboriginal cultures the practices of subincision, vaginal introcision and defloration tend to appear together rather than independently (vide Roth, 1897, p. 175). One might expect, therefore, that the Walbiri, who still carry out subincision, once conformed to this pattern.

But the people themselves deny that ritual defloration and vaginal introcision are, or have been, Walbiri customs. Some of the men told me that they were aware that neighbouring tribesmen, such as the Warramunga, performed the operations; but, they said, Walbiri men have no need to do so. As they take young (that is, prepubescent) girls to "grow up" as wives and copulate with them without delay, they simply rely on the acts of coitus to achieve this end. I discussed the matter privately with a number of men whose wives were from about eight to ten years old, and each man confirmed the statement.

The men all desire their wives to be sturdy and well-formed. So, for several nights after a young girl comes to live with him, the husband sits alone by his fire and softly sings *ilbindji* love-magic, which is thought to speed the growth of her breasts and buttocks. The songs, however, are not intended to develop her child-bearing potentiality or to enlarge her genitals, for in some obscure manner her *guruwari* dreaming determines the growth of these organs. Sometimes a group of younger married men gathers in the bush by day to sing these songs, in order to bene-fit all the young wives in the camp. The singers make mounds of sand to represent the girls' breasts and buttocks, over which they crouch as they chant in a harsh, staccato fashion. The atmosphere becomes electric with unconcealed eroticism, and there is much obscene joking and horse-play.

Conception and child-birth. A man who was previously un-married copulates regularly with a prepubescent wife soon after she joins his camp. A man who already has a mature and sexually active wife, however, sleeps less often with his second wife until she reaches puberty; then both wives share his bed in turn.

It is difficult to assess Aborigines' ages accurately, but it is probable that the menarche usually occurs when the girl is about 14 years old, although there may be about a year's latitude either way. At the first indication of the onset of the menses, the girl's mother and elder sister take her without ceremony to the widows' camp, where they dig a hole about two feet deep and three feet in diameter. They make a fire in this and then cover the coals with a thick layer of the leaves of *Acacia dictyophleba*. The naked girl squats on the leaves, so that the acrid smoke may "penetrate her vagina and make her strong". She sits there until the menstrual flow ceases, then fills in the pit and returns without formality to her husband's shelter.

The people associate the development of the girl's secondary sexual characteristics with the occurrence of the menarche, but they appear to have no theory to account for menstruation. The men are not (overtly) interested in the matter; it is "the affair of women". The women simply regard it as an event that occurs "every moon"; and irregular menstruation seems to be uncommon. Most women stated that their periods lasted for three days and were rarely accompanied by marked discomfort, depression, cramps and the like. There are no charms or spells to ward off such ill-effects, or to delay or hasten the periods. Although copulation during the menstrual period is not explicitly forbidden, it is regarded as physically distasteful. Normally a woman vacates her husband's bed during her periods, but she is not specifically debarred from ordinary social intercourse.

The Walbiri ascribe to human blood in general a quality of "strength", but only on particular ritual occasions does it become sacred. Menstrual blood is not in itself dangerous or evil; it is simply blood, and people need not take great care over its disposal. They may say that human excreta are physically offensive or "stinking" and should be covered with sand if deposited too close to the camp, but many people are in fact lax in this respect. (This attitude is also compatible with the rarity of "exuvial" sorcery.)

Thus, menstruating women are not regarded as dangerous or ritually unclean. People with whom they would ordinarily come into contact do not have to avoid them; they may prepare their own and their family's food; they may handle any objects or implements they normally use; they incur no special dietary restrictions; they may visit or care for sick relatives. Usually, however, they postpone setting out on strenuous food-gathering expeditions or carrying firewood and water. On the second day of her period, a woman is likely to retire to the widows' camp, or to a shelter near her husband's camp, and sit over a small pit in which her blood is caught. Neither she nor her husband undertakes any ritual or physical cleansing before resuming sexual intercourse, which may begin on the night her period ends.

Although most girls start copulating more or less regularly several years before they reach puberty, I have no record of any woman who bore a child before attaining the (apparent) age of about 17. The people themselves take this as a matter of course; women at that age have reached the stage of development appropriate to parturition and the effective action of the dreamings.

The native theory of conception is fairly elaborate. But, although it is clear that people in the past recognized the fact of physiological maternity, we cannot be sure to what extent they were aware of physiological paternity. The evidence surveyed by Ashley Montagu (1937) suggests that at least some of the neighbouring tribes appear to have been ignorant of the relationship between coitus and parturition. Moreover, Spencer and Gillen asserted that the Ilpirra (the eastern Yalpari) "firmly held that the child is not the direct result of intercourse" and believed instead that it develops from an "already-formed spirit-child who inhabits one of the local totem centres" (1899, p. 265).

I have already pointed out that the Walbiri postulate the existence, not of spirit-children, but of *guruwari* spirit-entities, which are by no means the same thing. It is true the people believe that a *guruwari* determines the child's sex to the extent that, in each incarnation, the same *guruwari* animates a child of the opposite sex to that in the previous incarnation. But they also say that this is being wise after the event, for nobody can know which individual previously possessed a particular *guruwari*. The *guruwari* are impersonal, homogeneous entities, whose course of incarnations through the ages cannot be traced in the way that those of the Aranda spirit-children can be known.

All the older men with whom I discussed the matter held that copulation and the entry of a *guruwari* into the woman are both necessary preliminaries to child-birth; but in general they thought the action of the *guruwari* to be more important, because it animates the foetus and helps to determine its future character or personality. A few men expressed additional opinions on the matter. One maintained that the father's semen carries some of his patri- or lodge-spirit into the child, which is partly formed from the semen. Another said that the semen mingles with the retained menstrual blood to create a foetus that the *guruwari* vivifies—a view resembling that of the Ooldea Pidjandjara (vide Berndt, 1945, p. 79).

The women, on the other hand, were emphatic that coitus is the significant antecedent of parturition; the entry of the *guruwari* is a secondary event that identifies the child formed of

the menstrual blood. Indeed, many of the women were surprised that my wife and myself had to ask for such self-evident
information. Warner had the same experience with the Murngin
of Arnhem Land (1937, p. 24).

It seems to me unlikely that this variety of opinions is merely
the outcome of the people's limited acquaintance with Europeans, for there is much evidence to demonstrate that desert
Aborigines change their beliefs very slowly on subjects that are
important to them, no matter how intensive European contact
is. Consequently, I agree with Warner and with Roheim (1954)
when they say that the Aborigines' answers to questions about
conception depend on who is asked and in what circumstances.
In ritual contexts, men speak of the action of the *guruwari*
as the significant factor; in secular contexts, they nominate both
the *guruwari* and sexual intercourse. The women, having few
ritual attitudes, generally emphasize copulation.

The people appear to make no use of contraceptive techniques
(if in fact they know of any apart from *coitus interruptus*),
and most married couples desire large families. As it is thought
that many acts of intercourse are necessary to lead to pregnancy,
lovers do not worry about the consequences of casual liaisons.
For the same reason, the inability of a married person to have
children may be blamed on his or her laziness; he has not
copulated often enough to enable the *guruwari* to act effectively.
Abortion, which is induced by manual pressure on the abdomen,
is uncommon and greatly deplored.

There are no magical procedures designed to ensure fertility,
other than those implied in the performance of dreaming-
ceremonies that maintain the supplies of *guruwari* in the
country. Women do not wear amulets of charms for this
purpose.

Although the people remark on the unfortunate decline of
sexual powers and appetites that accompanies old age, they still
consider it normal practice for men who appear to be quite old
(for instance, well over 60 years) to copulate nightly with young
wives. Women who have passed the menopause do not engage
in sexual intercourse so frequently, largely because their husbands turn to younger wives.

A woman takes the cessation of her menstrual periods to be

the first indication of pregnancy and looks for other symptoms, such as pains during micturition, nausea, and swollen breasts, to verify her assumption. She has little interest in calculating the expected date of the birth, but, if specifically asked, she may estimate that it is due in a particular season of the year—generally seven or eight "moons" after the first signs of pregnancy appear. This may well be knowledge acquired from Europeans, for women do not usually worry much about the matter; the child will come in its own good time.

When the woman is sure she is pregnant, she informs her husband, and they recall the locality in which they were residing when her menses were first interrupted. They assume that a *guruwari* from a dreaming-site in that area has entered the woman, either through her vulva or though a crack in the sole of her foot; this event has determined the child's conception-dreaming. Should the couple be residing continuously in that locality, they may wait for a further sign to confirm the identity of the dreaming.

> After living on Hooker Creek settlement for about two years, Liddy nagamara found that she was pregnant. The *guruwari* could have come from any of the several dreaming-sites near the settlement. The most likely were those of the mosquito and the wallaby, situated on the creek-bank; but for several months more neither Liddy nor her husband was prepared to specify any dreaming. One hot morning Liddy, who was then about six months pregnant, fainted while visiting my wife. This decided the matter, for our dwelling was only 50 yards from the mosquito dreaming-cave in the creek-bank.

A man with one wife usually continues to copulate with her until a short time before her child is born, and their intercourse is not thought to affect the foetus for good or ill. A polygynous husband may give up sleeping with a pregnant wife when her abdomen becomes too big for this to be convenient. A woman's everyday activities change little when she is pregnant. She still gathers food and firewood until a few days before the birth is expected, and I have known women to deliver children while on "walkabout" 20 miles or more from the main camp.

Dietary restrictions, however, come into force during pregnancy and continue until the child is weaned two or three years later. The woman must not eat echidna (which has spikes), possum (which has sharp claws), a species of *Varanus* goanna (which has a rough shingled tail), or a species of *Tiliqua* lizard (which has a spiked tail), lest the baby be still-born or deformed. She must not eat eggs or drink hot tea, lest these (for reasons which I could not discover) injure the foetus. The flesh of emu, bustard, or rabbit-bandicoot is "too strong" for pregnant women (and indeed for any young women); if they eat it, they are likely to have deformed or sickly children. It is not surprising, in view of the masculine bias of Walbiri society, that the men are not subject to such restrictions when their wives are pregnant.

At the onset of her labour pains, a woman goes with her sister or mother to the widows' camp or to a newly-erected shelter beside it. She lies naked beside a small fire, whose smoke drives away the flies. When she judges from the pains and abdominal contractions that the birth is imminent, she squats and a midwife kneels behind her to support her shoulders and massage her belly. The midwife, preferably a mother or a sister, is not recompensed for her services. It is unusual for other women to be present merely as spectators, and children are sent away. Men are never in the vicinity—this is "an affair of women".

TABLE 25
Selection of Walbiri midwives

Relationship to child's mother	Frequency
sister	17
mother	12
husband's sister	4
husband's mother	2
father's sister	2
daughter	1
mother's mother	1
total	39

chi squared (matrikin, others) $= 13 \cdot 56$, df $= 1$, p $\angle$ ·01
chi squared (m., sr., others) $= 4 \cdot 63$, df $= 1$, p $\angle$ ·05

The midwife takes the baby from the mother and severs the umbilical cord with the dirt-encrusted blade of a digging-stick, at a point about six inches from the child's navel. She makes a twist an inch or two behind the open end of the cord, which she packs with ashes or dirt to prevent bleeding, and then rubs the infant (whose skin is a greyish colour) with the fine ash of burnt acacia leaves. She also draws with her little finger a charcoal stripe across its forehead, to ward off hiccups and (I think) convulsions. She puts the baby beside the mother and lights a small fire to keep off the flies.

Meanwhile, in a hole about two feet deep and three feet in diameter, the midwife has made a fire, covering the coals with a layer of leaves of *Acacia dictyophleba*. The mother squats on the leaves in the dense smoke and sweats freely, until the placenta and cord are expelled into the pit. This may not occur for from four to six hours after the birth; any longer delay is thought to be dangerous, and the midwife massages the woman's belly to induce the movement of the placenta. She fills in the pit without any formality to prevent the dogs from eating the placenta, a substance which has no ritual significance or harmful attributes for humans.

As it is believed that the mother is unable to secrete milk for the first day after the birth, some other female relative (preferably an aunt) suckles the child. The mother remains with her baby in the widows' camp for about five or six days, sleeping most of the time until she feels "strong inside". She may also endure another session of smoking over the acacia leaves to ensure a copious flow of milk. Her mother or sister supplies her with food during this period.

The infant's umbilical cord is allowed to wither, the mother moistening it occasionally with her own milk to speed the process. She later buries it near the camp, so that the dogs cannot eat it. The site is not remembered. The father should not see the cord, for it is connected with "the women's business".

Difficult or protracted deliveries, which appear to be uncommon, are hastened by vigorous massage; magical spells are not employed. A prolonged labour is thought to indicate that the baby will be still-born, and the midwife may call on the advice of other experienced women in this case. The stress on the notion that child-birth is "the affair of women", however, prevents them from asking the help of the medicine-man. Should the mother die, her body is treated like any other corpse; but, because women of her matriline were present at the birth to help her, her kinsmen are unlikely to attribute the death to sorcery or to seek revenge on a putative killer. If the child survives, a co-wife or sister of the dead woman rears it.

The midwife buries a still-born baby without ceremony in the bush nearby; and she, or the mother, strikes a deformed child on the head or turns it face down in the sand to choke, then buries it at once. Minor disfigurements, such as birth-marks, moles and wens, however, are regarded lightly and vaguely as "dreaming-marks" inherited from a person who possessed the same *guruwari* in a previous incarnation. Surviving twins are rare (I do not recall having met any), a fact often remarked on by the women. As twins are unwelcome, the mothers probably destroy the female or the weaker member at birth; but I do not have definite evidence of this. The one infanticide about which I have detailed information occurred at Mount Doreen in 1954.

Ruby nambidjimba had two small children (one not yet weaned) when she again became pregnant. She and her husband then walked from Mount Singleton to Mount Doreen, so that she might be with her close relatives. On the day of the birth, Ruby's "mother" took her to the widows' camp in the usual way but then went off with the other women to collect rations. The baby was born soon after. Ruby later told me that she was angry and frightened at being left alone, and that, in any case, she did not want a third child so soon after the birth of the second. She hit the baby on the forehead with a digging-stick; the blow did not kill the child at once, so she pressed its face into the sand.

A "father's sister", who was returning from the ration distribution, saw that the child had been born, and she went to help Ruby. As she cleaned the baby, she found it was dead. Alarmed, she told other people in the camp, who in turn told the station-owner. Meanwhile, Ruby prevailed on her husband's sister, who was a close friend, to bury the body. Ruby's husband was furious when he learned of the affair, and he thrashed her several times.

Eventually, the police were informed of the death. Ruby, her husband and several "witnesses" were taken to Alice Springs, where Ruby was convicted of murder. Her long confinement while awaiting trial, however, was taken into consideration, and she was sentenced only to the rising of the court.

Walbiri who knew of the matter were inclined to lay most of the blame on Ruby's "mother", who, they said, had acted improperly in leaving Ruby unattended during the delivery. Their comments also made it clear to me that the rule demanding the presence of a midwife at every birth aimed partly at preventing infanticides.

When a woman goes to the widows' camp to deliver her child (whether or not it is her first baby), her husband retires to the bachelors' camp. As soon as the midwife shouts that the labour has begun, he strips naked, doffing even his head-band and armlets. He rubs his thumb down the side of his nose, or under his arm, to coat it with a mixture of sweat and grease and draws a red-ochre stripe from his chest to his navel. These actions are thought to facilitate the birth of the child. The husband should sit alone and silent, thinking only of his wife's "trouble", until the midwife calls across the camp, "It is born!" At once he resumes his dress and ornaments and is able to mix again with other men.

He resides in the bachelors' camp until the day his wife is to rejoin him. Then he waits quietly in his own dwelling for her. She generally arrives just before sunset. Without speaking, she sits and places before him tea and vegetable-food that she has prepared. When he has consumed these in silence, she sets the wooden trough containing the child in front of him. He draws a red-ochre stripe with his finger from the baby's chest to its navel, then lightly brushes both the child and the trough with his spear-thrower. The action "strengthens" the infant and indicates that the father accepts it as his own.

Although women stated that a couple can resume sexual intercourse immediately the wife returns from the widows' camp, in fact she usually asks her husband not to copulate with her for three or four weeks, until "her belly is stronger". The women also said that they do not menstruate again until the gradual weaning of the child is in progress, about two years after the birth; and they believe that, during this time, they are unlikely to become pregnant. I rarely encountered women whose children had been born less than from 18 to 24 months apart.

I have already described the general course of the first few years of the child's life. It acquires a personal name when about two years old, that is, after it has survived the many sicknesses that contribute to the high rate of infant mortality. A boy receives the name of a grandfather, usually of his mother's father, and a girl that of a grandmother, usually of her mother's mother. The grandparent decides without prompting to offer the name and informally tells the infant's parents of this. Later, when the grandparent dies, the bearer of the name is referred to as *gumindjari*, "no-name", for a year or so, then resumes the name.

Each name is a phrase in a dreaming-song. But, as names may be bequeathed in any line of descent, there is no necessary correlation between the subsection or moiety affiliation of the dreaming-song and that of the current possessor of the name.

Although most people know each other's personal names, they should never use them in the presence of the owners, nor should they utter their own names in the company of others. No matter how long a person has been dead, his (or her) name must never be mentioned in connection with him; it is an appalling solecism merely to speak the name in any context in the hearing of the deceased's close kinsmen. The only reason that people gave me for the strict observance of these rules was that everyone would experience great "shame" if they were broken. There was no suggestion that a personal name in any way expresses or contains the individual's power or virtue, or that indiscriminate use of the name would weaken or endanger the owner. The whole subject was one of such delicacy, however, that I was loath to pursue it at length, and it is likely, therefore, that I have not recorded all the data relevant to the matter.

There are several terms of address that might be applied to a person in ritual and secular situations. They are in approximate order of frequency of usage: subsection terms, kinship terms, European names and Walbiri nicknames, matrimoiety and age-grade terms for men, and direction terms (north, south, etc.) for men in small groups. The employment of terms of reference parallels this order but also includes the infrequent use of the special kinship terms of reference. Specification of conception-dreamings often has to accompany the reference term if "siblings" are to be distinguished.

To summarize the important features of betrothal, marriage and child-birth: contemporary Walbiri regard the announcement of a betrothal as an important, formal and public event, which redeems a pledge earlier made between two groups of relatives at the circumcision ceremonies connected with the initiation of a lad into his father's cult-lodge. The men of one matriline fulfil their promise to cede rights over one of their women to a man of another matriline. The betrothal also confirms a bond that was created when a man of the woman's patrilineage acted as the ritual guardian of the man (of another patrilineage) who is to be her husband. The structural significance of betrothal in the social system is obvious to us; it is no less apparent to percipient Walbiri.

The establishment of the marital relationship, which follows almost inevitably from the betrothal, attracts less publicity. The same social groupings as before are involved, but only those members directly affected have definite roles to enact. Nevertheless, the people see marriage as an element in a nexus of events that also includes circumcision and betrothal.

DIAGRAM 8

The pattern of exchanges connected with circumcision,
betrothal and marriage among the Walbiri

Actor	Event	Actor
wife's father,		ego
wife's M.B.		

circumcision, to "make ego a man" →
← payment of the circumciser
subincision, to "make ego a man" →
← payment of the subinciser
girl given in betrothal →
← bride-price given for girl
girl given in marriage →
← bride-price given for girl
gifts of food
← provision of aid in fights

Birth presents a somewhat different picture. Only the mother, her close female matrikin and her husband are concerned. The event does not create ties between hitherto unrelated groups but reinforces links already existing between groups of people. Thus, the extension of a man's conjugal family binds him more firmly to his wife's matriline; but the birth of his sons also involves him more deeply in the affairs of his patrilodge.

CHAPTER XVI

INITIATION

In this chapter I shall deal with the initiation of males into the totemic mysteries. In particular I want to show how the people who enact key roles in these ceremonies are members of social groups that are of great significance to the candidate for initiation, groups such as his patriline and patrilodge, his matriline and the matriline of his future wife. The Walbiri consider the ceremonies connected with circumcision to be in many respects the most important. In order to keep my account within manageable limits, I shall, therefore, treat these in some detail, while discussing subincision only briefly. The complex Gadjari cycle must await analysis elsewhere.

Circumcision. The data I present here derive mainly from five sets of ceremonies that I witnessed at Hooker Creek, Phillip Creek and Yuendumu, as well as from long discussions with many Walbiri men. Although the ceremonies exhibited differences of detail from one occasion to the next, arising in response to practical exigencies, the men deplored such deviations from the dreamtime norms.

A boy takes his first step into the secret life when he goes into seclusion preparatory to being circumcised. His kinsmen consider the extent of his mental and physical development before making the decision; but he is unlikely to be more than 13 or less than 11 years old at the time. In this respect Walbiri practice accords with that of the Kimberley Aborigines, who circumcise novices at or before puberty.

A few months before the summer ceremonial season is due to open, a sister's husband should draw the attention of men of the lad's patriline to the fact that he appears to be ready for seclusion. This action is largely a formality, for the father has been watching carefully for signs of his son's development, signs such as increased stature and the appearance of pubic hair. The close agnates of the boy discuss the matter with his mother's brother, M.M.B. and F.M.B., so that there will be no dispute when the father's father tells the sister's husband he is to take the lad into seclusion. The father, however, is expected to agree only reluctantly with the decision. The men advise the novice's mother of their intention and tell her she is not to worry about his welfare.

The father and elder brother also reassure the boy. They tell him that they, too, underwent this discipline in the past, and the elder brother says that he will always be on hand to protect him. The boy, in any case, has known for some time that he must be circumcised, and he has acquired from older lads a little knowledge of what to expect. Most boys desire to join the ranks of the bachelors, and they look forward to the occasion of their circumcision with both eagerness and trepidation.

The sister's husband who is to be the guardian prepares a camp in the bush a mile or so from the main camp, usually in a part of the "men's country" set aside for this purpose. Should several boys be ready for circumcision in the one season, they and their guardians all occupy one camp. (Novices who are "brothers" may be circumcised during the one series of cere-monies; others must wait in the seclusion-camp for the next series, and so on.)

When the camp is ready, the sister's husband and an elder brother come to escort the boy from his father's shelter. Unless, as rarely happens, the lad becomes frightened, he is not taken by force; his father and brothers simply tell him that he must go. The men signal their departure with shrill calls that warn all the women to remain out of sight until the party has left.

Later that night all the men come from the main camp and organize the first of the many revelatory rituals that the novice will see. Performed by younger men of both patrimoieties, it dramatizes an introductory episode from the myth of the two kangaroos, which is closely concerned with circumcision. (Wal-biri kangaroo ceremonies closely resemble those of the Pidjan-djara, and both have a common mythological rationale.) The actual and classificatory brothers, fathers and M.M.B. explain the significance of the ritual to the lad, who at this stage under-stands little of what they say.

The father then gives to the guardian a firestick with which to kindle a fire in the boy's camp; an elder sister, representing the women of the novice's patriline, has provided this firestick.

The father also leaves a supply of food and water. Several women who are potential mothers-in-law of the lad have prepared part of this food, and his mother (representing his matriline) has contributed the remainder. For the rest of his stay in seclusion, the mother alone provides vegetable-food. The boy is not allowed to eat meat until after he is circumcised.

Before they return to the main camp, his agnates exhort him to heed his guardian's commands at all times. Henceforth, although the novice is not expected to remain completely silent, he must keep his speech to a minimum and use manual signs to communicate his needs. Throughout the seclusion, his sister's husband (who represents the matriline of his future wife) regularly rubs him from head to foot with fat and red-ochre and binds up his hair into a topknot. While he is in the bush, he wears only a hair-string cincture, but he dons a loin-cloth whenever he joins the men to witness ceremonies.

Soon after dawn on the second day, all the subincised men assemble at a distance from the main camp in three or four contiguous groups, each of which comprises "masters" (men of the novice's patrimoiety) and "working men" (members of the opposite patrimoiety). In each group the masters supervise the working men, who paint on an oval, softwood shield a design that represents a dreaming of the lad's patrimoiety. The masters choose beforehand several dreamings that are the most important in the novice's (community) country, but they exclude that of his father's lodge, into which he is to be initiated. The masters and the working men chant the dreaming-songs during the painting, which may take an hour or two to complete, and the singing often develops into a vigorous competition among the groups. The decorated shields are hidden under a layer of branches, in readiness for display that night.

The men spend the rest of the day performing the ceremonies associated with the dreamings depicted on the shields, as well as with dreamings that belong to the opposite patrimoiety. That is to say, the occasion is of such importance that both patrimoieties, representing all the tribesmen, should participate equally. The dramatizations, which are intended also as increase ceremonies, are enacted in the usual way, following the normal patrilodge and patrimoiety rules. Youths who are already circumcised are called up to witness these rituals and have them explained; but the novice remains secluded in the bush with his guardian. He is not yet spiritually "strong" enough to come into contact with this element of the secret life.

After dark, everyone gathers in the main camp, where the elder brothers of the novice light many fires. The men sit in a group facing the east, with the women and children behind them. The boy and his guardian sit about 50 yards in front of the men. For three or four hours the men sing of the travels of a party of dreamtime women, *ganda,* from Gunadjari and of their encounters with an incestuous man, who was killed for his sins. The songs, which point a moral for the younger people present, are always sung on these occasions.

The men accompany the singing by beating the ground with their oval shields, while the women dance with an ungainly, loose-kneed shuffle. Many of the women, notably the mothers, sisters, fathers' sisters and potential mothers-in-law of the novice, have dreaming-designs painted on their bodies. An elder brother stands in front of the men and spurs on their singing with rhythmical yelps, just as elder sisters yelp to assist the dancers to keep time. From time to time, the boy's close mothers run in single file around him and brandish glowing firesticks at the guardian to warn him to fulfil his duties conscientiously. This is one of the few situations in which a woman can go near her "son-in-law". As the sun rises, the men tell all the women to go to the camp. Before they leave, the mothers and fathers' sisters weep over the novice, caress and admonish him, and tell him to be of good heart.

Once the women have gone, men of the opposite patrimoiety formally display the decorated shields to the lad, and his brothers, father and M.M.B. tell him something of their significance. The guardian then returns him to his camp in the bush.

This nocturnal assembly and the public farewells of the mothers mark the official beginning of the novice's seclusion. Up to this point, several structural groupings have been clearly involved in the various activities—the lad's patriline and patrimoiety, his future patrilodge, his matriline and his future wife's matriline. As we shall see, these are all emphasized in various ways throughout the ensuing ceremonies.

In the past, after this leave-taking occurred, the novice set out on his grand tour. Accompanied by his guardian and an elder brother (who supervised the guardian), he visited neighbouring Walbiri communities, as well as communities of other tribes. If several boys had been secluded together, they travelled as a party with their guardians and brothers. During the tour the novice learned about the flora, fauna and topography of the tribal territory, and his elder brother also told him of the totemic significance of various localities.

The travellers camped for a week or two at a time with each group of Walbiri they encountered. Men who were "fathers-in-law" of the boy fed them and arranged kangaroo ceremonies for the lad's instruction. If the local people had novices of their own in seclusion, the visitors camped with these. As they were leaving, the travellers invited their hosts to attend the boy's circumcision ceremonies, and his "fathers-in-law" accepted the invitation by decking him with skeins of hair-string to give to his father. The novice's party would wander about in this way for two or three months before returning home.

These tours still occur today in southern Walbiri country. Novices from Yuendumu, for instance, visit Mount Doreen, Mount Denison, Conistan and, occasionally, Haast's Bluff. But they rarely set out from Hooker Creek and Phillip Creek, because of the isolation of these settlements from other Walbiri camps. Thus, in 1953, older men at Hooker Creek wanted the candidates for circumcision to travel to Birrindudu and Gordon Downs. But the season was particularly hot and dry, and the fathers of the novices feared that the lads would suffer hardship on the long treks between waterholes. They refused to give their consent; and the public farewell to the boys was followed by a local seclusion.

When the novice returns from his tour and is again installed in the seclusion-camp, elder brothers from his patriline, assisted by M.M.B. who act as "siblings", prepare a clearing, *guridji*, in the "men's country", on which the circumcision ceremonies are to be held. The father's father should supervise the task. It is also the duty of the elder brothers to renovate the clearing at intervals during the ceremonies. Dreamtime heroes originally specified the form of this precinct; it must be funnel-shaped, running east and west, and widest at the eastern end (vide Diagram 9). Usually it is from 30 to 40 yards long, about 12 yards across the widest extremity and about 5 yards at the narrowest. The men use boomerangs to scrape the surface clean of stones and vegetation, and they bank the edges to a height of about 6 inches. At each end they construct wind-breaks, about 3 feet thick and 4 feet high, of piled branches (at W2 and W3 in the diagram).

From time to time, by day or night, the guardian brings the novice to a bough-shelter (S1) situated about 100 yards south or south-west of the clearing. (Women must later enter or leave

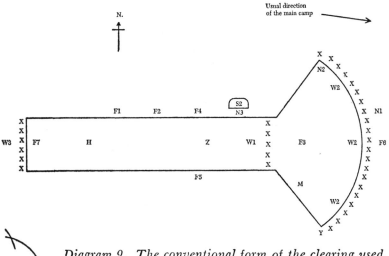

Diagram 9. *The conventional form of the clearing used in Walbiri circumcision ceremonies*

(The letters and figures refer to the locations of actors and objects mentioned in the text.)

the clearing to the north or the east.) Here his male agnates, close maternal kinsmen and his guardian join with all the younger men of the camp to sing the kangaroo "dreaming-line". The harsh staccato singing is unmistakable, as the chanting men sit in a circle and vigorously pound the earth with heavy billets of wood to simulate the thudding of kangaroo-tails.

(Throughout the kangaroo myths, songs and ceremonies, the symbolic equation of kangaroo-tail, spear and novice's penis is obvious.) Singing on these occasions may last for seven or eight hours at a time.

The boy, who is completely covered by a blanket (paper-bark, in the past), lies with his head on his guardian's thigh. He must remain silent and he may not look at the men. Thus, if he leaves the group in order to urinate, he has to keep his back to the singers; when given water to drink, he has to reach back over his shoulder to take it. During the singing, the guardian (his brother-in-law) frequently brushes the boy's head with the leaves of *Eremophila longifolia*, the badge of the novice among the Walbiri. This action closes the lad's mind to everything but the songs, the "strength" (but not the meaning) of which he now absorbs.

After the men have sung for some hours, the father, father's father and M.M.B. signal manually to the younger men to withdraw into the bush and decorate themselves for a performance of the relevant episode from the kangaroo myth. They leave noiselessly, and there is no break in the chanting to warn the muffled novice that something is afoot. The actors, who may number 14 or 15, later whistle, or howl like dingoes, when they are almost ready; and the other men move to the eastern end of the clearing. The father and mother's brother erect a bough-screen (W1), behind which the men sit with the boy, who is still covered. They sing and beat the ground until the actors file on to the western end of the clearing. The father throws down the screen, uncovers the lad and bids him watch closely. The actors mime (at H, with a fire F1 at night) various exploits of the two kangaroos, such as their meeting with wallabies, their fight with dingoes, their making a new tail. Each dramatization lasts for about five minutes, and several episodes may be enacted in succession.

The actors retire to the bush to remove their decorations; and men of the boy's patriline harangue him violently, explaining the meaning of the ritual and warning him on pain of death not to divulge the information to women or children. (All novices, whether singly or in groups, see these ceremonies, which are valid for all lodges in the tribe.)

When the actors rejoin the men, the whole party returns to the general camp. Holding their spears upright, the men form a wedge around the novice and, as they approach the camp, they repeatedly call *jo! jo! jo!* At this signal, all the women and children, except the lad's close mothers, hide in their dwellings. The mothers, however, may see him from a distance and assure themselves that he is still unharmed. His guardian then takes him back to his place of seclusion.

Older men, apart from the father's father and M.M.B., rarely attend the kangaroo rituals and never act in them. Instead, they meet daily in the men's country a mile or two from the camp to prepare the long, incised *jarandalba* boards for the coming circumcision ceremony. Each patrilodge possesses several boards associated with its dreamings; and men of the same community as the lodge, but of the opposite patrimoiety, spend hours each day rubbing the boards with red-ochre and fat and chanting the relevant dreaming-songs. They may also make new boards for the lodges to replace those damaged by termites or by exposure to the elements, or if those available are insufficient for the number of actors expected to participate in the later *jarandalba* ceremony. Men of the master patrimoieties, preferably members of the lodges concerned, supervise the working men, often marking out the designs to be incised; but it is unlawful for the masters themselves to complete these patterns.

The designs on the boards, as well as representing the particular dreamings, are also "maps" of the dreaming-countries or dreaming-tracks, so that the boards form part of a community's title deeds to its territory. Thus, when the Walbiri from Yuendumu came to Hooker Creek in 1952, they had no boards of their own to use in the first circumcision to be performed there. They obtained six boards (representing rain and wallaby dreamings) from the Wave Hill Walbiri, who in turn had procured them from other Aborigines at Limbunyah and Inverway. As these dreamings and patterns were intertribal, the Walbiri could keep the boards permanently; but men of the master patrimoiety had to give the extratribal masters large amounts of red-ochre and hair-string for the privilege. For the 1953 circumcision ceremonies the Hooker Creek men manufactured another seven boards of various dreamings, some of which were related to the Hooker Creek locality. The men told me that, until they possessed these boards of their own, they could not rightfully claim this country as their own, country that once had belonged to the Gurindji tribe.

The father and father's father of the novice, when not attending the kangaroo rituals, regularly visit the older men and urge them to make the boards ready in time for the ceremonies. Meanwhile, a mother's brother makes a small *windilburu* bullroarer (sometimes two), on which he incises the boy's conception-dreaming design. The boy will receive this object after he is circumcised.

At Hooker Creek and Yuendumu these sorts of activities continue until a day or so before the actual circumcision is to take place. At Phillip Creek, however, for four or five days before this event everyone gathers at the clearing just before dusk each day. The novice's close male agnates, his mother's brothers and (a Warramunga innovation) his "W.M.B." sit together at the western end and, led by an elder brother, sing the *ganda*, "travelling women", and the ŋ*arga*, "initiated men", dreamings. The women dance nearby, in time with the beating of the men's shields on the ground and with the yelping of an elder sister. The mothers, sisters and father's sisters of the lad (but no other women) wear plumes of the white corella (cockatoo) in their hair and have their bodies painted. His own mother dances with a glowing firestick held high. After each night's dancing, she extinguishes the brand and takes it to her camp in readiness for the next night. She must not let the firestick die while she dances, for the glowing coal symbolizes the boy's life.

Once the dancing is in progress, an elder brother and a "W.M.B." bring the novice from his seclusion-camp and seat him among a group of younger boys, his erstwhile playmates, so that he may farewell them. Then a sister lifts him on to her shoulders and leads all the women to another clearing in the bush, about 400 yards to the east. The women light a fire there and crowd around the lad, while his mothers and father's sisters rub his face and neck with the leg-bone of a kangaroo so that he will grow tall and strong. They caress him and weep over him, exhorting him to be courageous in the coming trial.

The men have remained in two groups at the eastern end

of the main clearing—the brothers, fathers, mother's brothers and "W.M.B." beating their shields on the ground as they sing ŋarga dreaming, the others pounding the earth with sticks as they sing kangaroo dreaming. The chanting is fast and powerful and soon becomes competitive. The women send the boy back to the men, and two brothers go to meet him. They place him on the lap of a "W.M.B.", against whose chest he hides his face as he listens to the singing. Once more he absorbs the virtue of the dreaming-songs, even though he does not understand them.

Later, the women, who have been dancing in the second clearing, run in single file along the main clearing. The kangaroo singers at once rush at them, shouting and hissing and threatening them with their sticks; and the women run screaming to the camp. Following this forcible separation of the women from the novice, his guardian takes him to his place of seclusion; and the other men leave for the general camp.

As this sequence of events is repeated each evening, the women dance a little farther along the main clearing (towards its eastern end), which cannot be used for the circumcision ceremonies until after the women have thus danced its entire length. Sometimes, before the women return from their dancing in the second clearing, naked bachelors who are the boy's "fathers-in-law" prance in turn down the clearing with grotesque steps, in time to the vigorous kangaroo singing, and pretend to spear the lad, in order to "mark" him as the victim of the coming operation. Then they dance backwards with the remarkably rapid "buck-and-wing" action that represents the dancing of the nightjars in the kangaroo myth.

The interpolation of all these activities into the general circumcision sequence is peculiar to the Walbiri at Phillip Creek; and I was unable to discover how or where this variant procedure originated. To judge from the reports of Spencer and Gillen (1904, p. 348) of Warramunga initiation, the practice has not been borrowed from these people.

To return to the general pattern of events leading to circumcision: when the men of the novice's patriline are satisfied that he understands something of the significance of his changing status, a final kangaroo ritual is performed on the main clearing. Immediately after this, without the boy's witnessing the operation, the men who have prepared the *jarandalba* boards bring these to the clearing, where an elder brother directs them to hide the objects under the eastern wind-break.

All the men then sing the emu dreaming and decorate as emus seven or eight men of both patrimoieties. The actors hide in the bush. An elder brother calls up the women and children, who sit behind the rest of the men; the mothers and father's sisters wear white head-bands to distinguish them from the other women. (Usually, when the men assemble in this way, the fathers, fathers' fathers, and mothers' brothers sit together in front, with the novice's brothers-in-law nearby, while the brothers stand before the group.)

An elder brother concealed among the trees nearby swings the *windilburu* bullroarer that the mother's brother has made for the novice, and the emu actors appear. In the slow miming that follows to the accompaniment of emu songs, the father's sisters take a minor part. Everybody, including the novice, may witness this performance; but the mothers and the father's sisters are the only women permitted to observe the emu dramatizations that follow it.

By now it is dusk. The elder brothers call all the women to stand again behind the men. As the men sing the ŋarga dreaming and the women dance, several of the brothers-in-law take the novice and all the small boys present to the eastern wind-break (N1). With much joking and hilarity, they grease the bodies of the novice, his elder brothers, and all the boys and then draw the conception-dreaming of each individual on his back. One elder brother lines up the boys (at X), with the novice at their head, and another lights a small fire (F2). Each boy jumps over the fire, "to make him grow tall", and rejoins the women.

The mothers and the father's sisters are permitted to embrace the novice for a few minutes before a brother leads him back to his guardians (at N1). Another brother makes a fire in front of the main company (at F3). The sisters' husbands again grease the lad, while all the younger men, clad in loin-cloths, grease themselves and tuck dry stalks of spinifex-grass into their head-, arm- and waist-bands.

To the exciting rhythm of the *jagingiri* (fire) chanting, they prance in single file (from N1) on to the clearing, led by a guardian who holds the novice's arm. After they dance once around the central fire (F3), the novice and guardian sit in front of the singing men. The young men circle the fire several times, while the mothers and the father's sisters dance together (at M). Then the men close in and hurl the coals and burning brands high in the air to fall on the dancing women. All the women and children run screaming from the clearing, pursued by the menacing shouts of the men. The mothers seize the novice as they go, and they lead the women to a clearing several hundred yards to the east, where they all dance for some time and take another farewell of the lad.

As soon as the women leave, an elder brother emerges from the shadow of the trees and swings a bullroarer to call the men together on the main clearing. They sit and sing the ŋarga dreaming. Another elder brother signals to them at intervals to change to the songs that refer to the *widi*, leafy poles held by the ŋarga men when they danced at Gulungalimba in the dreamtime. He also nominates in turn the younger men who are to participate in the *widi* dances on the following night. Each man jumps up in front of the group and executes the fast, hopping dance-steps, to demonstrate that he is a suitable choice. Shouts of laughter and ribald jokes greet his performance.

When the practice-session is over, the countrymen of the novice sit in two rows facing each other across the fire and sway rhythmically as they sing of the *jarandalba* boards. Men of the opposite patrimoieties produce the boards from their hiding-place in the wind-break and hand them one at a time to the singers, who inspect each board carefully before giving it back to its custodian. When all have been displayed, the custodians carry them to a bough-shelter (S1), where they spend the rest of the night painting the boards and singing the associated dreamings.

An elder brother recalls the women and takes charge of the novice. The mothers and the father's sisters sit at the western end of the clearing, and two of the brothers carry the lad to them, yelping as they do so. No sooner do the women begin to cry over him than the brothers snatch him up and run back to the men. The sobbing mothers chase them but are unable to recover their son.

Most of the people now prepare for several hours' sleep. Several of the novice's guardians place him on a bed (at N2) and sit beside him. His brothers sit nearby. Other married men seek their wives and settle down in family groups north and east of the clearing. The bachelors must sleep on the clearing in the firelight, where one or two of the old men can ensure that they keep away from the women. (At Phillip Creek, the novice's fathers and mother's brothers should also sleep near him on the clearing, so that he may draw comfort from their presence.)

In the sequence of events so far, the main emphasis has been on the lad's elder brothers (actual and close) as the active representatives of his patriline and its associated lodge. His fathers and father's fathers closely watch their behaviour and are ready to advise them; but, in all the ceremonies that I saw, the brothers took great pride in their ability to discharge their multifarious duties without aid or prompting. The part played by the father's sisters in these activities, especially their participation in the emu miming, also reflects the importance of patriline affiliation. This is one of the few occasions on which women may act in a ritual in company with men.

The roles of the mothers and the sisters, on the other hand, express their status as members of the novice's matriline; and the mother's brothers are ever alert to see that the women's privileges are not usurped or derogated. The mothers and the father's sisters together also represent the secular world that the neophyte is leaving, whereas his fathers and his mother's brothers stand for the secret life he is entering; consequently, throughout these ceremonies these four (sets of) relatives are referred to by one term, *julburu*, to distinguish them from all other close cognates.

Up to this point, the matriline of the lad's future wife, his marriage line, has had little to do. His guardians (his sisters' husbands) are its only active representatives and they are obviously over-shadowed by the boy's brothers, who direct the actions of the guardians.

While other people are sleeping, the brothers produce a *jarandalba* board, preferably one associated with the lodge of the novice's father, although, failing this, any board belonging to that patrimoiety will serve. Each brother in turn stands near the recumbent boy (at N2) and shows him the board as he explains the significance of its markings. When the exhausted lad falls asleep, the brothers return it to the bough-shelter, where the men selected earlier are still painting the other boards for the dawn ceremony; and they patrol the area, swinging bull-roarers to warn people to keep a safe distance.

Meanwhile, the guardians, who sit beside the sleeping novice, fasten a bunch of eagle-hawk or corella plumes to the butt of a hunting-spear and skeins of hair-string at intervals along the shaft. Each sister's husband present should contribute two skeins; if two "brothers" are to be circumcised together, a spear is prepared for each. Some of the elder brothers supervise the task; and they stick the decorated spear point-first into the ground beside the boy's bed, to indicate that he is indeed the candidate for circumcision. The spear represents his penis and the string his pubic hair and foreskin.

At about one a.m., when Orion is overhead, the brothers rouse all the sleepers for the next stage in the ceremonies. The men sit together (at W1), facing east, with the fathers, father's fathers and the mother's brothers in the front row. Several of the brothers, who hold boomerangs (the male badge), stand before them and shout rhythmically as the men chant ŋarga songs and beat the ground with their shields. The novice remains in his bed, attended by his guardians. The women hold digging-sticks (the female badge) and dance behind the men, urged on by the calls of the elder sisters. The boy's own mother dances with a firestick held aloft. The fire is his "life" and must burn throughout the night. The mother relights the stick on the next evening and finally extinguishes it when the lad is circumcised, when he dies only to be reborn. The Walbiri explicitly equate circumcision with ritual killing.

At a certain point in the singing, the brothers and guardians lead the novice through the ranks of the men and women to a fire at the western end of the clearing. All the women, except the mothers and the father's sisters, must cover their faces as the "victim" passes. At this, the fathers and the mother's brothers quietly signal to two men, whom they have previously nominated as his *jualbiri*—either his "fathers-in-law" or his "W.M.B."

These men push bones or quills through the holes in their noses and gather up their wallets. Hiding their faces and the wallets with upraised shields, they steal past the women, who bow their heads. Helped by a guardian, they silently grease and red-ochre the boy, bind up his hair afresh, and tie a hair-string round his waist. The *jualbiri* then pierce their subincised penes to draw blood, with which they fasten vegetable-down to the lad's body to form the *landjulgari* decorations. This dangerously "strong" design is associated with the moon and the "yam" (*Vigna lanceolata*) dreamings. Should the *jualbiri* belong to the opposite patrimoiety to these dreamings, a man of the master patrimoiety must also be present, lest the power of the design injure the boy or recoil on the decorators.

The *jualbiri* again conceal their faces and creep along the clearing, while the women cover their eyes. The two men hide behind the eastern wind-break (W2), where they sit side by side, facing the company. They drape strings of *landjulgari* den-talium shells from their heads, as the moon did in the dream-time, then light a tiny fire in front of them. An elder brother quietly parts the wind-break, and all the men chant the slow, haunting *landjulgari* songs.

At this signal, the *jualbiri* toss a few leaves on to their fire and are dramatically illuminated by the subdued flame. For some minutes they silently sway from side to side in time to the singing and then smother their fire. The women, except the father's sisters, must hide their faces during this eerie revelation; the power of the dentalium shells is inimical to females. Only the father's sisters may watch, for their indirect connection with the novice's patrilodge protects them. The boy witnesses the performance, but an elder brother must embrace him to strengthen him.

This display of the *jualbiri*, which they repeat several times, is a public declaration that they have befriended the lad and will ensure that he receives a wife in the future.

The men continue to sing the ŋarga dreaming, and the mothers and father's sisters dance. At irregular intervals a man of the rain-dreaming lodge shouts set phrases, which name and praise localities on the rain-dreaming tracks. He does this to protect the novice and the dancing women, lest the presence of the *landjulgari* shells and the *jarandalba* boards weakens their bellies.

As dawn approaches, an elder brother closes the gap in the wind-break, and the *jualbiri* hide their shells and return to the novice. While a brother holds him, they hang the shells on the boy so that he will acquire some of the dreaming-power. They then conceal the shells and take no further part in the proceedings.

An elder brother then tells the whole company to turn to the west and orders the women, except the father's sisters, to cover their heads. Two of the brothers run in wide circles around the clearing, throwing dust in the air to blind any demons that might be lurking ready to pounce on the vulnerable novice and the women (Meggitt, 1955a, p. 391). All the men chant the harsh *jarandalba* songs, as the father's sisters dance at one side and scatter handfuls of dust. An elder brother warns the novice to watch the western bush carefully.

Suddenly, in the shimmering light of the dawn, a decorated man springs up from the spinifex-grass, about a hundred yards to the north-west. He holds a painted *jarandalba* board in front of him, like a huge, erect penis (which indeed it is meant to represent), and moves it up and down in time to the singing. As he runs towards the clearing, another man appears to the south-west, then one to the west, another to the north, and so on until 20 or 30 men are running in from all directions. They stand in line on the clearing and swing their boards up and down in unison. Then, as the singing rises in a savage crescendo, they circle the group several times.

The actors run behind the company and hide the boards under the eastern wind-break. Other men drive the women from the clearing. One of the mothers or elder sisters carries the novice with her; and they all retire to the bush, where the mothers and the father's sisters again weep over the lad.

The elder brothers then embrace each *jarandalba* actor in turn and lead him to the boy's fathers and mother's brothers, each of whom also clasps him to his breast. The actors include men who are the novice's "fathers-in-law" and "W.M.B.", and, during the embraces, these softly ask the fathers and mother's brothers who is to be the circumciser. The men reply that they will make their choice later in the day, although, in fact, they have already decided in private on the man they want. Ritual friends then hold the fathers and mother's brothers and commiserate with them on the impending "death" of the boy. Following this, the brothers join with men of the matriline of the lad's future wife to perform a number of emu dances, which are obviously intended to dispel the atmosphere of gloom that has settled on the company. The exaggerated actions of the dancers soon have all the men laughing heartily.

One of the brothers summons the mothers and the father's sisters to the western end of the clearing and takes the novice from them. A guardian and several of the brothers then carry the decorated spear to the women. The men wrench off the hair-string, which they hand to the mothers to pass on to their husbands. The stripping of the spear indicates to the mothers the fate that awaits their son—the loss of his foreskin. By accepting the string, the women signify their willingness to surrender the lad to the men. At the same time, the passage of the string from the original donors (the brothers-in-law and guardians) to the women's husbands (the novice's agnates) expresses the intention of the guardians' matrikinsmen to provide a wife for the boy.

When the women return to the general camp, an elder brother removes the novice's loin-cloth and takes him to the western end of the clearing to show him the place where he will be circumcised that night. As the boy digests this sobering information, his brothers strip naked and prance towards him. They tell him to imitate their grotesque capering around a small fire. Each then leaps high in the air, and a brother helps the boy to do likewise, so that he will soon grow tall. Laughter and joking accompany these activities, which are clearly meant as a comic relief to alleviate the lad's fears and to relax the general tension. (Humorous episodes of this kind are commonly interpolated into ritual sequences that involve novices; and the men state explicitly that they relieve temporarily the emotional pressure on the youths.)

The naked boy faces the company of men. His brothers hold him and cover his eyes. One gives a stone knife to a M.B.S. or a M.M.B., who steals up and pretends to cut the lad's foreskin but does not actually touch it. In this way he shows the circumciser, who is in the audience, where to cut the novice that night.

The brothers place the boy briefly on the knees of his fathers and mother's brothers to show the men that he is unharmed, and they then muffle him. A naked elder brother slowly circles the group, swinging the *windilburu* bullroarer, which he buries in the sand beside the lad's head. The virtue of the object, which bears the boy's conception-dreaming design, is thus able to enter him. The brothers later uncover the novice, and they hop about like kangaroos in front of him. They bid him to do the same, until they are satisfied that he is proficient in this activity. In the evening he will have to hop around in public, to demonstrate to everybody that he has acquired a knowledge of the kangaroo rituals and songs.

It is by now seven or eight a.m., and most of the men are ready to return to the general camp to sleep for a time. A brother makes a bed on the clearing for the lad, at the place where the bullroarer is buried, and thrusts a *jarandalba* board in the ground at his feet. The boy is told to contemplate the markings on the board before he sleeps. His brothers and fathers place food and water beside him; and all the men depart, leaving the novice in the care of several of his brothers-in-law.

Although, in the group of activities just completed, the representatives of the boy's patriline and matriline have continued to play a major part, the performance of the *landjulgari* and *jarandalba* rituals has drawn people's attention to his future affines, especially to the matriline of his future wife. His *jualbiri* have formally promised their support in finding a wife for him, and the task of his circumciser has been explicitly defined.

During the forenoon, the guardians build a bough-shelter near the clearing (at S2), under which they and the boy sleep for a few hours. All the other men sleep in the main camp. At about noon, the male agnates and the mother's brothers of the novice, as well as a number of his older countrymen, assemble at another shelter (S1). Men of the opposite patrimoiety fetch the *jarandalba* boards, from which, after much discussion, the agnates select two for the construction of the string-cross that will symbolize their lodge-dreaming. Ideally, these boards should bear the design of that dreaming but, failing this, they may simply refer to any dreamings of that patrimoiety. While the boards are being chosen, the men may take the opportunity to invite subincised youths to handle the objects and to have their meanings explained to them.

As the other men look on and sing the relevant dreamings, the fathers and the mother's brothers grease and red-ochre the two boards and begin making the cross, *wanigi*. They lash the boards together at right angles with hair-string, which they lead around the arms of the cross to form a solid diamond about three feet wide. During the operation the men pierce their arm-veins, so that the blood spurts on both the boards and the string. Several pints of blood are used in this way to ensure that the object is imbued with the lodge patrispirit that the agnates share. The virtue of the songs associated with the lodge-dreaming also passes into the cross. Finally the men coat the surface of the diamond with a thick paste of charcoal and blood, on which they pick out the lodge-dreaming design with white down. They say that the *wanigi* must be made quickly (*sic!*), lest the actual circumcision be protracted and painful.

The fathers also rub grease and red-ochre on the *windilburu* bullroarers that the mother's brother has made for the novice. The elder brothers give these a trial swing and then place them at the foot of the string-cross to receive the arm-blood that drips from it.

One of the fathers sharpens the circumcision knife and stipples the blade with blood. Normally this is of stone, but nowadays a stock-knife or a razor may be used. The completed cross is placed on a bed of leaves, with the bullroarers and knife resting on it. The fathers and the mother's brothers crouch and sing harshly at the knife, so that it will cut "quickly and straight" on the night. The men leave all the objects under the bough-shelter until they are required.

While the fathers and mother's brothers are making the cross, they discuss and confirm their choice of the circumcisers, *djimari*. These may comprise from one to three men—the novice's "wife's father" (who is his "sister's son" or F.F.Sr.S.), his "W.M.B."

(who is his "M.M.B.S."), or his "M.B.S." Only one man, prefer-ably the "father-in-law", will actually perform the operation; but the others will be expected to find a wife for the lad if the operator cannot do so. The *djimari*, who must be present during the manufacture of the cross, are formally told of their selection.

At the same time, a brother-in-law of the novice produces a ball of hair-string, which he presses against the chests of 10 or 12 of the onlookers—men who are the boy's countrymen of any kin-category. They retire into the bush nearby to construct a long, double-armed string-cross, *warumbulga*, which is associa-ted with the kangaroo dreaming and will also be displayed that night.

When the cross is ready, the naked men return to the group, and each in turn offers his penis to the fathers, the mother's brothers, and the circumcisers to hold. He thus expresses his sympathy for the men whose boy will be killed and his confi-dence in the men who will kill the lad. The actual father and mother's brother of the novice, however, should refuse to touch the man's penis, for they are too deeply grieved at the thought of the boy's death.

Everyone then inspects the *warumbulga* cross and runs his hands over the design to make himself "strong and confident". By now it is almost sunset. All the men repair to the main clearing to await the first ceremonies. Each father and mother's brother plucks a leafy twig of acacia as he goes.

Meanwhile, in the other bough-shelter (S2), the guardians (the sisters' husbands) have greased and red-ochred the novice and all the elder brothers of his patriline and have painted each one's conception-totem on his back. The lad, who wears a small apron and a hair-string cincture and has his hair bound up, is told to kneel beside the clearing (at N3) until the other men arrive. His brothers demolish the shelter and pile up the wood in readiness for the night's fires (at F4 and F5). They also bring great quantities of firewood from the bush and then sweep the clearing with branches. While they are working, they hear the fathers and the mother's brothers "sing" the circumcision knife. Angered by these preparations for the death of their young brother, they shout abuse and hurl sticks at the fathers' bough-shelter.

Since about noon, in another part of the bush, most of the younger men have been making the poles they will carry in the *widi* dance that evening. Each man prepares a pair of poles about nine feet long, which he covers with leaves. The men have also decorated each other with designs that represent such things as fire, smoke, snakes, stone knives, *Canthium* and *Santalum* fruits—objects that figure in the myth of the ŋarga dream-time heroes, which provides the rationale of much of the circumcision ceremonies. Later, the men chosen to be the circumcisers join them.

When all the other men assemble on the main clearing, the fathers and mother's brothers stroke the novice's head with the acacia twigs, so that his mind will be rid of extraneous thoughts and he will be prepared for his ordeal. The men sit at the eastern end and chant ŋarga songs as they beat the ground with their shields. The elder brothers summon the mothers and the father's sisters, who have been waiting nearby, and then hop about the clearing like kangaroos. The boy does likewise to demonstrate his acquisition of ritual knowledge. At the same time the women flick the actors with switches of *Eremophila longifolia* (the badge of the novice) to "strengthen" their minds. The brothers place the boy on top of the bodies of several of his guardians, and the women embrace him and weep as they bid him farewell. All the other women then surge on to the clearing and take up their usual position behind the singing men.

The elder brothers light two big fires (F4 and F5) and, as the sun touches the horizon, one of the brothers formally opens the proceedings. He runs to the western end of the clearing and hits the ground with his shield, then runs back and hits the ground at the eastern end. At this signal, the *widi* dancers, who may number from about 10 to 30, emerge from the eastern bush, carrying their leafy poles. They congregate at a small fire (F6) behind the eastern wind-break and tie the poles to their legs. The men who are to act as circumcisers must stay apart from the other dancers, for they are potential killers.

The dancers line up in patrimoiety groups on either side of the wind-break (at X and Y). The singers change to the vigorous *widi* chanting, and the elder brothers call on the first dancer (always the most recently subincised youth) to perform. As he dances in front of the company (at W1), the brothers call out in time to the singing and beat his poles with short sticks. After a few minutes of this grotesque and exhausting skipping, he moves along the clearing (to Z) and stands with his back to the group. The brothers call dancers alternately from each patri-moiety, and each man dances briefly before moving down the clearing. The audience laugh and joke during the performances. Then the men dance in pairs, trios, quartets and so on, until all of them (except the circumcisers) are massed on the clearing, their poles swaying wildly against the evening sky. They make concerted charges at the frightened novice, who sits with his guardians in front of the audience.

(At Phillip Creek, during the *widi* dancing, a brother gives a glowing firestick to one of the dancers, a W.M.B., who holds the butt between his teeth. The brother holds up the novice, so that the brand burns the boy's chin. This ensures that he will later have a luxuriant beard. His mothers and father's sisters stand beside him and, when he is again set beside his guardian, caress and reassure him for the last time.)

After a time, the dancers halt and turn their backs to the company. All the women bow their heads, and the guardians cover the boy's eyes. To the accompaniment of slow singing, the circumcisers enter and dance for a few minutes, then stand to one side. A palpable tension builds up in the group.

At the far end of the clearing an elder brother lights a fire (F7) to reveal the *wanigi* cross stuck in the ground. The *widi* dancers form a single file, facing the group, so that their poles form a channel above their heads. The brother deftly passes the cross along this channel, in such a way that it appears to travel un-supported through the air towards the audience. As it hovers above the foremost dancer, the boy is told to open his eyes. At that moment two brothers snatch him up and press his chest against the design on the cross to enable the lodge patrispirit to enter him. The savage, guttural chanting rises to a crescendo, and the intense excitement of the men strikes the onlooker with the force of a blow. Then, with shouts and snarls, the men drive the women away to the general camp, as a brother carries the cross to the other end of the clearing.

Each of the circumcisers dances up to the novice and falls backward so that his poles strike the boy heavily to single him out as the intended victim of the killing. The circumcisers remove their poles and, led by one of the guardians, each sits between the knees of a father of the novice, who embraces him to show that he bears no animosity towards the killer of his son. The boy's own father covertly hands the knife to the actual circumciser. An elder brother then runs up with the cross and pretends to ram it into the belly of the dazed and terrified boy, before standing it in the eastern wind-break. There the cross faces squarely the opposite end of the clearing, where the operation will be performed; if it were askew, the foreskin would be cut crookedly. The brothers rub the lad's chest and, somewhat belatedly, tell him not to be frightened.

All the men burst into the rapid kangaroo-singing and furiously hammer the ground with heavy sticks. A brother signals with a firestick. Several naked men, decorated as night-jars, appear from the south-western bush and dance backward along the clearing in time to the pounding rhythm. As the trembling novice watches, two more naked men, decorated as kangaroos, rush towards him and brandish the long *warumbulga* cross over his head. They dance backward down the clearing, vigorously shaking the cross in the air. The nightjars reappear and dance to the frenzied singing. The elder brothers shout at the boy, threatening him with death if he reveals his newly-acquired knowledge to outsiders. To emphasize the point, they set fire to the *widi* poles and pretend to spear him with them. Other men dance and wave the burning poles back and forth.

The brothers tell several men (sisters' husbands, sisters' sons, or W.M.B.) to kneel in front of the western fire (F7) to form the circumcision-table. As the men crouch there, the circumcisers inconspicuously stand beside them. A brother seizes the novice and places him face upward on the table, with his feet towards the fire. Another brother straddles him and presses his pubes against the lad's face to silence his cries, while a third grips his legs. A brother holds the shaft of the boy's penis, in order to protect "the inside bone" from injury; one of the cir-

cumcisers stretches the foreskin several inches, and another cuts
it off with two or three quick slices. The rest of the brothers
watch closely, for it is their duty to kill the operator at once
if he mutilates the boy. (It is small wonder that some men are
literally grey with anxiety when they perform their first operation.)

The oldest brother examines the foreskin, shows it to the
others, and then throws it into the fire. Another brother, who
has held aloft a blazing *widi*, dashes the pole to the ground to
signal a successful operation. The mother, watching for this
from afar, extinguishes her own firestick; her son is dead. The
brothers order each of the *djimari* who did not actually cut the
boy to rub the blade of the knife across the bleeding penis. The
djimari then conceal themselves in the darkness. The brothers
praise the novice's fortitude and stand him for a minute or two
in front of the fire to relieve his pain.

Throughout the operation, the other men have been singing
loudly and harshly to drown any cries the boy might make.

With joyous cries of *jo! jo! jo!*, the brothers carry the novice
back to the men, who growl *jarara jarara* as they approach. The
brothers display the lad's wound and then seat him on a shield
resting on the thighs of each of the three or four men who have
been chosen to be his ritual friends, *bilarli*. These are usually
relatively young "mother's brothers", "M.M.B.", or, especially,
"M.B.S." The brothers again stand the boy in front of the men,
with his new *bilarli* around him, and tell him that these will
always be his mates, men with whom he must never quarrel. The
bilarli at once signify their friendliness by teaching him how
to click his fingers to drive away demons when he is to welcome
his circumcisers (Meggitt, 1955a, p. 392).

The brothers then summon the *djimari* to embrace the boy
and carefully explain to him the relationship in which they
stand; he learns that, although he must for some time avoid
these men, they will later ensure that he obtains a wife. The
circumcisers move away as several other "fathers-in-law" and
"W.M.B.", carrying *widi* poles, dance up in turn to the lad.
Instructed by the brothers and the *bilarli*, he pushes each dancer
flat on his back, "in retaliation for the pain he has suffered".
(It is of interest that he is not permitted to lay hands on the
actual circumcisers.)

Most of the men softly chant the ŋarga dreaming songs. Flanked by his *bilarli* friends, the boy sits on the knees of a sister's husband, who covers his eyes. A brother brings the *wanigi* cross, while another approaches swinging the *windilburu* bullroarer that has been made for the lad. The sister's husband puts a small stick into the novice's hand, and he and the *bilarli* urge the boy to hit the roaring *mindaba* demon that is coming to attack him. After the terrified boy makes several vain attempts to do so, the brother steadies the bullroarer so that he is able to hit it. The *bilarli* congratulate the lad on killing the demon. His eyes are uncovered and he sees the bullroarer making the noise. His brother hands him the object, explains its meaning, and tells him to guard and contemplate it while he is secluded.

Another brother limps in exaggerated fashion along the clearing, resting the *wanigi* cross on his right instep as he walks, just as the lame ŋarga man carried it in the dreamtime. The *bilarli* and the other brothers cry, "Who is this lame man? What does he carry?" They tell the boy to take the *wanigi*; but, as he reaches for it, the bearer snatches it away, shouting that it is "too dangerous" for a novice to touch. He limps away, only to return and give the cross to the lad to handle and examine. The *bilarli* press it against his chest, while the brothers explain how the lodge patri-spirit has now entered him.

A brother then shows the boy the circumcision knife. He points out the fresh blood on the blade. That, he says, has come from the novice; and it mingles with the older bloodstains (placed there earlier in the day) that have come from the lad's agnates. His elder brothers, his fathers and father's fathers have all been cut with the same (*sic!*) knife to make them into men. The brothers then warn the boy to be sparing with water that night, lest micturition make his penis bleed again. At this they give the dazed boy the *wanigi* cross and the *windilburu* bullroarer to hold. A guardian hoists him on his shoulders and carries him back to his place of seclusion.

The men thrust the *wanigi* in the ground by the novice's bed, so that he may think of all that has happened to him. When he falls asleep, a brother quietly removes the cross and dismantles it, returning the *jarandalba* boards to their cache in the bush. The other men talk on the clearing for a while after the boy's departure, praising each other and, especially, the elder brothers on a difficult task well executed. A man hides the *warumbulga* cross in the bush nearby, where some of its makers will demolish it the next day. By about nine p.m. everyone has returned to the general camp.

The latest stage in the sequence of ceremonies has been concerned with the induction of the novice into the ranks of the young bachelors and into his father's cult patrilodge. The events have also defined unequivocally the matriline into which the boy should marry. Not only has a particular man actually performed the circumcision, but he has also been singled out in the *widi* dancing so that all may recognize him. Moreover, after the operation the novice passes again into the care of his marriage line, in the person of the sister's husband who is his guardian.

Representatives of the lad's patriline and matriline have also played an important part. The mother's brothers have joined the fathers in making the *wanigi* cross that symbolizes the father's lodge and in nominating the circumciser(s). The mothers and the father's sisters have continued to be distinguished from all the other women throughout the events. The brothers, as usual, have organized many of the activities; and the father's fathers and, to some extent, the M.M.B. have stood by to give advice if necessary.

The apparent hostility expressed by the brothers when the fathers and the mother's brothers prepare the circumcision knife is of considerable interest. It may perhaps reflect the structural opposition of the alternate generation-levels; but it is more likely to be another manifestation of the general distinction between older and younger men that is made throughout the ceremonies. The kangaroo and emu actors, the *jarandalba* bearers and *widi* dancers are always drawn from the bachelors and young married men. Older men merely watch and, if they choose, criticize the performances. Similarly, the novice's ritual friends or *bilarli* always come from the younger men. This choice later has practical advantages with regard to shared interests and the provision of aid of various kinds.

There is, however, no rigid grouping of generation-levels in such selections. The *bilarli* may be "M.B.S.", "M.M.B." *and* "mother's brothers"; the actors and dancers may be of all kinship categories. The separation is simply in terms of relative age—the younger men versus the older. Moreover, this arrangement has the pragmatic function of providing situations in which the participants who are the centre of attraction still have their statuses clearly defined as young men. (The division is in line with the conventional psychoanalytic interpretations of *rites de passage*, as, for instance, that of Reik, 1931.)

After the novice goes into seclusion again, his mother continues to prepare his food, which his father takes to him daily. The men of his patriline and matriline visit him regularly to see if his wound is healing cleanly and if his guardian is caring for him properly. During this seclusion, the boy, naked and covered with red-ochre, roams the bush in the men's country a few miles from the general camp. He still may not eat meat, and he speaks to his guardian as little as possible. The sister's husband teaches him natural history, social rules and, occasionally, religious dogma.

The lad carries his bullroarer everywhere; he learns how to swing it and studies it carefully to absorb its virtue. After three or four weeks, his father secretly removes the object while the boy is sleeping. He may entrust it to a man of the opposite patrimoiety, to care for with other ritual boards, or he may give it to a kinsman who was unable to attend the circumcision ceremonies. The boy is never told of the ultimate fate of the bullroarer, and no special bond is thought to exist between him and the object in later life.

When the novice has been two or three months in seclusion, he is formally re-introduced to his circumciser, to whom he has hitherto been dead. Since performing the operation, the circumciser has been restricted to a diet of meat only. As the Walbiri are largely vegetarian, the man usually finds this fare inadequate; "he always feels hungry."

Ideally, the circumciser should join another community immediately after the circumcision ceremonies, because he "is sorry and ashamed at having killed that boy". Although the move would also effectively separate him from the lad's father, it is not specifically intended to do so; should the two men remain in the same camp, they may meet freely.

Whether or not the circumciser resides elsewhere for a time, he notifies the father of the novice when he is ready to meet the boy again. The men of the lad's patriline and matriline, together with his brothers-in-law, go hunting and cook a considerable amount of game, which they will give to the circumciser on behalf of the novice. They may add to the gift red-ochre, hair-string, boomerangs, spears, shields and, nowadays, clothes. The offering is partly a recompense for the ritual services that have been rendered to the boy's lodge and partly an anticipatory payment of his bride-price.

At dusk on the appointed day the circumciser sits at the outskirts of the general camp, with his back towards the seclusion-camp of the novice; his brothers hold vegetable-food cooked by his wife (or by the boy's future mother-in-law). The agnates and matrikinsmen of the lad, carrying their gifts, escort him from his camp and seat him with his back to the circumciser. They put the gifts (including the game) beside the circumciser's brothers, who place the vegetable-food by the boy. The novice eats some of the vegetable-food, while the circumciser eats some of the meat. Then the lad's elder brother gives the circumciser some of the vegetable-food to eat. The circumciser in turn rubs the boy's mouth with a piece of meat, after which he rubs the boy's body with his hands. He embraces him and shouts *bu!* (prepuce?), instructing the novice to follow suit. The lad takes the vegetable-food back to his seclusion-camp, and the circumciser carries away the gifts to share with men of his patriline. Both the novice and the circumciser may now revert to a normal diet.

Next morning, the boy is again brought to meet his circumciser, who produces a boomerang, demonstrates how it is held, and then throws it (in any direction). He retrieves it and tells the lad to throw it in the same manner. The two then laugh loudly in unison. The circumciser similarly shows the boy how to chop a tree-trunk with an axe, and the novice imitates him. He may now learn to make and use men's implements. The two again laugh together, for "they are happy, they are now friends." Nevertheless, for some months more, the boy behaves circumspectly towards his circumciser and tends to avoid him.

Following this formal meeting, the novice returns to seclusion for about a week, until his guardian tells the *jualbiri* it is time they cut his hair. They do this without ceremony in the general camp by day. The sister's husband and a *jualbiri* hold the boy's head, while another *jualbiri* uses a knife to hack the hair off in tufts—a very painful operation. The men softly chant the appropriate songs as they work. The *jualbiri* give the hair at once to the guardian; this is the first of a lifelong series of exchanges of hair-cuttings between the novice and his sister's husband.

The novice and his guardian reside in a shelter beside the main camp for another week or so. The boy stays near the shelter but may talk freely with any visitors. By now he has recovered from the effects of his sojourn in the secret and sacred realm; he is ready to return once more to his parents and to secular life in the camp.

Circumcision, with its accompanying ceremonies, firmly and unequivocally establishes a youth's status in Walbiri society. Should he fail to pass through these rites, he may not enter his father's lodge, he may not participate in religious ceremonies, he cannot acquire a marriage line, he cannot legitimately obtain a wife; in short, he cannot become a social person. I met only one lad who had not been circumcised within a reasonable time after reaching puberty; this was Wagulgari djungarai, a spastic moron. Men regarded him as insane, and not even his own father would insist on his being circumcised. All the men said that they would not take the risk of his divulging ritual secrets to the women. Consequently, Wagulgari is debarred from ever securing a Walbiri wife. The women, is any case, always asserted that they would never marry an uncircumcised man—it simply would not be proper for them to do so.

Sometimes, however, a circumcision may be delayed when the lad has been working for Europeans.

Although George djabanangga was still uncircumcised, he accompanied some kinsmen on two successive droving trips. By the time he returned to Hooker Creek (late in 1953) he had grown considerably and went to live in the bachelors' camp. Most of the older men were perturbed by this, for they thought (quite rightly) that he was now sufficiently developed to be sexually interested in young women. In theory, an uncircumcised youth who is detected in copulation should be knocked on the head and circumcised immediately; and the men were concerned to avoid such an outcome.

As George's own father and close agnates lived at Yuendumu, his classificatory "agnates" and "mother's brothers" at Hooker Creek decided to initiate him in the coming season without the consent of the father. In his travels, however, George had been filled with lurid tales of the ordeal ahead, and he flatly refused to be circumcised. His relatives threatened and cajoled him for weeks without success; but he stood firm, and they were unwilling to circumcise him forcibly without his father's permission.

Eventually, a party of men, who for some time had intended to walk to Yuendumu, decided to take George with them. When he reached Yuendumu, his father and his mother's brothers told him he must submit to the operation at once. Feeling more confident in their presence, he agreed and, after a brief seclusion, went through the usual ceremonies.

The incident nicely illustrates the tie that exists between father and son and also the father's importance in sanctioning the circumcision. George's classificatory kinsmen at Hooker Creek could have legitimately gone ahead with the affair; but in practice their action would have led to serious disputes with his own father.

Subincision and after. Provided a youth has been formally released from seclusion, he may be admitted to the first Gadjari ceremonies that occur after his circumcision; and matters are usually arranged so that he is able to attend. Similarly, he is permitted to witness all the lodge increase and revelatory ceremonies that take place throughout the year. His patriline affiliation and his marriage-line connections continue to be emphasized on these occasions. His sister's husband again acts as his guardian, while his agnates give him religious instruction. His matriline affiliation is not so important here; if his M.M.B. instructs him, he does so as an "elder brother" of the same patrimoiety.

When the youth is about 17 years old, the men of his patriline decide it is time he was subincised. They discuss the matter with his mother's brothers and M.M.B. and agree on the identity of the operator. They usually, but not necessarily, invite a man from the marriage line already established for the lad—the matriline of his future wife; but their final choice depends largely on their estimate of the girls likely to be available in a number of potential marriage lines. The men then tell the youth's sister's husband to take him into the brief seclusion that precedes the operation. No ceremony marks their departure. The two camp in the men's country for about a week and spend their time hunting. The lad is covered with red-ochre and wears only a hair-string cincture contributed by his guardian. He is under no dietary restrictions and may speak freely.

The elder brothers go out one afternoon and make a rough clearing near his place of seclusion. Late that night, the men of his patriline, matriline and marriage line assemble there, together with such of his countrymen as are interested. Other men are not obliged to attend, and women are never present. The men sit in a circle around the youth and his guardian and, for several hours, beat the ground with their shields as they sing of the episodes of the ŋarga (initiated men) myth that refer to subincision. The elder brothers are active in leading the singing, explaining the songs to the lad, seeing to his comfort, and tending the fires.

A couple of hours before dawn men of the opposite patrimoiety begin decorating the youth's father and one or two other members of his cult-lodge in readiness for the dramatization of an incident from the myth of the lodge-dreaming. Everybody chants the relevant songs, whose meanings the elder brothers also explain to the lad. All this activity follows the normal pattern of a lodge ritual and, when it is over, the brothers tell the youth what he has seen.

Just as the sun rises, the elder brothers tell two of the sisters' husbands to lie on their backs, side by side with their feet towards the fire. The brothers place the youth on his back on top of the men. Two "fathers-in-law" straddle him, one to hold his legs and the other to silence his cries if necessary. A brother leads forward the operator (a "father-in-law", "W.M.B.", "M.B.S.", or "M.M.B."), who has been concealed from the group until this time.

The brother hands the subinciser the knife, over which the fathers have previously sung to make it cut straight. To the accompaniment of loud chanting by the company, the man deftly slices open the youth's penis from the meatus to a point about an inch along the urethra. An elder brother also holds the penis, to ensure that the "inside bone" is not cut, while other brothers stand ready to kill the inciser if he bungles his task. The operator withdraws immediately he makes the cut; and the brothers stand the lad in front of the men to display the incision.

The youth's ritual friends, *bilarli*, then seat him on a shield held across the knees of one or two "mother's brothers", "M.M.B.", or "M.B.S.", who are to become additional *bilarli*. Each clasps him. The new *bilarli* then join the others in supporting the youth as the elder brothers bring the operator to embrace him. The patient squats over a small fire prepared by one of the brothers, so that the smoke and heat will alleviate the pain and cause the blood to congeal. After his brothers warn him not to micturate that day, they leave him in the care of his sister's husband, and all the other men return to the general camp.

Later in the morning, the mothers, elder sisters, father's sisters, and mothers-in-law of the lad, who have been in their shelters grieving for him, may, if they wish, be cicatrized to demonstrate their sympathy for him. Each woman simply asks any other who is known to be expert to perform the operation. The patient lies on her back outside her own shelter, and the operator uses a flake of stone or, nowadays, glass to make two or three parallel, shallow incisions above or between the breasts. Unlike men's cicatrices, the cuts (which are rarely more than four inches long) do not as a rule have dirt or down pressed in them to produce keloids. The whole operation takes but a few minutes. Although the operator does not receive any material recompense for her services, her social prestige is enhanced.

The subincised youth remains secluded in the care of his sister's husband until his wound has healed. After about a week he formally meets his subinciser at the outskirts of the general camp. Once again the men of his patriline and his mother's brothers support him and contribute hair-string, red-ochre, boomerangs and the like to the payment of the operator. The gift they make is also an anticipatory instalment of the lad's bride-price. The subinciser, who is accompanied by his own brothers, takes the articles and embraces the youth. Their mutual avoidance is now at an end. A few days later the lad returns to the bachelors' camp.

Sometimes, when a youth is subincised, other men present may take the opportunity to have their own incisions enlarged. They invite their brothers-in-law to perform the operation. In this way, a man's incision may be progressively lengthened until it reaches the scrotum. This sort of extension did not occur at the one subincision ceremony that I was able to witness, however; and I received a strong impression at the time that the whole affair was somewhat perfunctory as compared with the elaborate arrangements that accompany circumcision. Few men other than the youth's close kinsmen bothered to attend the ceremony, and indeed some did not know it had occurred until they were told the next day.

Men later informed me that my impressions were justified. They said that although subincision is an obligatory operation it does not have the same ritual significance as does circumcision; and their accounts of ideal subincision procedures did not differ substantially from the events I saw. Most of the men asserted that the chief ritual function of subincision is to ensure that, when a man later becomes *jualbiri* to a circumcision novice, he will be able to draw from his urethra the blood needed to decorate the boy; arm-blood is not "potent" enough for this task. On the other hand, urethral blood is rarely, if ever, used for body decoration either in lodge ceremonies or during the Gadjari rituals. Nor did I ever observe men displaying their subincised penes to novices during circumcision ceremonies, although this is said to occur occasionally at Yuendumu.

Despite the limited ritual implications of the operation, all the Walbiri men whom I encountered were subincised, and I did not hear of anyone who was not. (The fact that subincised men usually squat when they urinate makes their condition apparent.) Why should there be this general adherence to the norm? Roheim (1945), whose psychoanalytic account of subincision is fairly plausible, has suggested that it is the result of certain unconscious motives. The Walbiri themselves, however, point to one mundane reason for men's wanting to be subincised. Men and women both stated that the marked lateral extension of the erect penis, which is directly due to the slitting of the urethra, greatly increases their enjoyment of coitus. Indeed, some women said flatly that, for this reason, they would not consider marrying a man who was not subincised.

In theory, if a youth who is circumcised but not subincised is discovered in a sexual liaison, he is operated on at once; but I have no evidence that this has ever happened in fact. Similarly, a lad who becomes frightened and tries to evade the operation should be taken by force. I have heard of only one instance in which this is supposed to have occurred.

A Walbiri youth at Wave Hill had been absent on stock-work for some time. On his return his kinsmen decided that he should be subincised at once, without undergoing the preliminary seclusion. When his sister's husband escorted him at night to the creek-bed normally used for such ceremonies, his nerve failed and he escaped to the general camp. The men did not wish to pursue him and drag him away in the presence of the women. The lad then camped close to the station homestead for some days, judging correctly that the men would not try to seize him in the vicinity of the Europeans' houses. The men instead appeared to ignore him, and, his fears allayed, he returned to the main camp.

His agnates, however, had discussed the matter and agreed that the operation should be performed. One evening in the bachelors' camp several of his sisters' husbands suddenly pounced on him and hustled him off to the creek, where the other men were waiting. His elder brother clubbed him on the back of the neck, and his "father-in-law" subincised his penis before he regained consciousness. As my informant, who had been present at the affair, put it: "No matter how clever these young fellows think themselves or how hard they try to escape us, we older men know many stratagems that will defeat them."

It is clear that a man who has been forcibly subincised suffers a great loss of personal prestige, and other men never forget his cowardice. In any dispute his opponents are entitled to remind him of this in order to put him at a disadvantage. Moreover, the man who subincises him is under no obligation later to find him a wife.

There is no sudden or marked change in a young man's ritual status following his subincision. For a year or two he continues to participate in the Gadjari rituals as a neophyte;

he is still summoned to witness lodge ceremonies but cannot yet act in them. Nevertheless, his lodge "brothers" and the Gadjari leaders now gradually divulge more religious information to him and, in their own time, allow him to take a minor part in ceremonies. It is not until he is betrothed, a couple of years after he has been subincised, that the men begin to regard him as an adult.

Before this occurs, however, the young man's chest is cicatrized and, if he is a southern Walbiri, his nasal septum is pierced. (Northern Walbiri boys have their septums pierced at the age of about eight.) Neither operation is of ritual significance. Cicatrices are merely a form of personal adornment that attests to a man's physical hardihood and makes him more attractive to women. The presence of a hole in his septum enables him to wear a *marabindi* decoration (the fibula of a kangaroo, or the wing-bone of a bustard or eagle-hawk) to enhance his appearance on public or ceremonial occasions.

Both operations take place without formality. When it is time for a young man to have his septum pierced, his "W.M.B." or, less often, his brother-in-law mentions the matter and offers to make the hole there and then. This may be done in the general camp or when men are assembled in the bush. Few people watch the operation.

The patient sits with his back against the chest of the operator. This man holds the subject's head firmly in the crook of his arm and, spitting on the fire-hardened point of a thin wand of *Carissa lanceolata*, stabs it sharply through the septum. The brief operation is bloody and painful. The wand, which remains in place until the wound heals in a week or so, is occasionally twisted to prevent it from adhering to the scab. When the patient removes the stick, his father and brothers help him to make a small, private gift of hair-string, red-ochre and boomerangs to the operator, in order "to cure the headache that has followed".

Cicatrization usually occurs when men are gathered for lodge ceremonies. While they are singing or making preparations, a W.M.B. or, failing him, a sister's husband (in the young man's marriage matriline) quietly says that he is ready to cut the young man's chest. Nobody else is consulted, and few of the other men pay much attention to the activity.

A second W.M.B. kneels behind the seated patient and holds his arms. The operator draws two red-ochre guide-lines across the subject's chest above the nipples and then makes a shallow cut of about nine or ten inches along each stripe with a flake of stone or glass. Although little blood flows, the operation is obviously painful. The two men press the edges of the wounds apart and pack the incisions with a mixture of down and sand, blowing on the exposed flesh to ease the pain. All the other men then compliment the patient on his improved appearance and make him the butt of heavy-handed but good-natured sexual joking.

The cuts heal in a few days, forming the prominent ridges that are so desired; some stand at least half an inch above the chest. The operator then makes a small gift of boomerangs or clothes to the patient as payment for hurting him. At irregular intervals after this, the young man may ask any of his brothers-in-law, W.M.B., M.M.B., or M.B.S. to add more cicatrices to his chest. Most men are content with eight to ten, but on some I have counted 25, extending down to the navel. The cuts are usually made in the summer, because "they hurt too much in the cold time!" Some men also add clusters of small, vertical cicatrices to their own shoulders.

Cicatrization is not obligatory; nevertheless, I encountered only six or seven uncicatrized men, most of whom were younger than about 25 years. It is apparent that most men conform to the customary norm not only because they wish to look "flash" and attract women, but also because they do not want to be the object of a clearly-expressed satirical sanction. Uncicatrized men are likened to "cleanskins" or unbranded cattle, or to children. Sooner or later, in an all-male assembly, somebody will comment on their smooth chests and will question their courage. A quarrel is bound to follow, for no man can suffer this imputation with equanimity. The Walbiri place a high social value on the capacity of adults to tolerate, without flinching or outcry, physical pain caused by others.

CHAPTER XVII

DEATH

The kind of reincarnation after death that the Walbiri postulate involves the transmigration of impersonal spirit-entities. They do not believe that the human personality long survives unchanged the destruction of its corporeal shell or that it sojourns happily with departed kinsfolk in an intermediate after-world while awaiting rebirth. Instead, they see death as something final that marks the end of each individual personality as they know it. The previously unified personality disintegrates into its basic components, and the conception- and lodge-totems return to their spirit-homes, while the matrispirit soon dissipates completely.

Consequently the people are unable to regard the inevitability of their own or their relatives' deaths with any philosophical detachment or resignation. The passing of a member of the tribe generally sets in motion an elaborate sequence of activities, including disposing of the corpse, mourning, holding inquests and seeking revenge—all of which help to close the ranks of the survivors. On these occasions the rights and duties of particular categories of relatives of the deceased, notably the matri-kinsmen, are clearly and carefully defined.

The behaviour that follows the death of an adult differs in certain important respects from that which ensues when a child dies. Although I was able several times to observe the latter at first hand, no adult deaths occurred in any of the Walbiri groups with whom I was currently residing. As a result I had to rely for these sorts of data on oral and idealized descriptions of what should be done. I obtained such accounts in considerable detail from a number of men and women; but, as most Aborigines are reluctant to discuss certain aspects of mortuary activities, the analysis I present here probably suffers from some omissions.

The evidence I have, however, clearly indicates that the institutionalization of funerary practices among the Walbiri significantly resembles that of the Warramunga, whereas it has few elements in common with the usages of the tribes of the eastern Kimberleys or the southern desert (vide Spencer and Gillen, 1899, pp. 476, 497; 1904, p. 504; Kaberry, 1935, p. 33; Elkin, 1937, p. 275; Berndt, 1942, p. 189; Strehlow, 1947, p. 62).

The Walbiri generally count uncircumcised boys and unmarried girls as children; and, when a child dies, only those countrymen present at the time are specifically involved in the activities that follow. Actual or close mother's mothers or, less often, elder sisters (that is, women of the matriline) bury the corpse quickly and without formality in a shallow, unmarked grave in the bush near the parents' dwelling. The women are not ritually cleansed afterwards. The parents, in order to avoid the attentions of the ghost (which is the deceased's matrispirit in mobile form), vacate their shelter at once and build another about a quarter or half a mile away. Should the dead child have been very young, they simply leave the old shelter to decay. But if the child was more than three or four years old and had a personal name, its ghost is thought to be rather more dangerous. The parents, therefore, burn their old dwelling; and all their neighbours (their countrymen) also shift camp for a few hundred yards. They do not have to burn their abandoned shelters.

The countrywomen of the dead child then sit in a group in the general camp, where they may wail for about six to eight hours as they embrace each other. Women of the matriline of the child who are its close mothers cut off their hair; and they and their own mothers gouge their scalps open with sharp stones or digging-sticks, so that the blood streams down their faces and shoulders. The elder sisters and the m.b.d. of the child should try to prevent the women from injuring themselves too severely. Nearby, the child's father and brothers sit together, silently and mournfully.

Later in the day, several close sisters of the sobbing mother lead her to her husband's brothers, who condole with her. Her senior brother, who has been wailing loudly, gathers up his spears and runs towards her with the high-stepping prance reserved for formal occasions. He, the mother, and her sisters and brothers-in-law squat in a huddle as they clasp each other and cry. This action signifies the drawing together of the deceased's patriline and matriline in their hour of tribulation. The child's own father and brothers, however, are "too sorry" to participate. The mother then hacks at her head again, and her sisters take her back to the other women. They all keen for another hour or two before returning to their dwellings.

This ends the group demonstrations of sorrow, although during the next few months individual kinswomen may keen at night whenever they think of the departed child. Relatives do not carry out any inquest or attempt to avenge the death. Infant mortality-rates are so high that people tend to regard death in childhood as something that is almost normal. The relatives soon forget that the child ever existed, and they gradually drift back to their old camp-sites. Within a year or two, a field-worker collecting genealogies will have little chance of including that child in his records.

In the following account I deal mainly with the procedures that follow the death of a man, but I should point out that in most respects they are consistent with those which succeed the death of a woman.

When a man is thought to be dying, whether from wounds or from sorcery (internal illness), his brothers place him outside his shelter, so that the men of his matrimoiety may gather around him. Men of the opposite matrimoiety in turn surround this group. They all wail and sob as they kneel in the conventional mourning position with one arm covering the eyes. To indicate the depth of his sorrow, the man (usually a father-in-law) who originally circumcised the dying man asks the latter's brothers to paint on his back the design of the victim's conception-dreaming. He then withdraws from the crowd to weep alone. Occasionally the W.M.B. of the dying man does the same.

The women keen together some yards from the men. As the rules of avoidance should hold even in this situation, the victim's *djuraldja*, the mothers and mother's mothers of his wife's matriline, may form a more distant group. His wife and the wives of his patriline, the women of his patriline and matriline, and his mother-in-law tear off their garments and sit straight-

legged on the ground while they gash their scalps and toss handfuls of dust and ashes over themselves.

The men of the matriline of the dying man crouch over him
in turn and rub their chests against his. If he is the victim of
sorcery (and is still conscious), his brothers softly ask him
whether he has any clue to the identity of the culprit. He may
reply by making a sign that suggests a particular totem or
kinship category. Each of the other men of his matrimoiety
then lies on him, followed by the men of the opposite matrimoiety. All the men then turn their backs and hide their faces;
and the women (except the mothers-in-law and their mothers)
approach the dying man in the same order as above and clasp
him in turn. These actions, which doubtless loosen the victim's
feeble grip on life, are meant to induce his matrispirit in its
ghostly form to go from the camp and leave the survivors in
peace. (I could not discover whether the embrace was also
intended to transfer vitality from the living to the dying.)

A concerted shriek goes up when the medicine-man or a
brother announces that the man is dead. The brothers pile
leafy branches over the body. The fathers and adult sons of his
patriline, the men of his wife's matriline and those of his maternal kinsmen who are also his ritual friends, *bilarli*, at once gash
their thighs deeply with knives, despite the attempts of the
dead man's brothers and sisters' sons to prevent them. The men
bind up the wounds with hair-string in such a way that they
are forced wide open and the resulting scars will be very noticeable. This mode of expressing grief is lapsing today; I saw few
men under about 40 years who bore such scars. Some men said
that they have dropped the practice because the wounds interfered too much with their stock-work. (Apparently men never
cut their thighs when women died.)

Most of the deceased's close kinswomen wail unceasingly and
again gouge their heads. The women of his matriline, his
widow(s) and his mother(s)-in-law first hack off their hair and
then sear the wounds with firesticks. (Each woman later gives
the hair-cuttings to her mother's brother to spin into string.) The
man's own mother, his widow(s) and mother(s)-in-law also singe
off their pubic hair. His sisters and m.b.d. stand by, ready to intervene if the women are likely to do themselves serious harm.

The dead man's brothers then send his wife to the widows' camp, where she smears herself with ashes and keens all night. (I found no evidence that widows ever wore mourning caps or chaplets; vide Davidson, 1948; Spencer and Gillen, 1899, p. 503.) The widow may take only her digging-stick with her from her husband's shelter. His brothers tell a mother's brother to take charge of the deceased's own possessions, and they then set fire to the shelter and the rest of its contents in order to drive away the ghost. The dead man's goods are later given to the senior mother's brother of the matriline to share with the other mother's brothers of that line and, sometimes, of his community. When a woman dies, her daughters or sisters hand her possessions to her senior mother's brother to distribute to the women of her matriline. In neither case should the allocation precede the assembling of all the interested mother's brothers and mother's sisters.

If the death appears to have been caused by sorcery, a medicine-man visits the shelter before it is burned down and searches the site for evidence of the identity of the putative killer. He looks for such clues as the direction in which the grass is inclined, or the presence of animal tracks.

Everybody in the camp wails throughout the night following the death. Next morning the brothers carry the corpse a mile or two into the bush in the men's country. All the men of the matriline accompany them, except the mother's brothers, who must remain in the camp to supervise the other mourners. When the men find a suitable tree, they construct a substantial bough-platform in the fork about 10 to 15 feet from the ground. The brothers cut all the hair from the corpse and then stretch the body at full length on the platform, which they cover with branches. A man's head is oriented to his lodge-dreaming country and a woman's to her conception-dreaming country, in order to facilitate the return of the spirit, which is thought to emerge from the mouth (Davidson, 1948b). The brothers spin the hair from the corpse into a few feet of string and wind this into a small skein. When these tasks are completed, the men light a smoking fire in the spinifex-grass and set off for the camp, wailing loudly as they go. In an endeavour to confuse the ghost, which now hovers near the platform, the party takes a circuitous route through the bush.

At the camp the sisters of the deceased have been watching for the smoke-signal. As soon as they see it, they call out, and everyone assembles—the men seated in a group and the women standing behind them. The wailing and head-gashing continue. On its arrival, the inhumation party circles the company; and one of the brothers presses the hair-string against the belly of each woman and then of each man. He finishes in front of the senior mother's brother, to whom he gives the string. This man later makes it into a necklet or into arm-bands, which he carefully greases and wears to remind him of his duty to avenge the death. The string must eventually circulate among all the mother's brothers in the tribe; and none may keep it for more than a year or so lest its "potency" make him ill. When the string passes from the mother's brothers of one community to those of another, the recipients should make a counter-gift of weapons and food. The string may not be intentionally destroyed but should be worn until it disintegrates.

I was told that, when a very old man or woman dies, th' brothers simply inter the body in a shallow, unmarked grave, with the head pointing towards the lodge-dreaming or the conception-dreaming country. They spin the hair and bring it back to the camp; but the mother's brothers wear it only as a memento of the dead. In theory, the deaths of such persons do not have to be avenged; they have occurred "naturally" as the result of old age. Nevertheless, I gathered that, unless a man was very old indeed, few people would let his death pass unquestioned.

The body of a man who had a bad reputation as an adulterer, thief, or homicide may also be denied the dignity of platform-exposure. His relatives mourn his passing in the usual way; but they need not seek revenge, for his own actions probably led to his death. Despite this statement, I cannot believe that any matriline would voluntarily forgo the right to avenge the death of an adult member, no matter how dubious his social reputation might have been.

Once the brothers bring the hair-string back to the camp, nobody may utter the deceased's personal name in any context whatsoever. If another person already shares this name, he (or she) becomes *gumindjari*, "the nameless one". Dreaming-songs containing the name are dropped from the song-cycles. People should not mention the deceased's conception-totem in the presence of his close kin, especially of his brothers.

When the brothers press the string against the belly of the dead man's wife, her period of silence begins. This may last from about 12 to 24 months, until the ban on speech is formally lifted. Men at Phillip Creek asserted that the ban also affects the mothers-in-law, father's sisters and maternal kinswomen of a dead man and the husband's sisters, father's sisters and maternal kinswomen of a dead woman. This usage appears to be a Warramunga innovation; I encountered nothing like it among the other Walbiri, who stated that only the widow had to remain silent. Men do not suffer any corresponding restrictions when any of their relatives die.

During her mourning term, which the widow spends in the widows' camp, she should behave circumspectly lest she anger her husband's ghost. Thus, she should communicate only by means of manual signs (Meggitt, 1954); she should avoid her old camp-site at least until one wet season has passed; she must not take a lover (although I have known some widows who did so); she must remain in the company of other women and care for her children properly. Should her behaviour deviate from these norms, the irate ghost, which still watches over her, is capable of stealing her spirit, so that she becomes insane, wastes away and dies (Meggitt, 1955a, p. 399).

An old djungarai man died at Hooker Creek in September 1952; within nine months of this, his three widows had remarried. When I remarked that they seemed to have suffered no ill-effects, men told me that the deceased had been old enough to be buried without the formality of a platform-exposure. There was no need to avenge his death, and his ghost had no reason to remain near the camp. His widows could, therefore, cut short their period of mourning with impunity.

A day or two after the disposal of the man's body, his mother's brother leads the widow from the widows' camp to join her sisters, and he paints the deceased's conception-dreaming on the back of each woman. They kneel in line abreast, and their eldest or most senior brother, heavily armed, prances up to them. They all embrace him and wail for a few minutes, then return to their dwellings. This appears to end the formal, noisy mourning; from now on, the widow remains silent in the widows' camp.

In the past, after this ceremony, the whole camp was shifted for some miles to another waterhole, where new shelters were erected. The old dwellings were left to decay and the site was not used again until one wet season had passed. Nowadays, the people make much shorter moves within settlement limits.

If the death in question was not caused by wounds inflicted by a known person, people attribute it to the effects of sorcery. Some weeks after the death all the men of the deceased's matri-line assemble to hold an inquest. They accompany the medicine-man to the tree-platform on which the corpse lies, and there they employ several techniques to identify the putative killer. They combine and interpret various clues in order to arrive at an answer.

As the party stealthily approaches the tree, the medicine-man is alert for signs that the ghost (the deceased's matrispirit) is in the vicinity. (The ghost can manifest itself simultaneously near the corpse, at the site of the dead man's old dwelling and near the widows' camp.) In theory, every Walbiri can see ghosts in dreams; but only the medicine-man is able to see them when he is awake, for he has magical crystals and a certain lizard in his body (Meggitt, 1955a, p. 388). Sometimes he hears the ghost chattering to itself in the peculiar "popping" speech that ghosts affect. He questions it in the same fashion and repeats its answers to the other men. The ghost is not often detected in this way, however, and the party usually has to assess other clues.

The men carefully examine the tree-trunk and the surrounding earth. The general direction of the flow of exudations from the body points to the community country of the sorcerer; tracks of natural species near the exudations indicate his conception- or lodge-dreaming. The men strain their ears as the medicine-man draws their attention to a soft droning noise that comes from the direction of the killer's country. He tells them it emanates from the sorcerer's mind or conscience, which the murder has made uneasy. Everyone then climbs the tree and studies the corpse, looking for unusual fissures, discharges, bruises and other marks. The position of one of these may signify the kinship category of the killer relative to the victim; thus, the left shoulder denotes a "younger brother" or a "son's son", the right knee a "mother's father" or "M.B.S.", and so on (Meggitt, 1954, p. 6). (The Walbiri are familiar with modes of conducting inquests in some other tribes, such as the use of inquest-sticks in the Kimberleys and the hair-tugging in the Victoria River area; but they do not employ them.)

The men ponder the signs and come to a decision. Obviously, such clues are open to various interpretations, and the men's preconceptions must play a large part in determining the conclusions they reach. Moreover, an important part of the medicine-man's repertoire is his knowledge of all the current feuds and arguments, adulteries and elopements in the tribe.

Once the men think they know who the sorcerer is, they take steps to punish him. The medicine-man may privately perform rituals to inform the lightning of the culprit's name and place of residence, so that it may seek out and destroy him. More commonly, the medicine-man and the men of the deceased's matriline privately and individually "sing" the killer. Their actions and curses are projected through space and "solidify" as lethal objects inside him (Meggitt, 1955a, p. 387). In a recently developed technique, the avengers "sing" curses as they heat lengths of wire, with which they "spear" the sorcerer, wherever he may be. He experiences fierce pains in his body and, guessing their origin, he soon dies, for he knows that no medicine-man can aid him now. Some djabangari men at Hooker Creek who believed that two old djagamara men at Wave Hill had earlier "sung" and killed their young brother performed this wire-sorcery. The two djagamara died soon afterwards, an event that did much to popularize the new method.

In the past, if the deceased's maternal kinsmen learned that the killer had survived their retaliatory sorcery, the senior mother's brother was likely to organize a punitive expedition. The men of the matriline made emu-feather sandals (the well-known kadaitcha boots), which they wore to disguise their tracks, for desert Aborigines can identify individual foot-prints as confidently as a detective can distinguish among finger-prints. The raiders surrounded the camp of the killer just before dawn and each donned a *djiriŋana* head-dress made of leaves, hair-string and small *mandagi* bullroarers. This was believed to make the wearer invisible to the intended victim. The avengers despatched him with a volley of spears and escaped into the bush. Moving at a fast jog-trot, they took a roundabout path home in order to evade both the ghost and the relatives of their victim. Strengthening and purifying rituals (apparently similar to those of the Aranda) preceded and followed the foray.

Unfortunately, I could not obtain much detailed information about revenge expeditions, for the Walbiri are aware that most Europeans disapprove strongly of such practices. It is unlikely that any raids of this sort have occurred in the last 15 years or so; and the people nowadays prefer to attempt covert retaliation by sorcery.

Indeed, men told me of one procedure, which, they asserted, was a recent development intended to replace the punitive raid. It is likely, however, that people also employed it in the past in difficult inquests, when they could not identify the culprit in the usual ways. The men of the deceased's matriline do not expose the corpse on a tree-platform but, after the preliminary mourning, burn it in the bush. They lie down beside the fire and listen. As the thick black smoke ascends, the killer "sees" it, no matter how distant he may be. Burning pains at once attack him and he screams in fear, "*Warai! warai!* pity me!" When the men "hear" the cries, they know the pains are working on his conscience to destroy him. In any case, the direction taken by the smoke informs them where he lives, so that, if necessary, a revenge party knows where to look for him.

The only instance of corpse-burning about which I have information occurred in 1954 near Teatree. A group of Walbiri found the body of a Walbiri man lying in the bush. As he appeared to have died in suspicious circumstances, his maternal kinsmen burned the body in an attempt to punish the unknown killer. In consequence, the police later arrested several of the men and charged them at Alice Springs with illegally disposing of a human body. The ordinance under which the men were charged, however, had not yet been gazetted; and the case had to be dropped—an outcome that did not enhance the prestige of the Whitefellow law in the eyes of the Walbiri.

When the men of the deceased's matriline are following the normal funerary sequence, all of them (except the mother's brothers) again visit the corpse about a year or so after they have placed it on the platform. By now only the skeleton remains. The brothers smash the skull with their axes and use sticks to rake the bones into a wooden trough; they put the radius and ulna to one side. They knock the top off a termite-hill, tip the rest of the bones into the cavity that is revealed, cover them with the container and replace the top. They do not mark the site in any way, and other people do not know of its exact location.

If the putative killer has not yet been discovered, a medicine-man accompanies the party to the tree and makes further attempts to identify him. He again interrogates the ghost and may point the arm-bones in various directions and "sing" curses that will seek out and injure the culprit.

Whether or not he does these things, the brothers carefully bind the arm-bones together with hair-string and, soaking the bundle with blood from their arm-veins, decorate it with bands of white down and charcoal. (Black and white seem to be the colours characteristically associated with death throughout Central Australia.) They attach the package to the point of a spear, which one carries upright. The men light a fire in the spinifex grass and set off for the general camp, a few miles away.

The deceased's sisters have been watching for the smoke-signal, and they announce the return of the party. All the men in the camp sit in a circle around the mother's brothers; the women stand in an outer circle. The sisters dance to one side, while everybody wails.

When the maternal kinsmen arrive, they run round the group, shouting as they go. The brothers press the bundle containing the bones (still tied to the spear) in turn against the bellies of the women and then of the men. The mother's brothers are approached last, and the senior mother's brother present of the matriline retains the bones. Henceforth, only the mother's brothers may see the actual bones, which they must keep carefully wrapped and hidden in a bark wallet or a bag made of woven string. The bones circulate among the mother's brothers throughout the tribe, each man keeping them for no more than about 12 months lest he fall ill. When the bones pass from one community to another, the donors receive a counter-gift.

When a djuburula man died at Gordon Downs, his djabaldjari "mother's brothers" there sent his arm-bones via Inverway to his actual mother's brothers at Hooker Creek. After about a year these men handed the bones on to their "brothers" at Wave Hill, whence they should return to Hooker Creek to be carried to the djabaldjari "mother's brothers" at Yuendumu by the first available messengers. Counter-gifts of pearl-shells, hair-string and cloth have so far accompanied the transfers.

On receiving the arm-bones, each mother's brother in the deceased's matriline may use them in an attempt to injure the putative killer before passing them on to the other mother's brothers. He is most likely to employ them in the conventional technique of bone-pointing, in which he also "sings" curses.

He may, however, visit each community in turn, either alone or with other men of the matriline. To every group of Walbiri he meets he explains that he seeks the killer of his nephew. He then offers each man a container of liquid (in the past nectar mixed with water, nowadays tea), which also contains minute scrapings from the bones. The men must drink from it, for to refuse to do so is an admission of guilt. It is believed that, as soon as the actual killer (whose identity may still be unknown) tastes the liquid, his fingers and toes become contorted and he is unable to straighten them. The visitors publicly denounce him, and it appears that, in the face of this evidence, his own relatives refuse to support him. A formal duel may be arranged then and there, or the defendant may try to compound for the alleged crime by offering the avengers a son to circumcise. Sometimes the visitors return home without taking action and later organize a revenge expedition.

Some Walbiri at Phillip Creek told me that, when the brothers of the dead person press the bundle of arm-bones against the bellies of various women, the action releases the women from the ban on speech that has followed the death. This seems to be a Warramunga usage. Other men at Phillip Creek, as well as those at Hooker Creek and Yuendumu, stated that the ban (which affects only the widow) is lifted by the performance of a formal ceremony of "mouth-opening", analogous to that performed between a novice and his circumciser. Moreover, they said, the ceremony should not take place until the deceased has been avenged and his mollified ghost (matrispirit) has departed, apparently to dissipate in the sky.

Men of the dead man's matriline, especially his mother's brothers, decide when the widow's mouth should be "opened", and they warn her to prepare for the event. She cooks a large cake of meal and then daubs herself with white stripes. She goes to a low mound made in the middle of the general camp, around which silently sit a number of men holding switches of leaves. They include the men of the deceased's matriline and of his *djuraldja* line, his widow's matriline. The woman squats on the mound, crouching over the food. Each man strikes her on the head with his switch and rubs some of the food on her mouth in order "to open it". The widow eats a portion of the food and the men eat the rest. She gives one last wail and returns to the widows' camp; she may now talk freely. After this, the men of her matriline, in conjunction with the senior brothers of the dead man, may arrange for her remarriage.

This brief ceremony marks the end of organized mourning for the dead man; but for years afterwards his own and close mothers may indulge in bouts of keening and head-gashing whenever they think of him. Gradually people cease to call his name-sakes *gumindjari*, "the nameless ones", and dreaming-songs that contain his personal name may reappear in the song-lines—provided somebody thinks to replace them. Nevertheless, people will never refer to the deceased by name, and they will avoid mentioning his conception-dreaming in connection with him in the presence of his close agnates.

In the case of a dead woman serious mourning ceases much earlier, sometimes long before her death is avenged. Her husband does not have to wait for any prescribed period before remarrying and does not have to observe any behavioural restrictions for fear of offending her ghost. This difference is but another reflection of the superior status of men in Walbiri society.

I need say little to point out the significance of funerary activities as expressions of Walbiri social norms. From beginning to end, the main group involved is the deceased's matriline, although on occasions other members of the matrimoiety, especially countrymen, may substitute for them. Members of the *djuraldja* line of a dead man (his wife's matriline) have certain privileges and duties; the most obvious is the right to attend the mouth-opening ceremony of the widow, which precedes her remarriage. The deceased's agnates (except those siblings who are also matrikin) take little active part in the events after their initial outburst of grief and self-mutilation.

CHAPTER XVIII

"REACTION AND INTERACTION"

In this account of the Walbiri I have dealt not only with social relationships and groupings that were important in the recent past but also with those which are significant for the people today. In order to do this I have had to consider aspects of the culture, as well as the social structure and organization of the tribe. Analysis of the interconnections of statuses and groups has involved discussion not only of the institutionalized role-expectations associated with the statuses but also of the observed role-behaviour of the individuals who occupy the statuses and form the groups. I have tried, too, to indicate the effects on role-behaviour of the people's interactions with Europeans and, to a lesser extent, with other Aborigines. Although these effects are most clearly manifested in divergences of observed from expected role-behaviour, they are also perceptible in changes that occur in the expectations themselves.

During my sojourns with the Walbiri, I was impressed by the persistence of many traditional features of their society and culture in the face of increasing pressures from the European society that is now dominant in the Northern Territory. The norms of kinship and the totemic religion in particular continue to bind men into social groups, to orient their behaviour and to express values that they still believe are fundamental. Western society so far has not offered substitutes in these contexts that the people can accept. Indeed, the apparent absence of corresponding values among many of the Europeans whom they commonly encounter strengthens their opinion that, in such matters, the Walbiri norms are best.

Thus, few, if any, of the people are even "rice Christians". Men often told me that Christianity is a matter for White-fellows to discuss and practise; it has no relevance for the Blackfellows' way of life. In any case, some men asked, how could they accept a system of beliefs involving the patently false dogma that in the Northern Territory white and black people are equal in the eyes of God? Most of the Walbiri similarly find the Whitefellows' law baffling and inconsistent, and they heed what they take to be its injunctions only when disobedience will clearly invoke punishment by the White authorities. In all other matters, they say, it is best to follow the old law, "the Walbiri line", which is still the most reasonable code of behaviour for Blackfellows.

But, despite the people's cleaving to many of the old norms, Walbiri society has undergone some important changes, the most obvious being in the local organization and the economic system that supported it. Although the initial pattern of European settlement enabled the Walbiri to maintain for a time the traditional division of the tribe into four major, localized communities, this slowly broke down as the cattle-stations and mines attracted the younger men. Later, the Administration's policy of shifting relatively large numbers of people on to settlements merely hastened a process of change that had already received great impetus from the severe drought of 1924-8. As a result, some community countries have been emptied of people, whereas others now contain residents from all four communities.

Most Walbiri appear to be happy to exchange the uncertainties of living in the harsh desert environment for the security of settlement life. It is true that, for a few, nostalgia invests even the recent past with a roseate glow; and the country they have left is always better than the one they now occupy. Such men have told me how fabulously rich Tanami and the Granites were in game, how easy yet exciting life was there. Yuendumu by contrast is a poor and barren waste. But take the same people to Hooker Creek and Yuendumu becomes Elysium in retrospect.

The others, however, are under no such illusions. For the realists, life on any settlement and on most cattle-stations is more than comfortable when compared with the arduous existence in the desert. It is easier to receive a weekly issue of beef than it is to stalk kangaroos for miles, only to see them outdistance the hunting-dogs. It is better to be able to draw a bucket of clean water from a bore several times a day than to have to rely on a few pints of stinking slime in a rockhole to keep a whole family alive while walking 30 miles to the next soak.

Moreover, people can devote the time saved in food-collecting to singing and dramatizing the dreamings, to gossiping and brawling, to love-making and match-making—activities dear to Walbiri hearts. In short, many people count this intensification of social life as a great gain, and they are aware that the weakening of the traditional community affiliations and the loss of the old hunting and collecting economy have not necessarily cost them their independence in other fields of action.

More and more men nowadays are working for Europeans, on settlements and cattle-stations and, to a lesser extent, in towns. Some of the younger men do so not only to acquire money and new commodities but also to learn new skills and the English language. They believe that knowledge of this sort may help them to achieve a different social status in the plural society, one which, even though much inferior to that of the White-fellow, may place them in a stable context with clearly-defined rights and expectations vis à vis the latter. These men wish to be secure in their dealings with Europeans, to know where they stand in contemporary Territory society. They now see that, for better or worse, the future of the tribe is irrevocably linked with that of the Europeans; and a few realize that the major adaptation to the new situation must come from the numerically and materially weaker Walbiri.

But the young men are not yet prepared to break away completely from their own cultural background in order to attain a higher status. Thus, although as many as 20 to 25 per cent of the people (mainly men) work for Europeans for varying periods each year, they do not overtly challenge the old institutions. Men who can drive motor-trucks, who buy gramophones with their earnings, who wear sandals, socks and sun-glasses, still want to marry "straight" and to learn their lodge mysteries. They still wish to "follow the Walbiri line", a desire that in itself indicates the great vitality of that line.

The increasing dependence on European employment, together with the residential shifts to government settlements, however, has entailed consequences that as yet only a few of the men appreciate. As a result of the decline in local mining operations, there are not many employers within the Walbiri territory; there, Yuendumu, Mount Doreen and the handful of cattle-stations near Lander Creek are the only places of employment. Most men must therefore look outside for jobs —to the Victoria River stations, to the Barkly Tablelands and to Alice Springs.

I have already indicated that the government settlements are becoming the foci of new residential groupings. Will the outward migration to employment make the settlements into new communities with novel cultural traits? Will the members of each adopt practices and beliefs from the tribes with which their work brings them into close contact? To some extent, they have begun to do so. This was most noticeable at Phillip Creek, where the Walbiri were in continuous face-to-face contact with a smaller Warramunga group, an arrangement that was to continue when both moved to the new Warrabri settlement. The Walbiri have already taken over certain Warramunga norms concerned with initiation and funerary activities.

To a lesser degree, the increasing contact between the Hooker Creek Walbiri and the tribes at Wave Hill and neighbouring cattle-stations has facilitated the former's borrowing of religious rituals connected with the Gadjari cycle.

But we should not over-estimate the significance of such post-European intertribal encounters. The Walbiri have not accepted many ideas and practices from other Aborigines, largely because they have no great need of them. Their own culture is still rich enough to satisfy their interests. In any case, in view of the people's high rate of reproduction and territorial expansion, it seems likely that, long before they are ready to borrow new cultural elements in quantity from neighbouring groups, they will have absorbed the potential donors.

The most probable outcome of settlement residence appears to be that the mutual (geographical) isolation of the settlements and the obvious physical obstacles to their frequent intercommunication will limit the extent to which they can retain the traditional Walbiri culture unchanged and in common. The settlements will gradually diverge culturally as each community is involved in its own continuous interaction with Europeans and other Aborigines: three distinct but similar "neo-Walbiri" cultures will develop, all supported by basically the same social structure.

One question remains: why have Walbiri society and culture survived relatively unaltered, whereas geographically contiguous and culturally comparable tribes, such as the Ngadidji, have disintegrated and declined markedly in numbers? In answering the question I want to take data from the earlier chapter on Walbiri relations with Europeans and re-examine them in the light of the general analysis made by Elkin (1951) of the interaction of Aborigines and Europeans elsewhere in Australia.

Elkin has remarked that a common feature of the contacts with the early settlers was the tentative, yet amicable, approach of the Aborigines, who believed that the strangers were merely temporary sojourners in their tribal territories. But, before long, the competing demands of the food-gatherers and the food-producers for the land became obviously irreconcilable. Armed clashes followed and blood was shed on both sides.

As far as I can judge from the available evidence (such as from explorers' journals), the Walbiri at first made few overtures to the incoming Europeans. It seems that they quickly learned from tribes nearby (for instance, the Yanmadjari and Ngadidji) that the Whitefellows were there to stay, no matter what attempts the Aborigines made to dislodge them. The establishment of the chain of telegraph-stations from Alice Springs to Tennant Creek, as well as the retaliatory shooting of the Ngadidji involved in the attack on Barrow Creek, must have confirmed this opinion. Consequently, when the Walbiri first encountered Europeans in any number, during the Tanami gold-rush of 1909, they were from the start hostile and suspicious of them. In the ensuing disputes Walbiri were shot and their distrust of the Whitefellows intensified.

Their subsequent behaviour was consistent with this; they withdrew into their own country and as far as possible avoided the Europeans. They were able to do so only because their land was then relatively worthless to the Whites. The collapse of the Tanami gold-rush had temporarily discouraged extensive prospecting in the region, and cattle-men had selected suitable land elsewhere that was sufficient for their needs for some time. As the Walbiri territory did not connect any strategically or commercially important areas, the Administration had no reason to build roads or telegraph-lines in it.

Other tribes, such as the Ngadidji and Aranda, however, could not retire in this way in the face of early, unsatisfactory contacts with Europeans. The settlers spread too quickly across the dreaming and hunting countries, and there was literally nowhere else for the tribesmen to go. They had to accommodate themselves to the European occupation, to exist precariously in what were in effect small-scale slums on the outskirts of townships and at the back-doors of the station homesteads.

Thus the Walbiri at that time, because they lived outside the grazing areas, were not forced by economic necessity to seek employment with the Europeans. The settlers' herds had not entered their tribal territory. Nevertheless, in the next decade or so the isolation of the Walbiri broke down as younger men drifted on to the cattle-stations around the Victoria River and Lander Creek. Although they were ostensibly working for the pastoralists, these men were, in Elkin's terms, "parasitic on the local White society", a condition that became more apparent as their unemployable relatives followed them.

I must therefore qualify Elkin's assertion that "the Aborigines' reaction to White intrusion is not a matter of curiosity, imitation and acquisition" (1951, p. 165). In some instances at least, Aborigines who were members of relatively untouched and well-integrated communities moved to localities of European settlement long before the outsiders usurped their territories. To judge from the reminiscences of Walbiri men, sheer curiosity on the part of individuals of particular temperaments was an important motivating factor in the initial migrations.

It may well have been that this interest stemmed partly from the Aborigines' determination to learn something of the usages of the strangers, in case the latter advanced further into their country; the likelihood of such incursions must have been apparent to the people. At any rate, after the migrants came to the cattle-stations and mines, they developed new tastes and demands, while they lost old tastes and skills. This change tied them economically to White society; even though their lands were still there to support them, they could not return wholeheartedly to the traditional life in the desert.

The great drought of 1924, which hastened the Walbiri move to the stations, had two major consequences. Some of the refugees, emboldened by the numerical superiority and driven by hunger, resorted to force to secure the commodities they desired. The Europeans replied with harsh punitive action, which drove the survivors to new localities, such as Wauchope and Tennant Creek. At the same time, the number of other Walbiri increased greatly on stations where the Whites themselves were in serious straits; and the Aborigines' earlier relationship of "intelligent parasitism" changed into what we may fairly describe, in Elkin's words, as incipient or actual "pauperism". Indeed, so unsatisfactory were these connections with the cattle-men that, when the drought conditions eased after 1928, some of the Walbiri preferred to return to the arduous life in the desert rather than to continue them.

The gold-rushes at the Granites and Tennant Creek between 1932 and 1934 again drew many of the tribesmen into contact with comparatively large groups of Europeans. No serious disputes followed, however, for the Walbiri freshly remembered the Lander shootings of 1928 and realized the futility of trying to use force to improve their position. The outcome of these population moves was the emergence of two large communities of paupers, who worked sporadically for Whites at the two gold-fields until after 1945, when the Administration removed them to settlements.

The people who stayed on the cattle-stations appear at that time to have been in rather better circumstances, as they again achieved a relationship of parasitism on the pastoralists. Many worked periodically in the stock-camps and were able to provide some economic support for dependents and older relatives. The employers, however, did not try to teach the men more than the simplest techniques of stock-work, so that they remained comparatively inefficient workers. This incapacity in turn reinforced the reluctance of the employers to ameliorate the living conditions of the natives.

The Walbiri, nevertheless, were in some demand on the cattle-stations bordering their territory, for it had become increasingly clear that the considerable depopulation of the local tribes was already threatening future supplies of labour. A state of equilibrium was reached, therefore, in which the Walbiri worked sporadically and inefficiently in return for low material rewards and poor living conditions. This balance persisted until after World War II and was relatively unaffected by earlier changes in the ordinances that regulated the employment and care of Northern Territory Aborigines. After 1945, however, the Native Affairs Branch initiated an extensive welfare programme. Employers were required by law to provide wages and conditions attaining stated minimums, and the expansion of the patrol system facilitated the regular policing of the ordinances by disinterested government officers. This led to gradual improvements in the status of those Walbiri who had remained on the stations. The Branch also took the Walbiri who had been dependent on uncertain employment and charity at the gold-fields, as well as the unemployable people on the cattle-stations, and placed them all on settlements, where they could receive medical attention and regular issues of food and clothing. Schools were established on the settlements in 1950-1. The teachers not only drilled the children in the three Rs but also tried to help them understand the features of Western culture that they would encounter in later employment. The settlements also provided limited training for younger men in occupations not directly connected with stock-work, training they had rarely received on cattle-stations.

The changing figures for administrative expenditure on Aborigines from 1938-9 to 1954-5 give some idea of the extent of the Administration's welfare programme. The figures do not include expenditure on the salaries of the N.A.B. staff, which had increased from nine in 1938 to 60 by 1952, or on capital works.

TABLE 26

Annual expenditure on Aboriginal welfare by the Northern Territory Administration

Year	Amount £A
1938-9	17,327
War years	unknown
1946-7	63,486
1947-8	48,492
1948-9	70,208
1949-50	101,064
1950-1	175,094

1951-2	296,041
1952-3	278,492
1953-4	332,461
1954-5 estimated	492,000

As the number of Aborigines who benefit from such expenditures has remained more or less constant at about 15,000, the *per capita* outlay in those years has increased from about £1 to about £33 annually. In addition the Administration has raised the wages that private employers pay to Aborigines—directly, by passing ordinances, and indirectly by establishing settlements. To attract the Aborigines from the settlements, many employers have had to offer cash wages well above the statutory minimum.

The figures I have quoted, however, are significant not only as an index of the recent material improvement in the Walbiri standard of living, but also because they indicate that the Administration quickly implemented the plans it had announced for the betterment of native welfare. Up till this time, the Walbiri had been given nothing and promised nothing by the government. Consequently, they have had no reason to become disillusioned by broken promises or official apathy.

In other parts of Australia, such as in northern New South Wales, the Aborigines long ago indicated that they wished to enter White society and were promised by various official and quasi-official bodies that they would be helped to do so. But the delay of the Europeans in providing avenues of entry has been so great that it has engendered strong feelings of frustration, resentment and disillusionment among the people. This has led, in Elkin's terms, to "a return to the mat"—a rejection of Western values and a retreat into the remnants of the native culture; and the only relationship that the people can maintain with White society is one of parasitism or pauperism.

Now, although the Walbiri are still in a relationship of "intelligent parasitism" on Europeans, they do not have to remain in this situation indefinitely. They can, if they choose, move towards an "intelligent appreciation" of Western society and culture, with assimilation or some other form of integration as their ultimate goal. The conditions necessary for this sort of change in Walbiri life are already at hand—improved health and a rising birth-rate, increasing economic stability, greater educational facilities, and, among the Europeans, the emergence of more tolerant attitudes towards Aborigines. Some of the Walbiri are already aware of this and are adapting their aims and behaviour accordingly.

The official policy of the Welfare Branch in the Northern Territory is, to quote the Minister for Territories, "the policy of assimilation which has as its aim an advancement in the habits, the way of life, and the general outlook of the Aboriginal people so that eventually, as they are able to do so, they will come into our community as members of our community on the same footing as all other members of the community". The Minister has also pointed out that "it will be a long and difficult job to achieve the final goal of assimilation for all of the Aboriginal people in the Northern Territory. The job will require a great deal of patience. . . ."

Anyone who has worked with these Aborigines must recognize the pertinence of the Minister's warning; it will take years of imaginative planning and persuasive guidance to achieve assimilation or, indeed, any sort of rational integration of Northern Territory Aborigines with White society. Nevertheless, granted that such problems exist, I believe that the prospects of successful, long-term assimilation are nowhere brighter than among the Walbiri.

BIBLIOGRAPHY

Abbie, A. A. and Adey, W. R. The non-metrical characters of a Central
     Australian tribe. *Oceania*, XXV, 198-207. 1955.
Ashley Montagu, M. F. *Coming into Being among the Australian Aborigines.*
     London, 1937.
Baume, F. E. *Tragedy Track.* Sydney, 1933.
Berndt, C. H. Women's Changing Ceremonies in Northern Australia.
     L'Homme, I. 1950.
Berndt, R. M. *Kunapipi.* Melbourne, 1951.
     "Murngin" (Wulamba) social organization. *American Anthropologist*,
     LVII, 84-106. 1955.
Berndt, R. M. and C. H. A preliminary report of fieldwork in the Ooldea
     region . . . *Oceania Reprint*, 1945.
Berndt, R. M. and Johnston, T. H. Death, burial and associated ritual at
     Ooldea . . . *Oceania*, XII, 189-208. 1942.
Bleakley, J. W. *The Aboriginals and Half Castes of Central Australia.* Mel-
     bourne, 1928.
Buchanan, G. *Packhorse and Waterhole.* Sydney, 1933.
Calvert, A. F. *The Exploration of Australia.* London, 1909.
Campbell, T. D. *et alia* Physical anthropology of the Aborigines of Central
     Australia. *Oceania*, VII, 106-139, 246-261. 1936.
Capell, A. The Walbiri through their own eyes. *Oceania*, XXIII, 110-131.
     1952.
Chewings, C. A journey from Barrow Creek to Victoria River. *Geographical
     Journal*, LXXVI, 316-338. 1930.
     Back in the Stone Age. Sydney, 1936.
Davidson, D. S. Mourning-caps of the Australian Aborigines. *Proceedings
     of the American Philosophical Society*, 93, 57-70. 1948.
     Disposal of the dead in Western Australia. *Proceedings of the American
     Philosophical Society*, 93, 71-97. 1948b.
Elkin, A. P. Social organization of the Kimberley division . . . *Oceania*, II,
     296-333. 1932.
     Studies in Australian totemism. *Oceania Monograph* II. 1933.
     Initiation in the Bard tribe . . . *Journal and Proceedings of the Royal
     Society of N.S.W.*, LXIX, 190-208. 1936.
     Beliefs and practices connected with death in . . . South Australia.
     Oceania, VII, 275-299. 1937.
     Kinship in South Australia. *Oceania*, VIII, 420-452; IX, 41-78, 1938.
     X, 196-234, 295-349, 1939-40.
     Aboriginal Men of High Degree. Sydney, 1945.
     Reaction and interaction . . . *American Anthropologist*, LIII, 164-186.
     1951.
     Murngin kinship re-examined . . . *American Anthropologist*, LV, 412-
     419. 1953.
     The Australian Aborigines. Sydney, 1954.
Fortes, M. The structure of unilineal descent groups. *American Anthro-
     pologist*, LV, 17-41. 1953.
Fry, H. K. Kinship in western Central Australia. *Oceania*, IV, 472-478. 1934.
Giles, E. *Geographic Travels in Central Australia* . . . Melbourne, 1875.
Gluckman, M. *The Judicial Process among the Barotse of Northern Rhodesia.*
     Manchester, 1955.
Hernandez, T. Children among the Drysdale River tribes. *Oceania*, XII,
     122-134. 1941.
Hoebel, E. A. *The Law of Primitive Man.* Cambridge, Mass., 1954.

342 DESERT PEOPLE

Kaberry, P. M. Death and deferred mourning ceremonies . . . in north-west Australia. *Oceania*, VI, 33-47. 1935.
　Subsections in the east and south Kimberley tribes . . . *Oceania*, VII, 436-458. 1937.
　Aboriginal Woman: sacred and profane. London. 1939.
Lawrence, W. E. Alternating generations in Australia. *Studies in the Science of Society.* Ed. G. P. Murdock. New Haven, 1937.
Leach, E. R. The structural implications of matrilateral cross-cousin marriage. *Journal of Royal Anthropological Institute*, LXXXI, 23-55. 1951.
McCarthy, F. D. Trade in Aboriginal Australia . . . *Oceania*, IX, 405-438, 1939; X, 80-104, 171-195, 1939-40.
Madigan, C. T. *Central Australia.* Oxford, 1944.
Maine, H. J. S. *Ancient Law.* London, 1936.
Meggitt, M. J. Sign language among the Walbiri . . . *Oceania*, XXV, 1-16. 1954.
　Djanba among the Walbiri . . . *Anthropos*, L, 375-403. 1955a.
　Notes on the Malngjin and Gurindji . . . *Mankind*, V, 45-50. 1955b.
Murdock, G. P. *Social Structure.* New York, 1949.
Oliver, D. and Miller, W. B. Suggestions for . . . comparing political units. *American Anthropologist*, LVII, 118-120. 1955.
Piddington, R. Report on fieldwork in north-western Australia. *Oceania*, II, 342-358. 1932.
　Karadjeri initiation. *Oceania*, III, 46-86. 1932b.
Radcliffe Brown, A. R. The social organization of Australian tribes. *Oceania Monograph*, I. 1930.
　(Ed.) *African Systems of Kinship and Marriage.* Oxford, 1950.
　Murngin social organization. *American Anthropologist*, LIII, 37-55. 1951.
　Structure and Function in Primitive Society. London, 1952.
Rawson, G. *Desert Journeys.* London, 1948.
Reik, T. *Ritual: psychoanalytic studies.* London, 1931.
Reports on the Administration of Central Australia.
Reports on the Administration of North Australia.
Reports on the Administration of the Northern Territory.
Roheim, G. *The Eternal Ones of the Dream.* New York, 1945.
Roth, W. E. *Ethnological Studies . . .* Brisbane, 1897.
Schapera, I. (ed.) *The Bantu-speaking Tribes of South Africa.* London, 1937.
Smith, P. McD. *The Strenuous Saint.* Adelaide, 1947.
Spencer, B. *The Native Tribes of the Northern Territory . . .* London, 1914.
Spencer, B. and Gillen, F. J. *The Native Tribes of Central Australia.* London, 1899.
　The Northern Tribes of Central Australia. London, 1904.
　The Arunta. London, 1927.
Stanner, W. E. H. The Daly River tribes . . . *Oceania*, III, 377-405; IV, 10-29. 1933-4.
　Murinbata kinship and totemism. *Oceania*, VII, 186-216. 1936.
Strehlow, T. G. H. *Aranda Traditions.* Melbourne, 1947.
Stuart, J. McD. *The Journals . . .* London, 1864.
Sweeney, G. Food supplies of a desert tribe. *Oceania*, XVII, 289-299. 1947.
Terry, M. Journey through the north-west of Central Australia . . . *Geographical Journal*, LXXV, 218-224. 1930.
　Explorations near the border of Western Australia. *Geographical Journal*, LXXXIV, 498-510. 1934.
Tindale, N. B. Initiation among the Pitjandjara . . . *Oceania*, VI, 199-224. 1935.
Warburton, P. E. *Journey across the Western Interior of Australia.* London, 1875.
Warner, W. L. *A Black Civilization.* New York, 1937.
Worms, E. A. Die Initiationsfeiern Einiger Küsten- und Binnenlandstamme . . . *Annali Lateranensis*, II, 147-174. 1938.

INDEX

Arranged under the subheadings People, Places, Subjects, Tribes

People

Ashley Montagu, M. F., 272
Baume, F. E., 25, 47, 48
Berndt, R. M. and C. H., 43, 55, 165,
  168, 189, 196, 200, 211, 215, 236,
  263, 268, 269, 272, 318
Bleakley, J. W., 24
Braitling, W., 26
Brooks, —, 24
Brown, J., 20
Buchanan, N., 19, 20
Calvert, A. F., 17, 18
Chewings, C., 1, 21, 48
Davidson, D. S., 321
Durack Family, 19
Elkin, A. P., 32, 64, 71, 82, 146, 165,
  168, 186, 189, 196, 200, 215, 237,
  249, 268, 318, 335, 336, 337, 339
Farquharson, —, 19, 20
Fortes, M., 201, 211
Fry, H. K., 165, 168
Giles, E., 18
Gluckman, M., 91, 255
Gordon, —, 19
Gosse, W. C., 18
Gregory, A. C., 17
Hernandez, T., 236
Hoebel, E. A., 91
Johnston, T. H., 189
Kaberry, P. M., 55, 56, 165, 167, 186,
  188, 189, 268, 269, 318
Lawrence, W. E., 171, 172, 185
Leach, E. R., 201, 202
Madigan, C. T., 25
Maine, H. J. S., 91
Miller, W. B., 243
Murdock, G. P., 51, 83, 171, 265
Oliver, D., 243
Piddington, R., 237
Pierce, —, 21
Radcliffe Brown, A. R., 71, 82, 86,
  91, 171, 259
Rawson, G., 18
Reik, T., 307
Roheim, G., 273, 313
Roth, W. E., 269
Smith, P. McD., 22
Spencer, B., 23, 168
Spencer, B., and Gillen, F. J., 37, 39,
  44, 46, 65, 165, 168, 187, 196,
  203, 206, 208, 221, 223, 225,

Spencer and Gillen—continued
  236, 268, 269, 272, 290, 318,
  321
Stanner, W. E. H., 32, 56, 169, 193,
  268
Strehlow, T. G. H., 27, 40, 43, 47, 49,
  54, 55, 206, 215, 318
Stuart, J. McD., 17, 18, 47
Sweeney, G., 1
Terry, M., 25, 47, 48
Warburton, P. E., 18, 19
Warner, W. L., 32, 168, 236, 273
Wilkinson, —, 22
Worms, E. A., 237

Places

Alice Springs, 16, 26, 37, 334, 335
Anningie, 27, 30, 40, 55
Areyonga, 42
Banka Banka, 20, 37, 56
Barkly Tableland, 19, 30, 334
Barrow Creek, 18, 21, 39, 335
Birrindudu, 24, 26, 43, 153, 285
Bullocky Soak, 28, 167
Bungalow, 31, 40, 41, 73
Conistan, 1, 20, 24, 25, 27, 30, 31, 55,
  73, 285
Daly River, 32, 56
Darwin, 18, 21, 31, 36
Gordon Downs, 20, 24, 26, 31, 43,
  285
Haast Bluff, 28, 30, 31, 42, 63, 220,
  285
Hall's Creek, 19, 21
Hanson Creek, 2, 17, 20, 21, 24, 25,
  47
Hatches Creek, 26, 27, 40
Helen Springs, 37
Hermannsburg, 42
Hooker Creek, 1, 2, 17, 20, 21, 24, 29,
  30, 36, 37, 50, 52, 53, 55, 56,
  72, 73, 74, 153, 167, 170, 203,
  204, 222, 224, 226, 237, 238,
  285, 288, 325, 328, 334
Inverway, 288
Katherine, 36
Lander Creek, 2, 20, 24, 25, 48, 72,
  334, 336
Limbunya, 30, 35, 288
Macdonnell Ranges, 17, 18, 20
Mount Allan, 30

Mount Arthur, 17
Mount Barkly, 17, 40
Mount Davenport, 19
Mount Denison, 17, 30, 73, 285
Mount Doreen, 1, 3, 25, 26, 27, 48, 55, 61, 63, 65, 72, 285, 333
Mount Eclipse, 3, 19, 206
Mount Esther, 40
Mount Hardy, 3, 19, 26, 27, 63, 72, 212
Mount Leichhardt, 17, 40
Mount Singleton, 25, 26, 72
Mount Stanley, 19
Mount Stuart, 17, 18
Mount Treachery, 27
Mount Wedge, 18
Murray Downs, 39, 40
Newcastle Waters, 17, 37, 73
Ngama Cave, 68, 206
Ord River, 19
Papanya, 63
Phillip Creek, 1, 2, 28, 31, 37, 38, 39, 72, 73, 74, 96, 153, 162, 165, 167, 203, 204, 208, 222, 226, 228, 285, 289, 293, 302, 323, 328, 334
Powell Creek, 18, 19, 20, 37
Renner Springs, 37, 165
Reynolds Range, 2, 3, 17, 18, 47
Ryan's Well, 20
Stirling River, 19
Stuart Bluff Range, 18
Sturt Creek, 19, 20, 42
Tanami, 3, 19, 20, 21, 22, 24, 25, 27, 28, 42, 48, 72, 246, 335
Teatree, 1, 20, 28, 30, 40, 55, 326
Tennant Creek, 17, 18, 20, 24, 26, 27, 28, 37, 38, 73, 335, 337
The Granites, 1, 3, 19, 21, 22, 24, 25, 27, 29, 48, 61, 72, 337
Treuer Range, 2, 3
Vaughan Springs, 25, 73
Victoria River, 2, 3, 17, 19, 36, 334, 336
Warrabri, 28, 29, 334
Waterloo, 30, 153
Wauchope, 25, 26, 27, 39, 337
Wave Hill, 19, 20, 21, 24, 27, 30, 31, 36, 55, 73, 153, 220, 263, 325, 334
Willowra, 27, 30
Winnecke Creek, 2, 3, 19, 20, 21, 35
Yuendumu, 2, 28, 29, 30, 42, 48, 50, 55, 61, 62, 63, 64, 73, 153, 203, 204, 222, 226, 285, 288, 328, 333

Subjects
Abortion, 96, 98, 273

Age-grades, 233, 236, 237, 238, 239, 240, 250
Alternate generation levels, 141, 188, 189, 190, 203, 237, 306
Avoidance, mother in law, 138, 151, 154, 155, 190, 191, 268
circumciser, subinciser, 190, 304, 307, 308, 312
Bethrothal, 120, 121, 122, 126, 127, 131, 134, 139, 140, 146, 148, 156, 195, 196, 197, 198, 264, 265, 266, 295, 298
Blood, arm, 131, 149, 161, 162, 203, 204, 223, 227, 299, 327
menstrual, 271, 272
penis, 294, 312, 313
Cannibalism, 36, 42, 43
Cattle industry, Aborigines, 27, 30, 31, 36, 72, 332, 334, 336, 337
droving, 30, 31, 37, 43
pioneers, 19, 20, 22, 23, 26
Ceremonies, categories, 209, 220, 223, 225
description, 223, 224, 225, 226
Gadjari, 35, 36, 54, 55, 118, 119, 125, 131, 149, 162, 220, 227, 228, 229, 230, 231, 232, 234, 244, 248, 310
increase, 220, 221, 310
revelatory, 220, 221, 282, 284, 286, 287, 290, 310
secular, 35, 220, 244
women's, 189, 190, 209
Childbirth, 271, 272, 274, 275, 276, 277, 278
Childlessness, 96, 97, 273
Children, activities, 116
adoption, 97, 119, 132
care of, 124, 125
divorce, 102
discipline, 116, 118, 125, 128, 131, 137, 142, 147
food taboos, 233
Cicatrization, men, 315, 316
women, 312
Christian missions, 24, 28, 42, 331, 332
Climate, 1
Conception, 270, 271, 272, 273, 274, 278
Country, men's, 52, 53, 282, 285
women's, 52, 53
Death, deceased's bones, 327, 328
in childbirth, 276, 277
disposal of dead, 318, 321, 322, 326
infanticide, 277, 278
inheritance, 139, 140, 213, 321
inquest, 324, 325, 326
matriline, 200, 201, 202, 318, 319,

Death—*continued*
321, 325, 327, 328, 329, 330
matrimoiety, 200, 201, 202, 319, 330
mourning behaviour, 87, 120, 123,
127, 129, 133, 138, 139, 140, 141,
142, 146, 150, 155, 156, 157,
160, 162, 164, 246, 318, 319,
320, 321, 322, 323, 324, 327
name taboo, 222, 279
patriline, 319, 330
reincarnation, 317
revenge, 139, 192, 246, 322, 325, 326
self-wounding, 318, 320
speech ban, 323, 329
Demons, 59, 226, 295, 304
Disputes, community, 58, 245, 246
domestic, 94, 95, 98, 99, 105, 109,
111, 126, 135, 136, 173, 174,
175, 176, 177, 178, 179, 180, 181,
182, 183, 184, 277, 278
duels, 58, 101, 178, 182, 183, 328
intertribal, 38, 42, 245, 246
men, 95, 98, 99, 105, 107, 108, 119,
122, 126, 132, 133, 135, 136,
149, 150, 159, 160, 173, 174,
175, 176, 177, 178, 179, 180,
181, 182, 183, 184, 191, 239,
240
women, 95, 109, 123, 126, 128, 136,
147, 150, 163, 176, 182, 183
Dreams, 208, 227, 228
Drought, 24, 27, 38, 336
Education, 82, 108, 112, 118, 119,
128, 131, 136, 137, 142, 145, 148,
161, 220, 221, 225, 235, 244,
282, 284, 285, 287, 290, 294, 298,
301, 307, 308, 311, 315
Ethnocentrism, 34, 35, 44
Fauna, 10, 11, 12, 13, 14, 15
Flora, 3, 6, 7, 8, 9
Food, gathering and hunting, 49, 50,
52, 92, 112, 128, 244, 332
Food-taboos, children, 233
circumciser, 307, 308
novice, 283, 307, 308
pregnancy, 274, 275
totems, 208, 209
Footprints, 153, 325
Gambling, 116, 120
Ghost, 192, 208, 318, 320, 321, 322,
323, 324, 326, 329
Gift-exchange, 52, 56, 82, 128, 136,
139, 149, 154, 158, 159, 161,
162, 226, 231, 267, 268, 280,
283, 288, 308, 312, 315, 328
Hair, cutting, 309, 318, 320, 321
string, 161, 285, 294, 297, 299, 300,
320, 321, 322, 327

Initiation, age-grades, 237, 238, 301,
307
circumcision, 74, 206, 207, 233, 234,
281, 282, 283, 284, 285, 286,
287, 288, 289, 290, 291, 292,
293, 294, 295, 296, 297, 298,
299, 300, 301, 302, 303, 304,
305, 306, 307, 308, 309
fire-dance, 292
grand tour, 30, 46, 233, 285
ground, 285, 286
introcision, 269
matriline, 284, 293, 296, 298, 306,
307, 308, 310, 312
operator, 299, 302, 303, 311
patriline, 284, 285, 287, 290, 293,
298, 302, 305, 306, 307, 308,
310, 312
patrimoiety, 283, 284, 288, 291, 292,
294, 299, 301, 307
pole-dance, 292, 301, 302, 303
ritual killing, 294, 297, 303, 304, 307
season, 54, 55
seclusion, 233, 281, 282, 307, 311,
312
speech, 283, 287, 307
subincision, 234, 269, 310, 311,
312, 313, 314
women, 210, 282, 284, 289, 291, 292,
293, 295, 296, 301, 302
Insanity, 154, 155, 173, 174, 260, 309,
323
Killings, Aborigines, 19, 21, 22, 23,
24, 25, 40, 43, 159, 335, 337
Europeans, 21, 23, 24, 39, 335
Kinship, matriline, 195
patriline, 205
subsections, 170, 171, 184, 185, 186,
187, 216, 217, 218
system, 83, 188
terminology, 83, 84, 85, 109, 115,
123, 124, 129, 130, 137, 138,
141, 143, 144, 147, 150, 151,
152, 156, 157, 160, 161, 162,
163
Law, European, 154, 277, 326, 327,
332
Walbiri, 201, 212, 213, 251, 252,
253, 254, 255, 256, 257, 332
Leadership, 248, 249, 250, 251
Local groups, community, 51, 52, 54,
55, 56, 57, 58, 67, 69, 71, 211,
243, 244, 245, 247, 248
horde, 71, 187
kinship, 50, 51, 58, 69, 71, 187, 211
marriage, 56, 57, 69, 184
settlements, 72, 73, 74, 244

Marriage, abduction, 38
  brideprice, 267, 268, 280, 312
  community, 56, 57, 69, 184
  co-wives, 108, 109, 110, 111, 112,
    113, 114, 128, 136
  divorce, 102, 103, 239, 240
  elopement, 86, 99, 100, 101, 102
  intertribal, 35, 36, 37, 38, 39, 40,
    41
  levirate, 163, 174, 264, 265, 329
  matriline, 195, 196, 197, 198, 199,
    200, 264, 266, 280
  patriline, 198, 213, 214
  polygyny, 77, 78, 79, 198
  rules, 85, 86, 144, 145, 146, 147,
    163, 172, 173, 184, 185, 186,
    190, 192, 193, 196, 198, 199,
    200, 213, 214, 218, 266
  settlements, 74
  statistics, 86, 103, 199
  subsections, 62, 172, 173, 184, 185,
    186, 199
  widows, 133, 136, 264, 265, 323, 329
  wife-exchange, 88, 103, 104, 132,
    173, 183
Matriline, 83, 124, 138, 146, 155, 161,
    192, 200, 201, 202
  death, 200, 201, 202, 318, 319, 321,
    325, 327, 328, 329, 330
  initiation, 284, 293, 297, 298, 306,
    307, 308, 310, 311
  kinship, 195
  marriage, 195, 196, 197, 198, 199,
    200, 264, 265, 280
  ritual, 200
  size, 193, 194
Matrimoiety, 83, 190
  death, 200, 201, 202, 319, 330
  names, 191, 192, 203
  subsections, 186
Matrispirit, 124, 130, 138, 163, 192,
    193, 194, 207, 208, 317, 318,
    320, 329
Medicine men, 162, 249, 321, 324, 325
Menarche, 235, 270
Menopause, 236, 273
Menstruation, 111, 270, 271, 278
Mining, copper, 3
  employment, 26, 27, 28, 31, 72, 332,
    333, 337
  gold, 19, 20, 21, 22, 25, 26, 27
  mica, 3, 19
  tin, 3, 27
  wolfram, 3, 26, 27, 28
Mythology, 165, 167, 243, 261, 262,
    282, 287, 301
Names, sharing, 144, 145, 148, 278,
    279

  taboos, 222, 239, 279, 322, 323, 329
Northern Territory Administration,
    22, 23
  legislation, 22, 23, 26, 29, 338, 339
  Native Affairs Branch, 27, 28, 29,
    338, 339
  plural society, 34, 333, 334, 335,
    336, 337, 338, 339, 340
  Settlements, 27, 28, 31, 42, 72, 73,
    74, 153, 154, 250, 332, 334, 338,
    339
  Welfare Branch, 29, 340
Nose-piercing, 315
Overland Telegraph Line, 18, 20, 335
Paintings, body, 224
  ground, 223
  rock, 68, 220, 226
  shields, 283
Patriline, 68, 83, 137, 186, 195, 207,
    208, 211
  authority, 212, 213
  corporateness, 212, 213, 214, 215
  death, 319, 330
  depth, 212, 215
  initiation, 284, 285, 287, 290, 293,
    298, 302, 305, 306, 307, 308,
    310, 312
  kinship, 205
  locality, 211
  marriage, 198, 213, 214
  property, 213, 214
Patrilodge, 59, 68, 69, 70, 73, 74, 137,
    141, 186, 187, 195, 205, 206,
    207, 208, 209, 210, 211, 214,
    216, 218, 280, 299, 305, 311, 321,
  actors, 204, 219, 220, 222, 223,
    224
  numbers, 206
  recruitment, 207
  ritual rules, 203, 204, 222, 224,
    226, 228
  women, 209, 210
Patrimoiety, conception totem, 66,
    67, 207
  cult totem, 68, 186, 204, 221, 222,
    223, 227, 228, 230, 231, 232
  initiation, 283, 284, 288, 291, 292,
    295, 298, 301, 307
  names, 203
  subsections, 62, 186, 204, 215, 216,
    217, 218
Patrispirit, 130, 141, 206, 207, 208,
    210, 298, 302, 317
Penis-holding, 133, 262, 265, 299
Personality, theory, 208, 210, 221, 317
Political organization, 242, 243, 250,
    251

Population, densities, 32, 47, 48
  figures, 31, 32, 33, 47
  mobility, 30, 31
Property, inheritance, 139, 140, 213, 321
  land, 214, 288
  ownership, 93, 94, 112, 120, 214
Residence, bachelors, 76, 81, 120, 234, 278
  dwellings, 75, 76, 77, 94
  moves, 318, 321, 323, 324
  post-marital, 57
  widows, 75, 76, 81, 236, 275, 323
Residential family unit, 56, 77, 78, 79, 80, 81, 82
  statistics, 80, 81
Ritual friends, 191, 266, 295, 296, 298, 304, 305, 306, 309, 312, 320
Ritual objects, bullroarers and boards, 213, 226, 228, 229, 230, 231, 288, 289, 291, 292, 293, 295, 296, 297, 298, 299 300, 303, 304, 305, 306, 307
  shells, 260, 295, 296
  string-cross, 41, 118, 139, 161, 206, 207, 223, 299, 300, 302, 305, 306
  temporary, 223, 224, 225, 228
Sanctions, physical, 53, 92, 93, 95, 96, 97, 98, 100, 101, 102, 123, 252, 258
  satirical, 53, 54, 252, 258, 316
  social, 184, 252
  supernatural, 226, 249, 258, 260, 261, 325, 326
Sexual relations, extramarital, 53, 97, 98, 99, 100, 102, 104, 105, 106, 107, 108, 122, 123, 163, 176, 177, 180, 182, 184, 234, 240
  incestuous, 86, 123, 127, 134, 138, 140, 147, 148, 153, 163, 261, 262
  magic, 105, 181, 270
  marital, 88, 89, 90, 111, 269, 270, 273, 274, 278
  premarital, 163
  sodomy, 183
  subincision, 313
Shame, circumciser, 190
  mother in law, 153, 190, 192
  names, 279
  ritual friends, 191
  subinciser, 307
Singing, 222, 223, 226, 283, 286, 290, 299, 303
Sorcery, 36, 41, 122, 139, 176, 246, 249, 320, 321, 324, 325, 326, 328

Subsections, age-grades, 238
  alternate generations, 188
  couples, 62, 186, 216, 218
  diffusion, 168, 169
  kinship, 170, 171, 184, 185, 186, 187, 216, 217, 218
  marriage, 62, 172, 173, 184, 185, 186, 199
  matrimoieties, 186
  patrimoieties, 62, 186, 204, 215, 216, 217, 218
  system, 61, 169, 170
  terms, 165, 166, 167, 170
  totems, 62, 215, 216, 217, 218
Totems, 59, 60, 61, 62, 63, 64, 65, 69, 70, 73, 205, 209, 210
  classificatory, 63, 64, 70, 215, 216, 217, 218
  conception, 66, 67, 70, 73, 124, 207, 208, 272, 274, 317, 319, 321
  cult, 68, 69, 206, 207, 218, 219, 220, 221
  dreamtime, 60, 252, 253
  eating, 208, 209
  guruwari, 65, 66, 67, 73, 96, 167, 207, 221, 270, 272, 273, 274
  heroes, 59, 60, 61, 63, 206, 212, 227, 230, 284, 289, 292, 301
  localization, 48, 49, 59, 60, 61, 63, 64, 65, 66, 68, 69, 70, 73, 74, 187, 205, 206, 211, 288
  spirit children, 65
  subsections, 62, 215, 216, 217, 218
Trade, 35, 40, 56
Tribal territory, area, 1, 32, 35
  climate, 1, 2
  topography, 2, 3, 47, 48
  divisions, 47, 48, 49, 50, 51, 52, 67, 68, 242, 243
Vesteys (Australian Investment Agency), 20, 29
Visiting, intercommunity, 52, 53, 54, 128, 230, 231, 244, 285
  intertribal, 44, 45, 46, 231
  messengers, 46, 132, 230, 231
  sponsorship, 45, 46
World War II, 27, 28

Tribes

Aluridja (Luritya), 146, 166, 201
Arabana, 196
Aranda (Arunta), 23, 32, 40, 41, 43, 44, 47, 49, 54, 55, 166, 168, 187, 200, 201, 206, 215, 225, 236, 268, 272, 336
Arnhem Land, 168, 200, 211, 215, 273
Bard, 236
Daly River, 186, 268

Dieri, 200
Djauan, 166
Djingili, 17, 37, 193
Gurindji, 17, 19, 35, 36, 166, 263, 289, 325
Ilpirra (Walbiri), 17, 40, 208, 272
Karadjari, 166, 196, 202
Kimberley, 32, 166, 170, 186, 188, 215, 234, 236, 268, 269, 281, 318, 325
Kukata, 43
Kukatja, 43, 44
Lander (Walbiri), 17, 20, 25, 38, 40, 47, 48, 49, 61, 72, 73, 272
Lungga, 43, 167
Malngyin, 35, 36, 263
Matuntara, 55
Mudbara, 19, 35, 36, 166, 193, 263, 325
Murinbata, 32, 169, 193
Murngin (Wulamba), 32, 168, 196, 202, 211, 215, 236
Ngadidji (Kaitish), 17, 39, 40, 41, 44, 335, 336
Ngalia (Walbiri), 18, 19, 26, 28, 41, 47, 48, 49, 55, 56, 60, 61, 64, 68, 72, 73, 190, 206, 285
Ooldea, 43, 168, 234, 236, 272
Pidjandjara, 18, 28, 41, 42, 60, 63, 189, 236, 263, 268, 269, 272,

Pidjandjara—continued
282
Piladapa, 200
Pintubi, 41, 42, 43, 44, 55, 61, 166, 168, 169, 201
Unambal, 236
Ungarinyin, 215
Walmalla (Walbiri), 19, 20, 24, 25, 47, 48, 54, 55, 56, 60, 61, 68, 72
Walmanba, 17, 37, 40, 41, 44, 56, 228
Walpari (Walbiri), 208
Waneiga (Walbiri), 20, 21, 37, 38, 47, 48, 49, 54, 55, 56, 60, 61, 72, 206, 228, 246
Waringari, 37, 38, 42, 43, 44, 56, 170, 246
Warramunga, 17, 24, 28, 37, 38, 39, 40, 44, 46, 72, 166, 193, 203, 204, 208, 215, 221, 222, 223, 228, 268, 269, 289, 290, 318, 323, 328, 334
Wolmeri, 188, 189
Worgaia, 37
Yalpari (Walbiri)—see Lander
Yalyuwara (Illiaura), 40
Yangman, 166
Yanmadjari (Anmatjira), 17, 18, 40, 41, 44, 45, 167, 335
Yantruwanta, 200